MW00522835

Julia Domna

Julia Domna's influence on her age, unlike that of most women of ancient Rome, has not been underestimated. Throughout history she has been regarded as one of the most important figures to operate behind the imperial throne. In fact, as the Emperor Septimius Severus' prized and respected wife and the loyal mother of Caracalla, who joined them and their armies in their travels, she was on hand for all the Emperors' decisions and a figure visible throughout the Empire.

Yet her fame has come at a price. As part of a dynasty which used force and violence to preserve its rule, she was distrusted by its subjects; as a Syrian, she was the object of prejudice; as a woman with power, she was resented. Such judgements have been persistent: some modern historians blame Julia and her dynasty for the century of crisis that followed their rule, for the corruption of the Empire, civil war, oriental despotism, and exotic novelties in the imperial cult.

On the other hand, Domna was the centre of a literary circle considered highly significant by nineteenth-century admirers.

This book contains an overdue reassessment of these assumptions:

- Was Julia more powerful than earlier empresses?
- Did she really promote despotism?
- How seriously is her literary circle to be taken?

This book covers Julia's life, and charts her travels from Aswan to York during a period of profound upheaval, seeking the truth about this woman who inspired such extreme and contrasting views, exposing the instability of our sources about her, and characterizing a sympathetic, courageous, intelligent, and important woman.

Barbara Levick is Emeritus Fellow and Tutor in Literae Humaniores at St Hilda's College, Oxford. She is the author of *Claudius* (1990), *Vespasian* (1999) and *Tiberius the Politician* (ed. 2, 2000), and co-editor, with Richard Hawley, of *Women in Antiquity: New Assessments* (1995).

Women of the Ancient World
Series editors: Ronnie Ancona and Sarah Pomeroy

The books in this series offer compact and accessible introductions to the lives and historical times of women from the ancient world. Each book, written by a distinguished scholar in the field, introduces and explores the life of one woman or group of women from antiquity, from a biographical perspective.

The texts will be authoritative introductions by experts in the field. Each book will be of interest to students and scholars of antiquity as well as those with little or no prior knowledge of ancient history or literature, combining rigorous scholarship with reader-friendly prose. Each volume will contain a guide to further reading, a brief glossary, and timelines, maps and images, as necessary.

Women of the Ancient World will provide an opportunity for specialists to present concise, authoritative accounts, uncovering and exploring important figures in need of historical study and advancing current scholarship on women of the past. Although there is a growing body of excellent scholarship on the lives and roles of women in the ancient world, much work remains. This series will be the first of its kind.

Olympias, Mother of Alexander the Great
Elizabeth Carney

Julia Domna, Syrian Empress
Barbara Levick

Julia Augusti, The Emperor's Daughter
Elaine Fantham

Cornelia: Mother of the Gracchi
Suzanne Dixon

Terentia, Tullia and Publilia: Semi-detached Wives
Susan Treggiari

Julia Domna
Syrian Empress

Barbara Levick

LONDON AND NEW YORK

First published 2007
by Routledge
2 Park Square, Milton Park, Abingdon, Oxon OX14 4RN

Simultaneously published in the USA and Canada
by Routledge
270 Madison Ave, New York, NY 10016

Routledge is an imprint of the Taylor & Francis Group, an informa business

Typeset in Sabon
by Keystroke, 28 High Street, Tettenhall, Wolverhampton
Printed and bound in Great Britain
by Antony Rowe Ltd, Chippenham, Wiltshire

British Library Cataloguing in Publication Data
A catalogue record for this book is available from the British Library

Library of Congress Cataloging in Publication Data
Levick, Barbara.
Julia Domna, Syrian Empress / Barbara Levick.
p. cm. – (Women of antiquity)
Includes bibliographical references and indexes.
1. Julia Domna, Empress, consort of Severus, Lucius Septimius, Emperor of Rome, d. 217. 2. Empresse–Rome–Biography. 3. Rome–History–Severans, 193–235. I. Title.
DG298.7.J85L48 2007
937'.07092--dc22
[B]
2006033887

ISBN10: 0–415–33143–9 (hbk)
ISBN10: 0–415–33144–7 (pbk)
ISBN10: 0–203–39241–8 (ebk)

ISBN13: 978–0–415–33143–2 (hbk)
ISBN13: 978–0–415–33144–9 (pbk)
ISBN13: 978–0–203–39241–6 (ebk)

This book is dedicated to my friend of more than forty years, Beryl Roden

Contents

Illustrations

Plates appear between pages 86–87

Figures

The coins are reproduced by kind permission of the Trustees of the British Museum

Maps

Acknowledgements

It was Sarah Pomeroy and Ronnie Ancona who invited me to write on a Roman empress, and the idea was already in my mind. They gave me the opportunity of tackling a new theme, but one linked to long-term interests in imperial power, the Roman Empire in the east, and women in ancient society. They have also patiently read my text and suggested many improvements. My greatest debt has been to A. R. Birley, not only for his classic study of Septimius Severus, which a glance at the notes will show I have consulted throughout, but also for helpful comments on the original proposal and many bibliographical references and suggestions provided then and since, after he kindly read the completed draft; obligations mentioned in the notes are only a tiny proportion of the whole.

Indeed, the generous help and advice I have had from friends and colleagues have been one of the greatest sources of enjoyment that I have had in writing this book. Long ago Attilio Mastino gave me his work on the titulature of Caracalla and Geta; more recently I owe warm thanks to Jona Lendering, and Fanny Vito, to Emily Hemelrijk, for her help with Chapter 7, Martijn Icks, who has made many improvements to Chapter 9, Olivier Hekster, for the gift of his illuminating book on Commodus, Annika and Christina Kuhn for data on information technology, and Karen Forsyth, a candid reader. St Hilda's College Library, the Bodleian, Sackler, the Taylorian (Slavonic and Greek) libraries have provided all I could have hoped for, and St Hilda's information technology manager, Anne Wilson, has led me out of several difficulties.

I should like to offer special thanks to those who have helped me to obtain illustrations by generous advice and practical help on a particularly important aspect of this book. The list is headed by Jonathan Williams and Richard Abdy, Curators of Coins and Medals in the British Museum: the coins they have sought out are central to the illustrations, and they are reproduced by permission of the Trustees. It was through the good offices of Lindsay Allason-Jones that I am able to publish, by kind favour of the Museum of Antiquities of the University of Newcastle and the Society of Antiquaries of Newcastle, the photograph of the inscription from Carvoran, *RIB* 1791. I owe permission to reproduce photographs of the Kassel Cameo, through Rüdiger Splitter and Ingrid Knauf, to the courtesy of the Staatliche Museen Kassel, and of the bust of Domna, through Vinzenz Brinkmann and Irene Bösel, to that of the Staatliche Antikensammlungen und Glyptothek, Munich. From Ostia, Elvira Angeloni of the Soprintendenza per i Beni Archeologici di Ostia, Archivio Fotografico, kindly supplied a copy of the posthumous portrait of Domna as Ceres; from the Deutsches Archäologisches Institut Photothek Luisa Veneziano photos of three historical reliefs in Rome and Tripoli; the Governatorio, Direzione dei Musei dello Stato della Città del Vaticano, an image of the Vatican Domna; and Maria Daniela Donninelli of the Museo Nazionale Romano, Servizio di fotoriproduzione. Emilie Janvrin of the Bridgeman Art Library was most helpful in providing portraits of Domna and her family and other images. All have been most expertly handled by Amy Laurens, Editorial Assistant at Routledge, Classics, Archaeology, Religion and Anthropology. Since then the book has been in the expert hands of Christine Firth, Maggie Lindsey-Jones, Emma Wood and Ruth Jeavons, to whom I offer warm thanks.

B.M.L.

Abbreviations

Ancient works

Amm. Marc.	Ammianus Marcellinus, *History of Events*
Cic. *Att.*, *Fam.*, *Phil.*	Cicero, *Letters to Atticus*; *Letters to his Friends*; *Philippics*
Cod. Just.	*The Codex of Justinian*
Dig.	*The Digest of Justinian*
Dio	Cassius Dio, *Roman History*
Diod. Sic.	Diodorus Siculus, *Historical Library*
[*Epit. Caes*]	Anon. *Epitome of Aurelius Victor, Monograph on the Caesars*
HA Hadr., *M. Aur.*, *Avid.*, *Comm.*, *Pert.*, *Jul.*, *Sev.*, *Nig.*, *Alb.*, *Car.*, *Geta*, *Macr.*, *Diad.*, *Elag.*, *Alex.*	*Historia Augusta. Lives of Hadrian*, *M. Aurelius*, *Avidius Cassius*, *Commodus*, *Pertinax*, *Didius Julianus*, *Septimius Severus*, *Pescennius Niger*, *Clodius Albinus*, *Caracalla*, *Geta*, *Macrinus*, *Diadumenianus*, *Elagabalus*, *Severus Alexander*
Her.	Herodian, *History of the Roman Empire after Marcus Aurelius*
Inst. Just.	*The Institutes of Justinian*
Isoc. *Pan.*	Isocrates, *Panegyric*
Jos. *War*; *Ant.*; *Life*	Josephus, *Jewish War*; *Antiquities of the Jews*; *Life*
Luc.	Lucian of Samosata
Mal.	John Malalas, *Chronicle*
Pan. Lat.	Latin Panegyrists
Phil. *Apoll.*; *Soph.*; *Ep.*	Philostratus, *Life of Apollonius of Tyana*; *Lives of the Sophists*; *Letters*
Pliny *NH*	Pliny the Elder, *Natural History*

Pliny *Ep.*; *Pan.*	Pliny the Younger, *Letters*; *Panegyric on Trajan*
Plut. *Numa*; *Ant.*; *Artax*; *Mor.*	Plutarch, *Lives* (*Numa*; *Antony*; *Artaxerxes*); *Moralia*
RG	*Res Gestae Divi Augusti* (*Achievements of the Deified Augustus*)
Sen. *Dial.*	Seneca the Younger, *Dialogues*
Suet. *Caes.*, *Aug.*, *Tib.*, *Cal.*, *Claud.*, *Nero*, *Galba*, *Otho*, *Vit.*, *Vesp.*, *Titus*, *Dom.*	Suetonius, *Lives of the Caesars: Julius Caesar*, *Augustus*, *Tiberius*, *Caligula*, *Claudius*, *Nero*, *Galba*, *Otho*, *Vitellius*, *Vespasian*, *Titus*, *Domitian*
Tac. *Ann.*; *Hist.*	Tacitus, *Annals*; *Histories*
Vell. Pat.	Velleius Paterculus, *History of Rome*
Vict. *Caes.*	Sextus Aurelius Victor, *Monograph on the Caesars*
Xiph.	Xiphilinus
Zon.	Zonaras
Zos.	Zosimus

Modern works and collections

AC	*L'Antiquité classique*
Acta Arch. Debr.	*Acta Archaeologica Debrecenensia*
AE	*L'Année épigraphique*, Paris, 1893–
AJAH	*American Journal of Ancient History*
ANRW	*Aufstieg und Niedergang der römischen Welt*, H. Temporini et al., eds., Berlin, 1972–
Ant. syr.	*Antiquités syriennes* 1–6, H. Seyrig, Paris, 1932–66
Apokrimata	*Apokrimata: Decisions of Septimius Severus on Legal Matters*, W. L. Westermann and A. A. Schiller, eds., New York, 1954
Arch. Anz.	*Archäologischer Anzeiger: Beiblatt zum Jahrbuch des deutschen archäologischen instituts*
Ath.	*Athenaeum*
BAR	*British Archaeological Reports*
Barrington	*Barrington Atlas of the Greek and Roman World*, R. J. A. Talbert, ed., Princeton, NJ, 2000
BCH	*Bulletin de Correspondance hellénique*
BEFAR	*Bibliothèque des Écoles françaises d'Athènes et de Rome*
BGU	*Berliner griechische Urkunden*
BICS	*Bulletin of the Institute of Classical Studies*

BMC	*Catalogue of Greek Coins in the British Museum*, R. S. Poole et al., eds., London, 1873–
Bull. Com.	*Bulletino della Com. arch. comunale di Roma*
Bull. épigr.	*Bulletin épigraphique*, J. Robert and L. Robert, publ. in *REG*
CAH	*Cambridge Ancient History*, ed. 1, 13 vols., Cambridge, 1936–54; ed. 2, 1961–
CE	*Chronique d'Egypte*
CEFR	*Collection de l'Ecole française de Rome*
CIG	*Corpus Inscriptionum Graecarum*, A. Boeckh et al., eds., 4 vols., Berlin, 1828–77
CIJ	*Corpus Inscriptionum Judaicarum. Recueil des inscr. juives qui vont du IIIe siècle avant J.-C. au VIIe siècle de notre ère*, J.-B. Frey, ed., Sussidi allo Stud. delle Ant. crist. 1, 3; 2 vols., Rome, 1936, 1952
CIL	*Corpus Inscriptionum Latinarum*, Th. Mommsen et al., eds., Berlin, 1863–
CJ	*Codex Iustinianus. Corpus Iuris Civilis 2*, P. Krueger, ed., Berlin, 1877; repr. ed. 12, 1959
CP	*Classical Philology*
CQ	*Classical Quarterly*
CRAI	*Comptes rendus de l'Académie des inscriptions et belles-lettres*
Crawford, *RRC*	*Roman Republican Coinage*, M. H. Crawford, 2 vols., Cambridge, 1974
CREBM	*Coins of the Roman Empire in the British Museum*, H. Mattingly et al., eds., London, 1923–
DE	*Dizionario epigrafico di Antichità romane*. Ist. ital. per la storia ant, E. de Ruggiero et al., eds., Rome, 1886–
EJ[2]	*Documents Illustrating the Reigns of Augustus and Tiberius*, V. Ehrenberg and A. H. M. Jones, eds., ed. 2 rev. D. L. Stockton, Oxford, 1976
EPRO	*Etudes préliminaires aux religions orientales dans l'Empire romain*, M. J. Vermaseren, ed., Leipzig, 1961–
Fer. Dur.	*Feriale Duranum*, R. O. Fink, A. S. Hoey and W. F. Snyder, eds., repr. from *YCS* 7, New Haven, CT, 1940
FGrH	*Die Fragmente der griechischen Historiker*, F. Jacoby, ed., 4 parts, Leiden, 1923–63
Head, *HN*[2]	*Historia Numorum: A Manual of Greek Numismatics*, B. V. Head, ed. 2, Oxford, 1911
Henzen, *AA*	*Acta Fratrum Arvalium quae supersunt*, W. Henzen, ed., Berlin, 1874, repr. Berlin, 1967
Hist.	*Historia*
HSCP	*Harvard Studies in Classical Philology*

I.Ephesos — *Die Inschriften von Ephesos* (= *IK* 11–17) H. Wankel et al., eds., Bonn, 1979–
IG — *Inscriptiones Graecae*, A. Kirchhoff et al., eds., Deutsche Akad. der Wiss. zu Berlin, Berlin, 1873–
IGBulg. — *Inscriptiones Graecae in Bulgaria Repertae*, G. Mihailov, ed., Epigr. Poreditsa. Arkh. Inst. Bulg. Akad. na Naukite 6, 7, 9, 10, Sofia, 1958–97
IGLS — *Inscriptions grecques et latines de la Syrie*, L. Jalabert, R. Mouterde et al., eds., Inst. d'Arch. de Beyrout, Paris, 1929–
IGR — *Inscriptiones Graecae ad res Romanas pertinentes*, R. Cagnat et al., eds., vols. 1, 3, 4, Paris, 1906–27; repr. Chicago, IL, 1975
IK — *Inschriften griechischer Städte aus Kleinasien*, Bonn, 1972–
ILAfr. — *Inscriptions latines d'Afrique (Tripolitanie, Tunisie, Maroc)*, R. Cagnat et al., eds., Paris, 1923
ILAlg. — *Inscriptions latines de l'Algérie*, S. Gsell et al., eds., Paris, then Algiers, 1922
ILS — *Inscriptiones Latinae Selectae*, H. Dessau, ed., 3 vols., Berlin, 1892–1916, repr. 1954–5
I.Prusias — *Die Inschriften von Prusias ad Hypium* (= *IK* 27) W. Ameling, ed., Bonn, 1985
IRT — *The Inscriptions of Roman Tripolitania*, J. M. Reynolds and J. B. Ward Perkins, eds., Rome, 1952
JNG — *Jahrbücher für Numismatik und Geldgeschichte*
JÖAI — *Jahreshefte des Österreichisches archäologischen Institutes in Wien*
JRS — *Journal of Roman Studies*
JS — *Journal des savants*
Lat. — *Latomus*
LSJ — *Greek Lexicon* H. G. Liddell and R. Scott, eds., ed. 9, rev. H. S. Jones, Oxford, 1940; *A Supplement*, ed. E. A. Barber, 1968; *A Revised Supplement*, ed. P. G. W. Glare and A. A. Thompson, 1996
MAAR — *Memoirs of the American Academy in Rome*
MDAI(A)(I)(R) — *Mitteilungen des Deutsches Arch. Inst. (Abteilung Athen/ Istanbul/Rome)*
MEFRA — *Mélanges de l'Ecole française de Rome (Antiquité)*
MGH — *Monumenta Germaniae Historica*
Mommsen, *St.* — *Römisches Staatsrecht*, Th. Mommsen,3 vols., Berlin, 1^3, 1887; 2^3, 1886; 3^3, 1887; repr. Basel, 1952
MW — *Select Documents of the Principates of the Flavian Emperors including the Year of Revolution A.D. 68–96*, M. McCrum and A.G. Woodhead, eds., Cambridge, 1961

MZ	*Mainzer Zeitschrift*
NC	*Numismatic Chronicle*
OCD[3]	*The Oxford Classical Dictionary*, S. Hornblower and A. Spawforth, eds., ed. 3, Oxford, 1996
Oliver, *Gk. Const.*	*Greek Constitutions of Early Roman Emperors from Inscriptions and Papyri*, J. H. Oliver, Memoirs of the American Philosophical Society 178, Philadelphia, PA, 1989
P.Beatty Panopolis	*Papyri from Panopolis in the Chester Beatty Library Dublin*, T. C. Skeat, ed., Chester Beatty Monographs 10, Dublin, 1964
PBSR	*Papers of the British School at Rome*
PCPS	*Proceedings of the Cambridge Philological Society*
PDAR	*Pictorial Dictionary of Ancient Rome*, E. Nash, New York, 1961–2, rev. ed. 1968
PE	*The Princeton Encyclopedia of Classical Sites*, R. Stilwell, ed., Princeton, NJ, 1976
P.Fayum	*Fayûm Towns and their Papyri*, B. P. Grenfell, A. S. Hunt and D. G. Hogarth, London, 1900
PG	*Patrologia Graeca*, J.-P. Migne, ed., Paris, 1857–66
P.Giessen	*Griechische Papyri im Museum des oberhessischen Geschichtsvereins zu Giessen*, E. Kornemann et al., eds., Leipzig, 1910–12
PIR(2)	*Prosopographia Imperii Romani*, E. Klebs et al., eds., 3 vols., Berlin, 1897–8; ed. 2 E. Groag et al., Berlin, 1933–
PL	*Patrologia Latina*, J.-P. Migne, ed., Paris, 1844–64
P.Oxy.	*The Oxyrhynchus Papyri*, B. P. Grenfell et al., eds., London, 1898–
PP	*La Parola del Passato*
P.Strassb.	*Griechische Papyri der Universitäts- und Landesbibliothek zu Strassburg*, F. Preisigke, ed., 2 vols., Leipzig, 1912–20
RE	*Paulys Realencyclopädie der class. Altertumswissenschaft*, G. Wissowa et al., eds., Stuttgart, 1894–1980
REA	*Revue des études anciennes*
REG	*Revue des études grecques*
Rev. Phil.	*Revue de Philologie, de Littérature et d'Histoire anciennes*
Rhein. Mus.	*Rheinisches Museum für Philologie*
RIB	*The Roman Inscriptions of Britain*. 1. *Inscriptions on Stone*, R. G. Collingwood and R. P. Wright, Oxford, 1965; addenda and corr. by R. S. O. Tomlin, Stroud, 1995
RIC	*Roman Imperial Coinage*, H. Mattingly et al., eds., London, 1923–

RN	*Revue Numismatique*
Robert, *Hell.*	*Hellenica. Recueil d'épigr., de numismatique et d'antiquités grecques*, J. Robert and L. Robert, 13 vols., Limoges, 1940–65
RPC	*Roman Provincial Coinage*, A. Burnett, J. Amandry et al., eds., 1–, London, 1992–
SB	*Sammelbuch grieschischer Urkunden aus Ägypten*, F. Preisigke et al., eds., Strasburg, 1913–93
SEG	*Supplementum Epigraphicum Graecum*, J. J. E. Hondius et al., eds., Leiden, 1923–
Sel. Pap.	*Select Papyri: 2. Non-Literary Papyri*, A. S. Hunt and C. C. Edgar, eds., Cambridge, MA, 1934
Smallwood, *G-N*	*Documents Illustrating the Principates of Gaius Claudius and Nero*, E. M. Smallwood, Cambridge, 1967
Smallwood, *N-H*	*Documents Illustrating the Principates of Nerva Trajan and Hadrian*, E. M. Smallwood, Cambridge, 1966
SO	*Symbolae Osloenses*
Steinby, *Lexicon*	*Lexicon topographicum Urbis Romae*, E. M. Steinby, ed., 6 vols., Rome, 1993–9
Syme, *RP*	*Roman Papers*, R. Syme, eds. E. Badian (1–2), A. R. Birley (3–7), 7 vols., Oxford, 1979–91
TAM	*Tituli Asiae Minoris Antiquae*, R. Heberdey et al., eds., Vienna, 1901–
TAPA	*Transactions and Proceedings of the American Philological Association*
TDAR	*Topographical Dictionary of Ancient Rome*, S. B. Platner, rev. T. Ashby, Oxford, 1926
TLL	*Thesaurus Linguae Latinae. ed. auctoritate et consilio acad. quinque*, Leipzig, 1900–
YCS	*Yale Classical Studies*
ZPE	*Zeitschrift für Papyrologie und Epigraphik*

Family trees

The Dynasty of Emesa
(See Sullivan 1999: Stemma 6. with further details)

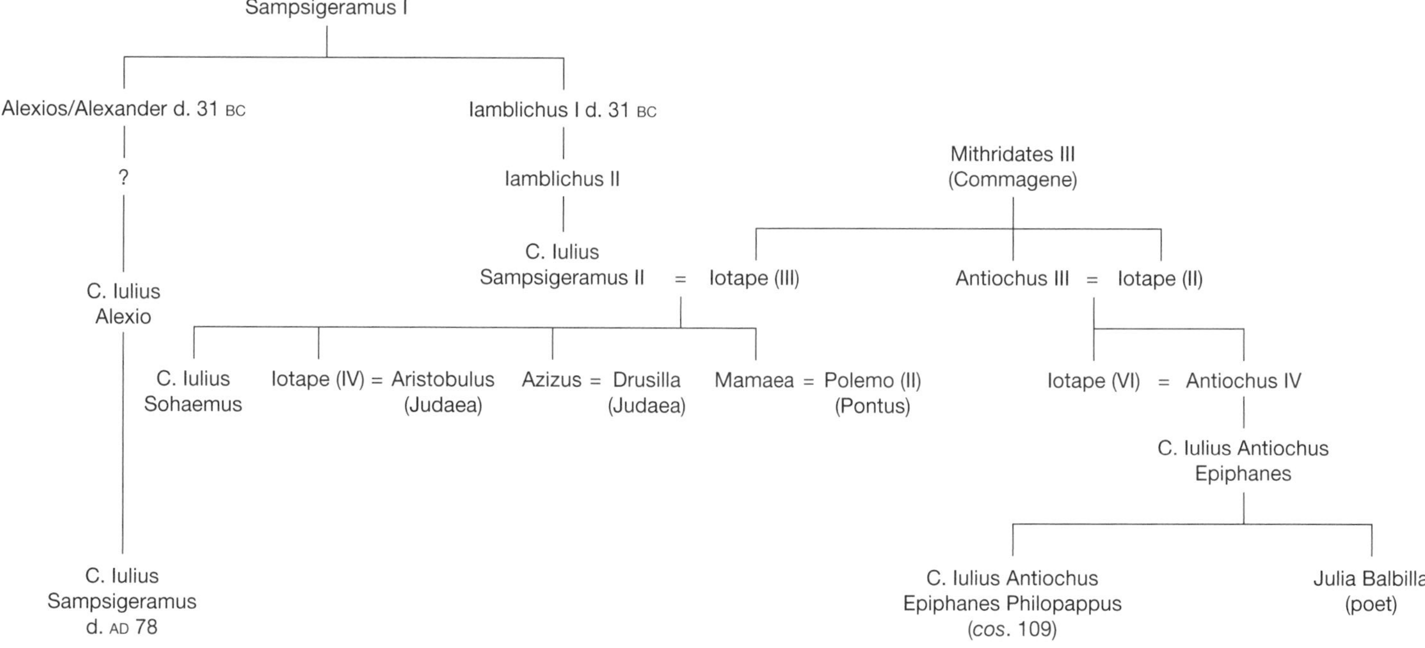

The Family of Julia Domna

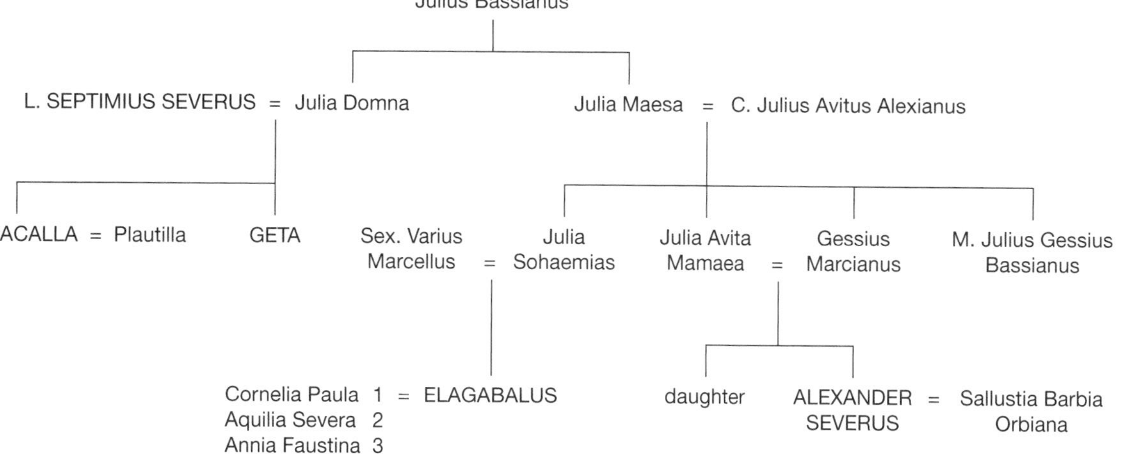

Descent of Septimius Severus
(for full details, see Birley 1999: 216f., with Chausson 2002)

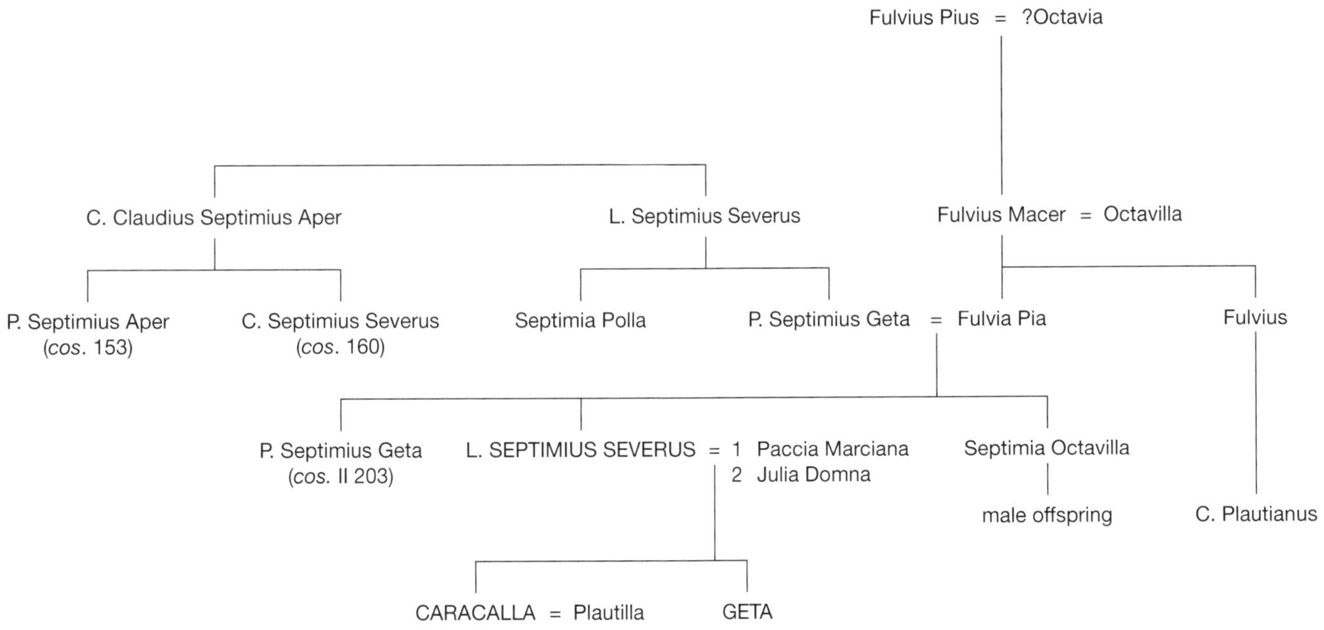

Maps

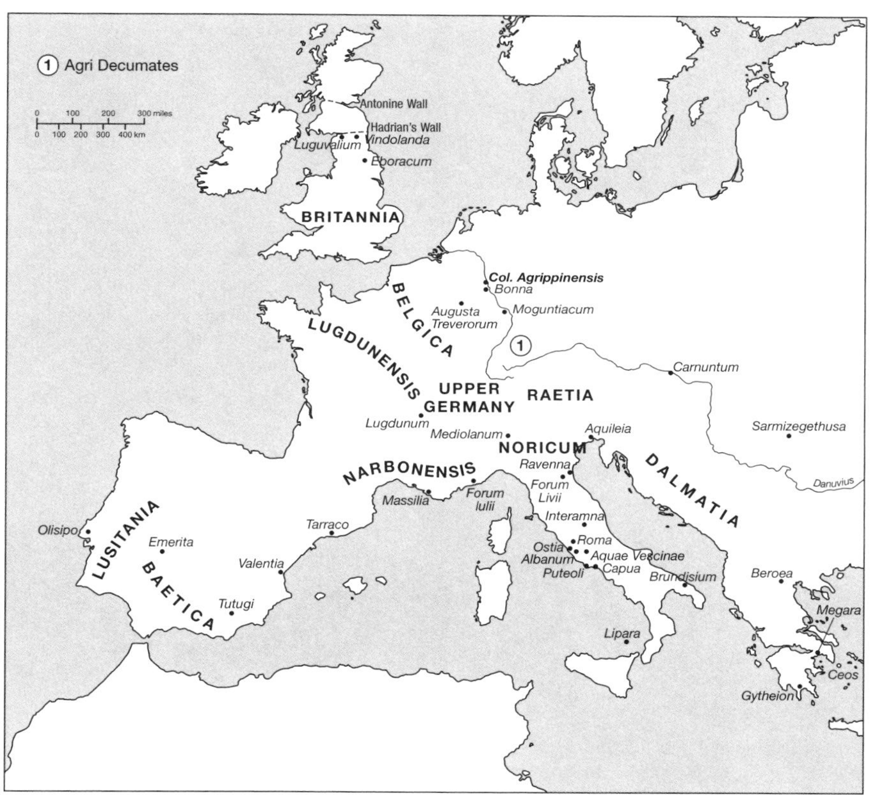

Map 1 The western provinces

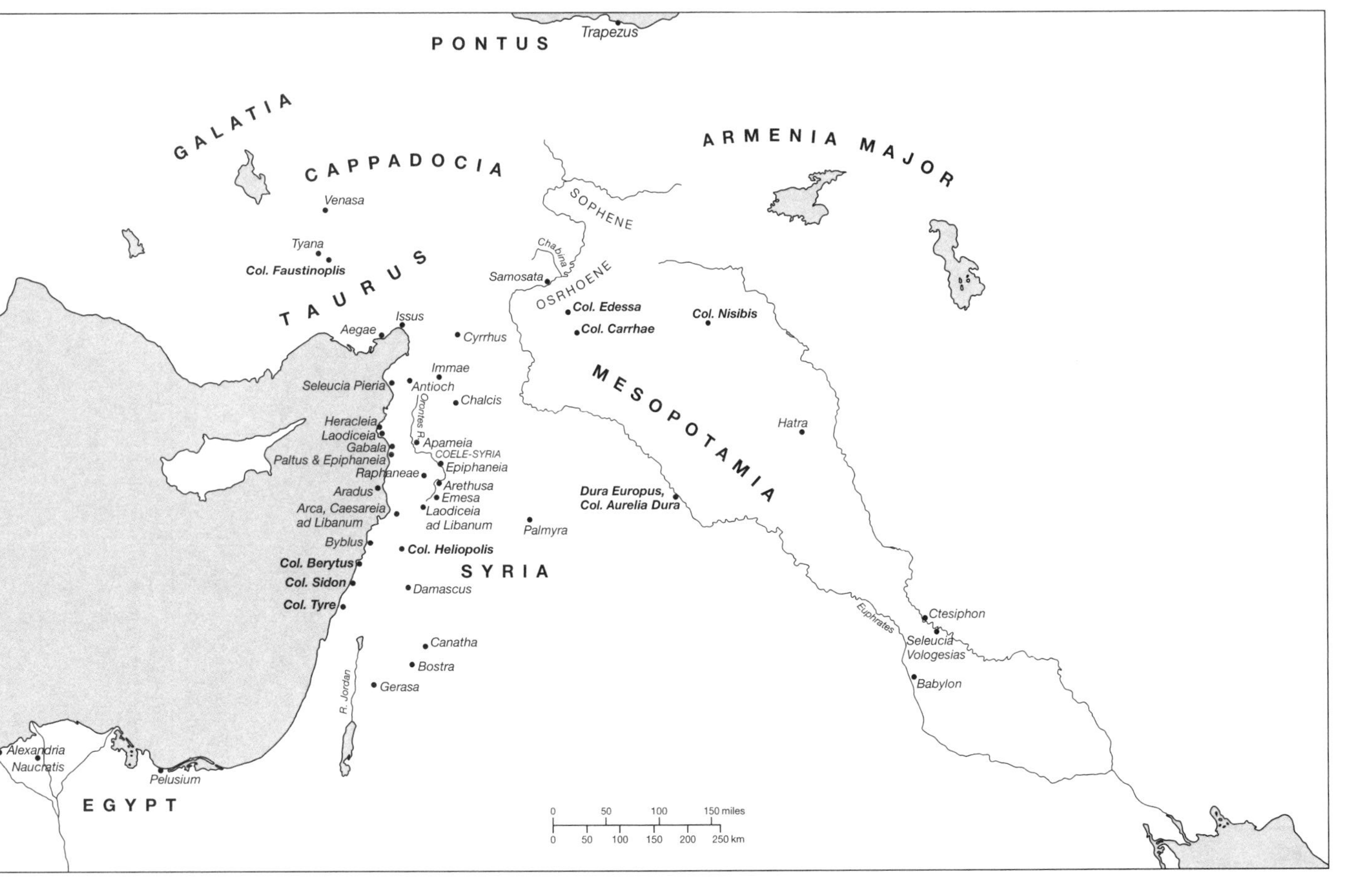

Map 2 The eastern provinces

Map 3 Asia Minor

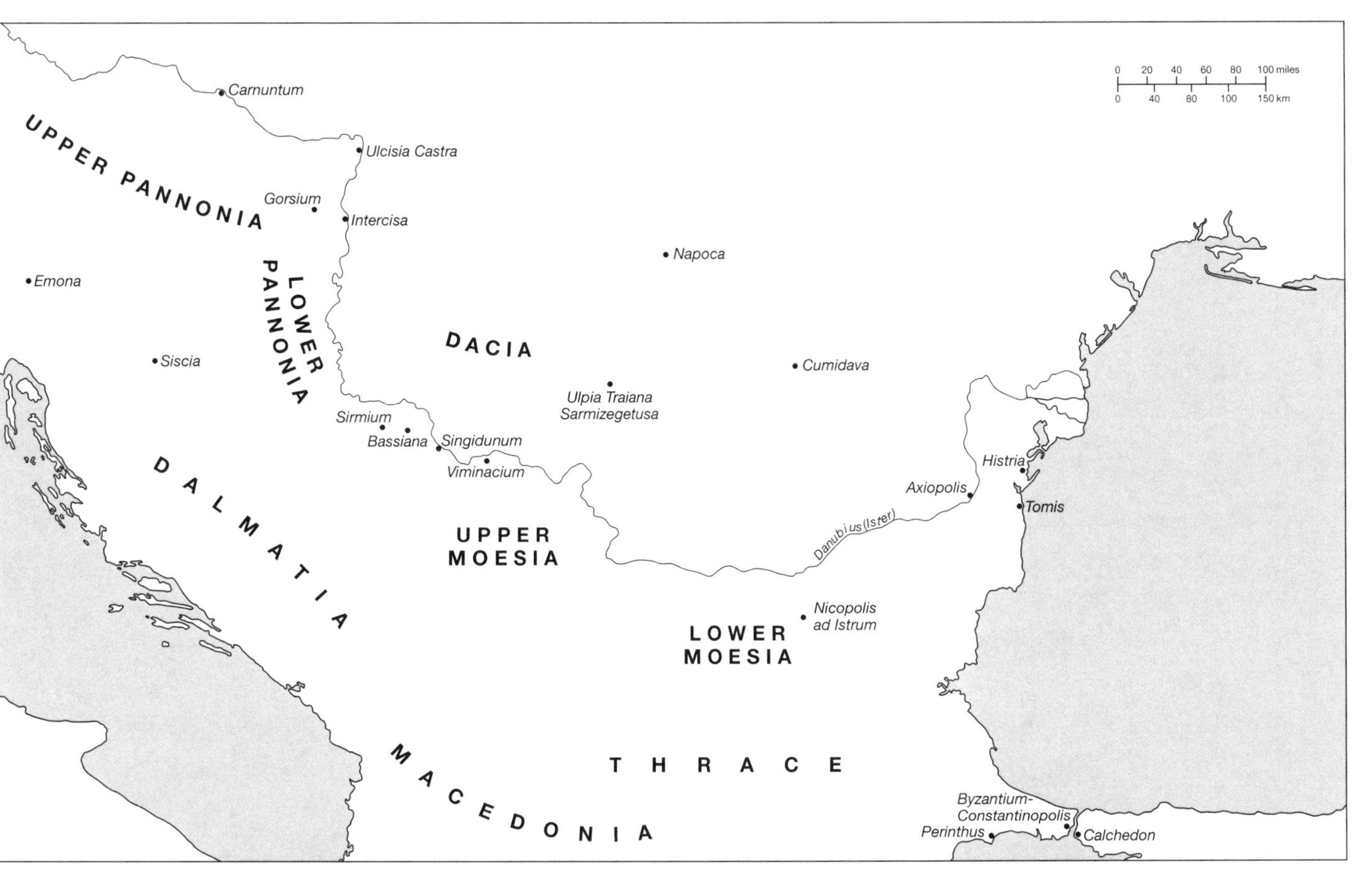

Map 4 The Balkan and Danubian provinces

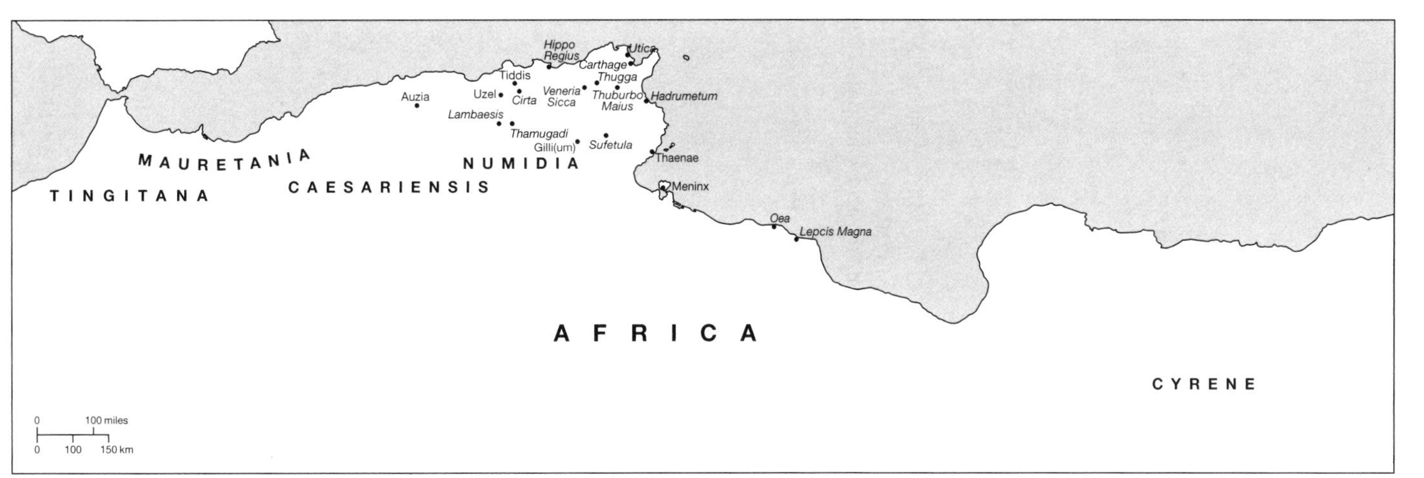

Map 5 Roman north Africa

Chronology

(See Kienast 1996; Halfmann 1986: 216–30; Leunissen 1989: 386; Birley 1999)

43 BC	Triumvirate formed by Mark Antony, M. Lepidus, Octavian (later Augustus)
30 BC	Defeat of Mark Antony and Cleopatra by Octavian
27 BC–AD 14	Principate of Augustus
14–68	Julio-Claudian Dynasty: Principates of:
14–37	Tiberius
37–41	Gaius (Caligula)
41–54	Claudius
54–68	Nero
69	'Year of the Four Emperors'
69–96	Flavio-Trajanic Dynasty: Reigns of:
69–79	Vespasian
79–81	Titus
81–96	Domitian
96–8	Nerva
98–117	Trajan
117–38	Hadrian
138–80	Antonine Dynasty:
138–61	Reign of Antoninus Pius
145 or 146	11 April. Birth of L. Septimius Severus
161–80	Reign of Marcus Aurelius (with Lucius Verus until 169)
170–4	Birth of Julia Domna
170 or 171	Severus quaestor
171 or 172	Severus quaestor in Sardinia
173–4	Severus legate in Africa
174	Severus tribune of the *plebs*; marriage to Paccia Marciana
175	Revolt of Avidius Cassius
?178	Severus praetor
?178–81	Severus *legatus iuridicus* in Asturia and Callaecia
180	17 Mar. to 31 Dec. 192. Sole reign of Commodus

?182–3	Severus legate of IV Scythica in Syria
?186–9	Severus governor of Lugdunensian Gaul
187	July or earlier. Marriage of Severus and Domna
188	4 April Birth of Caracalla
189	(spring) Birth of Geta
189–90	Severus governor of Sicily
190	(second half) Severus suffect consul
191–3	Severus governor of Upper Pannonia
192	31 Dec. Commodus assassinated
193	1 Jan. to 28 Mar. Reign of P. Helvius Pertinax
	28 Mar. to 1 June Reign of M. Didius Julianus
	9 April Proclamation of Severus at Carnuntum
	1 June Severus proclaimed emperor at Rome
	Mid-June to mid-July Sojourn at Rome
193–4	(winter) Sojourn at Perinthus?
194	(spring) Journey through Asia Minor to Syria
	Defeat of Pescennius Niger at Issus
194–5	(winter) Sojourn in Syria
195	(spring–summer) First Parthian war
	14 April Domna becomes *Mater Castrorum*
	(mid-year) Caracalla's name changed; title of Caesar used?
195	(end) to 196 Return to west through Asia Minor
196	(first half) Caracalla officially Caesar
197	19 Feb. Victory over Albinus at Lugdunum
	(beginning of June) Return to Rome
	(high summer) Departure for second Parthian war, via Brundisium
	Geta made pontifex
	(late summer to beginning of 198) Second Parthian war
	(late in year) Capture of Ctesiphon
198	28 Jan. Celebration of *Victoria Parthica*. Caracalla becomes Augustus, Geta becomes Caesar, and Domna becomes *Mater Augusti et Caesaris*
198–9	Sojourn in Syria
199	(early) Second siege of Hatra
199	(after Mar.–Apr.) Arrival in Egypt
	Nile voyage to border of Ethiopia
	Caracalla becomes Father of his Country
200	(towards end) Return by sea to Syria, followed by sojourn there
202	1 Jan. Joint consulship of Severus and Caracalla, entered at Antioch
	(early in year) Beginning of return journey to Rome
	(by 28 Aug.) Arrival at Rome; marriage of Caracalla and Plautilla

202	(late) or 203 (early) Journey to Africa
203	(shortly before 10 June) Return to Rome
204	26 May to 3 June. Secular Games
205	Caracalla (II) and Geta (I) consuls
	22 Jan. Fall of Plautianus
207	(late) or 208 (early) Departure for Britain
209	(at latest Sept./Oct.) Geta becomes Augustus and Domna Mater Augustorum
210	5 May. Severus in Eboracum
211	4 Feb. Death of Severus at Eboracum; accession of Caracalla and Geta; execution of Proculus Torpacion and other courtiers
	Domna, *Mater Castrorum et Senatus et Patriae*, also becomes *Pia Felix*
	Return of imperial family to Rome
	19 or 26 Dec. Murder of Geta. Domna becomes *Mater Augusti/Imperatoris*
212	*Constitutio Antoniniana*
212 or early 213.	Caracalla leaves for Germany and Raetia
213	Aug.–Sept. Caracalla's campaigns in Germany
	(end) Caracalla's journey to Pannonia and through Balkans; escape from shipwreck
213–14	Caracalla in winter quarters at ?Nicomedia, celebrating Saturnalia there 17 Dec.
214	Imperial family in Asia and Bithynia, including Ilium, Pergamum, and Thyatira (spring); journey through Asia Minor via Prusias ad Hypium, Tyana, and Tarsus
214–15	(summer) Sojourn at Antioch
	(autumn) Journey to Egypt
215	Dec. to 216 (spring). Sojourn in Alexandria; rioting repressed
216	(spring) Return to Antioch
216–17	Parthian campaign; Caracalla winters at Edessa
217	28 Jan. Caracalla's *Vicennalia*
217	8 Apr. Assassination of Caracalla between Edessa and Carrhae
	11 Apr. M. Opellius Macrinus becomes emperor
	(summer) Death of Domna
	Macrinus returns to Mesopotamia
	?Oct.–Nov.? Battle of Nisibis
217–18	Macrinus winters in Antioch
218	16 May. Mutiny at Raphaneae
	8 June. Defeat of Macrinus. Entry of Elagabalus into Antioch

218 (cont)	(early autumn) Departure of Elagabalus and Sohaemias from Antioch for Bithynia via Cappadocia-Galatia
218–19	Imperial party winters in Nicomedia
219	July–Aug. Arrival of Elagabalus in Rome after journey through Thrace, Moesia, and the Pannonias
221	June. Adoption of Severus Alexander
222	11 or 12 Mar. Deaths of Elagabalus and Sohaemias
222–35	(spring) Reign of Alexander Severus

Introduction

The story of Julia Domna is dramatic and powerful, even tragic. Surprisingly, it has not been made into a novel or a film for television or the big screen,[1] given the battle scenes, the wild backdrops of Yorkshire moors and the Taurus mountains, and the splendour of north Africa and Egypt. But Domna is not like Cleopatra VII, a notorious deviant from the conventions of her time, hostile as the chroniclers Cassius Dio, Herodian and the *Historia Augusta* are; it is her integration into ruling circles of Graeco-Roman society at the turn of the second and third centuries that make her a subject for history. Domna is both a personality who demands to be studied for her own sake and a Tolstoyan figurehead, carried along by events[2] – and serving to show how the currents are flowing.

Domna's story contains at least three dependent plots, all gripping, two of them of great historical importance. First comes the family romance of the dynasty of Emesa, dependent princes of the Roman Empire who, deprived of their realm in the first or second century AD, bounced back by marrying one of their women to a man who came to rule the whole Roman Empire, Septimius Severus. A second romance forms a sequel: of a powerful dynasty of Emesene women, Domna the first, who played an unprecedented part in running the Empire, so that in the last two reigns of the Severan emperors, those of Elagabalus and Severus Alexander, women seem to be its effective rulers. How powerful could a woman become, then, in comparison with earlier women in politics, and in the face of tenacious male hostility? Finally and most importantly comes a story of the society of Rome and the Empire: how it was orientalized in social life and especially in religion as a result of the dominance of a dynasty of north African and Syrian origins. The Severan age figures as a turning point for the Roman Empire – for the worse.[3] The Severan dynasty, in particular the Emesene women, in accordance with their own oriental origin and ways, were to be held responsible for taking Rome down a new road, towards oriental monarchy. Part of this change consisted in a change of personnel among the elite and the advance of 'orientals' to equestrian and senatorial posts; in particular it was the religion of the army that took this path toward orientalism.[4] The oriental monarchy was embodied in the notorious Emperor Elagabalus, as portrayed by his much older contemporary Cassius Dio and then by Herodian and others. Domna was primarily to blame: Severus was an African, but a thoroughly Romanized one. In this book the subject will recur more than once, but especially in connection with the imperial cult. As the word 'oriental', coming into English use in nineteenth-century historians, is often deployed as a term of abuse, it is vain to look for a satisfactory definition of it; it includes traits of religion, politics, architecture, art and music, language, and the morals and manners of society, thought to be peculiar to areas and peoples east of the Mediterranean and the Roman Empire; in short, in the abusive sense, extravagance, licence, and tyranny. Correspondingly intellectuals' 'orientalism', according to E. Said, is 'a style of thought based on distinctions an ontological and epistemological distinction made between "the Orient" and "the Occident", forming a starting point for theories' and involving 'dealing with' or 'conquering' the Orient.[5]

The three stories are interrelated, the last two in particular. The links between developing autocracy and orientalization are twofold. Democracy, or regulated oligarchy with some participation by the people, were the conscious creations of Greece and Rome. It was part of Greek and Roman beliefs about empires to the east of them, from Persia onwards, that they were ruled by despots, kings whose subjects were 'slaves'. The Persian Empire fell to Alexander the Great, and after his death his realms were divided up between successor monarchies, toppled one after another by Rome. In the Roman perspective, departures from equality between peers, notably departures made by emperors from equality with their fellow senators, besides being hated in themselves, could be seen in the light of alien practices and as a move towards monarchy and slavery. It was the weakness of Mark Antony's position as ruler of the Greek-speaking part of the Empire in the eyes of Italians and in the face of Octavian (soon to become Augustus) that he was politically and economically dependent on Cleopatra, as well as being her lover. But links between the ideas of developing autocracy and orientalization were not necessary: there had been at least one alleged tyrant, Tiberius, who could never be accused of eastern leanings (his interest in philosophy and art was something purely for his private life). And in the times of Nero, Domitian, and Hadrian mere philhellenism was the worst cultural insult yet to be hurled against an emperor hated by his peers.

All three stories have met severe criticism, separately or in combination. In particular, F. G. B. Millar has dealt with the first, I. Mundle, E. Kettenhofen, F. Ghedini and others with the second and third, Kettenhofen suggesting that the authority of Domaszewski had prevented attention being given to more fruitful aspects of the material.[6] But focusing on the dependent plots, all-important as they are historically, especially the third, must not draw attention away from the woman herself, Domna was a remarkable person, in looks, education, and character, and deserves considering for her own sake, in particular for the place she holds in the development of a woman's place in dynasties between Livia and Theodora.

Suetonius, biographer of the emperors from Caesar to Domitian, might well leave physical descriptions to the end of his works; physical and even intellectual compared with moral qualities displayed in action are to be seen as linked but trivial. To follow Suetonius' practice in the case of a woman would be misleading, no matter what her other qualities might be. Men could rise on merit, *uirtus*, but that was a quality of men, *uiri*; physical beauty played a more prominent part in the way a woman was perceived by her contemporaries, next to birth and property. A woman would know that and exploit it. Domna was attractive, as ancient writers say and her many portraits show. 'A striking, indeed beautiful woman, with fine and sensitive features', is how A. R. Birley describes her, also citing Gibbon: 'Julia Domna . . . deserved all that the stars could promise her; she possessed, even in an advanced age, the attractions of beauty, and united to a lively imagination a firmness of mind, and strength of judgment, seldom bestowed on her sex.'[7] A down-to-earth verdict was given a century ago on her representation on the Arch of the *Argentarii*: 'It is difficult to see any trace of beauty in her round face, even after making due allowance for all mutilation', but that was evidently due to a failing of the artist, for the great bust in the Vatican is allowed 'great charm'.[8] The hairstyle that Domna sported, and no doubt helped to make popular, a variant of the style initiated by Commodus' wife Bruttia Crispinilla, shows off a rich mane of wavy locks and would not have been possible without the generous hairpieces loathed by her Christian contemporary Tertullian, which are themselves claimed to be specimens of orientalization. The hair is parted in the middle and drawn back on either side (with little side-loops all her own emerging by either cheek), to be gathered at the neck into intertwined braids that were carried up the back of her head.[9] In 2001 a delicious hypothesis was put forward: that Domna was the model for the Venus di Milo, a production on its way to Syria in 217 with a companion piece representing Caracalla when news of his death arrived and the work became an embarrassment.[10] Beauty played a part not only in Domna's marriage but also in all that followed from it, notably her ability to work with her courtiers, friends, and subjects, and to get her own way.

Given the suggestion about the Venus di Milo, it is doubly interesting to consider the moralist Lucian's panegyric, in dialogue form, on a woman who belonged to a generation or so before Domna's: the beauty of this second century paragon is still owed in part to her resemblance to features of classic works of art such as the Cnidian Aphrodite of Praxiteles (her forehead and eyes, liquid and brilliant) and even Phidias' austere Lemnian Athena (the outline of her face and her shapely nose). Beautifully shaped hands with tapering fingers were also admired, like her exceptionally even teeth, which her admirers glimpsed in her hardly perceptible smile as she read, conversed, or sang in a voice that was not deep enough to be a man's but not womanishly high and weak; in fact rather like that of a prepubescent youth. She spoke pure Ionic Greek – not surprisingly in a woman from Smyrna, a settlement of Athens – had plenty to say and said it with great precision of language. She possessed the gifts of all the Muses and those of Apollo and Hermes as well. Interestingly too she was not only gentle, gracious, and modest, as all women were expected to be, but also shrewd and endowed with a good knowledge of public affairs. To cap it all, for all her position she never put herself above ordinary folk. Panthea of Smyrna was a courtesan, the mistress not the wife of the Emperor Lucius Verus, but she illustrates what was required of women at the centre of power: a touch of the masculine in all the femininity; alluring beauty and alert intelligence; proper devotion to her man. The beauty of Domna may well have been different from that of the Greek lady Panthea, and moulded to different ideals: there is no reason to believe that she was descended from Greek immigrants to the Levant rather than from an indigenous family.[11]

Sculptures and coins, even painting, remain to help students form their own opinion as to Domna's beauty.[12] We should not read too much into these representations. Her face has been written of as one on which the traces of the events of her time could be seen, and of her life lived at the highest of power and amid perpetual tension.[13] That is not what public portraiture would have aimed at. In any case, Domna's personality and culture are more enigmatic than her appearance. She came from Syria: how Syrian, how exotic, how Greek and how Roman was she? How far did she adapt to life at the Roman court? Did she refuse to eat pork, like her young kinsman, the deeply observant Emperor Elagabalus?[14] She was something at least of a philosopher; how seriously should we take her intellectual activities? Did she become, in maturity, the leader of a circle of literary men? Again, as the wife and mother of emperors, and one who certainly enjoyed a measure of power, her position fluctuated, and ended in utter defeat. How great did it become in comparison with the varied powers exercised at their peak by some of her predecessors, Livia, Agrippina the Younger, Faustina II, and by successors such as Theodora? Domaszewski offered a sweeping theory, but it implied development through time. The three stories in which Domna is involved will be dealt with chronologically, rather than in thematic essays, though culture and cult have called for separate treatment; the problems the stories raise will be reviewed in the concluding chapter.

Acute difficulties await the historian, and some of them have been lucidly expounded.[15] Biography as modern historians recognize it is impossible for want of evidence. Then the bias of ancient historians and orators has to be allowed for, as does the flattery of contemporary official documents, inscriptions, coins, and papyri; but when a prominent woman is the object of enquiry, a particular form of prejudice becomes evident, fear and derivative misogyny. That does not mean that historical narratives are to be discounted, even by feminists; rather the bias itself is part of the milieu in which the woman functioned, and something of which she would have had to take account. More radical still is the complaint that history is nothing but story, told by no matter whom. Rightly, Eck rejects that. All statements must be made by someone, in life as in history. It makes sense to distinguish between true and false, and to act accordingly. Verdicts can be reached and judgments passed.

I call Julia Domna by her *cognomen* throughout, because her *nomen* is too indistinctive to be useful; likewise I refer to her husband Septimius Severus by his *cognomen*, for brevity's sake. More controversially, their sons are denoted by the familiar names of Caracalla and Geta, no matter what name or title they were currently employing at any given moment; Geta's uncle of the same name is given his *praenomen* Publius. Caracalla was only a nick-name, the name of the Gallic cloak the emperor liked to wear, given him by the soldiery,[16] as their nickname for the Emperor Gaius, Caligula('Bootsie'), has no official standing but is conveniently unique; none of Caracalla's official names would be correct for the whole of his lifetime. For the same reason I refer to Varius Avitus Bassianus, who became the Emperor M. Aurelius Antoninus Augustus, by his later sobriquet Elagabalus; '(H)eliogabalus', the result of a false etymology connecting his name with the Sun god, does not appear until the mid-fourth century, nor was Elagabalus in use by ancient authors, except for the deity.[17] Severus Alexander is more sober and more acceptable as the working name for Elagabalus' successor, M. Aurelius Severus Alexander Augustus, born Gessius Alexianus Bassianus. Elagabalus' mother will be Sohaemias out of respect for its derivation from the Semitic name, despite Greek and Latin epigraphic evidence for Soaemias. As to the sheikhs and kings whose slightly variable name we shall find Cicero mirthfully exploiting, they are to be Sampsigeramus throughout, while Domna's native city will go in modern form by the familiar Homs, rather than the more accurate Ḥims.

1 The woman of Emesa

To understand Julia Domna's upbringing and mental horizons, as far as that is possible, her geographical, cultural, and religious background must be understood, and its complex development through space and time. Only then can she be set against it. Syria is a strip of land stretching from the Taurus mountains in the north to the confines of Egypt in the south; from west to east it reaches from the Mediterranean to the Iraqi desert.[1] This is the geographical term; political units called Syria, such as the Roman province and especially the modern state, have been more restricted. Geographers from the Arab period onwards have described the area as divided into parallel zones also running north–south.[2] Behind a narrow coastal plain lie broken mountain ranges separated from each other by the valleys of the Jordan and the Orontes. Further still to the east is undulating steppe and then the Arabian desert, watered at Damascus and elsewhere by rivers flowing from the mountain ranges or by local springs, as at Petra and Palmyra. The later Ottoman provinces of Aleppo and Damascus stretched to the Gulf of Aqaba, but they did not include the Mediterranean strip. The political result of the fragmented physical geography was that Syria was not likely to be a political unity but would be split into a number of small states, and, as the route between Egypt and powers to the north, whether based in Asia Minor or in Mesopotamia, a scene of conflict between them.

This geographical configuration meant that Syria was a crossroads for trade routes, most obviously up and down the coast and along the grain of the mountain ranges but more famously from east to west, through caravan routes. Against a background of village settlement there were towns on all these routes, several renowned, commercial dealings by caravan with the interior of Asia lending their names an exotic and romantic ring: Tyre and Sidon on the coast, Petra in the hinterland, Damascus and Palmyra in the desert. But the connecting river valleys were also important. 'The international route' has been described in some detail:[3] from Damascus the main highway turns west, crosses the Anti-Lebanon and shoots north following the Orontes through Kadesh (later Laodiceia ad Libanum) into north Syria. On its way through Kadesh it sends a branch that connects it with the Mediterranean through the Nahr al-Kabir (Eleutherus) gorge – a course which, Hitti pointed out, is taken by the modern railway that branches at Homs from the Aleppo–Damascus main line towards Tripoli.

The most important city on the Orontes route, Antioch, was the capital of the Greek Seleucid kingdom that established itself in this area; Emesa was one of the settlements further upstream on the Orontes, standing one and half km. from the bank, at 495 m. above sea level and owing its importance to its position at the head of the gorge and at the centre of a fertile, irrigated plain running north and south, a plain that is still heavily cultivated, with wheat and barley, fruit and vegetable gardens and vineyards, but no longer with the olives attested by presses left from antiquity; in the middle of the twentieth century shepherds engaged in transhumance were bringing their herds from Mount Lebanon into the hills round Homs for the winter. Emesa's connections were good: it stood on the Beroea–Damascus route, reached Antioch via Apameia and Tyre via Heliopolis, Palmyra and Aradus. Coins of the first century BC and of the reign of Augustus struck at Tyre, Aradus, and Seleuceia Pieria have been found in its necropolis, and a merchant from Salona in Dalmatia died and was buried there in AD 112.[4]

In 334 BC Persian suzerainty over Syria came to an end when Alexander the Great defeated Darius at the battle of Issus, but Alexander's death led to a struggle for control of Syria between the Ptolemies in Egypt and other successor dynasts to the north, reduced by the end of the century to Seleucus I Nicator (312–280), founder of the Seleucid dynasty and empire. The usual boundary of their spheres for the next century was the river Eleutherus, close to Emesa, but the Ptolemies lost their hold to Antiochus III (the Great, 223–187) in 200 BC.[5] We do not know how old the settlement at Emesa was, and that is the beginning of its historical obscurities.[6] It has been allowed 'some antiquity', with traces before the first century BC.[7] That is not surprising, given its situation, where the Bouqaia gap gives easy access at low altitude to the Mediterranean coast.[8] The Seleucids were responsible for colonies, refoundations, and the renaming of ancient communities in their kingdom. Twenty km. north of Emesa was Greek-sounding Arethusa, a native settlement with a name superficially hellenized under Seleucus I; still further downstream on the Orontes was biblical Hamath, which became Epiphaneia, while close by to the south was Laodiceia ad Libanum. These will have formed the northern and southern limits of Emesene territory.[9]

Antiochus IV Epiphanes (175–64) in particular promoted urbanization by granting autonomy and charters to a number of communities, including Jerusalem. He consciously gave an impetus to the hellenization of the area: the Greek language and nomenclature, Greek political institutions and styles in art were all being adopted. But the kingdom was beginning to break up. Antiochus III, after successful ventures into Asia, had taken on the Romans and was defeated at the battle of Magnesia in 189; that ended his claims to Asia Minor. The later second century BC saw the revolt of the Maccabees in 167 against the religious oppression of Antiochus Epiphanes and their establishment of an independent Judaea, the decline of the Seleucid monarchy, and the fragmentation of the kingdom into smaller independent units; Arabs under a dynast probably called Iamblichus – the name used by later rulers of Emesa, which brings us into contact with the earliest possible ancestors of Julia Domna that we can trace – were playing their part in the reorganization in 145 BC.[10] The last two rivals for control of the kingdom, Antiochus XIII Asiaticus (69–64) and Philip II Barypous (65–64), are said to have been put to death by two phylarchs, as the sheikhs were known to the Greeks, Azizus and Sampsigeramus I, the latter certainly a dynast of the Emesenes. (Cicero awarded the name Sampsigeramus to their patron Pompey the Great to make fun of Pompey's pretensions as an eastern potentate.) They did not succeed in taking the kingdom over but paved the way for Pompey, who brought it to an end in 63 BC. The core was annexed and outlying parts left to their existing dependent rulers as buffers against incursions from the east.[11] Emesa was not a candidate for the 'freedom' that Pompey granted many of the hellenized cities of Syria, but was left to its Arab dynasts under Roman suzerainty, and Sampsigeramus was confirmed in power. Arethusa went the same way and celebrated the change by adopting a new era, 64–63; according to the Augustan geographer and historian Strabo, Sampsigeramus governed it well.[12] Such men could police routes and preserve the integrity of the Roman Empire without cost to Roman manpower or to the Roman treasury; on the contrary, they probably paid dues for the privilege.

The next ruler of the Emesene district that we meet is the Iamblichus I, Sampsigeramus' son, mentioned by Cicero, who as governor of Cilicia in south-eastern Asia Minor was thinking of him in 51 as a possible ally against the Parthians.[13] Strabo writes of the territory of Sampsigeramus and his son Iamblichus at a time when the Emesenes had prudently given Julius Caesar support in Alexandria in 48; for he was their patron after Pompey had been defeated and killed.[14]

Power struggles between Roman politicians and the efforts of some to save the Republic naturally had an impact on dependent rulers. Doctrine was not important: what mattered as always was the nearness and effectiveness of the Roman commander in the area. There are variant stories of the fortunes of the Emesene dynasty during the Caesarian and Triumviral periods, from 48 to 31, but it looks as if Iamblichus, after a brief period in which he supported a governor of Syria who was one of Caesar's assassins,[15] acceded to Mark Antony in his government of the Greek-speaking provinces of the Empire. However, Iamblichus became suspect to Antony and was deposed and replaced by his brother Alexander.[16] In turn Julius Caesar's heir Augustus deposed and killed Alexander when he reorganized the east in 31 BC; for a few years the Emesenes were an autonomous community free of dynastic rule, though under the supervision of the governor of Syria.[17] Clearly, however, it was most convenient for the Roman government to deal with an individual in effective control. Augustus restored Emesa to his victim's nephew

Iamblichus II, son of Iamblichus I, after another decade,[18] and for a century, under Augustus and his Julio-Claudian successors, the ruling family need have had no doubt where its loyalties lay.

Another Sampsigeramus (II) was mentioned in 18/19 alongside Germanicus Caesar, who would have succeeded the Emperor Tiberius in power if he had not died on his mission to the east. That was in an inscription from the temple of Bel at Palmyra.[19] Emesa was closely linked for its prosperity with its neighbour Palmyra and Sampsigeramus may have acted as an intermediary between Palmyra and Rome.[20] By that time he was permitted the designation of 'Great King' that Agrippa I of Judaea enjoyed and that Ti. Claudius Togidubnus was to be allowed at the other end of the Empire in his realm of Hampshire, Berkshire, and Sussex: C. Iulius Sohaemus and his father Sampsigeramus, probably the man named at Palmyra in 18/19, were both honoured with that title in a Latin inscription from Heliopolis.[21] The position of all these monarchs in areas at the edge of direct Roman rule explains the advantages and prestige they enjoyed. Sohaemus was also patron of the Roman colony at Berytus. Sohaemus was the younger son of Sampsigeramus II, and succeeded his elder brother Azizus at the beginning of Nero's reign. He seems also to have been king of Sophene for a short while, and Arca (Caesareia ad Libanum), later to be the birthplace of Alexander Severus, was also under him, if all these men are identical.[22] Sohaemus, the last attested king of Emesa, survived until the 70s. He supplied troops to the governor of Syria when Judaea went into revolt in 66 and soon like his forebears had become involved in a Roman civil war, that of 68–69. He provided solid help to another formidable Roman soldier and politician, Vespasian, who won the struggle for power.[23] He was still providing troops when the Romans deposed his fellow client and cousin Antiochus IV of Commagene in 72 or 73.[24]

It looks as if the Arabs of the district were ruled for at least a century by a consistently successful dynasty, one that when necessary knew which potentate to follow and sometimes added to their domains for longer or shorter periods: Arethusa, Sophene, Arca. Julia Domna's ancestors, if that is what they were, were playing prominent roles in Roman dynastic policy and as kings loomed large among their fellow dynasts in the area. This successful politicking was reflected in and promoted by marriage alliances and other ties with their peers: the networks they created helped in their dealings with Rome. One of the dynasts, Azizus, who died in 54, married two years previously into the family of Herod the Great of Judaea. The bride was Drusilla, the sister of Agrippa II of Chalcis, notorious for her serial marriages. Their father Agrippa I had been king of Judaea, and they continued to hope that the family might still come into his entire kingdom.[25] Sohaemus' sister Iotape (IV), named after her mother, the child of Mithridates III of Commagene, whose wife was in turn a scion of the ruling dynasty of Media Atropatene, also married into the Herodian dynasty, redoubling the ties between the neighbouring principalities: her husband was Aristobulus, brother of Agrippa I.[26] Another marriage connection is possible but cannot be substantiated: a woman called Queen Julia Mamaea, wife of Great King M. Antonius Polemo II of Pontus (his second marriage), but the connection between her and the dynasty depends in the first instance on a relationship with her namesake the Empress, mother of Alexander Severus a hundred and fifty years later.[27] Such complex marriage connections between the families of dependent rulers were important: they gave enhanced prestige and potentially greater power, and they were not discouraged by the Romans, as long as there was no suspicion of independent policy or group diplomacy. The great independent power in the east, Parthia, was Rome's business, and Agrippa I came close to being deposed by Claudius for organizing a summit conference of dependent monarchs in the region: the conclave, which was dispersed by the governor of Syria, included Antiochus IV of Commagene, Cotys of Lesser Armenia, Polemo II of Pontus, and Sampsigeramus II – showing the current significance of Emesa.[28]

So how large was this Emesene kingdom? The city itself in the first century AD would probably have had a population measured at best in tens rather than hundreds of thousands, unlike the great city downstream, Antioch, which at an estimated quarter of a million was one of the largest cities in the Empire.[29] No doubt the population grew in the favourable conditions of the Roman peace, untouched by invasion or civil war until the struggle between Septimius Severus and Pescennius Niger. So evidently did its wealth grow, as the jewellery found at Homs in the necropolis of Tell Abu Sabun suggests, and the engineering work demanded by the dyke constructed along the lake.[30]

Cicero and Strabo followed earlier practice in designating the rulers of Emesa mere phylarchs, whether of the Arabs (Cicero) or 'of the tribe (*ethnos*) of the Emeseni' (Strabo), while Dio refers to the deposed Iamblichus I merely as 'king of some Arabs'.[31] Indeed, Strabo seems to include the Emesenes in the 'Scenite' Arabs; that is, they were pastoralists living in tents (*scenae*).[32] The central settlement, Emesa itself, may down to the time of Augustus have been a rudimentary township, possessing few of the constitutional structures, language and amenities of any town, let alone a Greek city-state (*polis*).[33] It is the people rather than the name of a town that is found in first century sources; certainly Pliny preserves 'Hemeseni' from his source. As to physical development, however, leaders as well placed as the dynasty of Sampsigeramus were likely to have made something of their tribal centre, if only to keep up with other dependent rulers such as Herod of Judaea and his successors, great builders. The swift development of Emesa has been compared with that of modern Kuwait.[34]

Syrian cities of antiquity and after have been divided into types: fortress, bazaar, caravan and sanctuary. Emesa has something of each of these about it: its basalt fortress looms 30 metres over the houses, while it would have made an important contribution to the caravans that Palmyra serviced and taxed, in the form of repairs and supplies (the mid-twentieth century route

Figure 1.1 Sun deity at Emesa.
AE. Obv. *AUTOKRATO. AI. TIT . . . AD.ANTONI . . . (IMPERATOR AELIUS TITUS HADRIANUS ANTONINUS)* Head of Antoninus Pius r., laureate. Rev. *EM ISE N (OF THE EMESENES)*. Bust of Helios or Elagabal r., radiate and draped. AD 138–61.

Source: *BMC Galatia*, etc., p. 238 no. 8.

from Emesa to Palmyra lacked wells over 88 km. of the journey).[35] At any rate it enjoyed enough vigour as a community to have maintained its identity and its name to the present day.[36] The site of the city has been built on, making it hard to estimate what lies beneath.[37]

But it is the institutions that made a proper Greek *polis*. The most miserable little community cannot be denied the title if it has the appropriate magistrates, council and assembly, and Emesa was 'a kingdom based on a city'.[38] When the operations of a city state began at Emesa is unknown; perhaps in the interregnum at the beginning of Augustus' Principate. Or they may have developed after the end of kingly rule; Emesa seems to have issued its first coins only in the second century, under Antoninus Pius.[39] It does not matter that on these coins, as well as in literature, it was the community, the Emeseni, that were still usually named, rather than the place, except when topography was in question. It was the same with decrees issued by the most sophisticated cities of the ancient world, such as Athens. By 217 Emesa is known to have had city councillors (*bouleutae*), but by that date it had passed beyond *polis* status and become a Roman colony.[40] All 713 inscriptions from the region of Emesene are in Greek, including funerary monuments.[41] It puts Emesa into a different perspective to look at it from Palmyra. There it was apparently only in Tiberius' time that architects began to turn their eyes towards Antioch and the west, and to copy the temples and colonnaded streets of hellenized Syria, giving the city the Roman imperial aspect that they still bear. Even the hellenizing of Palmyra came partly from the east, from Seleuceia-on-Tigris; Palmyra belonged to a cultural circle that included north-west India and centred on the Graeco-Parthian towns of Mesopotamia. Emesa was open both to Palmyrene influence (and so to Parthian) and to Graeco-Roman.[42]

Nonetheless, Emesa was a political backwater. There is no evidence that it was visited by any emperors before Septimius Severus, though the fact that it struck coins under Marcus Aurelius has suggested that he went there.[43] That is not a good argument: the mint was active under Antoninus Pius. Emesa faced the hinterland rather than the Mediterranean. For a young woman of spirit born there, the cosmopolitan political centre of Syria, Antioch, will have been a Mecca. It is significant that at Antioch, while the prestige of the status conferred on the sheikhs by Rome may have made them seem less like backwoodsmen, there is no trace of their becoming in any sense patrons or benefactors of the city, as they had been of Berytus. Julia Domna was to spend long periods of her life at Antioch; but by then she was the Augusta, wife of the Emperor of Rome, not the mere descendant (at best) of a superannuated princely family.

As to the territory of Emesa, the hills that linked Jebel Amariyeh in the north with Mount Lebanon in the south, and the north–south reaches of the river Eleutherus, were a possible geographical boundary to the west of Emesa; the city of Laodiceia ad Libanum lay only 25 km. to the south, blocking extension up the Orontes valley. But to the south-east a boundary stone at Qasr el Hair shows that in that direction Emesene territory stretched 90 km. towards that of Palmyra; Palmyra itself is only another 60 km. to the north-east of the stone. Further to the north lay country not yet thoroughly explored, where boundaries may have been left unclear or fluctuating.[44] Twenty km. down the valley of the Orontes was the community of Arethusa, which, as Strabo noted, had been under Emesene control in the mid-first century BC, in spite of its liberation by Pompey, but was lost in 20.[45]

Some indication of the population that the ruler of Emesa could command a century later, in relation to those of other dependencies, comes from accounts of the Jewish revolt against Roman rule that broke out in AD 66. A Roman expeditionary force opened operations against the rebels; Antiochus IV of Commagene, the greatest of the three princes as far as the size of his realm and no doubt its revenues were concerned,[46] contributed 2000 cavalry and 3000 foot-archers. Agrippa II, who at that time was ruler of territories in the Lebanon and Anti-Lebanon, with parts of Galilee and the Peraea, offered the same number of foot-soldiers, but fewer cavalry; and his cousin Sohaemus of Emesa provided 4000, one-third cavalry, the rest mainly archers. The Romans were defeated nonetheless, and command of the war taken over by the later emperor, Vespasian, who reorganized the forces engaged against the Jews. In 67 the three rulers are said to have provided equal numbers of troops: 1000 cavalry and 2000 infantry archers each. Evidently Agrippa II and Sohaemus were keen players and their territories could make a significant contribution. The Romans may have made uniform demands, or perhaps there was some collusion between the monarchs.

Emesa's ability to produce fighting men is confirmed after the dynastic period: auxiliary units of the Roman army bearing the name Emesene are found in Numidia and in Lower Pannonia. At Intercisa, where it remained at least until the mid-third century, the 'Thousand-strong Antonine Cohort of archers consisting of Roman citizen Hemeseni' is found dedicating to Deus Sol Aelagabalus for Severus and his sons. The unit was, as usual, smaller than the title implied, and after the first few years since its formation it would not all have been made up of Emesenes; even so, it was still loyal to its local gods.[47] It would have been piquant to Domna to have the chance of reviewing the unit when she was on her travels.

Just when Sohaemus might have felt that his dynasty had earned a secure place in the imperial scheme, it seems all to have come to an end with his death, probably soon after 72, when Antiochus IV was deposed, at any rate before 78. Turning his back on a family tie did not save Sohaemus' kingdom from Vespasian's inclination to extend direct Roman rule towards the east. Too close relations with the Parthians was always a plausible excuse for deposing the monarchs. But the occasion may have been nothing more sensational than the death of the incumbent. Then the principality of Emesa would have been incorporated into the Roman province of Syria rather than being granted 'freedom'. Of the three loyalists, only Agrippa II is known to have survived. This is the standard view, but nothing is said of the annexation in Josephus, and some scholars hold that the dynasty lasted until Domitian, Trajan, Antoninus Pius, or even Commodus.[48]

Whether it is right to hold that the dynasty continued in power and hence in control of Emesa's revenues beyond 78, even into the second century, is unclear. It is only after Sohaemus' time that the cult for which Emesa is renowned comes into view.[49] The family could have continued profitably in a 'republican' Emesa, keeping or acquiring a role as high priests of a burgeoning local cult and so enjoying great influence. The prestige and wealth attached to dynastic priesthoods, which could control local resources, may be seen from elsewhere in the east, notably in Pontus and Cappadocia.[50] Whatever their status, men who look as if they were members of the dynastic family were soon displaying the wealth that they would have stashed away in the palmy days of the Julio-Claudian dynasty. The chief monument of the Emesene necropolis was a two-storey funerary tower containing the remains of a C. Julius Sampsigeramus, 'also known as Silas',[51] of the Roman tribe Fabia, son of C. Julius Alexio; Sampsigeramus died near the end of Vespasian's reign. The Roman tribe shows that his family obtained its Roman citizenship from Augustus or Caesar, and he is evidently a connection of the dynasty.[52] Another Emesene worth noticing is M. Julius Avidius Minervinus, who erected an altar to the Good Fortune of Berytus and was honoured for it by the city council. That was in about 85, for it was on the hundredth anniversary of the colony's foundation. What makes Julius interesting is his name: an Avidius could be a forebear of the Syrian pretender of nearly a century later.[53] Later probable members of the dynastic family locally prominent are a Sohaemus and his son Sampsigeramus, who died in 137, and another Sohaemus, who was dead by 178.[54] One more man deserves mention in this context: he is Ti. Julius Balbillus, who in the late second century AD was priest of Sol Elagabal. He is unlikely to have been the chief priest of the day, but the cult was still of interest to a connection of the dynastic family: Balbillus' ancestry went back to Antiochus IV of Commagene, whose aunt had married Sampsigeramus II.[55]

Attributing Domna to the princely family gives her, for a Roman empress, what seem to be very exotic origins. The name of the last known ruler looks like the origin of the *cognomen* of Domna's niece Julia Sohaemias, or Sohaemis, as Dio and Herodian call her.[56] That of the Iamblichi, rulers in the mid-first century BC, was to become famous as that of two intellectuals: the Greek novelist of the mid-second century, author of *The Babylonian History*, who claimed to be a native of Syria and Aramaic speaking, and the more famous Neo-Platonist philosopher born at Chalcis in the mid-third.[57] There is nothing solid to connect them with the dynasty: the name may have had a cachet.[58] No more can the immediate family of Julia Domna be proved to be descended from the princely dynasty, although Emesa is attested as her family home.[59] The clear trail of the family ends with the owner of the pyramid tomb dated 78/9, in spite of the other members detected in second century Emesa and elsewhere. It is a fourth-century source that relates that Domna's father Julius Bassianus was 'priest of the Sun, whom the Phoenicians, from whom he sprang, call Heliogabalus (Elagabalus)'.[60] The name Bassianus sounds banal and authentically Roman, but Bassus itself, though borne by prominent Romans of the Republic and by a distinguished senator from Pergamum, Julius Quadratus, active in Syria, was excluded from a standard work on the Latin *cognomina*, and it could conceal a Phoenician title, *basus*, 'priest', which recurs in the name M. Aurelius Bazas, a veteran attested at Apameia.[61] Accepting this derivation makes it possible to go on to argue that the *cognomen* was allowed only to the older boys of Domna's family, so to her elder son Septimius Bassianus, later the Emperor Caracalla, and then to her elder great-nephew Varius Avitus, later Elagabalus.[62] This view should not go without question: Julia Domna's niece, the granddaughter of Julius Bassianus, was herself Bassiana, and when he was high priest Gessius Alexianus, the future Severus Alexander, was Bassianus. The placing of the name is equally well to be explained by the rules of Roman nomenclature, passing from maternal grandfather to granddaughter and elder grandson, while the second grandson took another, in this case Geta, with the desirable name being picked up again in the next generation, that of Severus Alexander, through Mamaea, while he was Alexianus from his maternal grandfather. But the 'priestly' connotation of the name offers an occasion both for its original appearance in the family and for the preference given to it by Severus for his older son over his own *cognomen* or his brother's. This preference would then be a clue to the sources of the changes that Severus supposedly introduced into Roman public religion. Those sources were his own ambition and the influence of his wife; when he was in virtual exile at Athens he had already imbibed 'oriental theosophy' and quarrelled with the Athenians.[63] Preference for a certain *cognomen* can hardly bear so much weight.

Even though the priesthood attributed to Domna's father comes from a late source, the *Epitome de Caesaribus* (though it may be relying on Marius Maximus), Emesa's chief claim to fame certainly became a religious one: a large and rich temple of uncertain date and a cult of a conical black stone or betyl, said to have come down from Zeus and to be an image of the sun; the deity was venerated beyond Emesa, 'satraps', as Herodian calls them, and barbarian princes vying with their offerings.[64] Investigations into the religious life in the area surrounding Emesa revealed the same mix of west Semitic, Babylonian, and Arab as at Hatra and Palmyra, though they conclude that the range of deities on offer there are restrained by comparison.[65] Chaldaean influence has also been detected at Emesa, and the mausoleum of Sampsigeramus is described as being of Mesopotamian type.[66] Topmost is the Semitic, Arab, and originally Babylonian deity El or Il. Then come Salman (Aziz) and Mun'im, two Arab morning and evening star deities, equivalent to the Greek Dioscuri.[67] These deities made up a triad such as the Phoenicians favoured, notably in the coastal towns of Byblus, Berytus, Tyre, and Sidon, but also at Hatra, Heliopolis, and Palmyra; Emperor Elagabalus carried a triad with him to Rome.[68] Finally both Arabs and Syrians worshipped female deities: Allât, who is equated at Emesa with Athena and had a temple nearby, and who was cultivated at Hierapolis as Atargatis, and Simia (Aphrodite). The Arab Sun cult of Petra involved a female principle which took two forms, that of a mother, the Meter Theon (Mother of the Gods) and of a young woman, here too given the Greek name of Athena.[69] Chad regards most of the deities as Arab, with those of Mesopotamian origin, such as Allât and Shams, adopted under the influence of a clergy given to Babylonian astrology, while the 'Dioscuri' Aziz and Mun'im appealed to herdsmen and caravaners. But such a grouping does not seem vital for the arrival of cults from the nearby river valleys.[70]

The nomenclature of the Emesene dynasts reflects religious beliefs. In fact the name of the deity Elagabal, misrepresented as Heliogabalus in fourth-century Latin writers, has nothing to do with the Greek word for the sun (*helios*), widespread though that cult was in Syria, notably at Palmyra.[71] It seems to be derived from two words, the first meaning 'god' and the second 'mountain' (the Aramaic *jebel*, common in place-names, is related) or 'creator'.[72] The Arabic or Nabataean name Iamblichus (a hypocoristic form of 'Yamlik'el', which would mean 'El reigns') occurs not only in Nabatene and Emesa but especially at Palmyra.[73] At least the first element of the Emesene dynastic name, Sampsigeramus, was Semitic, Aramaic or Arab, and did allude to the sun (*shamash*); Shams was a Babylonian deity worshipped by the Arabs and widely throughout the Middle East; he could be identified with El; the second element seems to be derived from a root

Figure 1.2 Altar at Emesa.
AE. Obv. *IOULIA DOMNA AUG* Bust of Julia Domna r. Rev. *EMESON COLONIAS* (*OF THE COLONY OF EMESA*) Altar, consisting of a massive base, placed on two steps and ornamented with a cornice and two rows of niches between two pilasters; each niche contains a statue; on the base rests a small altar, lighted. In exergue, *ZKF* = 527 of the Seleucid era = AD 215.

Source: *BMC Galatia*, etc., p. 238 no. 9.

GRM meaning 'decide', establish.[74] Aziz(os) was another theophoric name used in the dynasty and by others at Emesa and was very popular (it still survives among Muslims); the deity was a rider god, protector on the steppe, identified with Ares or Mars, the *Bonus Puer*.[75] Sohaemus is a name of Arab origin: SHM means an arrow; proceeding from the hands of Hada like storm lightning, it presages a rainstorm. It was also borne by the Arabs of Ituraea and Nabataea and at Hatra.[76]

When Emesa coined in the reign of Antoninus Pius, the conical stone or its surroundings, an eagle poised above it, almost monopolized its reverses. One type struck in the time of Julia Domna herself shows the deity's great altar, decorated; then under Caracalla and Elagabalus the stone appears within a temple, surrounded by a balustrade and shaded by two parasols.[77] The image of the eagle on the stone, with a dedication to Elahagabal in Palmyrene lettering, was found on a first century AD monument sited 80 km. south-east of Emesa and 100 km. south-west of Palmyra. The coinage reminds us that by the reign of Pius Emesa had some city institutions, and that by then the cult of Elagabal was highly important to it. Whatever other deities were worshipped there, they do not feature on the coinage. The deity of the stone had come to be bound up with the identity of the city.

> A double shift has . . . occurred. . . . A single divine name derived from a Semitic language has been re-located to a Greek-using context. Second, the cult-object, a large stone, has taken its place as the chief cult-object . . . of what was now a Greek city. . . . In the process, . . . the stone has come to be interpreted as a symbol of the Sun.[78]

The deity Elagabal naturally brought his city economic advantages as well as religious importance, from travellers and pilgrims. The trade route from Palmyra via Emesa to the coast was complex, but well used; an Indian plant arrived in Emesa in the second half of the second century.[79] Scholars differ as to how closely Emesa's rise to prosperity was connected with the trade of Palmyra, but there is no trace of the presence of Elagabal at hellenistic Emesa; the advance of Arab settlers into the mountains west of them may have carried the cult there.[80] Then the end of the semi-independent principality forced the Emesene authorities to pay more attention to the local cult as a focus of loyalty and a source of income: sacral authority rather than secular power began to confer prestige on leading families. Admittedly, the coin representations betray little of the self-awareness of individual citizens as Emesans; every *polis* displayed its protecting deity or, as at Athens with its owls, an emblem of it. The Emesan coinage also referred to the impeccably Greek games that it sponsored: Eleian and Pythian. But however remotely Domna's family was connected with the cult, and perhaps not at all by blood with the original dynasts, her father's name demonstrated a claim to belong to the religious elite of Emesa.

Even though Greek-speakers often adopted Roman *cognomina* as part of their own nomenclature without possessing any legitimate title to Roman citizenship, Bassianus was a Roman citizen, as the *nomen* of his daughter, Julia, shows. Barring fraud, they, like the original family, must have enjoyed that privilege since the time of Caesar or Augustus, at latest Tiberius or Caligula. Still, it is possible that Domna's family gained the franchise later, through the good offices of a governor of Syria called Julius, such as C. Antius A. Julius Quadratus or C. Julius Quadratus Bassus, C. Julius Severus, acting governor during Bar Kokhba revolt, or his son, or even Cn. Julius Verus in the mid-160s. Among their fellow Emesenes there was little sign of an extensive Romanized elite: two men are commemorated with the Roman *tria nomina*, sign of the citizenship.[81]

Dio's assertion, made of course in the latest stages of his work, that Domna's family was 'plebeian', not just technically, but in the sense of 'ordinary',[82] can hardly be taken seriously. Presumably it implies that they were not (as she claimed) connected with the earlier Emesene dynasty, or, more plausibly, with existing senators, as Dio himself certainly was;[83] but even that claim is inaccurate. Anyone sceptical of the tie and of the priestly status of Domna's family may stress rather its regional connections and an extensive participation in Roman imperial service, to a level not easily paralleled from any other Near Eastern city.[84]

After all it may not matter greatly if the descent from the earlier dynasty was genuine or a misconception on the part of ancient writers, or even one due to fraud on the part of Domna and Severus after their marriage: her immediate family had successfully annexed an important part of the power and prestige in the city. The two factors, sacral prestige and status in the Roman civil hierarchy, would work together in promoting the fortunes of the family; neither should be sacrificed. Domna's Emesene brother-in-law C. Julius Avitus Alexianus, when he was governor of Raetia in the first decade of the third century, is found dedicating an altar to 'the ancestral Sun God Elagabal'.[85] Her own second name, Domna, looks to anyone familiar with Latin like an abbreviated form of *domina*, 'lady', 'mistress' in Latin; so it would be equivalent to the Aramaic Martha, which means mistress, wife of a king. But that tempting and convenient etymology was false. A man who married Domna thinking that her name was an omen of his future greatness would have been deceiving himself. The origin of the name lies in the Arabic Dumayna, an archaic diminutive of *dimna*, and etymologically connected with the colour word for black.[86] We do not know what Domna was called at home. Her sister Maesa's name is also Arab, thought to be from a verb *masa*, 'walk with a swinging gait',[87] and one of her daughters has the feminine version of the dynastic Sohaemus (another word connoting blackness), the second, Mamaea, presents yet another Semitic name, bearing out the view that in Syria they continued in use for the women of a family.[88] It would have been strange if only Domna had been given a regular Latin *cognomen*. Nonetheless, there was a temptation, once she had become Augusta, for Latin-speaking outsiders to see her name as an honorific title, if they thought about it, and that is what has happened in some inscriptions.[89]

Domna's family must have been very well off indeed. The city itself was wealthy.[90] To attain primacy there, and to attract a senatorial suitor, would have required possessions and expenditure on a grand scale. The basic resources of the family may have been, as they were generally in the Graeco-Roman world, landed property, agriculture or flocks and herds; but this caravan city probably produced successful entrepreneurs. More property will have accrued if the family had once been a ruling dynasty; it would have taken its gains with it and even when only the priesthood was left there were still the offerings of devotees grateful for favours or revelations. Domna carried what must have been a handsome dowry with her, not only the property that under Roman law and custom was due to her husband, but also her beauty and accomplishments and the high descent she claimed; she can have lacked no adornment to enhance her attractions. After the marriage, the prudence of her father would have ensured that she (which meant he) kept sufficient control over the property to ensure that she would be comfortable during the marriage, and that if there should be a divorce she would not return to her family impoverished.[91] Another possible source of property for Domna is suggested by a text in the *Digest*, which records the contested inheritance by a Julia Domna from her great-great-uncle Julius Agrippa, a *primipilaris*, or former leading centurion.[92] Severus himself came from a very well-off family, though in 191, according to the *Historia Augusta*, he himself had only a modest residence in the city and a single estate in the territory of Veii, where his grandfather, Statius' friend and patron, had had property. Severus' consular cousins may have come into a larger share of the estate than Severus and his brother. At any rate, when his aunt Septimia Polla died, her heir and brother, Severus' father, set up a statue in commemoration of her: it was made of silver, 'the most expensive in Africa'.[93]

When Severus became emperor, Domna had no 'privy purse' that passed from one empress to another as the *patrimonium* passed down the succession of emperors.[94] But she could depend on her family wealth, on her husband's generosity, on the resources available to the imperial household, and on gifts that her position made it worth offering. Only the fall of her dynasty could impoverish her. The money was available for personal adornment, gifts to dependants, and construction. Livia, the first Augusta, spent some of her money on buildings at Rome. It is curious how rarely such activities can be attributed to her successors, even to Agrippina the Younger, Plotina, and Sabina. As the first-century emperor assumed a monopoly in the construction and restoration of public buildings at Rome, leaving no scope for his fellow aristocrats, perhaps he also encroached on the limited possibilities of what a woman might achieve.[95]

The date of Domna's birth is unknown – it was celebrated some time in the second half of the year – but if she was marriageable in 187 she was presumably at least 13 years old in that year and so born not later than 174, perhaps earlier, especially if this was a second marriage for her, but nothing suggests that it was. In the Roman marriage market girls of the highest rank were allocated soon after puberty, often after having been betrothed as infants; the less exalted might be as old as 19 when they first wed.[96] Since Domna's sister Maesa had a daughter Sohaemias, who was mother to Elagabalus, born in about 203 or 204, Domna, unless she did take Severus as a second husband, was necessarily the younger.[97]

Much emphasis has been put on the influence of Roman culture – language, architecture, and the like – in the Greek East of the imperial age, but it was a heterogeneous area; 'Romanization' is under-analysed and overgeneralized.[98] Culturally Domna had many choices and at various times: one ethnic, national or cultural identity does not preclude another, and language, manners, and dress may to be varied to suit an occasion. Syria, part of the 'fertile crescent' into which Arabs were infiltrating,[99] was an area in which Semitic languages, Aramaic, Hebrew, Arabic, and Phoenician, predominated. At Palmyra, Emesa's eastern neighbour, the great Customs Law of the second century was set up in both Greek and Palmyrene; the inscription mentioning Germanicus Caesar and the 'Great King' Sampsigeramus only in Palmyrene.[100] Emesa specifically had Arab roots, had been part of the Persian Empire and then ruled by a Graeco-Macedonian dynasty, the Seleucids, while being a close neighbour to the dominions of Ptolemaic Egypt. Greek culture was one of the two dominant in the Roman Empire. How far Seleucid rule had instilled it into the neighbourhood is unclear. The very lack of evidence has led a searching and sceptical survey to negative conclusions. Certainly, over-confident assumptions about what it was have tempted scholars into unfruitful generalization.[101] Each phenomenon, such as language, religion, or dress, has to be taken separately and assigned its place in the whole. So with nomenclature: Emesa's is strongly Aramaic and Arab; in that respect, then, it seems that hellenization lacked appeal, but that tells nothing of other spheres.[102]

Under the Principate there were three legions in Syria, and in their camps and in communities roundabout Latin was in use, although their recruits came from Greek-speaking provinces. Closest to Emesa was the camp at Raphaneae, 25 km. to the north-west in the Orontes valley. What was spoken in the Emesene street was probably a mixture of Aramaic and Greek, occasionally Latin, with graffiti in the vernacular dominating on walls, and we can be certain that we should have been listening to Aramaic inside private houses. Languages other than Latin and Greek survived in the Empire: it is entertaining that it should be the Tyrian jurist Ulpian, a contemporary of Domna's and a fellow Syrian, who should have considered the validity of points made in court by litigants speaking Punic or 'Assyrian'.[103]

Italian influence made itself felt in another language, that of architecture: the mausoleum of 78/9 was constructed in the *opus reticulatum* brickwork that was becoming fashionable in Asia Minor.[104] There are parallels to the pyramidal monument in monuments from Edessa and one dated 73 at Serrin, 75 km. distant on the Euphrates.[105] The monument belonged to a tradition that had spread to north Africa. At Thugga a Punic mausoleum of 139 BC presents the same structure as that of Emesa, though it had an additional storey. It is approached by rock-cut steps, and was built in three levels capped by a pyramid. The architecture mingles Greek with Egyptian-Near Eastern motifs.[106]

Instructive smaller scale grave monuments are not common. The architectural and decorative styles of grave monuments, the language and traditional phraseology of inscribed tombstones, difference in usage for and by men and women, bi- or trilingualism, or the particular use of Aramaic, Greek, or even Latin (as at Palmyra) on official monuments, nomenclature, and stress on ancestry or tribe on every type of inscription, would all have been informative. Certainly some Iranian influence has been detected in the style of dress that appears on monuments (strong at Palmyra).[107] Emesa's lack of a hellenistic past, like that of Palmyra, continued to affect its complex cultural life.[108]

What matters as much as how many tests for hellenization Emesa's inhabitants of all classes and callings could severally pass, is how they thought of themselves at any given moment, if it occurred to them at all. Emesa as a city with Greek legends on its coinage was Greek enough. Isocrates' famous claim, made already in 380 BC, was that what made a person Greek was *paideia* (education), which could be paid for. It was an idea that the conquests of Alexander helped to spread, and one welcome to Greek-speakers all over the eastern half of the Roman Empire, where the language was promoted still further by traders. The cultural roll is spectacular: Antiochus

Figure 1.3 Temple and conical stone at Emesa.
AE. Obv. *AUT K M AUR ANTONEINOS SEB* (*IMPERATOR CAESAR MARCUS AURELIUS ANTONINUS AUGUSTUS*) Bust of Caracalla r., laureate, wearing military cloak and cuirass. Rev. *EMISON COLON* (*COLONY OF EMESA*) Hexastyle temple; in pediment base of ?altar; a flight of steps leads to the central incolumniation, in which is seen the conical stone, surrounded by a balustrade and ?shaded by two parasols; in front of stone, eagle with wreath in beak; in exergue *ZKF* (AD 215).

Source: *BMC Galatia*, p. 239, no. 15.

of Ascalon, the intellectual who was a friend of the first century BC general Lucullus; Philodemus of Gadara, guru of Julius Caesar's Epicurean father-in-law Piso; Posidonius of Apameia, the Stoic philosopher whom Strabo considered the most learned of his contemporaries;[109] the Peripatetic philosopher, historian, diplomat, and biographer of Augustus Nicolaus of Damascus, completely at home in Greek; it was a Damascene architect, Apollodorus, who designed Trajan's column;[110] Flavius Josephus, former leader in the Jewish revolt of 66, was able, if perhaps with help, to produce a Greek version of his history of the war; his rival Justus of Tiberias was also a Greek-speaker;[111] Lucian of Samosata, the second century satirist, wrote brilliantly in his second language; Apollonius of Tyana in Cappadocia, whose *Life* was to be written up by Domna's friend Philostratus, was descended from the founders of another 'Greek' city, which certainly did not have a mainland Greek origin. All these men attest that the Greek culture that pervaded the east gave brilliant opportunities. 'Greek self-awareness' pervades Philostratus' *Life of Apollonius*, and in it the sage exhorts the ruler of Rome to maintain this Greek identity. It will have interested Domna that Philostratus makes a point of the languages that his hero Apollonius knows (all).[112]

The young Domna grew up in a society that had begun as 'tent-dwellers' but which had acquired wealth, status, and culture from its commercial and political dealings with bigger powers abroad. As she grew up in her dusty little city she 'knew' that she was of royal descent and of a family that had incomparable prestige with its neighbours for its connection with the main local cult. But as a girl she had no prospect of taking part actively in the religious ceremonies or publicly in local politics. Hellenization did not guarantee a woman a full Greek education; that depended on where one was born. Domna probably encountered conflicting ideas on the education of girls, but there was an overwhelming reason for her to get the best education available and proper in the district: she was a highly valued object of exchange between families in Syria and beyond, old dynasties and new imperial officials. She knew that and no doubt accepted it, but she could have taken to the education that was offered with real enthusiasm. Nor was she likely to have been kept close in purdah: what was on offer needed to be inspected. There was another corollary to her role: from puberty at least she will have dressed as sumptuously as her father's means allowed – he wanted a clever little doll.

As to her later dress, Domna is shown on the Arch of the *Argentarii* in the Forum Boarium wearing what is described as the severe unadorned dress of the Roman matron, the *palla*. It is in her gesture, that of the raised right hand, palm front, that oriental echoes have been seen, notably of a statue of a young woman of the royal dynasty of Hatra (AD 238).[113] As to language, she could always have used Greek at home and in polite society at Emesa and everywhere in the east. Her Latin was probably a later acquisition, though she might have been taught some as a child, or picked some up. Lucian of Samosata knew not only Greek but also Latin, which he probably learned on his travels to Rome and in Gaul; Domna's travels will have continued her education too.[114] Certainly her great-nephew Alexander Severus is said to have had both a Greek and a Roman upbringing, but that was when the family was already in its heyday, and in any case he was a boy.[115] Senators, equestrian administrators, and jurisconsults from the eastern provinces, all of them increasingly common in the second century, had to be at home in both.

As empress, then, Domna had to have mastered Latin, oral for use at court in Rome and the west and written for formal correspondence. Under Caracalla she was in charge of Latin as well as Greek correspondence.[116] Probably she used it when she conversed with her British acquaintance, the wife of Argentocoxus, though the Briton herself needed an interpreter.[117] Domna would never have disgraced Severus by deficiency in Latin and Greek, while his knowledge of Punic would have made it easy to him, while an officer in Syria, to have mastered Aramaic. It is a question whether she used Aramaic in her senatorial household; she may well have done to her personal servants, less so, perhaps, after she became empress and lived in a massive and evolving establishment.

2 Marriage

Domna's elder sister Julia Maesa married before her and it is worth comparing the two husbands. Maesa was given to a man apparently connected with the dynastic family of Emesa, and so with its presumed descendants. Julius Avitus, who is also called Alexianus by Herodian, is named by the literary sources as her husband, and he has been plausibly identified with C. Julius Avitus Alexianus, who is known from two inscriptions.[1] C. Iulius Avitus Alexianus began his career as the equestrian prefect of an auxiliary unit originally from Petra and stationed in Syria, and his equestrian career carried him only as far as the junior procuratorship of the grain supply at Ostia. He was clearly brought into the Senate by Severus in 193: being allowed to omit the junior ranks, he held the praetorship, then commanded the Upper Moesian legion IV Flavia, and probably during the war against Albinus, in 196, served as governor of Raetia. He became consul in about 200; in 208 he went with the imperial party to Britain in 208. While governing Raetia he dedicated an altar to 'the', or 'his', 'ancestral Sun God Elagabalus'. Maesa's husband looks like a man of worth in his town, one who was doing well in the junior ranks of the equestrian service – and who owed his further advancement primarily to the success of his sister-in-law's husband. Their daughters married knights and continued in the Syrian network: Sohaemias married Sex. Varius Marcellus of Apameia, by whom she had several children, and Mamaea, in a second marriage, Gessius Marcianus of Arca.[2]

Bassianus' younger daughter forged quite a different link. Her husband came from Lepcis Magna in north Africa. And at the time of the marriage Septimius Severus was already a senator, an ex-praetor, born in 145 or 146,[3] but not a man of great distinction as soldier or politician. Certainly in 186 he had no prospect of becoming emperor. It might be thought that if he had, it should have made him hesitate over the marriage, remembering the damage that Mark Antony's reputation had suffered in the west through his association with Cleopatra VII, and their marriage. More than a century after that, the Emperor Vespasian's son Titus had endangered his position through his affair with the Jewish princess Berenice, sister and co-ruler to Agrippa II, no matter that she was a Roman citizen. Unwillingly Titus rejected her when he became emperor in 81.[4] However, for Severus it was easier. Senators from the Greek-speaking half of the Empire were now commonplace and formed a substantial minority in the House. In 169 M. Aurelius married off his widowed daughter Lucilla to Ti. Claudius Pompeianus of Antioch; in 175 there had even been a Syrian claimant to the throne, strongly supported by the city of Antioch: Avidius Cassius, related by marriage to the Antonine imperial family.[5] Severus with his family members, Domna with hers, made a complementary dynastic structure with cultural ties well spread through the ruling elite of the late and post-Antonine age.

Nonetheless, there was another way of looking at this combination: Dio, who was a Roman senator and author of a history of Rome, as well as being a Greek-speaker from Bithynia, was ready to play the racist card. He considered that Domna's son Caracalla was a member of three peoples and possessed not a single one of their virtues, but a combination of all their failings: Gallic irresponsibility, cowardliness, and rashness, African harshness and barbarity, and from Syria, where he came from on his mother's side, cunning and villainy.[6] Dio's neat, rhetorical view incidentally equips Domna with another advantage as a political wife: she was, or could be seen as, an adept at political manoeuvring; Domna, like her elder son, was *panourgos*, a word that Rabelais appropriated as a name for his knave.

It would be a mistake, then, to discount the prejudices that regional differences inspired. Differences in clothing were noted with disapproval: even the fact that Arabs wore earrings, though not perhaps in the Senate.[7] The wealth of newcomers there was a recommendation, for they could share the costs of membership, but also a source of envy, as is shown by Tacitus' account of the reaction when Claudius proposed to admit men from northern Gaul in 48: rich as they were, they would fill the House and leave no room for Italians of modest means.[8] As to Greek-speakers, even those from old Greece, they were respected for their culture but liable to be despised as people who had been unable to govern themselves successfully, still less to resist Rome's encroachments. Besides, Greece proper was pitifully impoverished by comparison with the cities of Asia, Galatia-Pamphylia, and Bithynia. Dio was fortunate to live when Greek-speaking senators had been accepted; he might have remembered that superciliousness could once have been directed against him. The poet Juvenal had expressed Roman prejudice succinctly: 'My fellow Romans, I can't bear a Greek city'. He meant Rome; the Syrian Orontes had long since flowed into the Tiber.[9]

The prosperity of Africa, due to the cultivation of grain, vines, and olives, as well as to the trade in animals brought from the interior to supply wild beast shows, was growing in the second century and overtaking that of Spain, Gaul, and western Asia Minor, and there were increasing numbers of men of north African origin in the Senate, as well as *equites*, procurators or prefects in the equestrian service of the emperor.[10] They were a mixed bag, with differing talents. The first consul from the province, a man from Cirta, had held office in 80, while Suetonius Tranquillus of Hippo Regius, the biographer, was secretary to Hadrian.[11] Q. Lollius Urbicus, from Tiddis, was a noted soldier in the same reign and under Antoninus Pius; he constructed the Antonine Wall in Scotland.[12] In the wars that Marcus Aurelius had to wage at the beginning of his Principate, men from north Africa played their part; perhaps the best known was Sex. Calpurnius Agricola, governor of Britain, the second governor to bear that *cognomen* ('Farmer'). He probably came from Numidia, and may have had Severus' brother P. Septimius Geta serving under him as military tribune.[13] P. Salvius Julianus of Hadrumetum, consul 148, was a distinguished jurist;[14] then there was the celebrated orator and man of letters from Cirta, M. Cornelius Fronto, tutor to Marcus Aurelius.[15] Already a generation earlier Juvenal had described Africa as a 'nurse' of advocates.[16] More significant for the rise of the Septimii may have been the Prefect of the Praetorian Guard, holder of the most immediately powerful post in the Empire, at the beginning of Pius' reign, M. Petronius Mamertinus, who may already have been connected by marriage with the family, and seems later to be linked with it by another marriage.[17] Two relatives, probably first cousins of Severus' father, had held suffect consulships in 153 and in 160.[18] Severus himself was in all likelihood the younger son (as his *cognomen* shows, being different from his father's) of a P. Septimius Geta, a man born towards the end of Trajan's reign or early in Hadrian's who was not a member of the Roman Senate. That made Severus a 'new man' (*nouus homo*).

Severus' home town was Lepcis Magna in Tripolitania, at the mouth of a *wadi* and with fertile land behind it.[19] It was Phoenician, settled by Carthage and under its influence. When in 514 BC Spartan colonists landed nearby, it stood out against Greek expansion and they were driven off. But there was Greek influence also from the surviving Greek colony, Cyrene itself, which was to give its name to the Roman province. After two third-century wars, the second bringing Rome to near destruction at the hands of Hannibal, Carthage instead was destroyed by the Romans in 146. In the first century BC Lepcis enjoyed a period of independence, but the city backed the losing side in the civil wars between Caesar and Pompey and was annexed along with the Numidian kingdom. Caesar imposed an annual tribute of 3 million pounds of oil – testimony to the riches of its leading inhabitants.[20] Eventually Lepcis was made a municipality with Latin rights (that is, a community with a charter that granted Roman citizenship to its main magistrates at the end of their year of office) perhaps by Vespasian in the aftermath of the damage it had suffered during the civil wars of 68–9. The neighbouring people of Oea began by looting grain and cattle and went on to recruit tribesmen in the hinterland, the Garamantians, against it. In a further promotion it became a Roman colony in 110 under Trajan, as Colonia Ulpia Traiana Fidelis Lepcis Magna.[21]

The Punic pedigree was long, and Neo-Punic continued to appear on inscriptions after the promotion; at neighbouring Oea a youth of equestrian family might still in the mid-second century speak Punic and hardly any Latin.[22] Nonetheless, the integration of Lepcis into the Roman commonwealth went along with cultural change. How 'African' Severus was, that is, Punic, since the Berbers of the hinterland or Libya were outside the pale, has been a disputed subject, and the dispute has involved preconceptions: ancient writers and scholars hostile to Severus' regime stress alien origin, others ignore it or play it down.[23] His antecedents need scrutiny before we consider accounts of the man himself.

Attached as Severus was to Lepcis, his mother's family, the Fulvii, had been immigrants from Italy, though they had intermarried with locals who had Roman citizenship, notably the Plautii.[24] On his father's side the family had long liked to consider itself thoroughly Italianized, as a flattering poem that Statius addressed to a member of it in 95 explicitly reveals; everyone would take him for a native Roman.[25] The very fact that the point had to be insisted on tempts one to wonder in what ways they still might be considered north African, beyond the accidents of birthplace. Hostile individuals could make a lot of that. Defensiveness is more understandable if the family could not claim to be ultimately of Italian origin. A. R. Birley's attractive hypothesis is that a Lepcitane family received Roman citizenship under Vespasian, but did not, as was so common, take the name of the Emperor, Flavius. Their name may have been taken from an unknown senatorial senator active at Lepcis, or chosen for its assonance, because to Punic ears it resembled the plural form of the word for their chief magistracy, *sufes*, plural *sufetim*.[26] The first Septimius migrated to Italy and bought an estate at Veii. His son Severus, plausibly held to be the grandfather of the emperor, was born in Lepcis but grew up at Veii and was a pupil of Quintilian, who was also tutor to the imperial children and knew all the best orators. The elder Severus practised as an advocate; he did not, however, enter the Senate. Birley conjectures that the family enjoyed the friendship of one of the leading senators of Domitian's reign, C. Rutilius Gallicus, who had served in Africa regulating boundaries early in Vespasian's reign and may have been instrumental in raising Lepcis to municipal status; Statius wrote a poem in his honour too.[27] When Lepcis became a Roman colony and all its citizens Romans, L. Septimius Severus was one of the last two men to hold the old Punic office of *sufes* and of the first two to be *duovir* of the new colony (both offices were equivalent to that of joint mayor); he was also chosen to stand in for the emperor when he did the new foundation the honour of holding its duovirate.

The author who told his readers that some called the younger Severus 'a Punic Sulla' gave it away that cruelty and perfidy had been practised by patrician Romans against their fellow countrymen long since.[28] The history of his grandfather is enough to show that, provided the family remained prosperous, its members need not be faulted as Romans. That did not satisfy the ancient writers, who provided stereotypical personal descriptions. Severus in the *Historia Augusta* dresses roughly and eats sparingly, often without meat, and with a preference for his own African beans; he likes the occasional goblet of wine. That may be true, for Severus himself may have fancied parts of this picture. He is tall, with a long beard, grey curly hair, personable and with an impressive face; just like his statues, then.[29]

As to verbal culture, we have to remember that this also supplies materials for imperial biography and history, as well as the fact that such judgments are necessarily relative.[30] It would be good to be able to distinguish the observations of Dio, who at least knew the man, from the fourth century contributions of the *Historia Augusta* and the anonymous writer of imperial biographies; but they all allow him conventional Graeco-Roman culture. We also have to remember the various layers in Dio's work, which he began at Severus' instigation. Severus, who is ascribed a clarion voice, is said to speak particularly fluent Punic, but also to be a good scholar in both Latin and Greek, who when he was emperor devoted his afternoon walks to conversation in both languages, and who was fairly interested not only in oratory but also in philosophy. In fact he is said to have spoken of literary studies as well as military as leading to his success.[31] This claim is undermined by Dio's backhanded remark that Severus himself would have wished to have a better education. Dio, if reporting faithfully, was latching on to something that Severus would have wished later never to have said, or that he wrongly calculated would make him seem modest. In one unfriendly observation he is said to have kept an 'African' – Punic – accent into old age.[32] Vespasian had been twitted to his face with his Sabine vowels, and Hadrian over his Spanish accent, but, as A. R. Birley remarks, provincial ways were becoming fashionable and in the Senate of the mid-second century it was unlikely that a regional accent was still a real source of mirth or even comment, at least until a man became Princeps or offended in some other way. For entering the Senate and climbing the ladder of offices (many undesirable) was one thing, taking the supreme position of power quite another. Vespasian, who made a show of Sabine simplicity, was a shock in 70; the first emperor to come from the provinces was Trajan, a native of Italica in Spain, who like his kinsman and successor Hadrian, had Italian forebears. They had married into the wealthy aristocracy of Narbonensian Gaul, a province that was itself more like Italy than a province, Pliny had said already in the late 70s.[33] The Antonines were easily accepted. Half a century on, a Milanese whose mother came from Hadrumetum in Africa Proconsularis, Didius Julianus, and Severus, provided the next novelty.[34]

In 163 or 164 Severus ended his education at Lepcis by delivering a formal public speech; by the standards of his city, then, Severus was sufficiently accomplished, and he went to Rome to continue his studies, we are told.[35] It was probably different for the women of the family. An interesting story, not accepted by all scholars, tells of Severus' sister Septimia Octavilla, who may, like him, have married a Greek-speaking easterner. The story is that Octavilla approached Severus during the second Parthian war with her son, who was awarded the *latus clavus*. But Octavilla allegedly proved an embarrassment: she was evidently a native Punic speaker, perhaps a home-keeping woman, who knew hardly any Latin, and was asked to go home. On the charitable view, as the wife of a Greek-speaker, and so having spent her time in a Greek-speaking environment, she had forgotten her Latin.[36] One may suspect that the son was the problem, as a possible rival to Severus' own. But ignorance was a plausible excuse for sending her away. Whether Severus' literary accomplishments were enough for him to make a wife married as a mere girl into someone 'cultivated and refined' as Pliny the Younger says one of his own contemporaries, an ideal husband, had done at the end of the first century, is doubtful; but he may have improved Domna's Latin.[37]

With his cousins and his elder brother in the House to recommend him for the *latus clavus*, Severus can have met with no unusual obstacles in his career. Unlike his brother, he did not hold a military tribunate as a preliminary to entry in 170 or 171, and we do not know which post he held of those available in the other pre-senatorial post, one of a set known collectively as the vigintivirate; if we did, we should have some idea of the esteem in which he was held in his early twenties.[38] There is no sign of early distinction, then, and in fact Severus suffered a setback in the board-game of the senatorial career: he repeated the first post in it, the quaestorship, and found himself spending a year in a malarial backwater, Sardinia.[39] The first preserved record of his senatorial career comes from his home town in 174. Severus was serving as legate to his cousin C. Septimius Severus, consul probably in 160, proconsul of Africa, and their name and office appear on an arch dedicated in that year.[40] Things improved a little: when Severus was elected tribune of the *plebs* in 174 it is possible that it was with the emperor's support.[41] But the tribunate was not a post likely to bring distinction under the Principate, when the emperor's tribunician power overshadowed that of the office-holders themselves; they would not compete with him in wooing the *plebs* for its favour. Nor was there anything that we know of to mark out the praetorship and legateship in Spain that followed, or the command of a legion in Syria, the Fourth, Scythian.[42]

The death of M. Aurelius in 180 left his adolescent son Commodus in sole power, introducing an age of iron and rust, as Dio famously said, evidently thinking of domestic affairs, for under Marcus the Romans were already hard pressed abroad, on the Danube. But the new reign was saluted as an age of gold. There was nothing immediately to foreshadow the disaster of Commodus' incompetence and panicky purges, which led to his assassination twelve years later.[43]

The governor of Syria under whom Severus then served, in the early 80s, was P. Helvius Pertinax, the future emperor. Both men were involved in the case of the Quintilii, two consular brothers accused of plotting against Commodus in 182. The son of one of them, Quintilius Condianus, was hunted down in Syria, but was said to have escaped by feigning death and having a goat cremated in his place. The episode was no help to Severus' career. Pertinax lost his command and so, though not immediately, did Severus: his legateship of the Fourth, which was stationed near Antioch, made him the natural deputy for the governor. On leaving office he spent a period of time at Athens, for education, religious purposes, and tourism.[44] The downfall of Commodus' Prefect of the Praetorian Guard, Perennis, brought Pertinax and Severus into employment again, Pertinax in Britain, Severus as legate in Lugdunensian Gaul, and this was when his first wife Paccia Marciana died.[45]

Severus was well advanced in his career, then, when he took Domna as his second wife, conforming with the spirit of the legislation on marriage passed by Augustus and avoiding the penalties of celibacy.[46] He found his new wife far from home. Paccia Marciana, whom he married at the age of 30, when he was tribune of the *plebs*, belonged to a family of Lepcis, one of indigenous origin, as her names show, being derived from those of mid-first century governors of Africa who had arranged for Roman citizenship to be conferred on their protégés.[47] The story in the *Historia Augusta* that there were two daughters who reached marriageable age is not credited by modern scholars.[48] So Domna did not have the problem of acquiring stepdaughters little separated from herself in age, or more importantly of sons to stand in the way of her own. Paccia died after ten years of marriage, and Severus found nothing to say of her in his autobiography, written in part to justify his conduct as a private citizen. Later the *Lepcitani Septimiani* and three *curiae* or community divisions commemorated her on bases in their native city, as they did members of his own family.[49]

The former praetor Severus was much older than his new bride – up to twenty-eight years. But there was said to be a particular reason for his choice: her horoscope, which marked her as 'the wife of a future king' (he made enquiries about the horoscopes of all the candidates); his friends worked for the match, acting as intermediaries.[50] He may have thought that Domna's very name, in its transliterated Latin form (the origin of it was unlikely to be misunderstood by the Punic-speaking Severus), marked her out in the same way.[51] But the story of the horoscope is puzzling. Who first related it? How did Severus know about the horoscope of a young woman of Emesa? Why in 187 did he embrace such a dangerous bride? These are intertwined questions.

The plausible answer to the question of how Severus knew his future wife, or of her and her horoscope, is that he had indeed met members of her family during his legionary legateship in Syria.[52] The horoscope would have been brought to his attention – by *her* friends, who are likely to have put it out in the first place as bait for some promising local prince, or at least a member of some dynastic family, a person of Domna's own background. But a praetorian senator and legionary commander would have been a catch – if he had not already been married.

For Severus there was different kind of catch in making such a marriage: it betrayed ambitions that had often in the past proved fatal. If he did notice signs at that time he must have cherished ambitions, and there would be people to pass the information on to the sensitive Commodus.[53] At the end of Caracalla's reign the emperor's friend Flavius Maternianus was to try to reveal the ambitions of M. Opellius Macrinus, Prefect of the Praetorian Guard, in a letter telling of the predictions of soothsayers.[54] That makes the horoscope look like a *post eventum* creation designed to explain Severus' choice of wife ('he chose her because he knew that her royal destiny fitted his own'). Severus had married someone who could be made out by a contemporary to be 'plebeian' – but she was a plebeian whose husband would be king. Her name too, misunderstood by Latin speakers, made the story easy to develop. Becoming acquainted with her family in Syria, Severus later took a good-looking and potentially wealthy young woman to wife. Money and the family were the attractions.

The invention would come from the reign of Severus or during his struggle for power, to enhance Domna's prestige and value to the dynasty; ultimately, as A. R. Birley suggests, for Severus' own benefit because it enhanced his claims, especially in the east. Even as a creation of Severus', the story has its place, illuminating as it does one of the most striking features of his personality – and political strategy: his superstition, skill as an astrologer, and preoccupation with horoscopes matched by that of his rival Niger.[55] It is hardly surprising that like other rulers he discouraged unauthorized operations and issued a proclamation in Egypt in 199 forbidding the use of written documents and images to prophesy the future.[56]

In spite of Severus' particular reputation, his interest was shared by most Romans living in an age of anxiety and notably by Dio, whose first literary work to attract Severus' attention was a study of the omens that presaged his coming to power.[57] Severus himself wrote an autobiography that reflected Hadrian's interest in omens.[58] It gave an account of those that had come to him as signs of his future greatness. There is no need to ask whether either man was a believer or an unscrupulous exploiter of the material. They were both. Even in Spain, Severus claimed, he dreamt that he was instructed to restore the temple of Augustus at Tarraco.[59] Severus was naturally assiduous in informing himself about his future under an unpredictable monarch. As legionary legate he visited the authoritative, even imperious, oracle of Zeus Belus, 'Ruler of Destiny' at Apameia, half-way between Antioch and Emesa, and received a pair of lines from the *Iliad*, a flattering description of Agamemnon. On a later visit, dated by J. Balty to 201–2, he was warned, appropriately with a quotation from Euripides' *Phoenician Women*, of a bloody end to his dynasty – so we are told, hardly by Severus himself; that would be a late embellishment of Dio's, composed at the end of his work.[60] Severus, so the *Historia Augusta* alleges, had to face trial on a charge of consulting seers or astrologers, not about his own destiny but about the imperial position. That was in 190, on his return to Rome from Sicily; but he was acquitted.[61]

The story of the horoscope was one of the signs of Severus' future greatness that was essential to his claims to rule. It is of a piece with the tale that before the wedding Severus dreamt that it was attended by Faustina (II), wife of Marcus, and took place on her instruction in the temple of Venus and Rome.[62] The real reason for the marriage may have been the mundane one of the girl's real financial dowry, sanitized in a way that also benefited Severus. In Roman law, a woman's dowry passed to her husband, though he had to return it if they were divorced.[63] In other respects the importance of this marriage to Severus should not be exaggerated. In 307 Constantine, later 'the Great', married the daughter of his fellow ruler Maximian, and an orator of Gaul provided an epithalamian speech. But Fausta is never addressed in it. The important matter was the link between the two dynasts.[64] Domna's family was only of provincial importance, though she was a cut above Paccia Marciana.

Presumably Domna married Severus at Lugdunum, since his duties as a governor did not allow him to leave his province. She had come, of course, with a train of attendants and slaves, on the first of her journeys between east and west, making a leap in the dark, but inaugurating the contrast that has been perceived with Marguerite Yourcenar's Hadrian: he lived and worked successfully in both east and west, but as a stranger in both. Domna too moved from one end of the Empire to the other, but seems to have been comfortable in each.[65] Domna hardly knew her husband-to-be, if at all, but she was not worse off, as she descended to the port of Aradus or to Antioch and its port Seleuceia Pieria to leave Asia by sea, than overseas brides destined for English kings and princes over the centuries. She and Severus shared (ultimately) Semitic ancestry, at least two languages, Roman citizenship, high class, and ambition.

The marriage took place in 187, to judge by the birth date of Domna's elder son.[66] For Domna's fertility was quickly apparent: she soon produced two sons. The elder, later the Emperor Caracalla, was born at Lugdunum on 4 (or 6, if the *Historia Augusta* were correct) April 188,[67] and probably given his father's *praenomen* of Lucius to precede the family *nomen* of Septimius, while his *cognomen* was that of his maternal grandfather Bassianus, indicating the high standing of that side of the family, in local reckoning at least. Naturally the baby had a wet-nurse, and one interpretation of the difficult text of Tertullian makes it claim that she was a Christian. Allowing such contact would suggest a hint of tolerance, even curiosity on Domna's part. The Christian community at Lugdunum, many of whose members had been martyred in 177, was largely from Phrygia in Asia; a Greek-speaking nurse would by itself be an attraction. But the interpretation is wrong. Tertullian means that Caracalla knew that Severus had a Christian physiotherapist (Proculus Torpacion) permanently on his staff, who had drunk Christian 'milk' and had been a Christian from birth.[68]

Domna's time in Lugdunum cannot have been entirely tranquil: it was only a decade since disorders had led to the massacre of Christians and it was during the governorship of Severus that the revolt of the army deserter Maternus had broken out, affecting Gaul and, Herodian claims, Germany, Spain, and Italy. A serious outbreak came in Upper Germany, crushed in 186. The governor of Gaul would have been charged with repressing Maternus, and in a nice touch Commodus is said to have been dissatisfied with the efforts of Severus and his colleagues Pescennius Niger in Aquitania and Clodius Albinus in Belgica, sending them threatening letters.[69]

About a year after Caracalla's birth, probably in March 189, after Severus had left Lugdunum for Rome and drawn Sicily in the ballot for a proconsular province,[70] Domna was in Rome (not Mediolanum as the *Historia Augusta* claims to know in the face of rival versions, but contradicting itself) to give birth to her second son, P. Septimius Geta, whose original *praenomen* and *cognomen* were owed to his paternal uncle and grandfather.[71]

This is the place to deal with the story that Geta was actually Domna's only son, and that Caracalla was the child of Severus' first wife, but those of incestuous relations between the two of them may be left until later.[72] The first idea had several attractions, and for different groups: for Caracalla it allowed his birth date to be advanced, giving him greater seniority over his younger brother; for the public it helped excuse the implacable hatred between two boys; it accounted for the impression that Domna favoured Geta over Caracalla; and generally it mitigated the horror of the incest, once that story became an ingredient in the mix. In fact, however, it is likely that the story originated simply as the inevitable consequence of the antedating – at his own wish – of Caracalla's birth.

Domna's fertility might have been designed for the traditional dynastic plans of the Roman ruling family, and when Severus came to power the traditional pattern was followed. Already in the second decade BC Augustus had waited until the birth of his second grandson to his daughter Julia (in 17 BC) to go through the act of adoption that made Gaius and Lucius his sons and, by implication, his heirs. The same pattern had been followed in AD 4, when Augustus' adoptive son-to-be, Tiberius, himself adopted his nephew Germanicus, making him the brother of Tiberius' natural son Drusus. Again, when Claudius adopted the son of his new wife Agrippina in 51, so that L. Domitius Ahenobarbus became Claudius Nero, he was giving his own son Britannicus an elder brother. Sometimes the brothers were seen as potential joint rulers, sometimes (or by some contemporary politicians) as 'an heir and a spare'. Geta's forename of Publius was to be changed to Lucius, recalling, as B. Bleckmann suggests,[73] the name of Lucius Verus, Marcus Aurelius' co-ruler and fellow Augustus, when Caracalla assumed the full nomenclature of Marcus Aurelius. There is no support for any fantasy that Domna persuaded Severus to make both Caracalla and Geta his heirs: eventually Severus found that he had little option. The gap between the two youths was too small for Geta to be discounted as Domitian had been when Titus, twelve years older, was Vespasian's designated successor.

Domna probably coasted along the southern shore of Asia Minor to the Aegean and mainland Greece and Italy, unless she took the slow land-route through Asia Minor and the Balkans; in the beginning of her marriage she saw one of the great cities of the western Empire, the Roman colony of Lugdunum. Whether she passed through Rome on her journey west is another matter. Perhaps it was not until the end of Severus' governorship in Gaul that she had the overwhelming experience described by the fourth century historian Ammianus Marcellinus, himself a native of Antioch. Ammianus has it dazzling and bowling over the newly arrived Emperor Constantius in 357, with Trajan's Forum as the culminating vision.[74] Back from Sicily, and as the wife of a consul in 190, Domna would have been one of first ladies of Roman society, and even after Severus' short term of office was over, she enjoyed the permanent distinction of rank that it conferred. The members of senatorial families in the east were in the habit of alluding to themselves in Greek monuments as of senatorial family (*synkletikos*) or 'consular' (*hypatikos*).[75] It may be too that some of Domna's relatives followed her to Rome when she joined a senatorial family: her sister Julia Maesa for one, who is said to have spent long years in the Palace, perhaps with her husband, whose transfer to senatorial rank seems to have come soon after Severus' elevation.[76]

The marriage of Severus and Domna was apparently a success; naturally that is proclaimed on the coinage.[77] Stories of her adultery and incest have yet to be dealt with, but they were only to be expected when a woman has acquired power. What is more surprising is that the stories concern only her. Sexual licence is a commonplace of the biographies even of admirable married emperors: Augustus was supplied with mistresses by Livia herself; the *outré* Gaius committed incest with his sisters. His successor Claudius was the most uxorious of the Caesars, but he still had call girls (*paelices*) at his disposal. The sex life of Nero has been described as essentially heterosexual, but nobody has suggested that it was chaste.[78] Domitian, Trajan, and Hadrian certainly went in for boys or young men, while L. Verus had a gifted and beautiful mistress; most recently Pertinax had had his affair with Cornificia, perhaps the daughter of M. Aurelius.[79] No such information has come to light about Severus. Quite the reverse: he is criticized by the *Historia Augusta* for keeping Domna when she was not only notorious for her adulteries but also charged with conspiring against him.[80]

As Severus held his consulship and moved on in the following year to his last governorship, in Upper Pannonia, Commodus' Principate was spiralling downwards, with one 'favourite' succeeding another – Cleander after Perennis after Saoterus – to dominate the unfocused emperor, whose vanity and fears as well as their rivalries brought about one execution, or batch of executions, after another. Potential successors themselves were multiplying, with the name of Pertinax coming most often to the surface. It was a sign of the turmoil that Severus' consulship was one of twenty-five that graced his year.[81] Trusties and men whose support was needed were being rewarded. Exactly a century earlier, in 90, after a conspiracy against Domitian had been quashed on the Rhine, there had been thirteen consuls, an unusually high number in the Flavian period.

After spending one month in office during the second half of the year Severus passed some time without employment.[82] While Severus and Domna waited at Rome for his first appointment as an ex-consul, he continued to attend the Senate while she moved in the same high circles and took part in the dinners and entertainments arranged for them. Besides a town house, they had an estate that Severus bought before he went to Pannonia.[83] Some of the entertainments imposed a strain on the audience. One interest of the emperor was gladiatorial and hunting athleticism, which he would display before the senators as they sat in their privileged front seats at the arena (women were segregated in the gods). Death stared Dio and his colleagues in the face as Commodus killed an ostrich and brandished the head in front of them, causing nearly uncontrollable laughter – or near hysteria.[84] It came fairly close to Severus towards the end of Commodus' reign when it carried off an Emesene, a Julius Alexander, perhaps a kinsman of Domna, who according to Dio had killed a lion from horseback with his spear, outdoing the emperor. The charge though was conspiracy, and it is accepted as justified by the *Historia Augusta*: this was one of the two genuine conspiracies against Commodus before the successful one. Alexander killed his pursuers and his enemies among the Emesenes. That sheds unsurprising light on the internal politics of the city: the leading family will have had its enemies. Alexander took flight for Parthia, but killed himself and the boy lover he had with him when he was overtaken near the Euphrates.[85] Fifteen other victims are named, lending credit to the conspiracy theory.

Commodus' ultimate commander of the Praetorian Guard, Q. Aemilius Laetus of Thaenae, was the first known to have come from the province of Africa.[86] The emperor himself was contemplating a visit to Rome's greatest supplier of grain.[87] It was now that Severus returned to employment, and to a key position: the governorship of Upper Pannonia and its three legions. The appointment, and presumably that of Severus' brother P. Geta to Lower Moesia (two legions) was made on Laetus' recommendation. The Danubian provinces often went to men of experience. On this occasion presumed trustworthiness was evidently put first: Severus had never seen service on the Rhine or Danube. Didius Julianus was another man with African links who was supported by Laetus, and so was Clodius Albinus of Hadrumetum, who was sent to Britain.[88] But for whom was Severus trustworthy? To Laetus in the first instance, and he was prime mover in the assassination of Commodus. A. R. Birley has built up a picture of a constellation of officials put in place for the coming change. Any idea that Severus was first choice to take over from Commodus must be rejected: Pertinax was a better soldier and so a preferable candidate; but it is likely that Severus was brought in to ensure the support of his three legions.[89] Dio and Herodian make the assassination an improvised response to Commodus' plans for further executions, starting with the three leading conspirators, Laetus, Eclectus the Chamberlain, and Marcia, Commodus' mistress, followed, equally unsurprisingly, with a string of senators. That was a good story for the plotters to put out.[90]

3 Domna on her travels

There was not much of a role for a woman in the series of military coups and political crises that followed the murder of the childless Commodus at Rome at the end of 192. But if Domna's later habit of travelling with her husband was already established, she would have been with him in Pannonia and at headquarters in Carnuntum on the Danube when Commodus died and when Severus put himself forward, accompanying him south as he advanced. It is not certain, and the fact that Severus had to summon his children to security from Rome when he was proclaimed emperor may suggest that their mother was also there.[1] Other women besides Domna played small parts in the turmoil of 193, Marcia the most prominent of them; they illustrate what might be done, and what fates Domna might expect.

The death of Commodus left a vacancy as open as it had been when Domitian fell nearly a century before, but this time the emperor's death led to four years of civil war. The experienced politician, an Italian of low origin, P. Helvius Pertinax, who was currently Prefect of the City, and with whom Commodus had shared the opening consulship of 192, was the first choice. He had not joined Laetus and Marcia in the murder, but probably had reason to expect it.[2] Pertinax never won over the troops in Rome. They assassinated Pertinax on 28 March after a reign of eighty-seven days and replaced him with a man who was prepared to pay up and who might take after Commodus: M. Didius Julianus. But during his short reign there were other disturbances, and the distinguished treatment that Pertinax offered Ti. Claudius Pompeianus (M. Aurelius' son-in-law), and the patrician M'. Acilius Glabrio, has evoked the attractive, though not convincing, suggestion that Pertinax was always intended as a caretaker, perhaps for Pompeianus' eldest son.[3]

The precariousness of Pertinax's rule is nicely illustrated by the portentous dream that Severus allegedly enjoyed when he heard of the accession and took the oath of allegiance: a horse carrying Pertinax slipped and fell in the Comitium, unseating him; it then rose, carrying Severus into the middle of the Forum, to general applause.[4] Laetus is suspected of having engineered the attack on Pertinax in order to make way for Severus; they were on

Figure 3.1 Pertinax's Liberality to the people of Rome.
AE. Obv. *IMP CAES P. HELV PERTINAX AVG* Head of Pertinax r., laureate. Rev. *TR P COS II* (mid-field) *SC* (in exergue) *LIB AVG* (*TRIBUNICIAN POWER, CONSUL FOR THE SECOND TIME, BY DECREE OF THE SENATE, LIBERALITY OF AUGUSTUS*) Pertinax, togate, seated l. on a curule chair set on platform, extending r. hand and holding roll in l. hand at side; on platform, r., behind him, lictor, wearing tunic to thighs, standing front, head l., r. hand on ?chair and holding vertical staff in l., r. knee bent, r. leg drawn back behind, l. l. In front of him, Liberality, draped, standing front, head l., holding abacus up in r. and cornucopia in l.; to l. at foot of platform, citizen, togate, standing r., l. foot forward, in act to mount steps; he holds out in both hands fold of toga containing pieces of money (?). 1 Jan.–28 Mar., AD 193.

Source: *CREBM* 5, p. 8 no. 40.

Figure 3.2 Didius Julianus and the troops.
AV. Obv. *IMP CAES M DID IV LIAN AVG* head of Didius Julianus, laureate, bearded, r. Rev. *CONCO R D MILIT* (*HARMONY OF THE TROOPS*) Concordia, draped, standing front, head l., holding legionary eagle vertical in r. and standard vertical in l. 28 Mar. to near end of May, AD 193.

Source: *CREBM* 5, p. 11 no. 1.

friendly terms and Laetus was executed by Pertinax's immediate successor, Didius Julianus. The accusation cannot be proved.[5]

Other forces than the Praetorians wanted a say. In 96 the weak incumbent Nerva had survived because a determined military man, M. Ulpius Traianus, close at hand in Upper Germany and in command of legions, guaranteed his support. In an earlier contest still, that of 68–9, old Galba was supplanted by the champion of the Praetorians, Otho, Otho in turn by Vitellius, backed by the Rhine armies; but they had not been the final victors.

In 69 Vespasian transferred his war on the rebellious Jews to a struggle against Vitellius in Italy. Again in 97, though the man never openly declared himself, there was another potential candidate in the east. Now in 193, C. Pescennius Niger, who had distinguished himself in battle in the Balkans, was governor of Syria and its three legions and so able in turn to command the resources of the rest of the east, Egypt and Judaea. Niger was also favoured by the Senate and people of Rome, who hated Julianus for killing Pertinax, and saw Niger as a man to avenge him.[6] It was Niger that Didius Julianus feared, according to the *Historia Augusta*, and allegedly tried to have assassinated.[7] Historical precedent, the success of Vespasian, added to Niger's weight as a candidate, and to his popularity at Rome. For Domna his candidacy was particularly poignant. Her native country was behind him, and her kinsmen would have to lie low if they were not to be victimized; worst of all was the plight of any who had entered the imperial service and were on duty east of the Bosporus.

In 193, in contrast with 69, the three British legions had their own candidate instead of staying on the sidelines, as they had in 69: D. Clodius Albinus, a native of Hadrumetum who like Niger had distinguished himself in battle against the Dacians.[8] And by now the Balkans, which faced the most formidable threat from outside the Empire, contained the most formidable army, including in Upper Pannonia the three legions of Septimius Severus,[9] Even in 69 the Danubian troops were aware of their strength and made it felt: it is said that they were the first to declare for Vespasian.[10] Their commanders then were quietists, but an energetic legionary legate swept into Italy ahead of Vespasian's main expeditionary force and took Rome for him.[11]

Severus' proclamation in Pannonia must have antedated Niger's by several weeks. Early in193, perhaps even before, when the murder of Commodus was being planned, the Danubian governors will have been in consultation. As to the troops, the legions of Upper and Lower Moesia and of Dacia, as well as one of Severus' own legions, I Adiutrix, had served under the assassinated Pertinax, though not recently.[12] It was on 9 April 193, only twelve days after Pertinax's murder, that Severus had himself proclaimed emperor.[13] There could be no question of the adherence of Severus' brother P. Septimius Geta. He was probably governor of Lower Moesia, with two legions. C. Valerius Pudens, governor of Lower Pannonia or legate of one of the Upper Pannonian legions, significantly was later rewarded.[14] Julia Domna's kinsmen would have been reliable supporters in Rome. Against Severus Julianus tried the same evidently ineffective technique of assassination that Severus allegedly was to use against Albinus.[15]

The move into Italy came swiftly too, almost a lightning strike, by way of Emona, Aquileia, and Ravenna. Julianus' envoys went over to Severus and one of his last throws was to get the Senate to decree a division of Empire.[16] But his execution was essential to Severus: a single meeting of the Senate on 1 June, when Severus was still at Interamna,[17] voted him the official powers, deified Pertinax, whom Severus was avenging,[18] and condemned Julianus. Severus took and kept the *cognomen* Pertinax before the imperial title 'Augustus', later adding the particular title 'Pius' between the two designations in token of his loyalty – although it also recalled the first of the Antonine emperors, Pius.[19] Those who came to dislike the emperor said that he was well named: pertinacious and severe.[20]

From Interamna Severus was free to make for Rome in person – unlike Vespasian, who needed to secure his hold on Egypt and north Africa – and acted as an emperor, appointing consuls.[21] Didius Julianus was isolated in the Palace and his Praetorian Guard proved ineffective.[22] Severus entered Rome on 9 June, vindicating the late 'Princeps Senatus', and made the usual promise that he would not put any senator to death, that is, without the authorization of the Senate; he was not one of the few emperors who kept that promise. The populace turned out all in white to celebrate his arrival in a city brilliant with torches, flowers, and bunting; momentarily Domna could have believed that she and her husband and children were to enjoy a future of unclouded power and wealth.[23]

It was in this opening stage of his reign that Severus heard of Pescennius Niger's claim.[24] He split his potential opponents, who were closely linked, by offering Clodius Albinus the position of 'Caesar'.[25] That had been the *cognomen* of all male members of the imperial clan of the Julii, and so of Augustus and his male descendants. It was taken over by Claudius on his accession, and became the characteristic title of the heir, 'Augustus' being reserved for the reigning emperor. Severus, when backed by D. Clodius Septimius Albinus Caesar, as he was now styled, controlled the Roman Empire in the north and west and as far east as Byzantium, but not yet the city, which had to be besieged for more than two years.[26]

Romans were shocked when Septimius Severus brought in his provincially recruited legionaries to replace the previously Italian Praetorian guardsmen, many of whom he executed for their involvement in the death of Pertinax. To Dio, who mentions Italy, Spain, Macedonia, and Noricum as respectable sources for the Guard, they seemed a motley crowd recruited from different parts of the western Empire, many of them presumably from the Danube, and as uncouth to look at as they were terrifyingly wild to hear as they exulted in their capture of the capital. And then there was the question of class: these were not the elite of enlisted men that the Guard had had the right to expect, but peasants or sons of the legionary camp.[27]

Unless she had a few favourites among her husband's soldiers, Domna will not have had much to do with the abrupt changes that followed Severus' entry into Rome. When she went into the Palace for the first time as its mistress, she may have felt the same bewilderment as the wives of British Prime Ministers when they enter No. 10 Downing Street: the Prime Minister is swept off immediately on state business, the spouse left behind to wander the premises with no clear duty or function.[28]

Domna's first public act as Severus' consort may well have been to appear at the 'funeral' and consecration of Pertinax, perhaps wearing for the first time the combination of veil and diadem that is shown on the Arch of the *Argentarii*.[29] The effigy was brought to a shrine in the Forum, where the emperor and senators and their wives, clad in mourning, paid it their respects before Severus delivered the eulogy. For the future Domna led a life that was separate from her husband's, if not independent of it, and had her own interests. In the description that Dio gives of Severus' way of life – up before dawn and at work, then a walk in which affairs of state were discussed, riding, the gymnasium, a bath, lunch with his sons, and a siesta, more work, another bath, and dinner with friends, there is no mention of Domna, and room for her only at the luncheons and dinner parties. She was not in the room (before dinner, on one account) when the Praetorian Prefect Plautianus was killed in 205.[30] She was present on formal occasions, but could hardly hazard her influence then; promises to help courtiers and subjects could be carried out only behind closed doors.

Domna should now in June 193 have emerged from at least two months of acute anxiety for her husband, herself and her children, certainly since the declaration, probably since the death of Commodus, and possibly even before that. It is a question why the children were at Rome in the first place. It cannot have been for the sake of their education: even Caracalla at the end of 192 was still at the age when boys were being educated at their mother's knee. Perhaps Severus had to leave them at Rome as virtual hostages for his own good behaviour; that would have been likely long before Commodus died, for it was a practice of his to take governors' children hostage.[31] During Pertinax's reign Severus might seem more trustworthy; they could have gone underground when Julianus came to power and slipped away soon after.[32] Severus was more alert than Didius Julianus: he sent his commander of the Guard to take Pescennius Niger's children, and others, into custody as soon as he knew of the first serious opposition to his Principate; after eluding him for a while they were captured and eventually sent into exile with their mother. They were killed when Severus was about to deal with Clodius Albinus.[33] Niger in his provincial capital of Antioch had laid claim to the purple in late April, and the news cannot have taken more than a few weeks to reach Rome.[34]

Niger controlled the east, with ten legions and the granaries of Egypt. When he heard the news of Severus' coup he applied to the bordering monarchies for help, Armenia, Parthia, and Hatra. Armenia held off, but Parthia gave promises and Hatra sent archers. Severus began by blocking the way into Thrace, then, leaving Rome only one month after he had entered it, himself advanced by land into the Balkans, rejecting an offer of help from his brother, who was ordered back to his Danubian province.[35] Severus marched as far as Perinthus on the northern shore of the Propontis, about 80 km. west of Byzantium, and there seems to have spent the winter of 193–4.[36] Niger was first defeated in Bithynia, though Byzantium still held out, then destroyed at Issus in the south-west corner of Asia Minor. Niger was killed in a suburb of Antioch, or, as Dio damningly has it, as he fled from Antioch to the Euphrates.[37]

All through the war with Pescennius Niger, Domna had continued cause for anxiety. If Severus lost, he would eventually lose his life as well, and so might she, as a high-profile wife. Sometimes wives were spared, to be married off to nonentities, but certainly her sons would die. She had only to consider the fate of Vitellius' son in the aftermath of his defeat by Vespasian to know that, although his wife survived.[38] Again, while this was an anxiety less acute, her native city, and no doubt members of her family, were in the part of the Empire controlled by Niger.

Severus' defeat of Niger brought a new time for rewards and punishments. Individuals certainly suffered. Even if they did not die during or immediately after the campaigning, their careers faltered. Two instances may be mentioned:[39] C. Claudius Attalus Paterculianus of Pergamum and the later Emperor M. Antonius Gordianus (Gordian I), an easterner whose name recalls Gordium in Anatolia, famous for the knot cut by Alexander the Great. They were expelled from the Senate in 193–4 and restored by Caracalla. Gordian continued in favour with the Severi and became consul in 222. Gordian was safely tucked away as governor of Lower Britain when Caracalla was coming to the end of his reign in 216, while the less fortunate Paterculianus, who had become governor of Cyprus, was executed by Elagabalus.

As to communities, civil war offered a chance for old rivalries to vent themselves in something more serious than the traditional boundary suits and football hooliganism. Nicaea was set against Nicomedia in Bithynia, Tyre and Laodiceia against Antioch in Syria. Those who had backed the wrong candidate were penalized by the loss of prized titles such as 'metropolis', which were awarded to their rivals. Tyre, the mother-city of Carthage, and Laodiceia did better than that: they were awarded the valuable *ius Italicum*, which meant relief from taxation, as if they were built on Italian soil. Tyre also became the capital of a new province, Syria Phoenice, with one legion, for Severus now prudently divided up the great Syrian command. In the north Coele 'Hollow', Syria (an old name), which included Commagene, was left with two legions, still under a governor who had held the consulship. Niger's capital and mint Antioch for the moment lost its status as a city altogether and became a subordinate district of Laodiceia; supplying Niger was a valid reason, whether or not it was true that the

Antiochenes had made fun of Severus when he was legionary legate of Syria, as the *Historia Augusta* claims.[40]

Domna's home city of Emesa, like its trading partner Palmyra, was assigned to Phoenice, looking, in this smaller pool, like a bigger fish.[41] In the war Emesa might have been expected to opt for Severus, though it was a small place to stand up for itself and, as its earlier history shows, regularly acceded to the closer power. Besides, Niger had probably declared himself and secured local support against Julianus before news arrived of Severus' proclamation and march on Rome. It looks from coins as if the Emesenes had lost no time in displaying loyalty to Severus, but the issues are doubted. It was some time afterwards, under Caracalla, who had his own hereditary interest in the place, that Emesa was granted the status of a Roman colony, with the particular favour of *ius Italicum*, and 'colonial' coins were struck in the names of Caracalla and Domna – if they are genuine. The rank was not merely titular: there was centuriation, visible east of the town, with the two main roads intersecting at right angles at the city centre. This implies grants of individual plots, presumably to veteran soldiers. However, veteran settlement and loss of land can have been no part of an arrangement intended to be favourable. Natural difficulties may have led to depopulation; or, as W. J. Van Liere suggests, nomadic people were being encouraged to settle.[42]

After the battle of Issus, Severus with his family and court progressed through Asia Minor behind the troops. Their approach was celebrated by every city they came to (celebrations were an investment).[43] When an emperor marched in haste to war, requisitioning for troops notoriously imposed cruel burdens on his subjects. A progress on the part of the court was a different matter, although there were gradations between the two, as in this case. There was not only billeting to be arranged by local officials, but also ceremonies to be arranged and carried through with bunting and bands; the arrival (*adventus*) became an important part of late Roman protocol, tiring for the emperor too, if he had to listen to speeches of welcome standing up. His wife may have been excused that, but there will have been receptions in which she played a prominent part.[44] As to her role when they were in military encampments, nothing is known. Ancient inhibitions and censure may have restricted it, but the tributes paid her on inscriptions by the military and her title of *Mater Castrorum* and concomitant homage were liberating factors that may have brought her on to the imperial tribunal. Wherever she went, her presence stressed the dynastic aspect of Severus' rule, and so its permanence.

For the first time since her marriage, Domna was returning to her home province, and very likely to her home town. It was just in the upheavals and confusion that followed Niger's defeat that there was a role for an influential woman: she could intervene on behalf of Syrians who had taken the wrong side, although when entire communities had made the wrong choice, sometimes perforce, the offence was too great for the influence even of an empress. At the side of her bearded, middle-aged, relentless military man of a husband, Domna's beauty and comparative youth, her speaking Greek as a native, slightly accented, perhaps, but if so with a lilt that belonged to the region, were thrown into higher relief. It would always be noticed in the consort of an emperor, as in the emperor himself. Lucian in his *Portraits* notes that L. Verus' mistress Pantheia, besides her other charms, spoke the finest Ionic dialect; but other accents can be attractive. In Domna's case it was added to her appeal and authority as a mother and to the charm of her curly-headed, winsome little boys (unless the portraits are exceptionally misleading).[45] It will all have made her a high card in the hands of the new master of the Greek world.

Severus was prepared to linger in the east, consolidating his position there before he faced the last potential rival, Clodius Albinus, who could hardly be allowed to survive as ruler of the Gauls (four of Rome's richest provinces), Britain and perhaps Spain, and the Rhine armies. He began by dealing with breakaway subjects and adherents of Niger on the Euphrates who had laid siege to Nisibis, a Roman protectorate. With an army that contained contingents of the former supporters of Niger as well as his own men, Severus in spring 195 launched an expedition over the Euphrates into Osrhoene, Adiabene and against the Scenite Arabs, with Nisibis his first goal and base, and he remained in Mesopotamia until after the fall of Byzantium at the end of that year. A province of Osrhoene, minus the capital Edessa, was created in 195.[46] There was to be another war here, aimed at expanding the Empire beyond the Euphrates, but the first had helped unite the troops and won Severus prestige in the east. This made it possible for him to justify greater claims for himself than being the avenger of Pertinax, and left him free to deal with Albinus. Troops were on their way westwards already in 195.[47]

Domna's familiarity with the territory and its peoples made her more than an ornament for the expedition, which earned Severus his fifth to seventh salutations as *Imperator*. She and her kinsmen would have been a source of valuable intelligence, and that, as well as the morale-raising factor of the empress's presence among the troops, was recognized on 14 April 195, and celebrated annually thereafter: on a motion accepted in the Senate she became *Mater Castrorum*, 'Mother of the Camps'. The specific meaning of the title is obvious: the troops were under the protection of the empress, and she could expect their protection in return; more generally, it expressed the symbiotic relationship between dynasty and army.[48] Assiduous campaigning with modest successes was not the only source of Severan grip on the military; pay was much more important, but as long as that was secure Domna's symbolic patronage, or parental concern, contributed something. In one inscription cut in Italy under Caracalla, Domna seems to be identified with Victoria.

There was nothing orientalizing in the new title, as Domaszewski claimed: it went along with Severus' acquisition of titles of a traditional form, *Parthicus Arabicus*, *Parthicus Adiabenicus*, at a time when he was claiming adoption by Marcus Aurelius, and this connection with the Antonines is rightly stressed by C. R. Whittaker.[49] Gaius Caligula had styled himself 'Father of the Armies',[50] and Domna's title had already been awarded to Marcus' wife Faustina (II). Present in Marcus' northern base with her youngest daughter, Faustina received it in 174, when multiple incursions made the loyalty of the army all-important.[51] Portraits of imperial women from Livia onwards, and of imperial children, were also to be seen on military equipment; Domna herself appears on a helmet found in the river Jordan.[52] Now Domna, like Faustina, perhaps like Commodus' consort Crispina,[53] had her statue placed in the shrines of military units.

Whether Domna requested the honour that gave a mere Emesene notable the dignity of Marcus Aurelius' purple-born consort, the daughter of Antoninus Pius, and linked her by maternal ties of loyalty and affection to the army, the most significant estate of the realm, we cannot tell. Nothing is heard of any mechanism, whether a hint amid the pillow talk, a reference to Faustina at a banquet, still less of a blatant demand in public, nor of suggestions from any well-primed courtier or (perhaps most likely of all) a 'spontaneous' salutation from the troops when the empress appeared. Not that Severus would have needed many hints: the title was even more useful to him from the point of view of his position in the body politic, than it was as a personal sign of esteem to Domna.

Possession of a title that had previously belonged only to a woman genuinely of the Antonine dynasty added another bond to those that were already being created between Severus and the lost Antonines. From 198 the coins dropped the nomenclature of the assassinated Pertinax, whose true successor Severus had claimed to be, and the games that had been instituted to celebrate Pertinax's accession were given up. Instead Severus invented an adoption by Marcus Aurelius (who of course had died in 180).[54] Severus was proclaiming himself the 'son' and heir of Marcus and a continuation of the Antonine dynasty, so that Caracalla became M. Aurelius Antoninus.[55] This move, accompanied by the assimilation of Severan and Antonine portraiture, most notably, it is claimed, in the portraiture of Domna in relation to that of Faustina (II),[56] was not well received by senators; it could at best be understood as a promise of continuity with a great past, but it also meant the continuation of the Severi. Septimius was legitimizing not merely his own regime, but a dynastic scheme. However, they had no option but to accept it; wit as usual was senators' only refuge, and one joker of a governor allegedly congratulated Severus 'on finding a father', with implications about Severus' original parentage.[57]

Adoption was a long-standing device for conferring legitimacy on a dynast. Augustus himself had been the first to use it, in his own interest: his claim to be the adopted son of Julius Caesar allowed him the style 'Divi filius', 'Son of the Deified'. It was based on his position as chief heir in Caesar's will. For all the ceremony he went through as if Caesar were still alive and performing the adoption (this was vital), it was a fraud. Later emperors, Tiberius and Nero, were properly adopted by their predecessors, but lack of time before he was assassinated in 69 prevented Galba from going through the due rituals with his chosen heir. So the concept of imperial 'adoption' became looser as time went on and provided a solution to fresh problems. Nerva 'adopted' the absent Trajan, but Trajan did not trouble to take Nerva's undistinguished family name of Cocceius, and deified both Nerva and his real father.[58] Antoninus Pius and Marcus Aurelius, however, had acquired immense prestige, and Septimius Severus wanted their name.

The new connections, bogus though they were, carried Severus well beyond the near parity of his alliance with Clodius Albinus, and Albinus' title of Caesar, which would have allowed Albinus a claim if Severus died prematurely, but which was less useful without adoption, and which in any case Severus now began to deny him, became worthless to him.[59] Albinus enjoyed support in the Senate,[60] and any partisans of his still attending must have gritted their teeth harder than most as the changes were announced. The exact chronological relation between Severus' adoption of the Antonines, Caracalla's assumption of 'Caesar', with his image on coin obverses, Severus' denial of 'Caesar' to Albinus, and Albinus' declaration of himself as Augustus, is unclear.[61] If the title was conferred in 195 rather than in 196 it may have been that that was what provoked Albinus' move later in the same year. Caracalla was 7 years old, but Commodus had been 5: youth was no obstacle to the taking what had once been an inherited family name, though it now had constitutional significance in its relation to an Augustus. Caracalla and then Geta were next in succession, as provincial cities of the east recognized; as to whether Geta became Antoninus too, as the *Historia Augusta* claims, coins and inscriptions do not confirm it.[62] The advance of Domna's son and the hardening of attitude towards Albinus would have helped give rise to the story that it was Domna who egged Severus on against Albinus, as well as against Niger.[63] First, he hardly needed it, then the story of female intervention on behalf of a son is routine, and finally the hereditary principle of succession, whatever its failings, had long since established itself.

One of the most objectionable aspects of the 'adoption' was that it made Severus 'brother' of Commodus and after the death of Albinus involved the cynical consecration in due form of the Senate's recent *bête noire*, whom it had allegedly pronounced 'more savage than Domitian, more debauched than Nero'.[64] As Herodian noted, it was emperors with sons who were deified, but a 'brother' in need was better than nothing.[65] Senatorial opinion did not count. Severus had been enraged by signs of favour it had seemed to show Albinus,[66] and in any case the Senate was not the only constituency to be considered. In consecrating Commodus, as in conferring Domna's title of *Mater Castrorum*', he had the army in mind. S. Dušanić has pointed out that the dates of Severan military discharge *diplomata* awarding privileges to veterans coincide with and so celebrate the birthday and accession to power of Commodus. This was particularly valuable for Severus: recipients of these *diplomata* had been enlisted by the late emperor.[67]

Figure 3.3 Faustina II, deified, and as Mother of the Camps.
AR. Obv. *DIVAE FAVSTIN AVG MATR CASTROR* (*TO THE DEIFIED FAUSTINA AUGUSTA, MOTHER OF THE CAMPS*) Bust of the deified Faustina r., veiled, draped. Rev. *CONSE CRATIO Pietas* (Devotion), veiled, draped, standing front, head l., sacrificing out of patera in r., hand over a lighted altar l., and holding vertical sceptre in l., AD 176–80.

Source: *CREBM* 4, p. 488 no. 799.

Figure 3.4 Domna, Mother of the Camps.
AV. Obv. *IVLIA AVGVSTA* Bust of Domna, draped, head bare, r. The hair is elaborately waved, and the waving is divided by five horizontal ridges; large bun or chignon on the back of the head. Rev. *MATRI CAST RORVM* (*TO THE MOTHER OF THE CAMPS*) Julia Domna, veiled, draped, standing front, head l., sacrificing out of patera in r. hand over lighted and garlanded altar l., and holding box, with lid open, in l. hand; in front of her, l., two standards set in ground. Early in period AD 198–209

Source: *CREBM* 5, p. 164 no. 56.

News of Albinus' proclamation reached Severus and Domna on the journey back from Syria.[68] The imperial party seems to have followed the same route as on the outward journey, with a stay in Rome, where Severus made a dedication to his ancestor Nerva, who came to power in 96.[69] Again the outcome was a subject of acute anxiety for Domna. Not only had there been popular agitation in December of 195 at the games in Rome, designed to muffle Severus' strike against his rival, but also Albinus was making strenuous, if not always successful, efforts to broaden his base in the west, in Spain, Lugdunensian Gaul, the Rhine provinces, and Noricum; an attack on Italy through the Alps was considered possible, and Severus blocked the passes.[70] The stakes for the new dynasts were as high as ever.

Severus with his army passed through Pannonia, Noricum, and Raetia into Upper Germany; that left him poised to strike against the enemy centre, Lugdunum in Gaul. Whether Domna accompanied him all the way on this strenuous and, at its end, dangerous journey is not known. There was a nice balance of evils: in the front line the empress and her children were in immediate danger from a victorious enemy, but their presence would encourage the troops, while in Italy they might fall hostage to traitors in the rear.[71] One man in the entourage, in all likelihood, was L. Fabius Cilo, consul 193 and veteran of the eastern expedition; Caracalla was left with him in Upper Pannonia, Severus' old province, where Cilo stayed on as governor. It seems probable that Domna was with them.[72]

Albinus was finally defeated at the bloody and finely balanced battle of Lugdunum on 19 February 197. Severus had no mercy on him or the senators who had joined him, nor on his wife and sons, who had come with him from Britain. Their bodies allegedly went into the Rhône. Something like this, Domna must have reflected, could have been her own fate.[73] After the victory the imperial court moved with its master, not directly to Rome, but to Germany and Pannonia, and it was while it was in Germany that the Senate's embassy came to meet the emperor and reiterate its loyalty; they will have gone on into Pannonia to greet Caracalla. Altogether, the defeat of Clodius Albinus signalled a change in Severus' reign; he was free of rivals, and free to do his will. The victory was followed by executions, confiscations, and bullying of the Senate, who received a lecture when Severus returned to Rome on their relations with Commodus, just as they once had on their hostile attitude towards Tiberius when Caligula became disillusioned with them.[74]

On the way to the war, when the imperial party was at Viminacium in Upper Moesia, Caracalla had been displayed to the troops as Caesar, perhaps on his birthday, 4 April 196. Severus' elder brother P. Septimius Geta was also present; naturally the story was that the elevation of Caracalla was intended to put an end to his ambitions as well as to underline the degradation of Albinus.[75] But Severus' son was an asset to him in the struggle with Albinus: an emperor with an heir promised enduring stability along Antonine lines, a leading theme of the Severan age. Vespasian among others had found the same, to his political advantage, although Caracalla had none of the immediate viability of Vespasian's warrior son Titus.[76] We do not know how old the sons of Albinus were. Coins were struck in Caracalla's name on the theme of 'perpetual security' and – picking up and developing a notion that had been propagated on coinage since Claudius' time – 'unceasing hope'.[77] Nero had come to sole power at 16 and seemed likely to hold on to power indefinitely; but neither he nor Domitian had a male heir to avenge him, and both were toppled. No doubt at the triumphal procession held in Rome Severus had his sons riding by the horses that drew his chariot up to the Capitol, Caracalla on the right, Geta on the left. So had Augustus done with Marcellus and Tiberius in his processions of 29 BC. Claudius in AD 44 may have taken his infant son Britannicus into the chariot with him; the adult Titus, who had captured Jerusalem, actually shared Vespasian's triumph over Judaea; Marcus Aurelius was accompanied by a brood of both sexes, from 7 years old downwards.[78] These moves to advance Domna's elder son also included his holding the significant title *princeps iuventutis* (Leader of the Youth), which Ovid had long since neatly pointed out meant a boy destined one day to be a leader of the elders or the Senate.[79] In 197 the implication was to be spelt out in inscriptions that style Caracalla *Imperator designatus* or *destinatus* as well as *particeps imperii*. He was a sharer in the Empire who was 'destined' to become emperor or was officially, by vote of the Senate when Severus returned to Rome from Gaul, 'Emperor designate'.[80] These would have been welcome developments for Domna. In a society in which women could hold only the most limited official positions, their ambitions focused on the success of their sons. Roman society, like Jewish and Indian, offers striking illustrations of that: Cornelia, mother of the Gracchi; Aurelia, mother of Julius Caesar; Livia, mother of Tiberius; above all Agrippina the Younger, mother of Nero.

His behaviour shows Septimius Severus holding the tyrant's view – the Sullan and Triumviral view, it was thought – that he can bring resistance to an end by slaughter and confiscation. The violence leaves resentment behind and further repression is often required. At the same time the thinking tyrant makes efforts to win over hostile or wavering subjects over. Here women, with their conventionally softer image and dissociation from direct violence, have had their place. The paradigm is Livia, intervening with Augustus in the privacy of their bedroom on behalf of an old enemy of the Civil Wars, Cn. Cornelius Cinna, who had plotted against him once more. (The notorious influence of Claudius' wives was not so benevolent.)[81] The privacy of the occasion encouraged this perception of a Livia's role to develop, along with fictional but nourishing anecdotes: nobody knew what went on behind the scenes. In the aftermath of the coups and civil wars of the early 190s there could have been opportunities for Domna. We hear of no such Livian interventions. Either she was ineffective against a relentless husband, or the historians were too hostile to report what she did. Most likely as a woman new to Roman political life – Livia was born to it – she did not intervene.

Women in their role as positive links between male individuals and families were constantly important. Within the imperial entourage there was jostling for power, with Domna no doubt doing what she could for kinsmen and personal favourites; Livia is the paradigm again, celebrated both epigraphically and by Velleius Paterculus as a political support. Domna was vital to Septimius Severus as a representative of eastern aristocracies at court, stimulating their hopes and loyalty. That also contributed to her main aim, which, like that of any politician, was to maintain her own position. In her case that meant securing that of her sons. However directed, her influence would also have been resented by other courtiers and by the Senate.[82]

For additional security in Italy Severus had his Second, Parthian, Legion stationed near Alba Longa, south of Rome at a site that developed into a town known as Albano Laziale. His brutal purge gave strong motives to avoid attending the Senate three or more times a month. A few months after the victory in Gaul a new Parthian war demanded his attention. Severus' absence and his engagement with Albinus had given the Parthians their opportunity. They had invaded Mesopotamia and laid siege to Nisibis.[83] If he were to make a credible emperor Severus had to respond to this. Nor had Hatra been punished for adherence to Niger. The eastern provinces knew Severus by now, and he need not parade through them. In the summer of 197 the imperial family, together with the Praetorian Prefect C. Fulvius Plautianus, took ship at Brundisium and sailed to the port of Aegae in eastern Asia Minor.[84] Domna, valuable again on his second eastern expedition, probably resided in Syria once more – in Laodiceia, which was also granted special grain relief – while the campaigning was going on. There would have been time, though, for her to visit her native city again if she wished.

Severus arrived in Syria rather late for an extensive campaign, but after relieving Nisibis he invaded Mesopotamia, taking Seleuceia and Babylon, reached the capital Ctesiphon and captured it at the end of the year or at the beginning of 198. It was enough for him to celebrate his *Victoria Parthica* at the end of January. Like Trajan, though, he failed in a siege of Hatra, an important communications centre, and he gave up the campaign, entering into peace negotiations with the inhabitants. Presenting this as a victory seems to have called for strenuous propaganda efforts on the part of the emperor aimed at his own disgruntled troops and the Empire at large. At any rate Severus was able to recreate the Roman province of Mesopotamia, recalling Trajan's work of eighty years before.[85] The outcome appears on the Arch erected at Rome in 203 and on coinage as a success, an expansion of the Empire, with the local deity, Helios Shamash, supporting the Romans. The victory at Ctesiphon was celebrated on the day of Trajan's accession exactly a century before.[86]

Severus like Trajan became *Parthicus* – but Severus was *Parthicus Maximus* – and he chose the moment to advance the 9-year-old Caesar Caracalla to the rank of Augustus,[87] the step that Marcus Aurelius had taken with Commodus in 176, when his son was 15, and which was to be followed by third century emperors who wanted to assure the succession and deter usurpers. Philip the Arabian (244–9) and Philip II, Augustus at 10 years of age, are perhaps the best known examples. At the same time Severus raised his younger son to the rank of Caesar.[88] Julia Domna Augusta was now both the wife and the mother of an Augustus. There was not a cloud on the horizon.

This second sojourn in Syria was not wasted. There had been time since the war with Niger for healing and reconciliation. Most importantly, Antioch had its status as a city restored; it would have been unrealistic to give so powerful a community a permanent grievance. Severus' second visit to the oracle of Zeus Belos at Apameia, probably in 198, and perhaps one to that of the Jupiter of Heliopolis in 199 (an oracular response was involved), served several purposes: they showed respect to, and support from, powerful local deities. Belos had delivered a response that supported Severus' pretensions and the emperor remembered his obligations.[89] The touristic and cultural aspect of these visits, anticipating the coming cruise up the Nile, was also significant. It had obvious precedents, the leisurely tour of inspection in Greece, Asia Minor, and Egypt undertaken by Germanicus Caesar in AD 17–19, and the journeys of Hadrian in 129–131/2 and M. Aurelius in 175–6. Both sides, visitors and visited, benefited: imperial curiosity and vanity were satisfied, the prestige of local monuments was enhanced and the flow of private tourists and pilgrims increased. Such touring was a form of imperial activity in which female members of the family could play a prominent and gracious role, as the Elder Agrippina had done when she accompanied her husband Germanicus. The imperial women had always been recognized – almost advertised – by issues of Greek city mints and honorific decrees.[90] Such honours were not offered for nothing: they were an opportunity for repicrocal benefaction. Domna, her channelling role enhanced when her husband was absent on campaign, was a focus of civil business, and approached as a powerful go-between. In Syria she would have been in her element. More distant communities could benefit too: as the result of the help she gave an embassy from Athens – her 'kindliness working on their behalf' ('*philanthropias synergouses*') – the people of Athens called her 'saviour' of their city ('*soteira ton Athenon*'). Each year on her birthday the magistrates were to sacrifice to Good Fortune (*Agathe Tyche*) and make offerings to Domna and Athena Polias.[91] In case the influence of the empress should be exaggerated, it is worth recalling an illuminating instance of failure, on the part of Livia, because such cases are not often recorded. But Livia tried, unsuccessfully at first, to persuade her husband to grant freedom to the Samians; Octavian unchivalrously exposed her failure in his letter to the petitioners, and it was publicized in a luckier city, Aphrodisias. The exposure assured the Samians of her good will, while it showed that it was dependent on his own.[92]

In 199 the imperial household embarked for the seaports of Palestine and Pelusium in Egypt, where they entered the province (March or April)[93] and took up residence in the imposing, historic, and ever-restless city of Alexandria. The visit of Severus and Domna to Egypt (preceded by a precautionary ban on divination)[94] was a successful one. Severus had restored stability, and could be generous. Besides attending to the chronic, and recently acute, discontent in a province that had supported Niger, Severus reformed its administration in ways that included showing favour to the city of Alexandria. He promulgated a rule that villagers should not be impressed into compulsory service in their respective town centres (*metropoleis*); effective or not, it meant well towards the least of his subjects. We are specifically told that this was a time when 'the towns were still prosperous'.[95] As to Alexandria itself, Severus at last granted it the city council it had been agitating for since the reign of Augustus, giving it the full panoply of Greek city status.[96] There were limits. Severus was not the admirer of Alexander the Great that his elder son was to prove. His adversary Niger had adopted the champion of the Greeks as his patron, for clear propaganda purposes. Now Alexander's sarcophagus was closed.[97]

Then came the voyage up the Nile. Severus and Domna were able to view the antiquities, which he is said to have enjoyed,[98] at Memphis and Thebes and up to the border of Ethiopia. For Domna, visiting the statues of Memnon across the river from Thebes and the inscriptions on them, there was a reminder of earlier women of the imperial house who had been there: Hadrian's wife Sabina and the learned Julia Balbilla, a poet at that court and a distant and distinguished connection of the empress herself. Balbilla's tribute to Memnon and her own ancestors, naturally in verse, still survives and will have been read by Domna.[99] Balbilla and her brother Philopappus, consul in 109, whose great funeral monument looms up opposite the Acropolis in Athens, came from the client dynasty of Commagene, deposed in 72; both the princely family of Emesa and the savant who had advised Claudius and Nero, Ti. Claudius Balbillus, had formed marriage alliances with Antiochus IV.[100] The sojourn in Egypt, especially the Nile voyage, should have been one of the most satisfying episodes in the whole of Domna's life. Her husband's power was now unchallenged, the future of her sons assured, and foreign wars in abeyance. Only the presence of the overbearing Prefect of the Guard, C. Fulvius Plautianus, who was a kinsman of Severus on his mother's side (there was a story of a sexual relationship), and whom Severus referred to as his friend, was a threat to her happiness, and one that was to bring her hopes for her children, perhaps even her own life, into acute danger.[101]

From Egypt the court returned by ship to Syria (in the second half of 200),[102] and Severus entered on his next consulship, that of 202, in Antioch, with Caracalla as his colleague, two years younger than Commodus had been when he entered on his first in 177. Caracalla, already Augustus and perhaps since the end of 199 (grotesque though it would have been) 'Father of his Country', had only recently in 201 been invested with the *toga virilis*.[103] His every advance gave the regime additional stability by deterring conspiracy. Now on the journey from Syria back to Rome, which seems to have occupied the earlier part of 202, Caracalla was paraded on the route through Asia Minor, via Tyana, and Nicaea, into Thrace, Moesia, and both Pannonias; the exact route through the Balkans, by Viminacium, perhaps to Carnuntum, the site of Severus' proclamation, is uncertain. The opening of the tenth year of his rule was lavishly celebrated in April when the entourage finally reached Rome.[104]

When the family went on their travels again at the end of 202, wintering in Lepcis, or early in 203,[105] there were novelties. In Africa the primary objective for once need not have been military, although there had been incursions into the province. Again, Domna for the first time was in her husband's native province. It was not a novelty that they were accompanied by the Prefect of the Praetorian Guard. His daughter Plautilla was now there as the imperial couple's daughter-in-law: inscriptions from Timgad and Lambaesis, where they certainly stayed in 203, mention her. Plautilla and Caracalla had married in Rome, immeasurably strengthening Plautianus' position.[106]

This was not just a celebratory and ceremonial return of the native: Severus was also rewarding and encouraging loyalty. Carthage, Utica, and of course Lepcis were accorded the *ius Italicum*, and the adornment of Lepcis was begun which was to give Severus' home city the shape that makes it a wonder to tourists.[107] One of the most striking monuments of the new centre was the 'Arch of Severus', which was of such political importance that it was allowed to straddle the two intersecting main streets. P. W. Townsend's interpretations, stressing the commemoration of military victories in the province and Domna's role as Concordia, intended already to cover over the mutual hostility of her two sons, and the association of the ruling family with the Capitoline Triad, are not all equally convincing; certainly this interpretation of Concordia seems anachronistic.[108] Constructing Severus' forum, colonnades, temple, tetrapylon, and basilica, between the existing city centre and the river that empties into the harbour, was awkward and it has been judged that a single architect was necessary to make the overall plan a success. This architect was familiar with eastern Roman concepts and had access to eastern Roman craftsmen; the colonnaded street in particular recalls similar structures at Gerasa and Palmyra. But attention has also been drawn to the fact that some at least of Severus' craftsmen came from Aphrodisias, while the basilica recalls the basilica of Trajan's forum in Rome; some of the materials used came from Italy. It is wise, then, to avoid invoking the influence of the Syrian Julia Domna on the improvements made at Lepcis, and to conclude that what they demonstrate is the development of universal Roman styles.[109] To correspond with this adornment of his native city, Severus it seems was assembling in Africa all the eager rhetorical talents of the Empire.[110]

Severus was also concerned with the bounds of Roman power in the province, and advanced them southwards.[111] Domna is unlikely to have

Figure 3.5 Pescennius Niger and his horoscope.
AR (Antioch). Obv. *IMP CAES C PESCEN NIGER IVSTI AV(G)* (*IMPERATOR CAESAR GAIUS PESCENNIUS NIGER JUSTUS AUGUSTUS*) Head of Pescennius Niger r., laureate. Rev. *IVST I AVG* (?THE AUGUSTAN JUSTICE) Two Capricorns, back to back, r. and l., over small round shield, supporting large round shield on which are seven stars, the Pleiades. AD 193–4.

Source: *CREBM* 5, 1. p. 78, no. 304.

Figure 3.6 Clodius Albinus as Caesar.
AR. Obv. *CLODIVS AL BIN VS CAES* Head of Clodius Albinus, bare, bearded, r. Rev. *PROVID A V G COS* Providentia (*THE AUGUSTAN FORESIGHT; CONSUL*), draped, standing front, head l., holding wand in r., over small globe on ground l., and vertical sceptre in l. AD 193.

Source: *CREBM* 5, p. 26, no. 40.

accompanied her husband into the Sahara when he undertook an expedition against 'most warlike tribes', but both Caracalla and Geta, who needed like all imperial princes to win experience and prove their own worth (the mere presence would suffice, and their age would be forgotten), went with him, and their safe return to Lepcis, where presumably Domna was anxiously awaiting them, was celebrated in an inscription set up there by a centurion to the Syrian deity Jupiter Dolichenus. A. R. Birley notes that the abbreviation he used for *imperatores* ('*impp*p.') implies that there were now three emperors – the Caesar Geta being one of them.[112]

The imperial party arrived back in Rome to a gratifying reception.[113] The year 203 was one for celebration, in which the Arch of Severus and Caracalla, erected in the Roman Forum opposite the Arch of Augustus, was dedicated. Besides honouring the emperor and his sons for their victory over the Parthians, it proclaimed 'the restoration of the commonwealth': Severus had been in power for ten years, and had brought the state back to normality.[114] Severus or his agents designed a new spectacle for the Games. He and Domna and the young princes presided over an arena transformed by scenery into a huge boat containing four hundred animals. It was no ark: a shipwreck was staged that pitched the beasts out. Huntsmen were ready to begin the slaughter as the animals ran about in panic: bears, bison, panthers, lionesses, wild donkeys, and ostriches. It was a great success, giving a city-bound crowd a taste of the chase, as well as a sense of Rome's power over the world, even the world of nature. Whether the Greek-educated Domna enjoyed this quintessentially western entertainment we cannot tell. She may well have felt qualms about the sixty boars provided by the ambitious Plautianus, which Dio also mentions.[115]

The next year at Rome brought celebrations of something in which every citizen, male or female, could take pride, and in which there was scope for women: the achievement of another century in Rome's history since 753 BC, the Secular Games that under the Empire had first been held by Augustus in 17 BC, with purification of the people and games, and with a choir of twenty-seven boys and twenty-seven girls singing Horace's *Carmen Saeculare*. One hundred years, or on another reckoning one hundred and ten, had to separate the celebrations, so that no two such occasions could be witnessed by the same person. Later Games were timed according to the needs of the current emperor: Claudius held his in 47, Domitian his in 88, six years before the due date on the Augustan reckoning; Antoninus Pius followed the Claudian calculation in 148, and so did Philip the Arabian in 248, celebrating Rome's millennium. Now the aptly named Septimius, counting two hundred and twenty years from Augustus' Games, held the seventh and last, if we omit Philip's millenary festival. This occasion of 204 was billed as a celebration of the 'Good Fortune of the Age'. [116] The deities honoured were Jupiter Optimus Maximus, Juno Caelestis, and Apollo.

There were preparatory rites, but the Secular Games proper began on 1 June; Domna's role, as Livia's had once been, was to lead one hundred and nine matrons with children at the sacred banquets (*sellisternia*) held on the Capitol on honour of Juno and Diana during the three days of sacrifices. The great majority were her peers, the wives of senators; eighteen the wives of *equites*, a figure that curiously echoes the number of voting groups ('centuries') in one of the public voting groups of Rome, the 'Centuriate Assembly'; but it is likely that they were admitted to make up a shortage of senatorial ladies qualified and willing. Some senators were unmarried, or widowers; other women will have been abroad with their husbands on tours of duty; others kept from attending by imminent or recent childbirth. The eighteen were led by Domna's niece Julia Sohaemias, wife of the distinguished knight Sex. Varius Marcellus. Domna herself played a conspicuous part in these celebrations, notably on their second day, just as she was unusually depicted as playing a role in official sacrifice on the Lepcis Arch.[117] The very repetition of Augustus' rituals – a new *Carmen Saeculare* had to be written – was reassurance to the public: the State, the Principate, the dynasty were stable. A hundred years later, the Empire had passed through a series of violent changes of regime, military defeats and the collapse of the currency. It had a new form of government, the Tetrarchy, rule by two Augusti and two Caesars, and the senior Augustus, Diocletian, had just celebrated his *vicennalia*.

A. R. Birley calculates that up to 204 Severus had not spent more than twelve months at a time in Italy over the past forty years.[118] Since their marriage Domna travelled everywhere with him, except to the sharpest edge of conflicts, and her presence was acknowledged. Not until the last century of the Republic, and especially during the Second Triumvirate, did officials begin to take their wives with them on campaign or tours of inspection; as it was a novelty there were points to be made against it. Women got in the way, corrupted discipline, could even try to take over. It was a point to be made against Mark Antony that his wife Fulvia was with him in camp at Brundisium in 44 BC.[119]

There was a change under the Principate. Conditions were less volatile: the rulers and their aides spent long periods in the provinces, and Augustus and younger members of the imperial family could do as they chose. When Livia travelled north with Augustus in the teens BC we do not know how close she came to actual barracks; perhaps she stayed in Lugdunum, like Antonia, the wife of Drusus the Elder. Antonia gave birth to the future Emperor Claudius there in 10 BC. Health and safety were another factor that restricted women's travel: Tiberius, on his way to the Balkans at the same time, had left Julia the Elder in Aquileia, where she gave birth. She had already accompanied Agrippa on his tours of duty, although she remained in western Asia Minor while he travelled to Paphlagonia. Pregnancy was a reason to avoid the danger and discomfort of front-line positions, but Agrippina the Elder was not to be kept in the rear, pregnant or no: during the mutiny on the Rhine in 14 her gravid and ostentatious removal from camp helped bring the disturbances to an end. The following year, when a bedraggled Roman army made its way to safety across the bridge over the Rhine at Cologne, Agrippina was famously there to greet and tend the troops.[120]

The role played by Agrippina on the Rhine brings out another aspect of the presence of women in the provinces. She was the granddaughter of Augustus and on Germanicus' eastern mission played a prominent part in diplomatic engagements. Even this had its negative side, when her husband came into conflict with a tough-minded governor of Syria and the women joined in the dispute. The scandalous, even criminal behaviour of Munatia Plancina in Syria led to impeachment in the Senate alongside her husband Cn. Piso in 20. The next year a bold senator was railing against the presence of governors' wives in the provinces (he was probably digging at Agrippina as well). Debate was silenced when Tiberius' son Drusus Caesar declared how much comfort he derived from the presence of his wife Claudia Livilla with him in the provinces. There was more than comfort in it. Livilla, sister of Germanicus, was the daughter of the dead military hero Nero Drusus and granddaughter of Mark Antony, and so particularly welcome in Greek-speaking provinces where Drusus Caesar had been operating. The Elder Julia, as the daughter of Augustus and wife of M. Agrippa, had enjoyed even greater prestige, which was insisted on at Ilium when she had been left at the mercy of a swollen torrent. Augustus' grandson Gaius Caesar was equipped with a wife before he was sent on his fatal tour to the east, to enhance his authority – that same Livilla in her first marriage.[121] Naturally, after the debate of 21, which confirmed the legitimacy of imperial and senatorial practice but gave expression to conservative misgivings, reserve and modesty were still expected of lesser women such as the wife of the equestrian governor of Egypt, as Seneca's praise of one of them betrays.[122] And the fact that the mother of Pertinax accompanied him to Germany when he was in imperial service was still something to note.[123]

The first century of the Principate produces most evidence on these issues, partly because of the richness of the literary evidence, but mainly because of the social changes that the development of the Principate brought with it. Ideas changed too, if they did not always keep pace (it was the same with slaves and freedmen). The travelling empress had come into her own in the second century. As far as we know, Messalina had not accompanied Claudius to Britain, nor had Statilia Messalina accompanied Nero to Greece. But when Trajan moved east in 113 to open his campaigns against the Parthians both the Augustae, Plotina and Matidia, went with him, and so very likely Hadrian's wife Sabina.[124] Their base was probably Antioch in Syria, where Trajan himself spent time when not on campaign. In 168 the imperial brothers Marcus and Verus went north to deal with incursions there. They would have been accompanied by their wives; later Marcus' daughter Lucilla joined him at Carnuntum on the Danube with her husband the Syrian Ti. Claudius Pompeianus, who was to take charge of operations.[125] Of course junior male members of the family were in the entourage and benefited from it: in 172 Commodus was with his father in the north and received the resonant title 'Germanicus'.[126] When Marcus Aurelius marched east in reaction to the usurpation of Avidius Cassius in 175, he took with him his wife and at least two of his daughters to help stabilize the region; Commodus received the toga of manhood and the title 'Leader of the Youth'.[127] The long-standing presence of Faustina (II) at the scene of operations justified her title *Mater Castrorum*. She famously died in 176 on the eastern journey at Halala, an insignificant settlement in the Taurus Mountains in southern Asia Minor; its dignity was enhanced: it became Faustinopolis.[128] Again, two years later it was a family gathering that assembled on the Danube: Lucilla and Pompeianus, Commodus with his new wife Bruttia Crispina, and Annia Faustina, great-niece of M. Aurelius, with her husband Ti. Claudius Severus.[129] The presence of the emperor with his family spectacularly demonstrated and reinforced the ties of the family, notably the young heirs, with their troops.[130]

Domna's birth did not put her in the same class as Livia, nor in that of Faustina (II), who was ascribed imperial ancestry by Herodian that went still further than Antoninus Pius,[131] but she was a personage to reckon with in the east and always at Severus' side as he campaigned for his own position and sought to win friends on what had been hostile ground. Later, in Africa, she was a trophy-wife: the eastern princess won by the bourgeois from Lepcis. While Livia through her family history represented a 'Republican' and highly aristocratic element in the make-up of Augustus' regime, Domna was part of the new Empire in which Greek-speaking city leaders and dispossessed client princes entered the Senate and the imperial service, now finally the imperial family.

4 Empress

I have called Domna 'the Syrian Empress', and it is routine to refer to the wives of Roman emperors as empresses, right back to Livia.[1] That is misleading when the woman's position was inherently unofficial. The title implies legitimate and formal rights, usually derived from those of the husband, with attire, furniture, and ceremonial to match, as those of the most recent British Queen Consort Elizabeth matched those of the King Emperor George VI, although the crown might be smaller, the clothes less magnificent, or at any rate less military, the throne lower. The English title did not even exist in Latin. The question then is what did make a Roman 'empress', and the answer is that the position developed in various ways. From Livia's time there were garments or jewellery to be worn by women who married into the imperial family.[2] But even under Justinian and Theodora in the mid-sixth century we are told by Procopius that it was a novelty when subjects were required to offer her too the *proskynesis* (formal obeisance) that was afforded the emperor – itself a novel requirement, he says – in the extreme form of complete prostration.[3]

The Roman emperor's powers were of two kinds. First, the official authority, military and civil, conferred on him by the Roman People at the instance of the Senate (*imperium* and *potestas*). A woman could not possess the *imperium*, the power to command, or any other of the lesser prerogatives that were derived from magistracies tenable only by males, such as the tribunician power, that gave the emperor his official control of the army and his authority in Rome and Italy as well as in the provinces. But then he wielded *de facto* extra-legal powers, such as, at one end of the spectrum, the influence he deployed at elections, which was politely referred to as *auctoritas*, and, at the other, illegal extensions of his *imperium*, which he got away with, such as the summary execution of senators or making treaties with foreign peoples. The danger of relying on *auctoritas* was that it wore out with over-use, or was renamed by opponents as *potentia* – arbitrary power unsanctioned by law or custom. As time went on some of these powers (treaty-making) were explicitly incorporated into law, others simply accepted. This second type of power depended on, and in turn enhanced, the view of his position held by others, notably his troops.

As time went on, too, distinctions between the two types were neglected: nobody troubled to ask in virtue of what power the autocrat was acting. The amalgamation was markedly forwarded when Caligula and Claudius were granted all the legal powers at a stroke on the death of their predecessors, and the '*Lex de imperio Vespasiani*' of 70 included a clause that sanctioned in advance whatever the emperor 'deemed advantageous' to the commonwealth. The Severan lawyer Ulpian held that the emperor was exempt from the laws.[4] By the time of M. Aurelius, naturally followed by his son Commodus, the emperor was seen as 'Lord (or Master) of land and sea' or 'of the inhabited world' (*oikoumenes kyrios* or *despotes*); his political heirs Severus and Domna likewise, while Caracalla went one better still: he was 'Ruler of the Universe' (*kosmokrator*).[5]

Both types of power attracted respect and honour, the first receiving the uniforms and privileges prescribed for it, the second significantly battening on all that was offered. In the face of the autocrat the people of Rome, Italy and the provinces elevated him to a level above the human, and so incorporated his majesty in their world.[6] The empresses, in part precisely because of their position at the head of the imperial family, the 'Divine House', had a share of outward honour. So we learn from what Lucilla lost in 180 when her father M. Aurelius died: not just the seat in the imperial box at the theatre, where even the imperial children sat, but imperial *vexilla*, *fasces* wreathed in laurel and ceremonial torches carried before her.[7]

Roman women from old had been excluded from civil and state functions, most obviously and without discussion from military duties. So Ulpian tells us,[8] and it meant that they could not act as judges or hold magistracies or bring actions or speak on behalf of another litigant, or act as business agents. What power Roman empresses had was of the second sort, extra-legal and drawing largely on the influence that they wielded or were thought to wield over their husbands and so over the rest of the commonwealth. They might owe that influence in part to the prestige that they derived from their family (Livia with her aristocratic descent on both sides far outshone Augustus, though he had appropriated the Julian clan as his own). It was hardly due to their dowry, which they could carry off again if they opted for divorce, for it would be minute in comparison with the emperor's financial resources; above all they owed it to strength of personality. As the lawyers recognized, that was not something to be neglected even when formal power on the one side was virtually absolute: they ruled that if a master was intimidated into freeing his slave, the manumission was invalid.[9] On top of this influence they enjoyed as their menfolk did the subsidiary recognition and honours that attended and enhanced it.

What a woman could win from her emperor was considerable. Even of Livia it could be said that 'You draw eyes and ears to yourself, we pay attention to what you do, and what is spoken by the mouth of a leader (*principis*) cannot be concealed.'[10] That passage from a poem probably contemporary with Livia refers to publicity rather than power, but one flowed from the other, by example and fashion. The ultimate source of her power, however, is stated by Ulpian in the *Digest*: the empress is not exempt from the law, but the emperor allows her the same privileges as he enjoys. It is also nicely illustrated by Hadrian's rhetorical eulogies on his 'adoptive' mother Plotina and his mother-in-law Matidia the Elder. The former had made him many requests and obtained them all; Matidia on the other hand had 'never asked him for anything, and often refrained from asking things that he would gladly have granted.[11] It was clear how an emperor wanted things to be seen. Trajan had already been lauded by Pliny in 100 for the self-control and modesty of his women.[12] M. Aurelius in his *Meditations* thanked the gods that so obedient, loving, straightforward, and frugal a wife as Faustina (II) had fallen to his lot.[13]

All this meant that a woman's position depended on things outside her control, such as whom she had married, on her wealth and political connections, as well as on her own personality. Agrippina the Younger is the supreme example of these last two factors combined. Again, much of what we 'know' of these women comes from contemporary or later prejudice or speculation; the same claims recur, and the only difference is the tone in which they are produced. Tacitus makes Nero say that the day he had his mother murdered was the one on which he had received the Empire; a chronicler baldly begins the reign of Valentinian III at 450, the year his mother Galla Placidia died.[14] Agrippina had outrageously claimed to share with Claudius the *imperium* (here overall power) transmitted, or possibly acquired, by her ancestors; the poet Claudian meant no ill in 398 in describing Honorius' bride Maria as 'sharer of the imperial power' (*consors imperii*); admittedly her father was the great Stilicho.[15] Midway between these points Severus' contemporary Dio puts into the mouth of Augustus the phrase 'Don't you see how many are attacking me and our rule?' This was to Livia in AD 4, and it is an attractive suggestion that Dio is accommodating Severan sensibilities by admitting, against his own views, a notion of female co-rulership that less punctilious non-senators were already beginning to express.[16] In inscriptions that mention the entire family, Domna's normal position is after the two Augusti Severus and Caracalla and before the Caesar Geta.[17]

It was the military connotations of imperial power that had made it unthinkable for women. Agrippina, the daughter of the general Germanicus and mother of Nero, was not content with social position, public appearances, and influence behind the scenes; she was interested in developing the extra-legal side of the Principate in her own interest, as were freedmen and even knights. On one occasion in 51 when Claudius had the British captive Caratacus and his fellow Britons paraded before him in the Campus Martius, she mounted a tribunal close to that of Claudius, wearing the general's military cloak (*paludamentum*), and presided at his side. This was different from emperors' displays of their wives and mistresses as Amazons – Caligula and Commodus went in for that form of erotic titillation.[18] This was Roman and serious. As a favourite of the Praetorian Guard she was assuming trappings that went with their commander's power, and by implication his authority. As that derived from descent it was precarious simply because of her sex. No other empress before the Byzantine age approached it. The dynasty of Theodosius the Great (379–95) offers his first wife Aelia Flaccilla wearing the imperial insignia, the general's cloak that Agrippina had assumed. Another sign of change at that stage was the emergence of an anomalous dynastic name for imperial women, Aelia, taken from Flaccilla's *nomen*, which appears on their coins.[19]

The law was another sensitive area. A woman debarred from speaking in court except as a pleader in her own case *a fortiori* had no place on the presiding magistrate's tribunal or on the jury of an established court. But informal *cognitio* was a procedure that left the siting and conduct of a judicial enquiry in the hands of the holder of *imperium*. The emperor's 'friends' (*amici*) played an important part in day-to-day decisions and at times when they were left on their own – at the death of a Princeps.[20] The personnel and organization of the emperor's *consilium* had hardened since its early days under Augustus and Tiberius, not to such an extent that senior imperial women could be kept out of its deliberations. Occasionally it seems that they were in a position to play a dominant part – or to be ascribed one by malicious critics. He might have women in attendance if he chose, and we hear of a foreign princess, Berenice of Judaea, sitting in on proceedings at which her own property rights were being questioned, while court ladies were present when Claudius heard the case of two Alexandrian politicians.[21] Agrippina the Younger approached a dais on which Nero and his advisers were waiting for Parthian ambassadors, and Nero had to step down and waylay her.[22] Doubts about the propriety of this did not go away: Constantia, daughter of Constantine and Fausta, is angrily shown by Ammianus Marcellinus poking her head through a curtain during trials to ensure the condemnation of prisoners.[23]

Agrippina in 54 even listened to a debate of the Senate – but in the Palace and also from behind a curtain.[24] Only the boldest woman encroached on senatorial business in the House. Commodus' mistress Marcia, one of his assassins, appeared in the Senate behind Pertinax on the night of the murder, along with Laetus, Prefect of the Guard, so the *Historia Augusta* says; their presence was noted.[25] It is long before we hear of women's symbolic invasion of the House, with the empress's portrait displayed alongside that of the emperor, in the later fourth century that of Aelia Flaccilla, in the early fifth that of her granddaughter Aelia Pulcheria, along with those of Pulcheria's younger brother Theodosius II (408–50) and the western Emperor Honorius (395–423).[26]

Much female influence came directly, then, through their husband's orders or by his consent, but much of it was indirect, and due to courtiers' perception of their position. It differed greatly from one empress to another. When emperors themselves came to be recognized as holders of a unified position, beginning with Caligula and Claudius, they were approaching the status of an empress of the modern period, a tsarina or the wife of a British monarch. Before the Byzantine monarchy the strongly felt bar on *imperium* meant that they could not be a Catherine the Great, Maria-Theresien or Queen Victoria, a female emperor in her own right, or even act as a commissioned Regent as Queen Caroline did for George II when he was away in Hanover. Honorific distinctions, however, were frequent. Augustus made the first moves towards such recognition when he had Livia and his sister Octavia granted the sacrosanctity of tribunes of the people or Vestal Virgins in 36 BC, on receiving it himself. On occasion, to celebrate Octavian's victory at Naulochus soon afterwards, and in 7 BC, and AD 14, Livia gave banquets for the ladies of Rome while Augustus feasted their husbands, the senators.[27] She has been credited with a covert and baleful, even murderous, part in arranging the succession to her husband so that it came to her son Tiberius through his adoption by the old man.[28] It was ironical that Tiberius believed that women's public role should be limited.[29] Her power and Tiberius' efforts to restrict public recognition of it are part of the history of his Principate. His great admirer Velleius Paterculus, in his obituary of Livia, written in 30, the year after her death, insisted that she had used her power only to help men on or to relieve their distress. He was echoing the cautious praise of the Senate, uttered in the *Senatorial Decree on Cn. Piso Senior* of ten years before,[30] and we are reminded of how careful we need to be of such appraisals: a woman is to be lauded for not using what power she has.

Stories of unfair play are not always to be dismissed. Men's versions of how women work can illuminate their own attitudes but may reflect the truth. The *Historia Augusta* explains how Severus came to bestow the *cognomen* Antoninus on his younger son (he did not, but that only makes the need for an explanation more pressing). The author puts it down to Domna's skill in the interpretation of dreams: Severus dreamt that he would be succeeded by an Antoninus, and had given the title to Caracalla, thus barring Geta. The story is worthless, but the attribution of skill in interpreting dreams to Domna is interesting and plausible. A woman needed every skill she could muster, especially something beyond mortal comprehension and to which her husband was vulnerable.[31]

The extra-legal powers that women shared and on which they depended are represented by the residence that they also shared with their husband. The Palatium complex on the Palatine Hill had annexed public and sacral aspects even under Augustus: notably the adjunct Temple of Apollo in which the Senate could meet. It had been developing ever since the time of Augustus' originally modest private house,[32] and it conferred the lustre of its associations as the site of the *Domus Divina*. Caligula had made it grander, Nero had constructed a 'Domus Transitoria' intended to carry the house beyond the Palatine, but after that was destroyed in the fire of 64 he had begun his 'Golden House' in the low ground towards the north-east and on the slopes of the Oppian and Caelian Hills. The Flavians had other ideas and replaced part of the Golden House with a place of public entertainment, the

Colosseum. Domitian, however, made changes on the Palatine that have left the ruins that still dominate it. In the time of the Severi, one of intense building activity, especially between 200 and 204, Herodian claimed that the Palace, the *Domus Severiana*, was larger than a whole city.[33] Like all such complexes, including the less pretentious White House and 10 Downing Street, the Palace had both official and private space and functions. Of the domestic part of this Domna the Roman matron was the mistress. Daily salutations were accorded the emperor (as to Roman nobles in general) and Livia had been associated in them since her husband's death in 14, receiving senators.[34] When Agrippina was losing control over Nero she was sent away from the Palace to hinder her holding levées there.[35] Domna held her own levées, being greeted in the morning by women as well as men.[36]

Domna did not represent the end of a process. Nobody who has seen the portrayal of Theodora, in the chancel of San Vitale at Ravenna,[37] can doubt the grandeur with which by the mid-sixth century an empress came to be presented to the public. Her name, too, was inserted into official and public documents alongside that of Justinian, and officials took their oaths to both rulers; both were notified of the election of a Pope.[38] Later in the Byzantine period Empress Irene, widow of Leo IV (775–80), was to rule in her own right from 797 to 802, or at least as regent for her son, calling herself by the masculine term *basileus*, king. Irene's counterpart in the west was Theophanou, who took over from her young son Otto III (996–1002), referring to herself as *imperator*.[39] It is with these women, not with Domna, that the phrase 'a reigning empress', sometimes used of her, is legitimate.[40]

These developments took centuries and were considered remarkable. Whatever honour and power passed into a woman from her birth and marriage, there was still the deep-seated prejudice against her sex, embodied in law, and especially in societies that were fundamentally based on military might, that is, violence and the threat of it. Muscle told. Differences between Roman wives and empresses on the one hand and medieval and early modern queens are real because the powers that made the emperor were originally distinct and granted to an individual, while kingship was a unity, sometimes influenced by the Roman or Byzantine autocracy, conferred by descent or marriage or by decision of an electing body. Boudica had led the Iceni as the widow of their late king Prasutagus. Elizabeth I came to the throne as the last surviving child of Henry VIII, after the deaths of her brother Edward VI and of her older sister Mary. Some Germanic communities simply forbade the accession of a woman. Other restrictions were imposed on queens regnant that came from communal practice so strong as to make them equivalent to law: a king of England who marries simply makes his wife a queen, and it is a matter of dispute whether another arrangement is legal without enactment ('morganatic marriage' proposed in 1936 for Wallis Simpson, the title of 'Princess Consort' in 2005 for the former Camilla Parker-Bowles). But a queen has to find her husband an *ad hominem* title, 'Prince Consort', or a dukedom, or even, as with the wilful and besotted

Mary Queen of Scots in the mid-sixteenth century for the benefit of Darnley, 'King of this our kingdom'. The authority of Philip II, who had been allowed to become (uncrowned) King of England during Mary Tudor's lifetime, was to end if she died childless.

In the changing circumstances of the early Principate we need to be clear what is meant by an 'official' position (or, as it is called in connection with Livia, 'institutional'). Although powers granted and funded by the people in their assemblies, *imperium* and *potestas*, were beyond women, a less useful recognition was accorded them by the Senate, respect and places of honour at public functions. That too involved expenditure of public money. The Vestals were attended by lictors paid from the public purse; so were empresses, at least in the performance of their public duties as priestesses of the imperial cult.[41] The old association with Vesta was maintained by Domna, who may have rebuilt her temple.[42] Never did the number of attendant lictors reach even the five allowed the praetor, still less the twelve of the consul. The honour conferred by the grant was of a kind with the conferment of the name of Augusta.

In this category too belong prayers offered by priests of the state religion, notably the Arval Brothers for the welfare of the honorand; these were allowed Livia and continued for other women down to Mamaea.[43] The statues and inscriptions set up at public expense by the state or, at a lower level, by provincial assemblies and by municipalities represent temporary surges of regard for the honorand that were intended to survive as permanent tokens. Finally, the State could offer deification, a subject for a later chapter, good to look forward to but of less immediate benefit than local official honours, identification with an Olympian or some other deity. As far as the State went, it had much to do with the needs of an empress's son or other heir: it enhanced his own status. So it was in the case of Antonia, mother of the unimpressive Emperor Claudius, and Livia, his grandmother, and the Flaviae Domitillae, mother and sister of Titus and Domitian.[44]

It was a marked development in a patrilinear society when the mother of the emperor was recognized as such. An ironical and botched attempt was made to achieve this for Livia in AD 14 when the proposal was made that Tiberius should be dubbed '*Iuliae filius*', 'son of Julia Augusta'. Tiberius knew what was implied about how he had come to power.[45] No attempt was made to insult Nero in the same way, but later designations have been noted, Geta's as 'son of Julia', and an Antonine precedent, the prematurely dead child of Marcus, Annius Verus, as 'son of Faustina', but in each case the father is mentioned first.[46] Domna was being assigned a public role thought to be appropriate to her sex, her title as '*mater*' stressing it. In mid-May 213, the Arval Brothers gave her their good wishes as 'the mother of Augustus and the source of the Augustus they beheld'.[47] This went along with the increasing recognition of cognate relationships in the rules of inheritance during the first two centuries AD, but while her identity is bound up with her relationship with Caracalla, the reverse is not the case.[48]

Figure 4.1 Good Fortune of the Age.
AV. Obv. *SEVERVS PIVS AVG. P(ontifex) M(aximus) TR(ibunicia) P(otestate) X* Bust of Severus, laureate, draped, cuirassed, r. Rev. *FELICITAS SAECVLI* (*GOOD FORTUNE OF THE AGE*) Bust of Domna, facing, between busts of Caracalla and Geta, turned towards her, that of Caracalla laureate, cuirassed. AD 202.
Source: *CREBM* 5, p. 231, no. 379.

The title that specified Domna's relation to Severus' heirs was highly significant. It is misleading to suppose that his was nothing more than a military regime, as some accounts, relying on Dio, seem to imply. He was also preoccupied with its reception by the people at Rome and in the provinces,[49] and the key to that lay in his manifestly establishing a dynasty as stable as that of the true Antonine dynasty of 138–80, indeed a continuation of it. It is misleading too to speak of that dynasty as the 'adoptive emperors' (not the equivalent of a Latin phrase), as if they had chosen some new principle of government: adoption was second best, as it had been for earlier emperors, in the absence of a son. Not his own legitimacy alone was the object of Severus' 'adoption' of M. Aurelius, but the assurance he could now give that his regime was permanent. It was in this fact at the heart of the regime that the true importance of Julia Domna lies: she, with her fertility past and potential, embodied that continuity.

The most familiar honour conferred on a First Lady of Rome was the title Augusta, routine by the time Severus was recognized by Senate and people. As soon as he became the only man in the Empire entitled to call himself Augustus, his wife was given the corresponding title (probably from 1 June 193).[50] According to the *Historia Augusta*, Pertinax's wife was so honoured even while he was celebrating his accession on the Capitol, but he refused the title and the simultaneous elevation of his son to 'Caesar'. Dio invites his readers to share his suspicion that it was because she was too free of her favours, but the refusal of a title for his son makes that implausible.[51] Perhaps he was afraid for their safety – not that hesitation would have given the young man much protection. Most probably it was a political ploy demonstrating moderation. Nonetheless his wife bears the title on coins and inscriptions. Didius Julianus' wife and daughter received the title without demur, although they had hesitated to enter the Palace.[52]

It had taken time for the routine to develop, and it was still subject to modification. Augustus had accepted his new name in 27 BC, on a motion of the Senate. Livia had become Augusta only in 14 when her husband died and left a request that she should take his family name 'Julia' and that the Senate should confer his honorific name on her: it was a distinction for an elderly woman, widow of the old Princeps and, significantly, mother of the new one, Tiberius.[53] Gaius is said to have offered it to his grandmother Antonia, and she to have refused it. So it was not conferred again until Claudius awarded it posthumously in 41. Of Claudius' two 'empresses' only the second, Agrippina, was so honoured – the great-granddaughter, granddaughter and sister of emperors. When Nero came to power it was still apposite for her as the mother of the current emperor. Nero's wife Poppaea had also enjoyed the honour, but so did his daughter by her, who died an infant.[54] F. Ghedini and M. B. Florey justly stress the importance of the role of the woman as mother – the birth of a child to Faustina (II) was the occasion for her elevation – but the title had soon reached a wider circle. Nero's conferment of the honorific on Poppaea marks a step on the way to its development into a regular title.[55] Whatever the decisive stages, conferment was increasingly formalized. The very fact that the title implied no defined position made it more readily granted, By contrast a woman could not be a Caesar, for that was a *cognomen* of the Julii Caesares and also acquired clear status connotations under the Flavians: it marked a potential successor to an Augustus.

Nero's death led to a series of widowed or unmarried emperors, but the Flavians did not allow that to inhibit their use of the title: Titus' daughter Flavia Julia enjoyed it and that increased the danger to her husband under Domitian. Sisters too, could be brought in, as Trajan's Ulpia Marciana was, alongside his childless wife Plotina. Not all accepted the honour at once: the truly commendable female members of Trajan's family, as the Younger Pliny pointed out in his *Panegyric*, were reluctant to accept the title 'because they saw a greater distinction in being known as wife or sister of the emperor'.[56] Sabina, the wife of Hadrian, also modestly demurred, waiting for a suitable occasion. The anomaly of a man not emperor married to an Augusta was to occur again, this time without attendant danger: Marcus Aurelius was only Caesar when he was married in 145 to Faustina (II), who was already Augusta or at least became so when her first child was born in 147.[57] Antoninus Pius was fitting Marcus into his succession plans. 'The' Augusta, then, honoured by the Senate, on its own initiative or not, acquired *auctoritas*. That meant at least in its passive sense that she had earned their respect and homage, but the share in rule that it conferred was inherently undefinable.

As to titulature, the Severi could not afford to wait. Eventually Domna was to exceed all other empresses in the number and variety of her official titles;[58] 'Augusta' immediately appeared on coins.[59] Sometimes, as on many provincial inscriptions and on the imperial coinage mainly between 193 and 196, she bears her full name; sometimes in the epigraphy of Italy and the provinces and on Roman coinage from 196 to 211 she is simply Julia Augusta, like Livia in her widowhood.[60] Perhaps this was conscious imitation, flattering for Domna; more probably, as far as the coins were concerned, it was due to increasing familiarity. 'Julia' is the form used by Dio;[61] consequently her sister and younger female relatives needed their *cognomina* to distinguish them, as the granddaughters of Livia had needed theirs.

It was not far into Severus' reign, then, when fresh coinage assigned 'Julia Augusta' a distinctive and honourable place in numismatic iconography. It was one that was far-fetched, but predictable: her coins showed Venus Victrix and Venus Genetrix. The first deity had been Julius Caesar's patron in his struggle against Pompey and the Republicans, the second was the ancestress of the whole Julian clan. Nothing could be more natural for a Julia Augusta, but, as we have seen, Domna owed her name to a grant of Roman citizenship made to a forebear by Caesar or one of the earliest emperors. The types were generalized; they had none of the relevance of Severus' early issues, which alluded to his generosity, the fertility of the age and the false expectation of the succession of Clodius Albinus.[62] So in portrait sculpture four separate types have been distinguished for Severus, only two for his consort.[63] Closer to the immediate concerns of Romans were coins on which Domna appeared on the obverse with husband and sons on reverses, as assuring *AETERNITAS IMPERII* ('The Eternity of the Empire') and on reverses with the sons ensuring *FELICITAS SAECVLI* ('The Success of the Age').[64] The legend *SECVRITAS IMPERII* ('The Confident Stability of the Empire') is found only on reverses of Domna and Geta; they are guarantees of the future, Geta for obvious reasons, Domna for her fertility.[65] B. Bleckmann has pointed out that since the beginning of the third century the double portrait of the emperor and empress on coins was represented respectively in a familiar symbolism with the radiate Sun god's crown and the reflecting crescent of the Moon goddess, indicating her related but dependent power.[66] Besides, a wife was icing on the imperial cake, a gracious complement to the emperor, helping to set the tone of his reign. Hence *HILARITAS* and *FORTVNA FELIX* ('Light-heartedness', 'The Good Fortune that brings Success').[67]

Representations of Domna had not moved far from the guarded types allowed to Livia. She is explicitly named, while we cannot be sure that it is Livia who is represented at all. In this they are more like the named images of Caligula's sisters Agrippina, Drusilla and Julia, who adorn reverses as the Three Graces. Shocking as that was, it was one of the few ways in which Caligula could give his sisters the position that their kinship with him earned them.[68] Unfriendly interpreters of these excesses could attribute them to incestuous passions. They have more to do with Caligula's need to consolidate his own position as a member of a popular family oppressed by his predecessor Tiberius. So Caligula's dead mother Agrippina the Elder was honoured on reverses with a bust surrounded with her name and description as 'Mother of Gaius Caesar Augustus', while another reverse showed the ceremonial carriage dedicated by Senate and Roman People 'to the memory of Agrippina'.[69] His wives, women of undistinguished descent, had no place on the coinage.

A real innovation had come in 54, with *aurei* of Nero, when the portrait of his mother on the obverse was shown confronting that of her son, with her designation, 'Agrippina Augusta, . . . mother of Nero Caesar' in the nominative case; Nero's appeared on the reverse in the dative. In the following year their obverse busts were jugate, with Nero's titulature and Agrippina's on the reverse. In the dative case the legend implied that the coinage was issued in a person's honour, in the nominative that they were, if living, responsible for the issuing of coinage and hence in charge of the disposal of public funds.[70] Agrippina may indeed have exercised *de facto* control but later occurrences of the nominative may have been no more than gestures of courtesy, as the original significance wore away. So with Domna, as her husband came to power and established his position throughout the Empire.

Scholars encouraged by these obverses have credited empresses with a 'right to coin', with all the propaganda advantages that this brings – though surprisingly enough the great Theodora does not seem to have taken advantage of it. What the right meant, if it existed, is unclear. In its fullest sense it should be the legal possession or command of adequate quantities of bullion and control of how much was struck and when, and what appeared on the dies. There is no evidence for any woman in formal control of any of these things, none that any effective right to strike coins rested after Augustus on anyone but the emperor.[71]

To appreciate developments in the empress's complex position, other items than titulature and representation must be taken into account, especially those that might, like coin legends, assimilate her position to that of the emperor. Building is one indicator. A wealthy woman, like any Roman of substance, had a right to build, as any Roman of substance did, but there was a convention about the size and importance of constructions in the City. Livia had erected a shrine to Concord and later monuments to Augustus, along with Tiberius, but according to Dio the portico named after her was built by Augustus; Domna's rebuilding of the temple of Vesta and a structure in Trajan's Forum, perhaps the matrons' Assembly Hall built by Sabina, was within accepted parameters.[72]

Of course there were startling honours that earlier women had obtained in extraordinary circumstances and which Domna did not achieve: Caligula had from the first demanded that his sisters' names as well as his own be included in all public oaths.[73] Domna did not have the same value to Severus as Germanicus' daughters did to Caligula. But a new form of official recognition was granted to Domna, a new context in which she might be mentioned. The emperor's name and titles were recorded on milestones throughout the Empire, showing who was responsible for their construction. They had military implications, for it was the army that oversaw road-building, wherever the labour came from. In 196 Domna's name was mentioned on a milestone from the territory of Lagina in Asia Minor.[74] Twenty-five such milestones have been counted, mostly in Asian and Balkan provinces and set up when Domna's husband was still alive; in the west they are found only in Africa and during the sole reign of Caracalla.[75] This new distinction was later allowed to Julia Mamaea, both women achieving a visible place in one of the central and beneficial activities of the Roman state. It tells nothing of their place in decision-making, only of the way they were perceived.

Again, the return of an emperor to Rome had been celebrated since Augustus' time by dedications and altars to Fortuna Redux (the Good Fortune that brings him home). Under Severus for the first time the return of an empress was likewise celebrated in this way. (With two or three Augusti in different generations it would have been churlish to leave out the mother.) And when in 213 victory was celebrated it was (almost unthinkably in earlier times) Domna's victory as well as that of Caracalla that was commemorated.[76] Age and relationship to the young emperor made such developments easier. And when the sphere of activity was not defined, an empress might actually be envisaged as a sharer in the imperial power. So with Domna on an inscription from Syene in Egypt.[77]

The image of Domna that was projected over the wider Empire was beneficent. She responded to appeals, but did not play the role expected of modern royal women; there were no hospitals to visit, no charities in the Judaeo-Christian and Islamic traditions. But there were alimentary schemes dating back to the mid-first century AD: private benefactors such as the younger Pliny, then the emperor, beginning with Nerva or Trajan, supported the upbringing of children of both sexes.[78] The cost came from the interest on loans made to landowners, and Trajan's scheme was advertised on the coinage throughout his reign. Antoninus Pius gave such schemes a new twist to honour his wife Faustina (I), who died early in his reign; the lucky children were known as *puellae Faustinianae*, 'Faustina's girls'. M. Aurelius extended this benefaction to boys when he expanded it in honour of the marriage of his daughter Lucilla to his co-emperor, L. Verus.[79] It is the Empresses Faustina (II) and Lucilla who are shown on reliefs distributing the bounty to girls. We seem to see Domna as a patron of a scheme of this kind: coin reverses show *FELICITAS* carrying the cornucopia that represents bounty and accompanied by a bevy of six little girls.[80] The precedent makes the interpretation very convincing, and Domna's benefaction linked her too to the Antonine dynasty. All these women played a part in the theatre of beneficence.

So much for honour and state. We have already seen that they were not enough for Agrippina the Younger, who found that Nero drew a line where

Claudius had failed to do so. There had been occasions after her downfall when a woman had taken part in decisive political action. Domitian's wife Domitia Longina is reported to have been party to his assassination in 96. There are doubts about her guilt, but the structure of the plot remains interesting: the woman, who relied on the influence that her family and her marriage gave her, was associated with Palace freedmen, chamberlains and other servants, and a Prefect of the Praetorian Guard.[81] They depended for their positions on the emperor, as Domitia did. If he fell they as his associates would go too. The clever option was to act first and to take part in the installation of the successor. Twenty years later, when Trajan died, another empress, Plotina, took the initiative in the transfer of power to Hadrian by assuring that he was adopted before Trajan died, or so the official version ran. The manoeuvre was successful, and only one accomplice is named: another member of the court.[82]

In Domna's youth other empresses had allegedly been involved in trying to engineer the course of history in their own interest. Towards the end of the reign of M. Aurelius, when he had been ill in 175, came the revolt of Avidius Cassius. The story in Dio is that he had been tipped off by Faustina (II) to be prepared for the emperor's death, in which case she would marry him and so guarantee the succession of her children; in the *Historia Augusta* variant she simply encouraged the revolt in despair at her husband's state of health.[83] Another empress allegedly engineered a direct plot against Commodus. Lucilla, Commodus' sister, the widow of Lucius Verus, had speedily been married off to the provincial and, it was hoped, unambitious military man, Ti. Claudius Pompeianus of Antioch, whom she disliked. In 182 she backed an attempted coup. The motive alleged for it is interesting: envy of the new empress, Commodus' wife Crispina, who as wife of a living Augustus outranked his eldest sister; specifically, according to Herodian, it irked that she had lost her front seat at the spectacles. This affront may be taken as a symbol for the diminution of her influence and opportunities for its public recognition. Her main ally was Claudius Pompeianus Quintianus, clearly a connection of her husband; he was the man she intended as husband for a daughter she had by L.Verus, but he was also said to be her lover. Women operating in politics, especially in covert schemes, are always perceived, rightly or wrongly, as having sexual as well as political relations with their allies. Lucilla's fate is also paradigmatic: while some of her fellow conspirators were executed, she, a woman and a former empress, was exiled to an island, and, with particular consideration for her rank, it was the island of Capri. (She was later killed.) Any deeper motive for Lucilla's conspiracy remains unclear.[84] Apart from the senatorial Quintianus, the roll of men who were killed or forced to retire is significantly full of distinguished senators, including Pertinax and Severus, and *equites*. There is something paradoxical in this: the natural allies of a woman dependent on the emperor's power are others in the same position. A failed attack on the influence of the Praetorian Prefect Perennis is plausible, and Lucilla's husband would have been a likely successor, making Lucilla empress again. Less than a decade after Lucilla's fall, it was Commodus' next oldest sister Fadilla who was instrumental in bringing down another favourite: Commodus' former *tropheus*, the slave who looked after him in childhood, currently a chamberlain and in charge of some of the household troops, the freedman M. Aurelius Cleander. Herodian graphically tells how Fadilla ran to her brother and told him how Cleander's grip on the grain supply was antagonizing the hungry populace.[85]

Finally, Herodian is able to present Marcia, Commodus' mistress, as making another appeal. This was on her knees and against his plan to appear on 1 January 192 as a gladiator from the barracks.[86] (He notes that she had all the honours due to an empress but for that of being accompanied by the ceremonial fire.) Her failure led directly to the final conspiracy, involving the Prefect of the Guard, a chamberlain, and leading senators, and including herself. No matter that the story is suspiciously like that told about Domitian's assassination; the question is why an emperor's wife or mistress should join in his assassination, when her position apparently depended entirely on his. Either she genuinely believed that she and the other conspirators were in immediate danger, or she saw that her master already had no hope of survival. Afterwards she would have to rely on gratitude and the strength of other ties that she had already built up. Domitian's wife was allowed to live on in obscurity, Marcia died in months, when Didius Julianus came to power.

The privileged access of wives and mistresses has already been noted. Normally they were part of an informal band of advisers of the kind familiarly called in Britain, since the days of Harold Wilson and Marcia Williams in the 1960s, kitchen cabinets. No Roman politician could be found in a kitchen, as Oliver Cromwell was in his wife Elizabeth's, but the political structure was the same. Wherever a domestic influence has been exercised, it has been met with suspicion and exaggerated by official and traditional power-holders; Cromwell's imperialist interests in the Caribbean were attributed to Elizabeth's taste for citrus fruit. Women are prime favourites for leading roles in the 'tyrants' bad advisers' scenario.[87]

These groups wielded power and patronage dependent on the emperor's and in rivalry with each other's. Favours and advancement were obtained through them, and resented alike by the unsuccessful, probably by the successful too. The cheap and obvious charge was sexual misconduct. Messalina and the younger Agrippina, and Faustina (II) were notorious; only Livia and the elder Agrippina, whose entire success depended on that of one male, respectively Augustus and Germanicus, escaped with reputations intact. Domna was touted as an adulteress, even a conspirator. Such allegations were put about by her rival for influence, C. Fulvius Plautianus, as we shall see.[88] There might be a personal reference in the story of Domna's conversation with the Caledonian wife of Argentocoxus, in which she twitted the native with the open intercourse of native women with men, and was tartly answered with the comment that Roman women did worse, as they allowed themselves to be seduced in secret by the worst men. But the theme of the contrast between Roman and barbarian manners is too commonplace either to be interpreted against Domna or to show defensive prudery in her remark.[89]

If we set aside the occasional drama of Palace plots, and allow for the suspicions of those outside the court, it is reasonable to ask what the normal extent of an empress's power would be. There was no limit to areas in which she might offer advice in private: she could be envisaged urging an emperor to war,[90] and later we shall see Domna advising on army pay. Far more often she was concerned, like other Roman politicians, with the advancement and protection of friends and relations, a perfectly acceptable role. Domna acted on her travels for provincial communities. What happened at Rome was more significant. As well as making recommendation to appointments, a woman could use advantageous marriage alliances to help her protégés. Cornificia, daughter of M. Aurelius, lost her husband at the beginning of the 190s: he was M. Petronius Sura Mamertinus, executed by Commodus in 190 or 191. When she married again it seems to have been under her new 'brother' Septimius Severus, to L. Didius Marinus, whose *cognomen* could be Syrian. Marinus was only an equestrian official, but he was eventually at least to be allowed honorary senatorial rank, and Domna received two dedications from him.[91]

The number of men from north Africa who rose to high positions under Septimius Severus is remarkable. The trend began before his time and he was part of it, but he appointed too many men from north Africa to governorships and other important posts for this not to be a sign of favour to neighbours, friends, dependants, and partisans. The question is how far Domna too was able to exercise influence on the choice of postholders. Severus no more stuffed the Senate with Syrians, than he did with Illyrians and Mauretanians.[92] The influx of Greek-speakers, some of them distinguished men of letters, into the Senate and equestrian service had been extensive since the reign of Trajan, even since the Flavians. There were three overlapping types: descendants of Roman settlers; men eminent in such great *poleis* as Pergamum and Ephesus; and members of families that had once ruled as dynasts in Rome's dependencies. How high they had risen is clear from the career of Avidius Cassius of Cyrrhus; then there was the son-in-law of M. Aurelius who appears in battle scenes on the emperor's column in Rome, Ti. Claudius Pompeianus, son of an *eques* of Antioch, who is said twice to have refused the Principate after Commodus' assassination.[93]

Favour to Domna is shown by the appointment of her relatives to high positions, and they are mentioned here, although their careers (where they are certain) spanned the reigns of Severus and Caracalla, and as we shall see were probably checked for a while by the ascendancy of Plautianus. The empress's influence will have been a significant and constant factor in their original appointments and later advancement. Her brother-in-law C. Julius

Avitus Alexianus of Apameia was born into the equestrian order.[94] The last equestrian post Alexianus held was in 193, when he was junior procurator in charge of the grain supply at Ostia. The following year saw him promptly co-opted into Senate at the rank of an ex-tribune of the *plebs*. He went on to command the Fourth, Flavian, Legion at Singidunum in Upper Moesia. It was at Viminacium in this province that his nephew Caracalla was proclaimed as Caesar, and he continued in the military powerhouse of central Europe as governor of Raetia, probably at the time of the campaign against Albinus. He held the consulship in 200 or just before, for he was proconsul of Asia in 216–177. But his next known position was as *comes*, member of the staff of Severus and Caracalla on the British expedition of 208. Finally, before his governorship of Asia, a rewarding plum job, he had another turn in the Balkans as governor of Dalmatia. This is a remarkable career, though with an obvious check in the middle, before the British expedition, that it is natural to attribute to the decline in Domna's fortunes to be discussed in Chapter 5; he was not the only public figure whose career followed that pattern. It seems then that Domna's influence had its limitations, and that her feud with the Praetorian Prefect Plautianus involved her sister's family as well as her own. To follow Avitus' career to its conclusion, his last mission was given him by Caracalla in Mesopotamia: some special task in Cyprus. He died there of old age and illness.[95] His rehabilitation, then, had limits imposed by Caracalla, suggesting that restrictions on Domna's influence still remained. Caracalla gave him two consular provinces that were without troops, Dalmatia and Asia, and took him under his wing – and under his eye – on the eastern expedition. Nor was the equestrian procurator Gessius Marcianus of Arca (Caesareia ad Libanum), son-in-law of Maesa and father of Alexander Severus, co-opted into the Senate.[96]

Severus' decision to take his sons to Britain may also have marked the rehabilitation of Sex. Varius Marcellus of Apameia, husband of Sohaemias and father of the future Emperor Elagabalus, who like his father-in-law had undergone eclipse at the beginning of the century.[97] Varius Marcellus is known to have begun as an equestrian procurator in charge of aqueducts at Rome, but the core of his career has been a subject of dispute.[98]

At some time Marcellus had been appointed to a special post which looks as if it might have been held during the absence of the imperial family from Rome, when a particularly trusty person was needed to control city and troops. Marcellus was active in Britain, and on returning had become director of the emperor's private funds, the *res privata*. During the absence of the imperial family and apparently that of Plautianus the Guard Prefect and the Prefect of the City, Fabius Cilo, he was entrusted with the protection of security under the title of Acting Prefect of the Guard and of the City. After this period of eminence Marcellus embarked on a senatorial career: Prefect of the Military Treasury, commander of the Third, Augustan, Legion in Africa, and governor of Numidia. This senatorial career was certainly over when Elagabalus came to power: Marcellus was dead by then.

It was anomalous that the Prefect of the City should be absent from his post when the emperor himself was away: the post had been created to ensure that there was a high authority present even in the emperor's absences.[99] A political crisis has been suggested as the occasion for this extraordinary appointment. We are in the year 211, when Caracalla removed both Aemilius Papinian the jurist from his post as Prefect of the Guard, in which he had succeeded Plautianus, and Fabius Cilo, Prefect of the City for nine years.[100] Marcellus took up his procuratorship of the *res privatae* after 4 April 211 and the vice-prefectures between early summer and the death of Geta, or immediately after that. He would have held the purse-strings long enough to provide the Praetorian Guard with the necessary reward for their loyalty, but gave up the City Prefecture to the consul C. Iulius Asper before 1 January 212. Marcellus was co-opted into the Senate, probably at the rank of ex-praetor. He was sent to Numidia by Caracalla, probably to consolidate loyalty there, where the affections of the troops had been divided between the two brothers;[101] the fact that he did not reach the consulship was due only to his premature death. He was more trusted by Caracalla than the old consular Avitus, who in 211 was only in charge of the grain supply. This reconstruction makes it possible to find a similar pattern in Marcellus' and Avitus' careers. Marcellus' procuratorship in Britain coincides with the British expedition, and his nomination to control of the privy purse belongs to 211. The gap between the procuratorship of the aqueducts and that in Britain was again due to the enmity of Plautianus.

There is a difficulty in this elegant reconstruction: the gap between the fall of Plautianus in 205 and the rehabilitation of Domna's relatives seemingly in 208. But that gap may be only apparent and due to lack of evidence. Whether both Avitus and Marcellus or only the former suffered in his career, there is something else to be learnt from these years about Domna and her influence. When it came to choosing between her and Caracalla, Avitus and Marcellus were committed partisans of Caracalla against Geta, or taken by him to be so, while Domna naturally attempted to mediate, as she is seen doing in the final violent scene.[102] The same applies to Asper, the new City Prefect, who was an easterner from Attaleia in Pamphylia or Pisidian Antioch, and whose son had a dedication set up to him in Heliopolis in Syria. Perhaps he was another connection of Domna. Asper's own pride was short-lived: he was suddenly dismissed by Caracalla and relegated to his home town.[103] All this is not difficult to understand: the men were simply backing the side that they knew was going to win rather than adhering to loyalties forged in a joint enmity to Plautianus; that was not a choice open to a mother.

5 Plautianus and the struggle for the succession

Secondary politicians who depend on an autocrat are as likely to be rivals as allies. A famous scenario of AD 48 presents three of Claudius' leading freedmen, Narcissus, Callistus, and Pallas, promoting candidates in a contest to provide the emperor's next wife – who would be duly grateful. Pallas won the argument, supporting Agrippina. His main rival Narcissus did not survive the death of Claudius by more than a few days.[1] Domna accordingly had a foe whose importance was proportionate to her own, as well as allies, and lost influence in the middle years of Severus' Principate because of the ascendancy that C. Fulvius Plautianus, sole Prefect of the Guard since 200, gained over his boyhood friend (lover, if we believe Herodian's anonymous informants), a fellow native of Lepcis, a kinsman on the mother's side; Severus' maternal family shared his name. Among the protégés Plautianus took into service was a man who later held the same office of Prefect of the Guard: another man from north Africa, the Mauretanian Opellius Macrinus. Plautianus was already a trusted agent at the beginning of Severus' rule in 193, though attested in office as Prefect of the Guard only by 1 January 197, then as a *clarissimus uir*, a man of senatorial rank, on 9 June. Plautianus had previously held the post of Prefect of the Watch, and before that seems to have fallen into disgrace with Pertinax when the future emperor was proconsul of Africa.[2] Services to Severus won him positions of power, and he used those to acquire more. From 200 his rise seemed irresistible. Award of the consular ornaments was routine; they simply meant that, within the equestrian order, the holder was of a standing equivalent to that of a consular in the Senate; but in 203 he held the consulship itself, as Sejanus had held it with Tiberius in 31. To add to the distinction, the consulship was numbered 'II' as if it were the second time he had held it. The award of *ornamenta* was being treated as if it were equivalent to a substantive tenure of the consulship; only a second tenure now conferred much distinction. As a member of the Senate Plautianus was eligible for one of the two more distinguished priestly offices that senators monopolized: the pontificate, in the college of priests of which the emperor himself was chief as Pontifex Maximus. Plautianus was also awarded patrician status. His rise to power led, we are told, to the production of more statues of him than of the emperor himself, and on a larger scale. This must have been one of the complaints against him, as it was noticed that Tiberius could see (evidently through others' eyes, as he was a recluse on Capri) gilt portraits of his prefect Sejanus venerated everywhere.[3] But Dio explicitly says that Plautianus' power was greater than Sejanus' had been. It is not surprising that a statue of Plautianus has been recognized in the 'colossal image' set up at Athens and placed alongside one of a Caesar, presumably Caracalla.[4] Caracalla had multiple reasons for hating Plautianus: such equations with himself and fears for his own future might have been aggravated by anger on his mother's account, especially if he had heard the tale of Plautianus' earlier relations with Severus.

If Plautianus had a firm plan, rather than, as one may suspect, improvising a series of formidable defences against the rivalry of his fellow courtiers, it was, like Sejanus', to become the emperor's partner in power, or if Severus died while his sons were still immature, to take power in a coup. In 202 Caracalla's marriage to Plautianus' daughter Publia Fulvia Plautilla (at the emperor's request, we are told) was celebrated with a sumptuous and, according to Dio, semi-barbaric banquet, and wedding presents streamed in. The wedding party, and the celebrations for the *decennalia* and the Parthian success, went on for seven days.[5] Severus, whose health was not good, saw the Prefect (and no doubt his cohorts) as a vital part of government and he was now formally admitted to the dynasty. Sejanus had courted the widow of Tiberius' son Drusus Caesar to make himself the protector of Drusus' son Tiberius Gemellus. For Plautianus, once Severus was dead, his son-in-law, the new emperor, would be malleable or dispensable, and his younger brother Geta would certainly have been. Plautianus may even have repeated Sejanus' technique of putting the brothers against each other, as Sejanus had done with Germanicus' sons, Nero and Drusus Caesars. Caracalla's advance to a position in which he was the guarantee of the dynasty – and perhaps of his mother's life after Severus' demise, made him the focus of Plautianus' attention, and the marriage dealt with him. Naturally Caracalla loathed his father-in-law, but the views of the 14 year old were disregarded.[6] It is unlikely that Domna hoped to become a grandmother as a result of this marriage. In spite of an apparent allusion in the inscription that relates to the Secular Games, and coin types of the same bent, the explicit statement of Herodian that Caracalla refused to sleep or eat with his wife, and even threatened to kill her and her father when he became emperor, makes it improbable that the marriage proved fruitful.[7] Coins issued to celebrate their union bore the slogan *CONCORDIA* ('Mutual Harmony') that was often associated with married couples, as also with political relationships, in the second case at least often betraying relations anything but harmonious.[8] To Domna the danger was obvious. Plautilla, as Caracalla's wife, became Augusta, like her mother-in-law, who had been *the* Augusta; in company with Plautilla, Domna was merely one of the two Augustae; an inscription honouring Plautilla thereby honoured the kinsman of the emperor.[9] Domna had also to fear for her position, as charges of conspiracy against Severus were also being levelled at her; like all imperial women she was particularly vulnerable to accusations of that kind, and had to endure them.[10] The story that she was put on trial for adultery may not be literally true and it is a fanciful notion that the reverse legend *PVDICITIA* ('Chastity') displayed on her coins was a riposte to these accusations. It is more plausible to hold that the rumours were a hostile comment on a well-established coin legend. In any case, Dio says that Plautianus made Domna's life an agony, and that would have been due to public eclipse as well as private fear. The paucity of Domna's coin reverses during his ascendancy made for a period of standard and unobtrusive types.[11]

The blow to Domna represented by Plautianus' extraordinary advance was twofold: not only did he hold the delegated *imperium* of the Guard Prefect, but also he was addressed as the fourth Caesar, intruding into the imperial family structure as a member of the 'Divine House', taken to be an integrated member of it, and as *comes* accompanying the emperor on his expeditions – just as Domna did; and he too was waited on by senators.[12] Plautianus' prominence and honours were explicable, but what Dio is stressing in his account is the flaunting of power that, while theoretically dependent on that of the emperor, and the more galling to Domna because of that, came apparently to be felt by senators to outstrip Severus' own. As he rose, what had been rivalry with Domna and her sons passed into rivalry with an emperor who had already disposed of two would-be emperors. But Plautianus controlled the Praetorians, and even Tiberius had feared his prefect at the end.[13] His usefulness had been translated into power; that eventually generated fear in the emperor – and so in turn in the Prefect.

It is less shocking to us than it was to Dio that at his native city, Nicaea, Severus depended even for the supply of a local speciality mullet on the Prefect – an emperor could hardly involve himself in procurement of victuals. Dio had become sensitized to the man's power. More seriously at Tyana Severus failed to gain admittance to the sick Prefect's bedside without giving up his escort:[14] the emperor was visibly reduced to the ruck of senators and the like. The refusal of the official in charge of the schedule of court cases to bring forward a trial without Plautianus' orders proved that the emperor's *imperium* was effectively no longer *maius* than that of this particular appointee.[15] Severus is reported as saying in a letter that he was so fond of Plautianus that he prayed to die before him.[16] That was incautious, even if it contained a hidden threat: it looked placatory, and could be over-interpreted by an ambitious politician, or taken for a presage by a superstitious one. A glimpse of what was in store had come when Plautianus saw off Q. Aemilius Saturninus, a Prefect of Egypt who had been promoted to share his command of the Guard.[17] A grant of formal powers to Plautianus would be a deferred death warrant for Caracalla.[18] Dio reports that he kept his own wife in purdah, away even from Severus and Domna. He was afraid perhaps that the anonymous wife might have let something slip.[19]

Figure 5.1 Plautilla as Augusta; Family harmony.
AV. Obv. *PLAVTILLA AVG* Bust of Plautilla, draped, head bare r., hair waved vertically in eight ridges, with low bun at back of head. Rev. *CONCORDIA AVGG (HARMONY OF THE AUGUSTI)* Concordia, wearing *stephane*, draped, seated l. on low seat, holding patera extended in r. hand and double cornucopia in l.; her feet rest on stool. AD 202–5.

Source: *CREBM* 5, p. 237, no. 416.

Domna, however, was still wife of the emperor and mother of his sons, and they had all been used to popularize Severus' regime and guarantee stability. They could not have been totally eclipsed. A dedication from Vindolanda exemplifies the vitality of the conception of the imperial family, the *Domus Augusta* or *divina*: it was familiar Empire-wide under Severus as it had been under the Flavians – a reason for Plautianus to join it. The conception is embodied in the first century AD by the 'Grand Cameo of France'. The cameo presents members of the Julio-Claudian dynasty in three registers, the current emperor and his female companion, usually taken to be Tiberius and Livia, on the central stage. The consort at the emperor's side, it has been suggested, presents eloquent support for his legitimacy, while male members of the dynasty attain world rule and immortality through military victory; the lowest register, which is the base of the triangular composition of which emperor and empress form the apex, is occupied by cowering defeated barbarians. The permanent relevance of the conception is clear: it was recut to fit the needs of the dynasty of Constantine in the early fourth century.[20]

Tensions and balance in the disposition of power are embodied in a contemporary monument. Between 10 December 203 and 9 December 204, near the end of Plautianus' ascendancy, Domna and her children were honoured at Rome in the inscription cut on the 'Arch of the *Argentarii*',[21] that was one of the entrances to the cattle market, the Forum Boarium. The donors of the monument were the *argentarii* and *negotiatores*, bankers and businessmen of the Forum, expressing their devotion to the *numen* of the

Emperors Severus and Caracalla, to Geta, the Empresses Julia Domna and Plautilla, and probably to Plautianus. It was all done for public display with the approval of the imperial family, in gratitude for a privilege, perhaps according to their specifications.[22] The overall theme of the decorations was military. Severus in the main panel on the right limb of the gateway appears as chief priest (*Pontifex Maximus*) pouring a libation over a tripod altar; beside him is Domna, in a position that may reflect the prominence of her role in the Secular Games.[23] The figure of Geta was obliterated after his death. To the left is Caracalla with an altar on which he is making offerings; Plautianus seems to have been represented along with Plautilla, his link with the *Domus*, but their figures have been chiselled off. Originally there were almost two imperial families in balance. Yet the prominence given Domna on the Arch is unmistakable, echoing her central role on the Lepcis Arch of 203, on which in the sacrificial scene on the north-east attic panel she seems to attract attention away from the emperor himself, and where she has been said in a certain sense to be an incarnation of the dynasty.[24] Her function is different from that of the passive presence of Livia and Julia on the Augustan Ara Pacis. It is highly dubious, though, whether these monuments, mutilated and fragmentary as they are, one of them the work of provincial sculptors, can be shown to signal more than the broadest political developments. Certainly they suggest the empress's lively interest in religious ceremony; and at Lepcis the sacrifice may be offered to the Genius of the Emperor.[25]

Plautianus, his humble beginnings and current wealth, the alleged debaucheries he could afford (carrying on from an earlier relationship with Severus, they might think) were not loved by the common people of Rome, who called out derisively at the Circus about his possessions and his pallor and tremulousness.[26] Plautianus' ascendancy with the emperor also had its slips, one perhaps during the second Parthian war, another in its declining stage, when Severus stripped him of some powers.[27] It was in 204 that signs of Plautianus' decline were seen. The matter of statues caused the trouble. Too many, thought Severus, or in the wrong place, among those of his own kinsmen and relatives. This is strange when the Prefect appears in monumental groups with the emperor and his immediate family, but the offending pieces may have been free-standing bronzes inserted by Plautianus, on the strength of his marriage tie, into collections representing Severus' family. This was probably in Rome, since news of Severus' order is said to have spread to the provinces. An eager court-watcher, the governor of Sardinia, Racius Constans, moved fast and ordered a melt-down; he soon paid for misinterpreting the scope of Severus' snub.[28]

The signal for Plautianus' downfall early in 205 came when the emperor's brother Geta died, so we are told. Geta had not stood up against him; he knew that Plautianus' influence on the emperor, backed up by the threat of the Praetorians, would outweigh his own. It was only when he was dying that he dared to speak.[29] That convenient tale, told of an unbiased and eminent informant (now dead) helped to justify the outcome, whichever version of it was accepted.

An official story, however garbled and rhetorical (and what Severus put out after Plautianus' death must have been full of rhetoric), seems to be recounted by Herodian.[30] Plautianus, stripped of some powers, planned to assassinate the emperor. He instructed a tribune of the Guard, a Syrian called Saturninus, in return for a promise of the Prefecture, to make away with 'an old man and a boy'. Saturninus demanded, and (incredibly) received, written authority. This he took to Severus, who suspected that the story was a trick of Caracalla's. Such a touch was unlikely to be part of any 'official' version; indeed, it has struck Herodian's commentator as his rejection of Dio's rival story. At any rate, Saturninus offered to trick Plautianus into thinking that he had actually carried out the murders. The Prefect entered the Palace and was seized by Severus' bodyguards; even so, he was so persuasive that it was only when his clothes were torn aside and his breastplate revealed that the truth was confirmed. Then Caracalla's anger overcame him; on his orders the Prefect was killed on the spot. Euodus, Caracalla's former infant teacher, and Saturninus were brought into the Senate to give their evidence and were duly praised for loyalty. These services were not enough to save them from being executed by Caracalla after his father's death; perhaps they wanted rewards he was not prepared to pay, but Herodian suggests that they perished as adherents of Geta.[31] Plautilla was divorced; she and her brother were banished to Lipara, to linger in penury, or with adequate means, according to whether one believes Herodian or Dio, until their execution during Caracalla's reign.[32] Thenceforward Caracalla remained unmarried, and there is no evidence that Geta was ever married at all. The provision of an heir was important, but Caracalla was probably strong enough to exercise his own will in the matter. He had had enough of marriage, and any woman presumably was available to him. As to Geta, Caracalla may not have wanted him producing heirs older than any that he himself might have; or, more generally, the family wanted to keep hopeful nobles with marriageable daughters dancing attendance on them without making the commitment that had proved so dangerous with Plautianus.

Dio's account,[33] earlier than Herodian's, is different, and not only in trivial details such as the time of day in which the murder was carried out (in the afternoon rather than at night). It makes Caracalla engineer Plautianus' death by exploiting Severus' fear of the Praetorian Guard. Using Euodus as a go-between, he suborned three centurions of the Guard to tell the emperor, just as the imperial family were about to dine on the evening of 22 January, that they and seven others had been ordered to kill Severus and Caracalla. To back up what they said they had a letter, allegedly written by Plautianus and ordering a tribune to carry out the assassinations. Plautianus was summoned, and the gleeful story went that he arrived with such eager speed that the mules of his vehicle collapsed in the courtyard. He was made to enter the Palace alone (a nice answer to his rebuff of Severus at Tyana).

Severus calmly asked why he plotted to kill him. As he began to make his defence, Caracalla, evidently afraid that it would be successful, attacked him physically. Restrained by Severus, Caracalla ordered an attendant to kill Plautianus. The defence was never heard.

Elements of the 'official' version, including public scenes with witnesses in the Senate, were used for Dio's more convincing scenario. It seems highly unlikely that the Prefect would plan to rid himself of the Augusti unless he had cast-iron plans for his own immediate take-over. Like Tiberius when he had to bring down Sejanus in 31, Caracalla knew that the enemy had to be killed promptly, before he could rally the troops he commanded. Like Titus when as Vespasian's heir he disposed of two old allies of the emperor, he knew the value of documentary evidence. Titus found a seditious speech on the body of one of the 'conspirators'. Vespasian's son was known as an excellent forger; Caracalla could have a good penman among his friends.[34]

In each of the accounts Severus is an innocent victim, in Dio's a dupe. That is not plausible. Severus was more likely the good policeman in a script that he left to Caracalla. His professed incredulity and unwillingness to allow a summary execution, if historical, kept him in the clear, but he must have been glad to lose the over-powerful Prefect without taking responsibility for it, as Claudius rid himself of a threatening descendant of Augustus through the agency of his wife and freedman.[35]

When the murder took place Domna and Plautilla were in a separate room. Tufts of Plautianus' beard were brought in, according to Dio before the women knew what was going on. 'Here's Plautianus for you!' they were told. It was a peculiar gesture, as if the beard were a trophy for Domna, or proof of what had been done, the words a taunt for Plautilla. It showed Plautilla her fate at once, but proves nothing about Domna's role in the conspiracy; we can be sure what she wished, not what she knew, let alone what she may have planned.[36] Yet if the detail is not mere rhetoric, it might be that Domna was with Plautilla to keep an eye on her. Caracalla was 16, and adults other than Euodus may have helped him with the scheme. Domna is a prime suspect, though all that implicates her is the fact that one of the men involved in denouncing Plautianus, Saturninus, was a Syrian, centurion in Dio, tribune in Herodian, and with Syrian cunning.[37] It is a less plausible theory that Domna was behind a conspiracy of Palace guards and freedmen. Their collective interests were marginal. That does not mean that there was none in the plot; they would follow their patrons as their individual interests allowed.

The power of Severus' Prefect of the Guard had loomed threateningly over Domna's entire family, even, as we have seen, over the relatives by marriage, Avitus and Marcellus, whose careers seem to have suffered setbacks during his ascendancy. On his death Domna's influence at court was restored. Plautianus was replaced by a pair of Prefects of the Guard, to prevent any individual from accumulating the power and wealth that Plautianus had achieved. One of them was Aemilius Papinian the jurist. He was on excellent terms with the emperor and is said in the *Historia Augusta* to have been a kinsman by marriage, 'through his second wife'. Some are inclined to interpret this ambiguous phrase as referring to Severus' second wife, Domna, which would mean strong revival of her power. But one wonders why, if the celebrated empress is meant, she is not simply named; the second wife of Papinian may be meant.[38] There is nothing then to connect the rise of this man specifically with Domna.

After the domestic revolution of January 205, our main sources have little to tell for the next three years. This phase of Domna's coins produces her last new type (209) with *HILARITAS*, *CERES*, and *PVDICITIA*; naturally portrayals of family members are also stressed. Domna is shown with her husband and the boys on the reverse: the result is *FELICITAS PVBLICA* guaranteed by *PERPETVA CONCORDIA*.[39] What there is in the literary sources concerns the consolidation of Severan power through the uncovering of conspiracies. One was of uncertain date, but an inscription from Ephesus implies that Severus and Caracalla, along with Domna, were the intended victims of a plot, 'baffling the murderous hopes of traitors by their forethought'. It may relate to another plot, attested in 208. Overlapping with events of that kind came a final settlement with the relics of the real Antonines: M. Peducaeus Plautius Quintillus was one of M. Aurelius' sons-in-law, and he died as a conspirator. So did Popillius Pedo Apronianus and others for dabbling in astrology.[40] Women were less harshly treated, being

Figure 5.2 Harmony of Caracalla and Geta.
AE. Obv. *IMP CAES. P. SEPT GETA PIVS AVG* Head of Geta, laureate, bearded, r. Rev. *CONCORDIAE AVGG* (in exergue) *S C* (*TO THE HARMONY OF THE AUGUSTI; BY DECREE OF THE SENATE*) Caracalla and Geta, in military dress, standing front, *vis-à-vis*, heads l. and r. respectively, clasping r. hands over garlanded and lighted altar in centre; each is crowned by a Victory, winged, draped, standing behind him, facing l. and r., respectively, and holding palm in l. hand. AD 209–11.

Source: *CREBM* 5, p. 391, no. 178.

married off to men of equestrian rank who could not aspire to the Principate: Cornificia we have already seen wedded to L. Didius Marinus; Vibia Sabina, who lost her first husband in a purge (187) went to a man called L. Aurelius Agaclytus, whose name shows him to have been the son of a freedman of Emperor L. Verus.[41] It would be good to know what view these ladies took of the upstart empress.

How important the succession was to Severus is shown both by the appearance of *SPES* (Hope) on coins and by Domna's titulature. She was '*Mater Caesaris*' from 196,[42] mother, that is, of young Caracalla. Domna's title changed automatically with the status of her sons: necessarily she was '*Mater Augusti et Caesaris*' from, probably, 28 January 198.[43] That title was officially upgraded to '*Augustorum*' when Geta was elevated during the British campaign; but it is found anachronistically on documents dating from 199–200, making three Augusti – in essence three emperors.[44] There were no precedents: the first two Augusti to be in power together were Antoninus Pius and L. Verus from 161 to 169; then there were M. Aurelius and Commodus, father and son. It was ironical that Commodus had had a twin brother, perfect for the joint succession of a pair of Augusti; it was a fact celebrated on the coinage, which showed the two infants playing on a ceremonial couch, with *SAECVLI FELICITAS* ('The Good Fortune of the Age'), but the twin died.[45] Marcus had to make his son his partner in power, and Commodus was Augustus at just 16.[46]

Orientalism has been detected in Domna's titles of '*Mater Caesaris*' and '*Mater Augusti*' or '*Augustorum*'; they have been seen as the age-old titles of honour of the Sultan's mother. This is wrong, as the development of honours to imperial mothers from the time of Livia shows.[47] Informally the title 'Mother of Augustus' had been in use since the time of the two Agrippinas.[48] But the logic of the title in the two different situations was also different: in the harem the mother of the legitimate heir would be distinguished from concubines whose offspring had a lesser status; in Severus' court the safe succession of his sons, one or both, was vital to him, and everything was done that could be to enhance their status; his wife was naturally to be honoured for being their mother. In 197 she became the mother of the 'Future Emperor' (*Imperator destinatus*),[49] and the real innovation is the use of that phrase, with its insistence on Caracalla's coming status. In the past, if a man was *imperator*, it was because his army had formally saluted his military success by conferring the title, or because he had assumed it as a *cognomen* or, as with Augustus, Vespasian and all later emperors, as a *praenomen*; hence in due course its development into the equivalent of 'Emperor'. The word *destinatus* in Roman electoral vocabulary means 'intended' rather than officially 'designate'; but nothing (we are to understand) would baulk the determination of Severus – or the compliance of the Senate, if it conferred the title officially.

Severus' dynastic plans have been pinned to the time when Caracalla took the toga of manhood. Coins are inscribed *AETERNITAS IMPERII* and

CONCORDIA AETERNA ('The ever-lasting life of the Empire'; 'Everlasting concord'). That indicates thinking, not the form it took. It was finalized only when Geta's rise to the status of Augustus inspired an eloquent *CONCORDIA AVGVSTORVM* issue.[50] It is not evident when the process of regulating the succession began, that anyone but Caracalla was in question. In 195, the people of Aezani in Phrygia passed an honorific decree and we have Severus' reply, engraved on stone in the city (as Severus indicated!): the emperor says that he has clearly understood the pleasure that the people of Aezani take in his successes 'and in the rise of his son M. Aurelius Antoninus with good fortune to the hopes of the Empire and to a position alongside his father'.[51] That is, Caracalla was to come into partnership with his father, as Tiberius had with Augustus.

Later Severus showed signs of advancing his sons along a path that had been familiar since the beginning of the Principate, although there had never been two 'Augusti' until the joint reign of M. Aurelius and Lucius Verus. He even used the same interval of three years to distinguish between his sons when he gave them their first consulships, though they were less than a year apart in age. That three-year interval had actually separated the first two Caesars who were intended for power, the grandsons, sons by adoption, of Augustus, C. and L. Caesars, perhaps too the second pair, Germanicus and Drusus Caesars.[52] Finally in Britain Geta too was raised to the rank of Augustus, presumably at the end of the campaigning season of 209: the news was celebrated in Athens and, in the wording of the authorities there, Geta was made equal partner with Severus and Caracalla.[53] Accordingly his *praenomen* Publius was changed back to Lucius, the name that had belonged to Severus himself and which recalled the original family of Lepcis.[54] Over-enthusiastic dedicators even ascribed the supreme pontificate to Geta – a privilege reserved for the leading Augustus.[55] The new changes indicated that Severus had in mind a joint Principate for his sons, like that of Marcus Aurelius and Verus. They had been adopted; the *Historia Augusta* paints Severus on his deathbed rejoicing in his superior success.[56] But there was a more recent pattern for Caracalla to notice: his father allowed his helpful brother P. Geta no share in real power, perhaps because the latter had a son of his own; Caracalla saw his own father as an autocrat.

The scheme of a dual Principate went back far beyond M. Aurelius to Augustus himself, who simultaneously adopted his grandsons Gaius and Lucius and henceforward kept an array of pairs in place; so did Tiberius with his sons Drusus Caesar and Germanicus (adopted), and with their offspring; Claudius was adumbrating the same scheme when he adopted Nero as a brother for Britannicus. The advantages were obvious: the death of a single successor would not provide an opportunity for usurpers, or for the Senate to be rid of dynastic rule. The disadvantages were equally clear from the Triumviral periods: mutual jealousy ending in civil war. The paradigm was the republican consulship, and it is amusing that historians developed a similar scheme for the earliest years of the monarchy, to provide a model: Romulus, attacked by the Sabine ruler Titus Tatius, took him on as a colleague. That lasted until Tatius was assassinated – with Romulus a suspect.[57]

The delay in Geta's rise to Augustus (the three-year interval should have brought it to him in 199) implied that Severus had not intended to make both his sons his near equals, but, like Vespasian with his partner Titus and the much younger Domitian, to keep one in reserve. The change needs explaining. It may be that as he felt his end coming this final advancement was the only step Severus could take which might secure Geta's future position[58] – or, at its most brutal, save Geta's life by making an attack on him highly dangerous.[59]

The advancement of Geta may have been the trigger for Caracalla's near-assault on his father probably in early spring 210, otherwise unexplained except as an outburst of impatience. Severus was now committed to bequeathing his position to both brothers – or rather, leaving the stage with two partners in power in place and reviving the dual Principate that had worked in the early years of M. Aurelius. The *Historia Augusta* even says that Severus ordered the silver statue of Fortune shared by M. Aurelius and L. Verus to be placed in their quarters on alternate days.[60] The question of Domna's influence arises in an acute form in connection with Geta's advancement. It has been held that she was behind Severus' creation of a double Principate of the Antonine type.[61] That cannot be shown. It is not even certain that she welcomed it, if she understood her relentless boys. Whatever the dangers, though, the move was politically necessary, in case Caracalla died; and leaving out Geta would not necessarily have ended their mutual hatred.

It was after the fall of Plautianus, according to Dio, that Caracalla and Geta broke out of tutelage and took to rivalrous debauchery and loutishness, which on one occasion resulted in Caracalla breaking his leg when he was thrown out of a racing chariot. Herodian, however, who insists on how insufferable Caracalla became after he was free of Plautianus, claims that although they were both mad for the theatre, chariot races and dancing, their quarrels went back to their earliest childhood, when they were expressed in quail- and cock-fights or in wrestling. They backed different factions at the games, and had diametrically opposed tastes in theatrical performance and recitals, presumably by sophists.[62] Plautianus had provided the external threat that made for internal cohesion. Caracalla's strike had made the dynasty secure, but by embarrassing Severus and opening the way to dissension.

Dio alleges that Severus' expedition to Britain was motivated in part by the wish to shock Caracalla and Geta out of their mutually destructive behaviour.[63] Someone thought that idea up at the time, perhaps at a dinner party at which the prospects of the expedition were discussed. Severus had already been suffering from gout during the second Parthian war, engaging a permanent physiotherapist, and he was now 62 years old, approaching the notoriously dangerous 'grand climacteric'.[64] The reasons for the expedition (beyond glory) were serious and pressing: trouble from the tribes north of Hadrian's Wall and uncertainty as to which line, the Hadrianic or the Antonine, if either, could be held. Its military aim according to Dio was to dissolve that problem by conquering the whole of Scotland.[65] This was the time when, as we have seen, Domna's connections Avitus and Marcellus seem to re-emerge. They were useful men in themselves, and C. Julius Avitus Alexianus doubly so as a member of the council of an ailing emperor and his unruly sons.

In 208 Domna went with her husband to Britain, following a road system in Gaul that had been overhauled in preparation, and probably accompanied into Gaul at least by her sophist friend Philostratus.[66] She made Eboracum her residence during 209; Geta remained with her (at least according to Herodian), engaged in civil administration with the help of a board of advisers, while Caracalla campaigned with his father. Not only age but also his presence on active service with his troops, warring in the mists against the allegedly naked, tattooed foe, gave Caracalla the edge over his brother. The courtiers in attendance were also split; it could be claimed that Caracalla and Geta had set up separate 'courts' in Britain.

Caracalla was evidently emboldened by his new position and Dio was persuaded that he was so impatient for power that he had to be restrained from putting Severus out of the way with a stab in the back, in full view of Roman troops. (As Ronald Syme pointed out, travel or residence in foreign parts can bring out the worst in people.) Severus' reaction was to call a council of Caracalla, Papinian, and Castor, a freedman whom Caracalla had already tried to have lynched. Severus lay back on a couch and invited Caracalla, if he liked, to order Papinian to kill him.[67] It is hard to take this story, with its parallels in Roman history and elsewhere, at face value, certainly the second part of it. By allowing his son to kill him, Severus would have assured Caracalla a brief and stormy Principate. On the other hand, Caracalla's lack of self-control is well attested by stories such as those of the deaths of Plautianus and Geta. In a fit of rage he may well have chased his father brandishing a sword, not necesssarily with the intention of harming him. Even that would give Severus and Domna cause for serious concern and it gives the theme of *concordia Augustorum* – 'the unity of the Emperors' – sung out on the Lepcis Arch an ironical and discordant cadence.[68]

On a lighter note, we may return to the conversation that Dio records between Domna and the wife of the Caledonian – presumably a chieftain – Argentocoxus. Whether this was simply a way of passing the time in a province which was the furthest from Rome (in the cultural sense) that she ever travelled – though York was to be a Roman colony – we cannot tell.[69] It may have had an intellectual component: the women discussed sexual *mores*, an engrossing subject, but one that can pass for philosophy. In any case, for the chieftain's wife, and the man himself, such conversation with the empress was prestigious, and helped to cement cordial relations between the government and its vital supporters in Britain.

All this was interrupted by Severus' death at York on 4 February 211, which Dio inevitably suspects was hastened by Caracalla, while Herodian takes another line, admitting that Caracalla had not succeeded in persuading his father's attendants to make away with him: Severus had been ill for a long time and finally died of grief.[70] It was an event weeks away from the authorities at Rome, the Senate and People, who alone could recognize and so fully legitimize the succession of his son, or sons, and it put Domna in a position in which her weight as the emperor's widow was significant. But the military men were vital and must immediately have aligned themselves with the heirs, one or both. There may have been a purge of courtiers, including Euodus, Castor and Proculus Torpacion, Caracalla's childhood attendant, but the entire army in Britain was behind Caracalla and Geta – even if there had been rivals elsewhere who were prepared to fight. But the soldiers were unwilling to accept Caracalla as sole emperor by confining their oath of loyalty to him (the death of Geta would soon have followed). They refused, according to Dio, because they knew Geta and noticed how closely he resembled his father.[71] Caracalla falsified the year of his birth, making himself out to be two years older than he was. The most important reason for that, apart from the astrological fact that in 186 Caracalla's birthday fell on Monday, the day of the goddess he particularly revered,[72] would be to acquire seniority not only in general but also over Geta, who was actually less than a year younger than himself.

At Eboracum Domna and members of Severus' entourage patched up the quarrel. Journeying to Rome with Caracalla and Geta, she would have found dedications set up for their safety, victory and return, as in the territory of Aquae Vescinae.[73] Educated men and women who read their Tacitus would have remembered the passage in the *Annals* in which the people of Rome speculate about the fate of the Empire in the hands of two youths, Germanicus and Drusus: they would oppress it, and eventually tear it apart.[74] Domna did not need to read Tacitus, however, to see what was likely to happen and to know that she would finally be torn between her two sons.

Plate 1 Bust of Julia Domna (front). See Baharal (1992: Fig. 5), stressing the change in coiffure after 211 from the style of Faustina II.

Source: Staatliche Antikensammlung und Glyptothek München 354

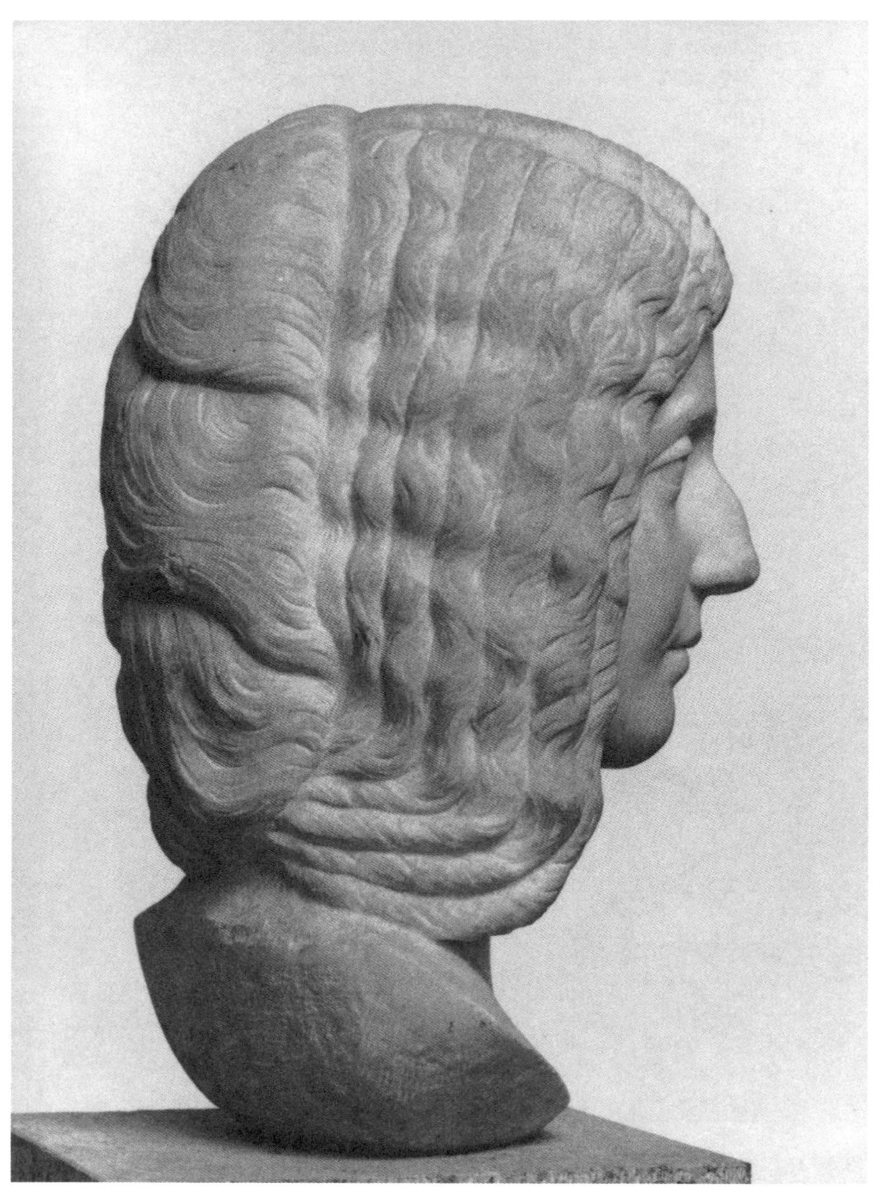

Plate 2 Bust of Julia Domna (right profile). See Baharal (1992: Fig. 3)

Source: Staatliche Antikensammlung und Glyptothek München 354

Plate 3 Cameo of Julia Domna as Victoria. Winged, seated figure with cuirass below, holding wreath in r., palm branch in l., 16.3 by 10.7 cm.

Source: Staatliche Museen Kassel, Antikensammlung, Ant. Gemmen Kat. 55. Photo S. Luckert

Plate 4 Arch of Septimius Severus, Lepcis Magna. (Tripolis, Archaeological Museum)
Severus and Caracalla shake hands; Geta between them, Domna, to l., watches. To r., a soldier, perhaps the Praetorian Prefect, Fulvius Plautianus, perhaps followed by the City Prefect, Fabius Cilo. Severus' head is ascribed to a type popular 207–11 (McCann 1968: 77), or to a *decennalia* type of 202 (D. Soechting (1972) *Die Porträts des Septimius Severus*, Bonn, 231). Caracalla's portrait is of the 'Gabii' type.
Source: Deutsches Archäologisches Institut, Rome 1961.1701; Photo Koppermann

Plate 5 Arch of Septimius Severus, Lepcis Magna
(Tripolis, Archaeological Museum)
Relief of sacrifice (r. side), Senatus (the Senate) central, Domna to l.
Source: Deutsches Archäologisches Institut, Rome 1961. 1699 Photo Koppermann

Plate 6 Arch of the *Argentarii*, Rome (east pier, internal panel).
Severus and Domna, sacrificing, Geta chiselled away, r. The dedicants have stressed the divine aspect of Severus, whose pose is hieratic and frontal. His bust is of the 'Serapis' type, with four rows of curls and long, parted beard (McCann 1968: 58). Domna wears a crescent diadem and her hairstyle is of the early 'Gabii' type.

Source: Deutsches Archäologisches Institut, Rome 1970. 0993 Photo Singer

Plate 7 Largest extant portrait of a woman in Antiquity. Vatican, Ingresso Superiore, W. Helbig, *Führer durch die öffentlichen Sammlungen klass. Altertümer in Rom* (ed. 4 by H. Speier, Tübingen, 1963) 5 n. 5).

Source: Governatorio, Direzione dei Musei dello Stato della Città del Vaticano

Plate 8 The Berlin tondo. The Emperor Septimius Severus with his wife Julia Domna and sons, Caracalla and Geta (roundel, pigment on panel).

Source: Staatliche Museen, Berlin, Germany/ The Bridgeman Art Library

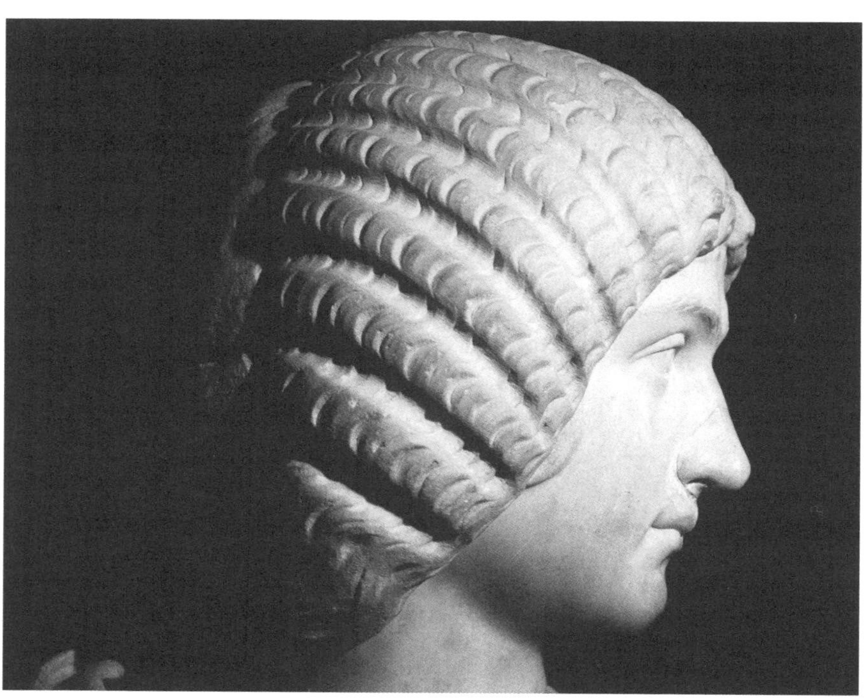

Plate 9 Julia Domna. Detail of marble portrait (right profile)
Source: Louvre, Paris, France/ B. de Sollier and P. Muxel/ The Bridgeman Art Library

6 The reign of Caracalla

Like 'the new Julia Augusta' – Livia in AD 14 – Domna was a significant factor in the continuity of the imperial regime.[1] The constraints on power that derived from her relation to her husband and son were different from those that limited Livia's scope: Tiberius was a man in his mid-fifties, an established politician and soldier; it was principle and regard for his own constitutional position and status that made him restrictive. Caracalla's position was more like Nero's. He had all the necessary constitutional powers, only his use of them, except on campaign, had not been proven. His mother's sixteen years at the centre of power gave her high authority; but Caracalla was impatient of advisers.[2]

When Septimius Severus died, the army and then the Senate duly recognized both his sons as joint emperors and at their request deified their father.[3] Severus' cautious succession plans were too strong for any alternative schemes. Although both had enjoyed *imperium* and the title Augustus before their father's death, 4 February was marked in calendars as Caracalla's accession date (*dies imperii*), a move from 28 January, when he had first been made Augustus; Geta probably intended to make the same move.[4]

As they made their way back to Rome with Severus' ashes consigned to a purple urn, probably blue-john (fluorspar) from Derbyshire,[5] Herodian claims that the feud broke out again, despite the efforts of Domna and the imperial counsellors, and one may well believe him.[6] Caracalla's coins of 211 veil the story, with their depiction of the brothers sacrificing in the presence of Concord, while Geta's of the same period, *CONCORDIA AVGVSTORVM*, show them clasping hands.[7]

Herodian tells graphically how Domna used every means she had, including tears, in an attempt to prevent one solution, the geographical division of the Empire, west and east, between the brothers, with Caracalla receiving the west (including the north African provinces up to Greek-speaking Cyrenaica) and Geta the east, with Alexandria or Antioch as his capital; the Senators were to divide according to their origins and troops were to be stationed at Byzantium and Calchedon.[8] As if Caracalla would have been satisfied with that as a solution, even though the Rhine and Danubian armies would have been in his portion! It was nearly a century before Diocletian was strong enough to see through a division of responsibilities, and even then a panegyrist of 289 told him and his colleague that 'by your unanimity you maintain the advantage of an undivided empire'.[9] If anyone considered it in 211 it would have been with the scheme of the latter part of the Second Triumvirate in mind, the division of the Empire between Octavian and Antony, and Geta cannot have forgotten the outcome of that. The exemplary Augusti M. Aurelius and L. Verus (161–9) had certainly divided their work, and Verus had gone east against the Parthians, but there had been no such final division of responsibility and powers. Herodian, seeing in his own time the possibility of a divided Empire, and a possible resolution of the quarrel between the brothers, invented a role for Domna to account for its not having been adopted. The impassioned rhetoric he puts into her mouth is a far cry from the dignified words of her letter to the Ephesians – but so it would have been:

> Your mother! How are you going to divide her? How am I to be cut up and assigned to the two of you, God help me? You had better kill me first, then each of you can cut me up and bury each part. Then I can be shared between you, like the land and sea.

So saying she threw her arms round the young men, trying to reconcile them. Not surprisingly, everyone present was overwhelmed with pity and the Council was adjourned.

Fiction, but illuminating, for it shows how the empress and her place in government was perceived by Herodian and any source he used. First, while she was present at the deliberations and able to speak, Domna never entered the contenders' calculations at all until she drew attention to herself: effectively she was a disposable cipher. On the other hand, the emotional effect of her plea, her symbolic role as mother of the Augusti, made the debate collapse. She is advisory, powerless, but powerfully symbolic.

Domna had the reputation of being fonder of her younger son, and her contemporary Dio claims that she remained implacably hostile to Caracalla.[10] Assuming that the remark is not just wishful thinking, born of his own dislike, one wonders how he knew. He was not her confidant, and it must have been through some indiscretion on her part, or perhaps through personal or reported observation of her body language. Even if he is right, and in view of the public cooperation of Domna and Caracalla to the end the claim must be an oversimplification, and at most means that she did all she could to safeguard Geta and his position. It does not authenticate the story of the proposed division. She could only try to reconcile the brothers and so save Geta's life. It may have been these efforts that earned Domna a nickname: Jocasta, mother of the warring Theban brothers Eteocles and Polynices, but, as we shall see, that was not the only part of the Theban story that was referred to her.[11]

When they arrived in Rome to a warm welcome from the people, who waved them on their way with laurel branches, and an address from the

Senate, the brothers divided the huge and symbolic Palatium between themselves. They are said even to have closed off access between the two parts of the residence, which meant a change in use of the rooms. Now they could keep their housekeeping and tables apart, avoiding the danger of poison. Presumably Domna occupied her old set of rooms.[12] However, there were occasions when Caracalla and Geta had to appear together, first and foremost at the interment and consecration of their father.[13]

Not too much is to be made of the contrast drawn by Herodian here between the character and interests of the two brothers: it is not consistent with his earlier claim that they were equally licentious and brutal. Here he gives Geta credit for more winning ways, serious studies and distinguished literary men as companions, while Caracalla was a rough soldierly character, given to violence and threats.[14] Brutal and sudden in defence of his own interests Caracalla was, but, as C. R. Whittaker has pointed out, he too cared for oratory, poetry, and music and was capable enough of writing verses of thanks when he was saved from shipwreck between Europe and Asia.[15]

Herodian's story of the proposed division of the Empire is a fine melodrama, worthy of the Victorian stage. What followed was more Jacobean, but this time there is substance in the tale: an emperor was killed. Geta had part of the Praetorian Guard attending on him, and even on his side, besides the fans of his circus faction. But it was not enough: he did not survive beyond December 211. Whether the violence had been preceded by abortive attempts at poisoning, as Herodian claims, we cannot tell.[16]

In Domna's neutral quarters, perhaps just after the Saturnalia of 211,[17] Geta met his brother, but Caracalla had the room surrounded by armed men, centurions. Geta ran to his mother for protection, the story goes, irresistibly recalling the inappropriately comic episode of the *Iliad* in which Aphrodite protects her son Aeneas and, goddess as she is, is slightly wounded. But Geta was killed in her arms and Domna herself wounded in the hand.[18] So Dio, with Caracalla dedicating the fatal sword in the aftermath. It looks as if Herodian was not content with this story: in the more graphic version, Caracalla, who had planned the attack,[19] struck the blow himself, after which he rushed out of the Palace begging for the help of the soldiers against the intending assassin.[20] Such was the confidence of Caracalla: he had no other rivals. It is tempting to recall Nero's impudent letter to the Senate after the murder of his adoptive brother Britannicus: Nero told them that he was the only surviving male heir of the dynasty (the Elder Agrippina, as a woman, could not come into consideration).[21] Caracalla went to the Praetorian barracks at once to denounce his brother's attempt on himself and demand the support of the entire Guard. A donative and increase in pay made it easier for them to believe him. Prudently, the pay rise was extended to the entire army. Caracalla had more trouble in winning over the Second Legion, Parthica, which had taken over the role of the Guard at Albanum, but they too yielded to his money offer.[22] Next day he went into the Senate with his bodyguard and wearing a breastplate under his robes.[23] The formal charge against Geta was brought out: plotting to poison Caracalla and disrespect towards Domna. That is an interesting detail: it publicly committed Domna to Caracalla's side. However, the *Historia Augusta* goes on to say that on the following day, when he found Geta's mother weeping for her son in company with other women (the author was committed to the view that Domna was Caracalla's stepmother), he was on the point of killing them too.[24] Geta was declared a public enemy and it was only after Caracalla's and Domna's deaths that his remains were admitted to the Antonine and Severan tomb.[25]

Serious doubts arise about accounts of Geta's murder. A planned, open assassination in the presence of witnesses, and especially of their mother, seems implausible when quieter methods were available: a single assassin or (with patience) poison. It may be that there was something in Caracalla's account, at least to the extent that the murder resulted from a quarrel at a meeting intended to reconcile them that turned into a brawl of the kind the brothers had enjoyed in the past; Caracalla simply got the better of the scrap.[26]

Now that Caracalla was liberated from dynastic rivalry he could remove other obstacles to untrammelled supremacy. A bloodbath followed, went on into 212, and ended in the booing of Caracalla's favoured charioteer in the circus and an indiscriminate rampage against the audience by his soldiers.[27] The numbers of Geta's followers given by Dio – 20,000 men and women alike in the imperial residence – are not easily believed, but he has the names of distinguished victims. The clear-out included powerful politicians and Prefects of the Guard: Valerius Patruinus, L. Valerius Messalla Thrasea Priscus, consul 196, and the great jurist Papinian, who had tried to protect Geta, struck down in Caracalla's presence; Papinian's son, who was old enough for the quaestorship and so potentially dangerous, was also killed. The Prefect of the City Fabius Cilo, a faithful adherent of the Severi but one who had tried to reconcile the brothers, is said to have had a narrow escape and also had to step down. The consul of 212 and City Prefect C. Julius Asper, who may have been involved in the attempt on Cilo, himself soon had to retire.[28] Aelius Antipater, Caracalla's teacher, killed himself. Besides that there were potential rivals such as the son of Pertinax, also consul in 212, and Plautianus' son and daughter, Caracalla's divorced wife; Ti. Claudius (Aurelius) Pompeianus, grandson of Marcus Aurelius and regular consul in 209; Caracalla's cousin C. Septimius (Severus) Aper, regular consul in 207; the elderly sister of Commodus, and so 'sister-in-law' of Domna, Cornificia, who consoled Domna on the death of Geta (her husband L. Didius Marinus survived); and the intellectual Serenus Sammonicus. The governor of Baetica was executed, a man of African origin, with whom Caracalla may have had a personal quarrel, for his province was no springboard for a coup. Neither was Narbonensis, whose governor perished likewise. These distinguished people, known to Domna, gave her fresh reasons for grief – which she would have to hide. No mourning for Geta was allowed.[29] There was an additional cause for grief if two of Domna's closest kinsmen by marriage, Julius Avitus Alexianus and Varius Marcellus, took the part of the elder brother against the younger.[30]

All this came after the first shock. One son was dead at the hands of the other, and the survivor himself was in danger if the legions refused his offers out of loyalty to Geta. Everything that Severus had built up was tottering; on top of the personal loss it was a crushing political blow. There was nothing for a woman used to danger and power to do but to give her dead son a decent burial and rally to Caracalla. Loyalty to the memory of her husband and a taste for her entrenched position, not to say fear, reinforced each other.

A monument of 212 set up in Africa seems to embody the official mood: a veteran from Lambaesis, L. Propertius Martialis, made his dedication in recognition of the perpetual flaminate conferred on him by the city council to Jupiter Best and Greatest, 'preservers of the Emperor and of Julia Domna'.[31] If this interpretation of the stone is right, it looks as if Domna was being put into the category of a potential victim of Geta, as she was in Caracalla's account to the Senate – absurd though that would be. Domna was being brought on side in the sight of the whole Empire. Inscriptions set up in honour of Geta were defaced like his images and in many cases re-cut, with the substitution of extra titles for Caracalla and Domna, shattered if they were statue bases.[32] It is notable that inscriptions honouring Domna as '*Mater Augustorum*' survived Geta's murder, still more so that a stone recording her as the mother of Geta alone was not destroyed: respect to the mother of the emperor outweighed the need to eradicate Geta's memory.

The question is what change in power and prestige Domna underwent when the Empire passed from the near-joint rule of three Augusti, with Caracalla in particular an effective 'Emperor' (as Severus himself is made to express it in the particularly poignant context of Caracalla's supposed attempt on his life),[33] by way of the months of struggle, to the sole rule of Caracalla. The same question has been asked of Livia, when she became Julia Augusta in 14, and conflicting answers have been given. On one view, with the title Augusta Livia received an official position which Augustus had previously denied her and which Tiberius strongly deprecated; another denies that the title itself had any such significance, and it is surely right.[34] There is nothing substantial to call upon in support of the idea of any formal change. Rather Livia achieved her position by a gradual development over the reigns of Augustus and Tiberius, as her influence became entrenched and taken for granted, to be enhanced when the emperor was no longer the founder of the Principate but his unpopular adoptive son. Julia Domna's position likewise developed over the years, and in any case she had possessed the honorific title since the beginning.

There could have been a change for the worse: dowagers live in dower houses away from the family seat; they are displaced by the incumbent's wife, and the wife is prime. But both Tiberius and Caracalla had been divorced and soon lost their former wives altogether: Augustus' daughter dead of starvation at Rhegium in 14, Plautilla executed. Livia and Domna had no daughters-in-law to take their place. Their position depended on two factors: the extent to which the emperor felt that he needed them as props to his regime, and his malleability in the face of maternal authority. For Tiberius, with his austerely constitutional view of the Principate, Livia was a threat to his planned position in the state. For Caracalla, as far as continuity was indeed a concern to him, Domna represented a valuable connection to his father Severus, and one with the eastern reaches of the Empire. In the exercise of his power when he felt threatened it is hard to see Caracalla, a soldier emperor if ever there was one, allowing himself to be ruled by his mother, but G. W. Bowersock is probably right to see Domna's political influence growing greater under the new regime, at any rate in day-to-day matters.[35]

Besides her experience, an important factor in Domna's enhanced importance was Caracalla's military activity: much of his reign was taken up with campaigning, first in the North, from spring to autumn 213, then in the east. The eastern journey lasted until his death, and a proportion of it, when he was in the field, would have been spent away from any political centre. Domna was the person whom Caracalla knew he could trust with routine questions and in the first instance with more serious matters. To what level his trust extended, and how heavy Domna's responsibilities were, are different matters. As for trust, he knew that with him gone she had nothing to look forward to (as it proved).

The murder of Geta made the perennial problem of the Principate – the succession – acute. Augustus had begun by holding quasi-magisterial powers, which originally had time limits. By combining an accepted private-law principle of inheritance from father to son with a clever scheme of providing his partners and destined heirs with their own overlapping powers, he had overcome the difficulty. After that there was a precedent to follow, but no officially recognized rules.

Domitian succeeded his brother Titus in 81. If Caracalla had died in 211, Geta, on the 'overlap' scheme, would not have succeeded him but would simply have continued as Augustus. When Geta died Caracalla was likewise childless, and unmarried. He had achieved his father-in-law Plautianus' downfall at high personal cost. He would not want to risk repeating that experience. There was also an understandable tendency for the imperial dynasties to marry within the family, avoiding not only the dissipation of power outside it, but also, as intrigues over the marriages of King Henry VIII showed, the invidiousness of favour conferred on a single family outside it. It is possible that there was a young female member of the Septimii or the Julii of Emesa who would have grown up into a suitable consort. Whether Caracalla in his early twenties would have given thought for what might come after him is another question.

Severus' widow, however, had to think about it; she owed it to her dead husband and herself. Much as she had hated Plautilla, a son even of hers would have continued her line and guaranteed the Severan Principate. Whatever she wanted, Caracalla had not remarried. And now his brutality had deprived him of an avenger if he were assassinated, besides making him a more likely target by blackening his reputation. The precedents of Gaius Caligula, who killed his cousin and heir Tiberius Gemellus, and Nero, the killer of Britannicus, his adoptive brother, and Domitian, who made away with his cousin Flavius Sabinus, were obvious. All died by violence, while Augustus and Vespasian, who shared military power with members of their family, died in their beds. Who was available on Severus' side of the family is not clear; Domna's own is better documented, and Caracalla's eventual successor, Elagabalus, born in 203 or 204, was a potential candidate for grooming. Elagabalus' distaff descent, from the empress's sister, was no serious impediment. Augustus had already been succeeded by his wife's son Tiberius (although he had adopted him as his son); Nero's connection with the house was through his mother the younger Agrippina. In due course Caracalla might have adopted Elagabalus, who was 7 or 8 when Geta died. He would have been a poor substitute for a grandchild of her own.

Julia Maesa, the child's grandmother, and his mother Sohaemias would have been enthusiastic advocates, but there may have been an insuperable obstacle: Caracalla himself, unreceptive to the idea of preparing for his own death and supersession. Without his consent, no preparations, powers and titles could be put in hand. There was nothing that the sisters could do. Elagabalus may have been at court: he seems to have been with Caracalla at Thyatira. His mother presumably stayed, at least for a while, with her husband, who was certainly at Rome until he went to Numidia; and the children, who joined with her in setting up his funerary inscription, might have been expected to be with her; but they might not have personally supervised the interment. Until the court reached Syria his entourage could not make much of Elagabalus' position there (whatever it was) or consolidate local support for him and his family. Maesa was certainly living at court with Domna, but that did not help to bring Elagabalus any recognition.[36]

On the disappearance of Geta, Domna's full titulature evolved into '*Mater Augusti/imperatoris et castrorum et senatus et patriae*', 'Mother of the Emperor, of the Camps and the Senate and her Native Land'.[37] Her motherhood was almost as all-encompassing when it was designated '*Mater populi Romani*'.[38] This was a title that showed her as enjoying the informal authority of a mother, not only in a military context, but also over the supreme council of state, once an assembly of kings, and over the entire body politic. And that authority was (as ever) whatever its holder could make it.

The original *Mater Castrorum* had been long in use; *Mater Senatus* was formally a novelty, but Claudius had been saluted as 'Father of the Senate', which has implications of paternal power, so that it is no surprise that Commodus had the title on the coins of his later years; and those

Figure 6.1 Domna devoted and fortunate; Venus Genetrix.
AE. Obv. *IVLIA PIA FELIX AVG* Bust of Domna, draped, l.; hair with seven horizontal ridges. Rev. *VENVS GENETRIX* (in exergue) *S C* Venus, draped to feet, seated l. on throne, extending r. hand and holding vertical sceptre in l. AD 212–17.

Source: *CREBM* 5, p. 470, no. 217.

connotations are naturally absent from the innocuous female version.[39] The last two titles '*senatus et patriae*' were probably accorded after the death of Severus, though an earlier date has been proposed. *Mater patriae* in particular would trip off the tongue after the routine *Pater patriae* of the emperor's titulature. They are likely to have occurred in orations and in unofficial inscriptions before they were formally endorsed; Trajan's title of *Optimus Princeps*, 'Best of Emperors', offers a parallel.[40] The new titulature put the august institution, and all Rome and Italy, into Domna's care along with her surviving son; at once bringing them all together and offering Domna a uniquely high distinction to console her widowhood. It embodied that protective capacity that had won approval in Livia. In the old days between 202 and 205, when Domna had been honoured alongside her daughter-in-law Plautilla Augusta, who had no titles other than that of being Caracalla's wife, she had had to do without her own.[41] Once granted, *Mater patriae et senatus* was available to Domna's successors, at any rate to Maesa and Mamaea.[42] This most elaborate and developed form of Domna's titulature has been taken by scholars to be further evidence both of her power and of its orientalizing tendencies.[43] It is extraordinary, then, that the extreme and even anomalous versions of them occur not in the east but in north Africa.[44] The development had an internal logic and was in no need of external stimulus.

A less specific title that Domna was awarded, or assumed, was *Pia Felix*. That combination had entered the male imperial titulature gradually. From Trajan onwards, new titles began to be bestowed on emperors, besides the 'geographical' sobriquets such as *Germanicus* and *Parthicus*, derived from peoples they claimed to have conquered. *Pius* and *Felix* were in this new category; then, after Commodus, they were taken in combination by Caracalla and all his successors, and apparently accorded by him to Julia Domna.[45] *Felicitas* (Good Fortune) was a quality that was essential for the successful general, as Cicero had pointed out in connection with Pompey.[46] *Pietas* (Devotion) was a quality demanded of every Roman towards the State and senior family members, and exhibited above all by the ultimate founder, Aeneas, towards his aged father and his people. It proliferated on coinage at the end of the Republic and Pompey's son Sextus had taken Pius as a *cognomen* to demonstrate allegiance to his late father's memory. *Pius* was one of the sobriquets declined for Tiberius as heir to Augustus. More recently in Trajan's last years *PIETAS AVGVST(AE)* had been inscribed on a reverse of his niece Matidia which showed her with her daughters Sabina and Matidia the Younger, and the adjective came to the fore when Hadrian's successor T. Aelius Caesar Antoninus acquired it, largely for his devotion to the memory of the Emperor, whose consecration the Senate had opposed. It became, with *felix*, a regular ingredient of the imperial titulature, in the abbreviated form '*p.f.*' on Caracalla's obverses.[47]

Possession was not a formality: when the assassinated Commodus was buried, the tombstone omitted these titles.[48] For a woman it was an unprecedented novelty. Taken separately, '*pia*' was unexceptionable: a woman simply owed her devotion to all the men in her family, Domna in particular to the emperor who had been her husband and the emperor who was her son. '*Felix*' should have lacked the military focus that it had for men, but Julia Domna was always among the troops, enjoyed other 'military' titles, was associated with the emperor in his greetings to the Senate; her 'good fortune' became relevant to the State, and in any case the two titles must be taken together, as they were with the Augusti. Domna was simply being granted one of the distinctions that had been prerogatives of the emperor himself. So the name Julia Augusta Pia Felix, followed by the familiar string of 'motherhood' references that balance Caracalla's *Parthicus Maximus, Britannicus maximus, Germanicus maximus*, came to track that of her son, *Pius Felix Augustus*. It was another small step towards the unreachable assimilation and the creation of a royal pair. In themselves the adjectives were not exotic or un-Roman. They are the product of the internal dynamics of imperial power and ideology, and in combination (it has been suggested, not quite convincingly) of changing attitudes to the Empire among provincials who no longer saw it as a coherent whole.[49]

Domna continued to hold her receptions of front-rank politicians, and her recommendation of a sophist to the chair at Athens during the time she and her son were at Rome together was enough to secure it. That was exactly the approved sphere in which Trajan's wife Plotina had operated.[50] In the east, by 217 at latest, she had part of the Praetorian Guard assigned to her; perhaps this was routine when she was apart from the emperor.[51] Moreover, Caracalla entrusted her with his Greek and Latin correspondence and his replies to petitions.[52] These secretarial functions were normally performed by freedmen or *equites*, who had titles, '*ab epistulis Graecis et Latinis*', '*ab responsis*', and a staff of slave clerks. When Vitellius is said in 69 to have transferred such posts from freedmen to *equites*, what is meant is that he put *equites* in at the head of the bureaux without disturbing the rest of the structure.[53] The same thing may have been done for Domna, but it is highly unlikely that she was offered (given the ban on women's tenure of official posts), or would have accepted, a title that had belonged to freedmen and knights.[54] The occasion for the development is obscure: the death of one of the key *chefs de bureau*, perhaps some slip on the part of the staff which the emperor did not want repeated, or an effort to tighten imperial control. Perhaps the role had developed gradually with the absence of Severus on campaign in Scotland and his increasing weakness. On all imperial expeditions there would have been a full impartial staff, in Britain and in the Balkans. But Severus at the end of his reign was faced with intense problems, mostly in connection with his sons, while Caracalla after the murder of Geta had provided himself with infinite grounds for suspecting the men who surrounded him. Domna could be trusted by each of them.

It is in the east that Domna's role can be glimpsed, because of the survival of epigraphic records of transactions. We have an example of her work in her letter to the authorities of Ephesus, later embedded in a pavement of the gymnasium. It is connected with benefits conferred by the emperor or, less probably, with a visit of his; the letter may also have to do with the city's request for a third neocory (temple warden of the imperial cult). Domna recognizes the city's pre-eminence – it is a school of Hellas – and promises to work for it with her 'sweetest son'. Domna's work is correctly estimated and praised in patronizing terms by J. and L. Robert: she performs no act of government nor even of administration and is in no way indiscreet.[55] No doubt the surviving letter is typical of what she could do (all emperors had secretarial advisers at their disposal). How many she drafted and what she did beyond this are unknown. E. Kettenhofen is surely right to warn against phrases that imply that she was 'administering the Empire' and to insist that the idea of everything being left to her needs revising. Her official position and power should not be overestimated, and terms such as 'co-regent' and 'queen-mother' are to be avoided. Kettenhofen draws attention to the inscription from Dmeir which shows Caracalla himself involved in the domestic and judicial affairs of the Empire.[56] Domna did not decide the question of the neocory: it was the emperor's business. But we should not be too hasty. We do not know what part the advice of Domna played in forming Caracalla's decision. As Kettenhofen remarks, the document illustrates how difficult it is to estimate Domna's influence. Enhancement explains, in B. Bleckmann's view, the increasingly devoted character of the dedications made to her in Caracalla's reign, and gives meaning to the conferment of the enhanced 'motherhood' titles.[57] But that may be due to affection and regard for a stabilizing factor in government.

Domna can be found offering Caracalla advice, if in a staged fiction. Caracalla, true to his father's dying injunctions, paid attention to enriching the soldiers (disregarding everyone else).[58] The money he spent on their increased pay came largely from increased rates of taxation, the creation of new citizens who would be liable, and then by manipulating the coinage. Senatorial purses suffered, and it was a bitter grievance. Domna, the obvious foil for critical historians, was given the credit for trying to curb his expenditure: 'There is no longer any source of revenue available to us, legal or illegal.' (Evidently it was plausible to present Domna as having access to the account books.) For what it is worth, Caracalla is not portrayed as irritated by her interference: he merely showed her his sword: 'Cheer up, mother; as long as we have this we shall not want for money'. Dio envisages other failures, against acts of violence and breaches of the law, and describes her (rejected) advice as 'sound' (*chresta*), whether for its advantage to the general interest or to Caracalla's is not clear; probably both. But the notion entertained by M. Grant that Domna was at least partly responsible for the *Constitutio Antoniniana* rests on no foundation, other than her concern for controlling expenditure.[59]

Exaggerated ideas of Domna's power have grown up because some scholars were hypnotized by the conception of the eastern princess imposing eastern notions of 'mother-right' on the patriarchal Roman establishment. Those conjectures have been reinforced with notions in Dio and Herodian of the power enjoyed by her kinswomen Maesa, Sohaemias, and Mamaea, during the reigns of the boy-emperors Elagabalus and Alexander Severus. Petticoat government, by alien and eastern women, was a Roman nightmare, glimpsed in the flesh of Cleopatra and Berenice, and nothing is heard of that in sources contemporary with Domna. Not that 'mother-right' was likely to be dominant in a Syria that in part had been hellenized since Alexander's conquests and Romanized since those of Pompey the Great. Further, Caracalla's own lust for power was too great for the picture to be convincing. The contrast with Nero and his relations with Agrippina in the earliest years of his reign could not be clearer. At first the 16-year-old Nero, who owed his position to his mother's marriage to Claudius and to her prompt actions on Claudius' death, was obedient, and swayed into disobedience only by warnings from his advisers Seneca and Burrus and his own inclinations. Nero's preoccupations as emperor were with performance and popularity rather than with the exercise of power. Caracalla, who had been on the trail in beleaguered provinces from infancy, and who became sole emperor at 23, kept his mother on, but evidently did not always take her advice. W. Eck has justly written of the age of Gaius, Claudius, and Nero as one in which the prominence and power of women were exceptional, not to be reached again until the time of Elagabalus.[60]

It seems that the population of the Empire accepted Domna's status and titles at their face value and, as we shall see, considered her worthy of attention that bordered on deification. Perhaps the most revealing indications of where Domna stood in the minds of Rome's subjects, at least, come from forms of words apparently unconsciously adopted in which the lead of official pronouncements was followed. In 214, a *lauacrum* (washhouse) was built at Timgad, and dated by using the imperial titulature in the ablative case. That was a commonplace in Roman epigraphy; pairs of consuls had been used in this way from the early Republic, and the years of an emperor's tribunician power had been used in the same way. Now, however, this African building was dated, not just with a mention of the emperor, but with one of the empress mother as well.[61]

However cautiously, personal relations between Domna and her murderous son must also be probed, as they were by ancient writers. The murder of Geta, shocking as it was, had been predictable, and the roles of murderer and victim could have been reversed. Whatever her grief, Domna may well have been conscious of this, and her anger assuaged by it. However, there is contrary testimony to deal with. First of all, Dio insists on Domna's hostility to Caracalla, and preference for Geta, who is given a more agreeable character in some sources.[62] This is unsurprising when Domna is the foil to a villainous emperor. Indeed she is described as being a 'stepmother' to Caracalla. Some writers seem to mean this literally, and this picture of Domna would spread more easily (even in face of the fact that his original *cognomen* of Bassianus was that of Domna's father) because she was Severus' second wife and because there was confusion over Caracalla's date of birth. In one view the story was a way of explaining the unnatural hostility between the brothers, but it is surprising that at Rome, one of whose founders, Romulus, killed his brother Remus, that would have required explaining.[63] Whether meant literally or metaphorically, the idea of stepmotherhood has all the advantages of ambiguity. A stepmother is also prone to fall in love with her stepson, as the doomed heroine Phaedra had with Hippolytus. Hence a source of enjoyable scandal: incest between Domna and Caracalla. Sexual relations with a stepson were incestuous, hardly less so than sexual relations between a mother and her son by birth, such those between Jocasta and Oedipus. The incest is taken quite for granted by writers of late antiquity. Some versions make the pair actually marry, evidently after the death of Geta.[64] Domna's nickname of Jocasta, a jibe of the Alexandrians made against the dowager during Caracalla's sole rule,[65] was as apposite for the incest as it was for Caracalla's fatal quarrel with Geta.

Given the intrinsic implausibility of the entire incest story, apart from its value as a gross presentation of the political partnership between mother and son after 211, the question remains as to how it developed.[66] Attempts have been made to find one originator, such as Plautianus or Macrinus. Neither is plausible, Plautianus because he fell before the story seems to have become current, Macrinus because, during his short reign, he was preoccupied with the future and securing his own position rather than with smearing his dead predecessor and that man's doomed mother with irrelevant gossip. Dio, writing under Alexander Severus, has nothing to say of incest; if he had one would have expected it to take the form of a rape, to blacken Caracalla still.[67] Its first appearance is in Herodian, decades after the deaths of the protagonists, and it is developed in the later, Latin, sources. No straightforward linear development can be found, and that makes it likely that there were several strands in its origins, popular and literary; writers who perpetuated it could choose the version that would mean most in their culture, and opt for or devise variants, such as which of them took the initiative, that fitted their view of the dynamics of Caracalla's reign.[68] Such is the plasticity of rumour and hence its value.[69] G. Marasco is convincing in uncovering a source in Alexandria, a city that had good reason to detest Caracalla after his visit of 215–16. Personal attacks on the ancestry and private life of emperors were a commonplace in the popular accounts of local champions of the city who had been tried and executed by earlier emperors from Augustus to Commodus.[70] As to the development of the story among the historians, it took two forms, one part of a tradition hostile to Caracalla, the other of an attack on Domna. As to Domna's involvement, she was after all the mother of the villain and to an extent responsible for him; and there was a recent precedent for sexual misconduct on the part of imperial women: Faustina (II).[71] There is a less plausible theory that Domna's eastern origin played a contributory part: it plays on incest as practised in Phoenicia and Syria and taken up among the Sassanian Persians from the Persians of old,[72] but these were brother and sister marriages. In particular Domna was compared with Semiramis, who was killed by her son after she propositioned him.[73] Even weaker is the invocation of Julia Maesa, who strengthened Elagabalus' claim to the Empire by putting it about that he was really a son of Caracalla's by her daughter Sohaemias (Caracalla was also to be credited with Alexander Severus' parentage).[74] This neglects the desperate need of both these young claimants to legitimacy of any kind in their bids for power; and the incest theme was very weak: Caracalla was only a cousin of Soaemias and Mamaea.

Some part in the literary development of the story is also played by the notorious tradition, available in Tacitus and Dio, of an incestuous relationship between Nero and his mother Agrippina, in spite of real differences in the stories. Tacitus too mentions variants from earlier authors that ascribe the sexual initiative to one or the other partner. The precedent of Nero and Agrippina survived in ancient thinking: some sources mention a plan of Caracalla's to kill his mother, as Agrippina had been killed.[75] The germ may have been a comparison between the two emperors, elaborated as time went on. Later imperial parallels could then be seen by the fourth century Latin writers: Penella suggests that Domna may eventually have been assimilated to Fausta, the ill-fated wife of Constantine the Great, by Eutropius and Aurelius Victor, the contemporaries of Constantine's successor Julian.

From the military point of view – and it was a presage of emperors' lives for the coming century – Caracalla's reign was a continuation of his father's, with few intervals of peace between campaigns. It may have been little more than twelve months after the assassination of Geta, in early 213, that he travelled north, as (the excerpted) Dio says to deal with the Alamanni. They were an increasingly threatening group of tribes in southern Germany which has given French a name for the entire country – Allemagne. The campaign itself, conducted from Raetia and Moguntiacum, took place in August–September of 213, and has been seen as little more than a diplomatic mission, 'showing the flag'. What followed is not clear, but there may have been a tour of inspection of Rhine bases and a victory on the Main as well as reconstruction of roads in the Agri Decumates.[76] Herodian's claim that Caracalla was driven north by his guilty conscience is a dramatic fantasy.[77] Caracalla was consolidating his own position with the army and winning independent military glory.[78]

It is not clear either where Domna was while these wide-ranging operations were going on. She may have preferred to be away from her son after the assassination. She went north probably as far as some centre such as Carnuntum, Lugdunum, or the effective base of operations at Moguntiacum, and she may have moved about as the scene shifted.[79] However far removed Domna may have been from the action, her role as a bringer of Victory and as an associate of that deity was not lost, as a relief from Warsaw seems to attest: holding a palm branch she crowns a Caracalla who stands by a trophy of 'northern' type. The Aphrodisias relief of the younger Agrippina crowning Nero comes to mind, though the *décolleté* of the Severan mother is excessive enough to suggest that there is more Victoria than Domna in the representation.[80]

When Caracalla turned east, Domna's presence was imperative. The importance of her image there was obvious enough, but so was precedent. Domna had twice accompanied Severus on his eastern expeditions; if she failed to accompany her son, that would reveal a breach and deprive him of the strengthening authority of her presence, apart from giving her scope for intrigue and independent action at Rome. Her authority, weak and marginal as it might be, could not be neglected.

Caracalla does not seem to have returned to Rome after the campaign of 213 and before setting out on the journey traced in the *Antonine Itinerary*, which set out the intended halting places and became a road-map for later emperors. Indeed, there was no time for it if he spent the winter of 213–14 at Nicomedia, nor for the extended stay in the Balkans after his victory over the Alamanni of September 213 that has also been postulated.[81] Domna, even if she had previously been in Rome, joined the emperor before they set out together for the east.

The journey will have revived memories, of the months of anxiety nearly twenty years before during the war with Niger, when she and Severus wintered at Perinthus in 193–4 and followed their victorious armies into Syria; then of the confident progress in the summer of 197 to the second Parthian war. She will also have thought of journeys made in the reverse direction. The first was not a return at all but the journey, though probably made by sea, that was to take her to her future husband in Gaul. The second, with extreme dangers still to face, carried her towards the confrontation with Clodius Albinus and the relief that followed. The third came after a war that had not ended gloriously, but which had culminated in a progress on the Nile, and it ended in 202 at a Rome that was fully under Severus' control, though the arrival may have been poisoned by knowledge of the power wielded by Plautianus. As the entourage advanced, the familiar routes and countryside, the familiarly fulsome welcomes in cities and hamlets, with magistrates, perhaps the sons of those she had met on earlier journeys, coming out garlanded and dressed in white to greet the imperial party, cannot have failed to give Domna confidence that on her return this time too, after more victories over the Parthians, who were torn between rival claimants to the throne, she would find another warm welcome, however she felt in private about her son.

At the same time, Caracalla's extravagant identification of himself with Alexander the Great, which had to be given expression in his portraits, was alarming, given the Roman track-record against the Parthians. Earlier emulators of Alexander, Mark Antony, Nero, and even Trajan, she would remember, had not achieved anything permanent. Her son was evidently determined to outdo his father's performance in the east, and his preparations for the campaign were elaborate.[82] But 'Alexander' was for Greek consumption too: Severus had taken over the east by force; Caracalla, half Syrian, Greek-speaking, could make it his own. One element in the strategy for bringing Parthia under Roman control was Caracalla's proposal of marriage with the daughter of one of the pretenders, Artabanus V. Alexander, was again an ultimate precedent, far outdistancing what Severus had done in marrying a mere Syrian royal.[83] For Domna one personal result of her son's preoccupation with Alexander would have been her own identification with Alexander's mother Olympias, reinforcing her prestige. That identification has indeed been suggested by E. Nau for a sardonyx bearing a portrait in profile, the head crowned and veiled, with a sceptre in the right hand.[84] The identification of the portrait is problematical, but Domna's enhanced status as the mother of a new Alexander can be accepted.

Caracalla and Domna crossed into Asia Minor perhaps after another stay at Perinthus.[85] Caracalla narrowly escaped shipwreck on the crossing; Domna, if she was in the same vessel, perhaps even if not, will have met the same danger.[86] The first cities named in their journey through the peninsula, Ilium and Pergamum, were familiar; whether they had been to Thyatira before is not known. Ilium was of particular interest to Domna, because Apollonius of Tyana, the guru whose biography she urged Philostratus to write, had likewise visited the tomb of Achilles, and advocated its restoration. Caracalla decorated it with garlands and flowers. Whether it was still in a state of disrepair is uncertain.[87] In Pergamum the bases of statues set up in honour of the imperial pair have been found, one dating precisely to the year 214. This was the year in which Pergamum was granted its third neocorate.[88] After this, it is now generally agreed, the entourage and the army passed from Nicomedia through Prusias ad Hypium towards the east, staying longer perhaps in the richer and more inviting provinces of Asia and Bithynia and speeding up as they went though Galatia-Cappadocia by way of Ancyra, Caesarea-Mazaca, Tyana – Apollonius' home city – and the Cilician Gates down to Tarsus.[89] Favours granted the cities by the emperor sometimes coincided with his visit, as did his grant of its own assize district (*conventus iuridicus*) to Thyatira, which would guarantee it a regular and profitable influx of visitors, as well as convenient access to the governor's court for its inhabitants.[90] Approaching him directly – Caracalla was forbidding beyond the usual for an emperor, although the inscription from Dmeir exhibits patience[91] – could have been alarming and Domna may sometimes have played the gracious intercessor.

Once in Syria, they were warmly greeted at Antioch: Caracalla was to grant the city colonial status. It was a sweet contrast to his father's original attitude. In 215 and 216, Caracalla and Domna also spent some time in Laodiceia, almost Domna's home ground which likewise received imperial favours. Towards the end of 215 she and the emperor moved to Egypt and Alexandria *via* Pelusium, where donkeys were being requisitioned for the visit.[92]

The stay in Egypt was noticed by the imperial mint at Rome: Caracalla is shown standing on a crocodile and holds the corn ears associated with Isis. Grain and the law and order recently breached again would be in Roman minds, taxes and privileges in Alexandrian.[93] After Caracalla's arrival, perfumed and celebrated as it was, riots broke out, and there are reports of extreme brutality on Caracalla's part. The people of Alexandria, once the capital of a great hellenistic monarchy, had been intermittently restive under the Principate. Caracalla was a hard man who had dealt ruthlessly with Plautianus and Geta. Rioting Alexandrians were to be treated in the same spirit. There was a massacre, not without danger to Roman soldiers.[94]

The visit had a very different tone from the earlier one, although there may have been a sight-seeing tour. At any rate it did not last long. In March or April Caracalla and presumably Domna were back in Antioch, and that is where Domna seems to have stayed. Caracalla's campaigns against the Parthians were begun on the pretext that his marriage proposal for the daughter of the Parthian monarch had been turned down, according to Dio, less plausibly in Herodian as a sheer act of treachery against Artabanus. They took place in northern Mesopotamia and Adiabene, and occupied him in 216 and 217; he wintered in the colony of Edessa, his campaign headquarters. Only for a short time in December did he return to Antioch.[95]

Caracalla's reign ended in his assassination after only six years, just failing to break the record held by Gaius Caligula (under four years) for an emperor who came to power peacefully. The question of Caracalla's sanity has exercised scholars from Dio onwards.[96] It always does with emperors whose extreme behaviour helps bring about their death (Caligula is the model). In

Figure 6.2 Caracalla 'Germanicus'; Jupiter.
Double *AV*. Obv. *ANTONINVS PIVS AV G GERM(anicus)*. Bust of Caracalla, bearded, radiate, draped, r. Rev. *P(ontifex) M(aximus) T(ribunicia) P(otestate) XVIIII COS IIII P(ater) P(atriae)* Jupiter, naked to waist, seated l., on low seat, holding Victory on extended r. hand and vertical sceptre in l.; at his feet, l., eagle standing front, body inclined l., head turned back, r. AD 216.
Source: *CREBM* 5, p. 460, no. 157.

the absence of the patient, no diagnosis should or can be given. These men were in extreme situations and hence without experience. The limits of what seemed unlimited, godlike, power had to be tested; and knowing that they caused anger and fear caused them to fear in turn, and to use terror to keep themselves in power. Subjected to journalistic interviews, they could rationalize their behaviour without raving or babble (Caligula was a shrewd and witty fellow). Caracalla was at a disadvantage, first because of Geta, then because of Geta's murder. Prestige and popularity had to be won, and that, especially if it were achieved by warfare, cost money. Caracalla in 212 or 214 gave Roman citizenship to free inhabitants of the Empire, completing a process that had been kick-started by the Social War waged by the Italians against Rome in 91–88 BC, hastened by the manpower and political needs of dynasts such as Caesar and Pompey (support from provincial communities helped to make up for the resentment of their peers), cautiously continued by Augustus for the same reasons, overtly supported by Claudius, and forwarded by the Flavians and Hadrian. Their work is shown in the indexes of epigraphic collections by the numbers of Pompeii, especially of Julii, Claudii, Flavii, and Aelii. Caracalla, mass-producing (Marci) Aurelii, only completed the long process. There were disadvantages to becoming a citizen: one might if without wife and children become liable to the unpopular inheritance tax, and it is the revenue from tax that Caracalla was alleged to have been after. His own fragmentary pronouncement on the issue, if the Giessen papyrus does refer to it, suggests, however, that it was a measure of gratitude to the gods for his preservation. If this refers to Geta's alleged assassination attempt, we may be witnessing a bid to win over the unenfranchised of the Roman world.[97] Caracalla's campaigns in Germany and the east were disliked for their expense and derided as charades. Even without the campaigns his dependence upon the army, and what it cost, were a thorn to the propertied classes.[98]

In 217 Caracalla set out for his expedition against the Parthians.[99] Domna settled in Antioch. It was there that she is said, in her charge of the imperial correspondence, to have received a letter from Flavius Maternianus, commander of the city troops. It denounced M. Opellius Macrinus, her son's Praetorian Prefect and future assassin. The message, addressed to Caracalla in Syria, reported the spread of a prophecy that Macrinus and his son Diadumenian would succeed Caracalla; but it was delayed by arriving on Domna's desk first. (In Herodian's version the letter reached Caracalla when he was getting into his chariot and he passed the letter to Macrinus to deal with.) Another letter, written by Ulpius Julianus, who was then in charge of the census, was sent directly to Macrinus, so that he advanced his plans.[100]

The apparently trivial content of the letters should cause no surprise, given how seriously cultivated Romans such as Dio took prophecies and omens, while Severus and Caracalla, who lived even more dangerously than run-of-the-mill senators, were notorious for their faith.[101] Besides, the rumour may have been deliberately provoked as a means of supporting Macrinus or preparing men's minds for his accession, and for that reason alone it was worth attention. It looks as if Macrinus took action to save his own life when he was denounced, whether or not he had actually entertained hopes of taking over from Caracalla (the story might have been thought up by a rival in the imperial suite).

Caracalla was killed early in April 217, after he went aside to relieve himself on the road between Edessa and Carrhae, where he was to visit a temple of Sîn, the Moon god. The assassin was Martialis, a soldier who had been refused promotion to a centurionate, but several officers are implicated by the sources, and unless Macrinus was opportunistically taking advantage of Martialis' violent act, he had at least encouraged the assassin.[102] At first his low-born but experienced colleague in the Prefecture of the Guard, Adventus, was mooted for emperor: Herodian says that the Parthians were on their way. Adventus refused, and on 11 April the soldiers elected Macrinus.[103] News of Caracalla's death arrived at Antioch in a day or two, soon followed by the urn of ashes on their way to Rome. Maternianus warned Domna to flee from Antioch.[104] He did not survive long into the new reign.[105]

With the murder of Caracalla it seemed that the dynasty of the Severi had come to an end. But, if Caracalla had not been a gifted strategist, and was loathed by the Senate, he had known how to follow his dying father's advice and appeal to the army, in part with money, in part by sharing the hardships of his men, which in the east included one or more of his

Praetorian cohorts.[106] Macrinus had no hold on them, even when he took the name Severus and the title Augustus.[107] This was the first time that an *eques* had come to power, though Tiberius' Praetorian Prefect Sejanus had been close to it. Macrinus had risen from procuratorships to the Prefecture of the Guard. In fact, he had been a protégé of Plautianus and in 205 when Plautianus fell owed his life to the intercession of Fabius Cilo.[108] He had no reason then to love Caracalla, or Domna if she was involved in Plautianus' downfall.[109] Still, his takeover was well received by the Senate: he was not Caracalla, at any rate.[110]

Domna must have asked herself whether she could have saved Caracalla if she had been at his side on the journey, instead of at Antioch, and the question has been asked in modern times.[111] It has to be answered in the negative: the causes of Caracalla's downfall were too deep for them to be obviated by any individual. She would have met the same fate as Sohaemias and Mamaea, who were to die with their imperial sons. Domna was now powerless, even in danger. If Macrinus was indeed a former protégé of Plautianus, that would be an extra reason for Domna to hate and fear him; she might not realize that Macrinus, who was pretending not to have organized Caracalla's murder, and deified him, might have had strong doubts about assassinating her too. Moreover, the new regime would allow acts of vengeance. Domna was not to know that the reign of Macrinus would last only a year and that his place would be taken by her own great-nephew, the grandson of her vigorous and wealthy elder sister Julia Maesa.[112] Young Elagabalus derived his *cognomen* from the service as high priest that he was rendering, as his great-grandfather was said to have done. Still only 14 years old, for a while he would be strictly under the control of his elders, as the 16-year old Nero had been when he came to power in 54. Not that the precedent would have been a comfort to Domna, if she read history. Nero's mother Agrippina the Younger had allegedly been afraid of the influence over him that his indulgent aunt Domitia Lepida enjoyed; and Lepida had been destroyed.[113]

Dio's scepticism about grief as the cause of Domna's first attempt at suicide (Herodian presents it as successful, and attributes it to her despair at the loss of her two sons – or enforced by Macrinus) is well justified.[114] To be sure, in the first paroxysm as she mourned a man that she had 'hated' during his lifetime, she struck herself a blow on the chest that according to Dio reactivated the tumour that she had long suffered from. But she was a strong woman. Geta's death had not killed her. Dio's explanation is that she could not bear to live as a private person, but there is probably more to it than that; it is unclear that Macrinus would have allowed her to survive, whether or not she entertained ambitions of her own. Other empresses had lived on after the assassination of their husbands – Domitia, the wife of Domitian, for example, although she is alleged to have been part of the conspiracy against him – and she had no threatening male relatives. But the insignificant Caesonia, wife of Caligula, had been killed in 41 along with her infant, and Licinius in 315 would think it worth while to eliminate Prisca and Valeria, wife and daughter of his predecessor Diocletian.[115] It was not likely that Macrinus would allow a woman who had been so close to the throne for twenty-five years to survive for long. And in her agony Domna allowed herself lengthy and atrocious abuse of the new emperor.[116] However, Macrinus was trying to legitimize himself by establishing connections with the preceding regime. He appropriated the name Antoninus for his son: that was meant to please the troops.[117] He allowed Domna to keep her former state and her bodyguard and sent her a positive message.[118] Domna did not reply: she was beginning allegedly to entertain hopes of keeping on her high political role.[119] It is not clear whether she was effectively in custody, but it was only after a last vain appeal to the soldiers, who had been mostly loyal to Caracalla, that she finally put an end to her life.[120] She evidently had no cause for hope from her sister and nieces and their sons at Emesa. She had already heard that there was nothing to be hoped for from Rome: Caracalla's death was welcomed there in aristocratic circles at least. It is not clear either what an appeal by Domna would mean: it could not be on her own behalf, as a prospective Semiramis or Nitocris, as Dio claims.[121] A woman could not rule, so probably it would have been on behalf of Elagabalus who was indeed to take over in a few months. Her eminence made any candidate she supported a danger to Macrinus. He ordered her to leave Antioch, where she was known to government and city officials and to their attendant troops. Presumably she would lose all or most of her retinue military and civilian, and no doubt she was afraid of being stripped of all her titles, some of them now manifestly inappropriate. She was no longer the Mother of the Emperor. Domitia, wife of Domitian, had never formally been stripped of the title Augusta, but was certainly never called by it during her long widowhood and had lived in retirement in the country.[122] Macrinus simply ordered Domna to go where she chose, but she probably saw herself being virtually confined to Emesa, like Maesa.[123] She did indeed leave the scene, by starving to death with the same command of herself that she had always shown.[124] News of reactions at Rome could have arrived about three months after Caracalla's death; Domna's then would have followed in about mid-July.[125]

7 Cultural activities

Julia Domna is one of Roman history's most famous women of culture; in fact, she is the final point of a study that takes Cornelia, mother of the Gracchi three and a half centuries earlier, as its beginning. Not that she did not have successors in the later Empire: Domna's association with philosophers was not unlike the situation at Rome from the 380s to 410, when aristocratic Christian women gathered around Jerome or Pelagius; of course allowance has to be made for her special position as empress. But what does her culture amount to? The prime items in Domna's cultural life are her education, as far as we can assess it, her friendship with the celebrated sophist Philostratus, member of a distinguished family originating in Lemnos that produced literary men in several generations,[1] the biography of Apollonius of Tyana that she urged Philostratus to write, and above all her being the centre of a 'circle' of eminent literary men and a significant patron. Of this extreme views have been held, at first romantic and exalted and, it must be admitted, sensationalist, more recently severely reductionist.

As a child and young girl Domna will have received an education appropriate to her sex and class, whatever that was for an aristocratic girl of Emesa. We have seen the cultural mix, Arab and Greek, that Emesa was likely to have been. She was also a Roman citizen, though that would have made less difference for a female, probably seen as the repository of native tradition. The value to a groom, expecting a dowry, of a literate, numerate, and cultivated bride was too obvious for her education to have been less than the best; even from a financial point of view, education was a good investment. In the first and second centuries AD there is a steep increase in evidence for the education of girls; that evidence declines in the third,[2] whether because there was less money about or because there were simply fewer and different sources. There will have been no shortage of money in Domna's family during her mid-second century youth. She may in any case have continued her education as a grown woman, even as empress. Men did that: in his mid-thirties one of Tiberius' pretexts for retiring from politics to the island of Rhodes was that he wanted to continue his education.[3] A Roman husband (especially one who had read the letters of the younger Pliny)[4] might well think of educating his wife. Severus was not a boor, and whatever he had to teach, Domna could have learnt. But while Domna is the first woman as far as we know to have studied rhetoric since Cornelia, we should not put overmuch weight on the silence of the sources.[5] Certainly Mamaea, Domna's niece, is presented as a woman capable of supervising the education of her son Alexander Severus. His invented sister is said to have been imbued with the refined accomplishments of the Greeks, but the sources, Herodian and the *Historia Augusta*, often draw on their own imaginations. The dynasty of Emesa had been raised to greatness before it was Mamaea's turn for education.[6]

Domna's friend Philostratus of Athens – for he held civic office there – was a sophist, and later in life he wrote a set of *Lives of the Sophists*. The literary and philosophic activity of Domna that is surveyed here is connected with the 'sophistic movement' that was so prominent in the first three centuries of the Principate, especially in the Greek east. Propagation, style and content would all have been affected by it.

Sophistry originated in the Greek world of the fifth century BC. It was primarily technical, and aimed at training speakers in persuasion, an essential skill in societies that depended on oral communication, with public assemblies and political decisions dominated by good speakers. What had become famous in fifth-century Athens took on new life in the Greek east under the Roman Empire. This burgeoning may be seen as a product of the leisure and affluence generated by the Augustan Peace; the period of bloom began in the Julio-Claudian age.[7] The Greek cities, especially those in Asia Minor, were prospering. The way they were run still mattered to local politicians, usually members of the wealthy elite who could afford the intensive training that the accomplished sophist required, as well as the expenditure that holding office entailed. The new wave of sophists, besides teaching, gave recitals in their home cities and elsewhere that sometimes were merely entertainments, demonstrating the practitioners' skills, but sometimes had a serious political, social, or philosophical purpose. Naturally, historical and in particular patriotic 'Churchillian' themes had a particular resonance for Greek-speakers under Roman rule: discourses harked back to better times, when Greece was free and heroic. Not everybody thought it worth dwelling on that.[8] Some sophists lectured on topics deeper even than Dio of Prusa's political harangues on harmony made to xenophobic or faction-ridden cities. They aimed to improve their fellow beings.

Sophists belonged mostly to families wealthy and distinguished enough to have sons educated to the highest level and were qualified, like Philostratus himself, to take a full part in the government of their cities, for which they might undertake embassies, to other cities and even to the imperial court. For Greek *poleis* regarded themselves as engaged in diplomacy with each other, and with the central government; the embassies to the emperor demanded keenness, boldness and skill, as Plutarch insisted.[9] So oratorical and political talents gave some sophists access to the highest political life of all, at court, and they could advise the emperor himself. Emperors, who had also to speak in public persuasively and hold their own in intellectual conversation at the dinner table, valued the same skills, and listened to the practitioners, as ambassadors, entertainers and sometimes as political counsellors. To be seen listening to principled advice was a good sign in an emperor. Dio of Prusa himself produced addresses on kingship for the Emperor Trajan. Not that they were always heard with appreciation or even understanding. On one occasion Trajan's reaction to Dio, the 'golden mouthed', as he was called, was good-natured bafflement.[10] The less forbiddingly intellectual practitioners enjoyed a vast following in the second century; according to Philostratus Adrian of Tyre performed in the Athenaeum at Rome under Commodus, and senators came running.[11]

We are not dealing with a simple phenomenon, and the 'Second Sophistic', as it was dubbed by Philostratus in his biographical work,[12] was not universally admired. Striving for technical perfection brought the temptation to make an effect, by charming or stunning, sometimes to the detriment of content, so that candour suffered. One of the characteristics that the Stoic Emperor M. Aurelius found to praise in his predecessor Pius was that he 'was not a sophist'.[13] In the ancient world there was a rift between philosophy on the one hand and rhetoric or sophistry on the other that went back to Greece of the fifth century BC and was made canonical by Plato's *Gorgias*; Plato mistrusted the facility of preaching professionals and the skills they taught, though he was not unaffected by the style. Accordingly a lost work of Plutarch – a philosopher if ever there was one – attacked the sophists.[14] The rift found famous expression in the career of Dio of Prusa, who has been supposed to pass from being a sophist to practising philosophy.[15] 'Philosopher' remained the more prestigious term, and 'sophistical' still has an unfavourable sense. Both claimed attention and influence. Philosophers had long lived in the households of leading Roman politicians and had been present at the imperial court since the beginning as advisers and teachers of the heirs. Some philosophers, such as the impressive, beautifully bearded Euphrates, and Artemidorus, whom Pliny the Younger revered,[16] acquired the status of gurus. These two were connected with the Stoic politician Musonius Rufus and lived through the reign of Domitian. In the second and early third century philosophers were assuming the enviably charismatic aspect of sages, such as they were were to become in fully-fledged Neo-Platonism.[17]

Nonetheless, like the senators who came from the Greek-speaking East in increasing numbers from the reign of Vespasian onwards, and perhaps more effectively, sophists gave that part of the Empire a voice in government, both by direct advice and by the power of their personalities. A sophist might himself be a senator: the most famous was the brilliant Herodes Atticus, member of Athens' most distinguished and wealthiest families and consul in 143.[18] Their influence too was often enhanced by careful attention to their personal appearance; at least one allegedly used pitch-plasters and cosmeticians to remove body hair.[19]

There is no equivalent in the modern world to a sophist, or rather there are a number of partial equivalents: inspirational preacher; television pundit; political adviser; mystic guru. (Philostratus made his hero Apollonius an incarnation of Proteus.)[20] These partial equivalents leave out what scholars regard as the core element. The sophist was a virtuoso artist in extempore declamation on historical or imaginary themes; he did demonstrations, gave tuition and was paid for it, helping his pupils to cope with the political world and perhaps to become practitioners themselves.[21]

Domna is said, like other politicians in eclipse, such as Cicero in the late 50s BC and the younger Seneca after AD 62, to have taken to philosophy when Plautianus was supreme in authority, that is, between about 200 and early 205, perhaps even as a calculated manoeuvre for her own safety.[22] But associations between Greek intellectuals and eminent Romans still active in politics went back into the second century BC: one need think only of Scipio Africanus and Panaetius, Ti. Gracchus and Blossius of Cumae, who was killed in the purge that followed Gracchus' assassination in 133 BC.[23] Domna was likely all through her life as empress to encounter learned men and charlatans alike, because this period coincided with travels through the Greek east, Egypt and Africa. The court was a magnet. The first occasion in the reign of Severus when men of culture are mentioned as being assembled at court is during the imperial tour of Africa, when the emperor gathered 'men of talent from all over the world'.[24] Given that the author of this remark was a sophist and biographer of sophists, it is probable that some of these men were philosophers and sophists as well as architects and sculptors destined for the building operations at Lepcis. But when Domna first encountered Philostratus is unknown. The hoplite generalship at Athens, with which he was entrusted at some point, perhaps the beginning of his career, was a demanding post that he can hardly have held in absence, and he became a member of the city council (*boule*).[25] It is a plausible suggestion that Philostratus made himself known to the court in 203, on its return to Rome from Africa.[26] He claims in the *Life of Apollonius* to have seen the tides of Ocean,[27] and this has led to the convincing idea that he was present with the imperial family in Gaul and even went over the Channel to Britain, 208–11. He might have obtained his commission to write the *Life of Apollonius* at Rome in 212 or at the court in Nicomedia in the winter of 214–15, or even, most appropriately, at Apollonius' birthplace of Tyana when the rulers passed through Cappadocia in 215.[28] When he recalls a discussion on sophists with a Gordian, one of two future emperors of that name, themselves of Anatolian origin, which took place at Daphne, a suburb 8 km. out of Syrian Antioch, he may even then have been on tour with Domna or domiciled with her in Syria, and there is no reason to believe that he ever left her entourage.[29] Not every sophist need be after public office; proximity to the court was also prestigious.[30]

Insight into the relationship between the sophist and his imperial friend should be provided by the *Letter* to her that is ascribed to him. It urges her first to believe that Plato really admired Gorgias and imitated his rhetorical style, which was more elaborate than that of Aeschines the Socratic, favoured by Domna; she is to persuade Plutarch not to be annoyed with the sophists. It was probably Plutarch's lost attack on the sophists to which the *Letter* refers.[31]

The obvious problem that makes G. W. Bowersock deny the authenticity of this *Letter* lies in this last section.[32] Domna is told that she will know what name to call Plutarch if she fails to persuade him to change his mind – a name that the writer knows but cannot utter. The writer ineptly assumed, then, that Plutarch was still alive at the turn of the second and third centuries. The motive of the imposter would have been to enhance the reputation of sophists by showing the eminent Philostratus vigorously enlisting the aid of an imperial patron in their defence. But Bowersock has a second reason for rejecting the *Letter*: its verbal and thematic resemblance to Philostratus's life of Gorgias, making use in particular of the concepts of *apostaseis* and *prosbolai* (the use of detached phrases and 'stabs' at a subject); Philostratus' biographies were written some years after Domna's death, as the dedication to Gordian shows. This reason is not compelling. As R. J. Penella points out, Philostratus could have plundered his own earlier letter or drawn twice on material that was always available to him, including the two technical terms, a linked pair. As to the apparent mistake over Plutarch's life-span, which is gross, it might rather be a playful allusion to the fact that Plutarch's opinions were in fact beyond changing, even by an empress; Philostratus is exhibiting his familiarity with her. C. P. Jones convincingly argues that Philostratus was ornately attacking Plutarch's *work*, not a living Plutarch. It would perhaps be safest, then, to entertain the idea, acknowledged by E. Hemelrijk, that the *Letter* is authentic in the sense that it is the work of Philostratus, but that it is a literary creation of his, never sent to Domna, but presenting topics that were in the air and perhaps actually talked over by them; clearly it is intended to be seen as a continuation of an earlier discussion. The *Letter* that precedes it, 72, is addressed to Caracalla but contains material that cannot possibly have been sent to the living emperor. The author, after the death of his patron, was insisting on his influence with her and her son, perhaps exaggerating it.[33] Certainly he boasted about being a member of her 'circle'.

Philostratus describes Domna as a 'philosopher', or, more broadly 'a lover of wisdom', in our terms perhaps an 'intellectual', who loved literary discussion and had a 'circle' (*kuklos*) of savants round her.[34] Such a feature of Severan court society would have had a precursor in the group of men round Hadrian's wife Sabina, which came to an abrupt end when C. Suetonius Tranquillus the biographer and others were found by Hadrian to be too familiar with her.[35] Domna's 'circle' on the other hand has been presented in exalted terms, coming to scholarly attention in an age, the nineteenth century, when women's education and capacities were being vehemently urged – and pruriently watched. It was admiration that swayed ideas of

Domna's 'circle', except when Messalina was brought into comparison with her.

In Domna's own time wealthy women who interested themselves in philosophy and even engaged personal tutors had been the subject of innuendo and open ridicule, even to male scholars, as Lucian's skit makes clear:

> And yet, I suppose, what men do is bearable. But the women! This is another fad of women, to have educated men at their disposal, who are living with them on a salary and dancing attendance behind their litters. They think that it is a singular accomplishment, if it is said that they are educated, and philosophers, and write odes that are not much inferior to Sappho's. And it's on that account that they themselves hang about hirelings, practitioners of rhetoric, literature, and philosophy, and listen to them – when? (Here's another ridiculous thing.) When they are in the middle of their toilet or their hair is being dressed or as a distraction at dinner. They have no time for it otherwise. It often happens that just as the philosopher is expounding something, the ladies' maid comes in and proffers her a *billet doux* from her paramour, and those arguments on chastity hang fire until she has written a reply to the paramour; then she trips back to hear them.

These allegations of shallowness and bad manners are an enlightening counterpoint to the praise of the serious Roman philosopher and senator Arulenus Rusticus, who perished under Domitian, and who once, when listening to a discourse of Plutarch's, refused to read a letter brought to him from the emperor himself until the lecture was over.[36]

Hostility to *femmes savantes* has remained until recent times, but it is in part because of the over-excited interest that the 'circle' aroused that the construction has been attacked, proved vulnerable, and in the view of many scholars demolished, as a 'welter of error and misunderstanding'. G. W. Bowersock, opening his attack, noted the enthusiasm of those who believed in the importance and seriousness of Domna's 'circle': it made her an alluring combination of Catherine de' Medici, Queen Christina of Sweden, and the Empress Messalina (that is, of political acumen and caprice, intellectualism and vice).[37] Indeed, Domna has been tantalizingly compared with Aspasia,[38] the learned and influential mistress of Pericles of Athens, and that is enough to raise eyebrows: a statesman's mistress is hardly fit precedent for an emperor's wife, still less for an emperor's mother. One can only suppose that Aspasia's extraordinary intellectual qualities overlaid her anomalous social position. The philosopher whom Domna admired, Aeschines of Sphettus, had admittedly written a dialogue named after Aspasia, but a recent comparison that made use of Aspasia was still with an imperial mistress: Lucian compared her with Lucius Verus' mistress Panthea.[39]

Bowersock traces the origin of the lists of members of Domna's group back to Victor Duruy's *Histoire de Rome* of 1879: 'the current notion of Julia's circle, . . . with the list of its members and a nice allusion to Renaissance courts, is nothing more than a nineteenth-century fabrication'.[40] In 1907 K. Münscher named other literary men, apart from Philostratus and the sophist Philiscus of Thessaly, who, according to Philostratus, joined 'geometricians and philosophers' associated with Domna at the beginning of Caracalla's sole rule, when he arrived in Rome to defend himself in a legal action.[41] Caracalla's tutor Aelius Antipater of Hierapolis in Phrygia and in charge of Greek correspondence by 200, was also a plausible contact,[42] and so was Philostratus' future dedicatee (and future emperor) Gordian, whether I or II. Münscher also added Aspasius of Ravenna, 'Oppian', the author of the poem *Cynegetica* dedicated to Caracalla, a native of Apameia in Syria,[43] and the prose writer Aelian, perhaps born a slave in Praeneste, but a celebrated stylist in Greek, most famous for his *Natural History of Animals*.[44] Poetry is not prominent; it was at a low ebb at the end of the second century. Then there were the lawyers, Papinian, probably of African origin, Ulpian, who came from Tyre, and Julius Paulus, of unknown origin; the medical profession was represented by the shadowy figure of Serenus Sammonicus, one of Caracalla's victims in 212, but whom Champlin finds 'a scholar, a translator, and a poet', and by Galen of Pergamum. It is unfortunate that the work that most intimately links the great physician to women members of the imperial family, perhaps Domna and Maesa, as well as to the emperors themselves, Severus and his sons, was the digression on hair dyes that he reluctantly composed for them.[45]

The consular historians Cassius Dio of Bithynia and Marius Maximus were obvious candidates.[46] Indeed, C. R. Whittaker has suggested that the account of Domitian's murder in 96 given by Dio is made as close as possible to the circumstances of Commodus' murder – the essentials, assassination organized by a palace cabal, carried out by a servant – precisely for the benefit of Domna. She revered Apollonius of Tyana, and he prophesied the earlier assassination.[47] But this is a tenuous link: literary as well as political reasons could have suggested the parallels, and the factual basis was similar.

Other Greek luminaries, included in the list drawn up a decade after Münscher by M. Platnauer,[48] were Apollonius of Athens, Athenaeus of Naucratis in Egypt, author of the *Philosophers at Dinner*, Heracleides of Lycia, Hermocrates of Phocaea,[49] and Alexander of Aphrodisias, the influential commentator on Aristotle. The best known of Platnauer's candidates is Diogenes Laertius, author of *Lives of the Philosophers*. Diogenes addressed his book to a woman, unnamed but usually identified with Domna or with Arria, an aristocratic friend of Galen – who was herself ascribed to the 'circle' by M. Platnauer, for she was interested in philosophy, especially in Plato.[50]

To substantiate the high claims made for Domna's 'circle', then, all the possible well-known intellectuals of the age of the Severi have been enlisted. Not only was there a long and resounding roll of members, but also it has been felt that the tone was set by Domna's origins in Emesa: the 'circle' bore an eastern character. Whether even the most inclusive list of members justifies that idea is questionable. Most of the enlisted men are Greek-speakers, but so were the majority of intellectuals. It is Asia Minor that predominates, with mainland Greece also doing well, and Apameia, Tyre and Naucratis are the only cities to produce possible members of the 'circle' outside traditional Greek-speaking areas. Any 'oriental' tendency must be dismissed at once.

In a further claim, the 'circle' allegedly was not of a purely literary character: in a society where politics were personal, it has been assigned a political significance. Domna's 'circle' has been taken to be favourable to Geta because she is supposed to have preferred him and because of his supposed mildness in comparison with Caracalla's bellicosity.[51] Names have been mentioned, those of Aelius Antipater, who was forced into suicide on Geta's death; the elder Philostratus, on the basis of a letter of reproach sent to 'Antoninus' (nonetheless he stayed at court after 211); Serenus Sammonicus, whose works, dedicated to him, were Geta's favourite reading, according to the *Historia Augusta*; Gordian; and Dio, who as a propertied senator suffered from the cost of Caracalla's campaigns and from the autocratic rule of the Severi. Then there is the historian Asinius Quadratus, who may have held the proconsulate of Asia under Caracalla and seems to have dedicated a statue to him, showing no genuine devotion, only self-interest and common prudence.[52] Such judgments on the political colour of the 'circle' are fanciful, and a gratuitous refinement on the basic concept. That is what has to be assessed.

The tenuousness of the entire network is immediately clear if we ask how many of these men were without doubt known personally to Domna besides Philostratus and Philiscus: the two historians Dio and Maximus; the three jurists Papinian, Ulpian, and Paulus; Antipater and Galen. Bowersock's acute and harsh critique makes the nature and membership of the salon markedly less exciting than the received accounts. Most of the intellectuals on modern lists cannot be shown to be members. As to others who might genuinely belong, Bowersock is prepared to admit the Gordian who conversed with Philostratus outside Antioch, where Domna spent many months. Even so, if Gordian I is meant rather than Gordian II, that does not guarantee that he was there as a courtier rather than as governor of the province of Syria. Not only that: in Bowersock's view the real members will have been second-raters, those whose official duties did not give them something better to do, men whose names would mean nothing to us if we knew them.[53] Mobility was a feature of Roman official life: ambitious men from the Greek-speaking cities of the Empire went on to chairs at Athens or Rome and to positions in the imperial service.[54]

These criticisms do not demolish the 'circle' altogether. Other men than the few named may well have been known personally to the empress. Again, the very uncertainty about what took a Gordian to Syria is suggestive. First, a sharp distinction between membership and non-membership might be hard to maintain; it raises the question of what membership of a 'salon' or *kuklos* might mean. Regular plenary meetings, as of a statutory committee, must not be presupposed, nor even the regular 'Thursdays' of a European hostess. Again, the larger the 'circle' the less tight the structure becomes, because of the variety of interests and extraneous commitments involved. So with Gordian I and other senators and equestrian officials employed intermittently on official business: the guest membership of a governor on a temporary basis (and afterwards by correspondence) is not ruled out. Domna may have been in the habit of entertaining her gurus as she found them, in small groups of two or three at a time, according to their expertise, literary or philosophical. It is a question then how far the men Domna consulted were linked one with another to form Philostratus' single 'circle'. We do not know what form the séances took, joint discussions, separate consultations, or a mix. Practical considerations suggest that the lower-ranking professional intellectuals joined in common discussions with amateurs too, except when official duties carried these men elsewhere. They might also have been split by the irreconcilable rivalries of courtiers, but it would have been in the interests of each to know what the others were saying, and to adapt his own discourse to what the patron and her other advisers were discussing. Suetonius draws an amusing sketch of the savants attendant on the Emperor Tiberius trying to discover what he had last been reading, but Domna is unlikely to have frightened her 'circle' quite so much.[55]

Another factor to take into account, besides the Empire-wide duties of any high-ranking members, is the mobility of the imperial court itself. Except where officials attached to the person of the emperor were concerned, there must be something almost aleatory about Domna's encounters with career intellectuals committed to official business. Those who could control their own careers – making professional tours such as the Prusan Dio's – could be much more regular attenders. Certainly only those of dependent standing, not senators and superior *equites* with official duties to see to, would have accompanied Domna on her travels. The exceptions would be prefects of the Praetorian Guard, jurisconsults and others whose duties kept them with the moving capital that the court was becoming.[56]

If one recognizes that the structure of the *kuklos* must necessarily have been loose and thinks less of 'membership' than of 'participation', there is no need to relegate participants more or less wholesale to second-rate status. Domna's activities may rightly be compared with those of her intellectual niece Mamaea, who is said to have summoned Origen to visit her in Antioch, probably in 232–4, so that she could learn from his knowledge of divine things.[57] Probably Domna enticed some big fish to attend on her for short periods; to be sure, constant attendants may have been lesser fry who congratulated themselves on their luck. Such a view of a *kuklos* flexible in size and composition makes it unnecessary to hold that such great figures as Papinian and Antipater were too important to waste time as members of a salon.[58] Culture was an integral and paraded part of the lives of the greatest men of the second and early third centuries. And the leader of the group was the wife of their master. Whatever our difficulties, it seems that Philiscus, coming to Rome from his native Thessaly, evidently had no difficulty in recognizing which men were connected with the 'circle'.

Another factor, time, also contributed to the fluidity of the *kyklos*, not only through deaths and retirements natural and forced. It could have meant something different to Domna at different periods of her life. She is said to have turned her attention to intellectual pursuits because of the enmity of Plautianus when she fell out of favour with her husband; so G. W. Bowersock dates the beginning of the 'circle' to the late 190s. Intellectual activity filled a gap left during Plautianus' ascendancy,[59] but it survived as she returned to the centre of power and even when she was engaged on routine duties during her last journey to the east. Nor need one hold that a woman strenuously engaged in political life and the development of the new Severan imperial court would have no time to cultivate a literary circle; that might have been part of the development, so that Domna's existing involvement in cultural matters simply became more prominent when she had to avoid conspicuous political activity. Half a century later a queen reigning in Palmyra, Zenobia, emulated Domna and gathered round herself what R. Stoneman has called 'a cabinet of intellectuals'.[60] As with the male politicians in retirement whose example she may have been following in the years of Plautianus' dominance, an interest in philosophy and rhetoric became for a while the sustenance of her life.

The men she talked to will have changed too. During the period of eclipse, association with Domna could have been damaging to an ambitious man's career; some may well have avoided her. After 205 she could have thrown the net wider, and those who had failed to put in an appearance before would have been eager for acceptance. Dio has her devoting herself in Caracalla's reign to receiving the most prominent men and studying philosophy with them.[61] The upheaval of 211 cut out at least two of her probable friends, Papinian and Antipater, but as her influence did not diminish under Caracalla there was no reason for a break in 211–12. And in her double bereavement the consolations of philosophy could have become even more important to her again.

Dio's assertion about the participation of leading men is more significant than the fact that Philostratus cherished his own and thought it deserved mentioning, as Eusebius also found Mamaea's summons to Origen something to record. In claiming that Domna's philosophers were not very different from those ridiculed by the second century satirist Lucian for hiring themselves out to the rich and powerful,[62] Bowersock might have nuanced his criticism a little. Discussion between Domna and eminent men does not make them hirelings: there was a stock of intellectuals all over the Empire; she would have had the pick wherever she went, unless they were in pursuit of offices more readily available from other patrons or were out of reach on official business. And she worked for her protégés, demonstrably for the lesser ones. The Empress Plotina had interested herself in the Athenian schools of philosophy, securing the Epicureans the right to appoint as its head a man who was not a Roman citizen; no doubt the school had a particular candidate in mind, whose application was blocked because he lacked Roman citizenship. Now Domna played her part in the appointment of a candidate for the chair of literature that Vespasian had established at Athens, Philiscus of Thessaly, though Caracalla did not allow him exemption from the public duties he owed his maternal community, the Heordaeans of Macedonia. This transaction seems to have taken place at Rome, so not later than 212.[63]

Domna earned the epithet 'the wise', or 'the philosopher' from Philostratus (admittedly not a disinterested witness), and she may well have gone as deeply into that subject as any woman could, or thought she could, in the ancient world.[64] The question is that of the ideological content of her studies, as well as of their depth. If philosophical in the narrowest sense, they were likely at that point in history to be essentially Platonic, for this was the school that was in vogue, as Christianity was to come to be in religion, with the two ways being found to be mutually reconcilable.[65] On the basis of the revival of dogmatic Platonism in the first century AD, the 'middle Platonists' of the second century forged from Plato's dialogues a body of systematic doctrine. Early in the second century Plotina's protégés were Epicureans of the school at Athens; Marcus Aurelius was a distinguished and articulate Stoic. However, the heyday of those sects was over; Neo-Platonism was the coming doctrine, offering ground on which argument on vital issues could be fought out. Here at last it seems legitimate to suspect Syrian input. J. Balty has discovered links between Neo-Platonism and the city of Apameia, next door to Emesa. The oracle of Zeus Belos there existed in a 'climate of magic', and the possible founder of the Neo-Platonic school, Numenius, taught there. The city was staunchly loyal to its deities even when in the Christian fourth century the performance of pagan rites was actively being discouraged. It had always been less open to new influences such as Christianity than the cosmopolitan centre of Antioch, where Christians had made an early appearance and received their name (though probably as a derisive nickname – 'Christ-men') in the early 40s AD. But the philosophy handled by Domna was already mainstream.[66]

Perhaps we should not be too restrictive about Domna's interests, even about particular areas of intellectual interest. Our possession of Philostratus' work pushes us in the direction of philosophy and rhetoric, so that little or no attention is paid to her possible interest in, say, poetry. But she is credited by Philostratus with love of all rhetoric, which she encouraged, and that does not suggest limited cultural horizons.[67] Of all the intellectuals mentioned as possible members of her 'circle', three she certainly knew personally were the jurists, Papinian, Paulus and Ulpian, probably the most powerful thinkers of the age, Papinian especially acute, but Ulpian usefully devoting himself to the exposition of Roman law for the benefit of Caracalla's newly enfranchised citizens. Paulus' daughter may have been the first wife of Domna's great-nephew Elagabalus (220).[68] But we know nothing of any engagement of Domna's with these men.

Besides philosophers, Philiscus found Domna in conversation with 'geometricians', and that may indicate, however unsatisfactorily, one of her other interests. Whether these 'geometricians' were actually astrologers has been a question, and the mystical aspect has been seen as deriving from Domna's oriental background.[69] Severus was certainly devoted to astrology, and although his particular interest was noticed, it was no disgrace. Astrology, linked with the Stoic doctrine of the unity of the universe, was a reputable study. Tiberius was adept, and he was the close friend of another expert, Ti. Claudius Thrasyllus (who was also renowned as a Platonist), founder of a remarkable dynasty of intellectuals and imperial aides that came to be linked with the first century dynasty of Emesa.[70]

Nonetheless, the juxtaposition of geometricians and philosophers favours the alternative interpretation that the former were practitioners of 'liberal studies', including mathematics itself. That links well with philosophical studies. Mathematics was part of the stock of Platonic and Pythagorean philosophers, and J.-J. Flinterman has gone on to argue that Domna's disputants were 'a variegated assortment', including Platonic or Pythagorean philosophers and sophists and (with some probability) that one of the subjects of discussion was the relative merits of philosophy and rhetoric, a subject echoed in the notorious *Letter*.[71] The Neo-Pythagoreans, who went back to the hellenistic age, claimed to be following the teachings and way of life of the sixth-century philosopher. Scientific theories on number symbolism and harmony ran parallel with sectarian religious practices, notably vegetarianism, which followed from belief in the transmigration of souls.[72] Plato himself had favoured Pythagorean ideas, and Neo-Platonism followed suit.

Philosophy was part of literature, certainly for Philostratus and presumably for Domna too: no clear distinction of the two activities is to be expected.[73] Literature naturally meant 'all forms of eloquence', in Philostratus' words, and it could be studied for its style. He describes Domna as 'a lover of all rhetorical discussion' and also as a 'philosopher of Aeschines', meaning that she had studied Aeschines' Socratic dialogue: its 'remarkably restrained style' interested her.[74] Plato too was a model of style, and was imitated by Dio of Prusa, according to Philostratus; but even Plato was influenced by Gorgias.[75] However, even if Domna's interest, and that of other students of philosophy in the second and early third centuries, was largely in style, it must at some level include an interest in content as well.[76]

As to the standard at which Domna pursued her studies in whatever fields, A. R. Birley may be right to be sceptical: he is judging from the content of Philostratus' *Life of Apollonius* and considers that they meant 'a combination of religious superstition with somewhat pretentious erudition'.[77] Still, however superficial and fragile the achievement, something lofty along lines currently in vogue was certainly the aim. Especially in her encounters with the most distinguished intellectuals of the age Domna will have done her best to hold her own. Even leaving aside the glorious classical models of philosophical debate provided by Plato, she and her friends may have seen themselves recreating the discussions envisaged by Plutarch, whose work Domna evidently knew. Such serious philosophical symposia had been parodied by Lucian, as in his *Symposium, or, the Lapiths*. A more recent model than Plutarch's dialogues, in symposium form, was Athenaeus' *Philosophers at Dinner*, completed in the early 190s. This work is a holdall of excerpts, but its framework is suggestive. Besides philosophy, literature, law and medicine are discussed. The Roman host was an historical character, and Galen is also introduced. Whatever the level of Domna's discussions, she and the other participants would have been conscious that they were justifying and so testing their credentials as intellectuals.

One thing that Domna was certainly responsible for was encouraging Philostratus, probably when the court was travelling abroad in the east, to compose his work on the first century thaumaturge and sage Apollonius of Tyana, a man who was 'wise, a Greek, and a good counsellor'. This work, which has been ascribed 'assertive hellenism', is the tangible relic of Domna's intellectual preoccupations, which have to be approached through it.[78] The composition of Philostratus' *Life of Apollonius* did not begin until after Severus' death, but Domna's interest in the sage may have persisted over a number of years.

The content of the *Life* is simple but sensational. Apollonius had wandered the Empire from the time of Tiberius, gone to India and encountered and outfaced the most eminent and formidable persons, such as the Emperor Domitian (forty-four years separated these two reigns), offering them rebuke and advice. He was built up into a figure fit to match Christ himself, with his own miracles, and without the disadvantage of being embedded in an alien Judaism, and he was long revered; but he had not become the founder of a reformed paganism. Necessarily, too, the work is suspect in its sources and in its details, even if some of the stories it tells were not so obviously tall.

The question is how far the book reflects the philosophical and religious beliefs of the empress who commissioned it. Philostratus continued his work after Domna's death, which explains why he did not dedicate it to her, completing it some time before 238, perhaps by 222,[79] and even if that were in part due to respect for her memory or at the behest of her surviving relatives in the dynasty, it suggests that there was a wider audience for the story and its moral. Domna's taste and outlook were not unduly eccentric. In fact, stripped of the miraculous trimmings, the views that the work embodies are hardly startling. They are simple as well as conventional, and not systematized. The messages conveyed by the biography include reverence for traditional religion, supported and made more graphic by techniques learned from a newer cult; an attitude towards emperors, especially predatory emperors, that eastern aristocrats, even if they were not members of the

Senate, might well entertain; and a predictably high estimate of the power of sophists' discourse over their hearers. The advice conveyed by Apollonius to Vespasian is trite and simple: the monarch has to be liberal, not to let his absolute power descend into arbitrariness, to check subversive movements only by making it certain that they will be punished if put into action; the emperor must respect the laws, yielding to them when his private interests are concerned, and he must pay particular regard to the gods; he must be careful over the education of his sons, and they must be controlled; freedmen too have to be kept in check. Finally, the selection of governors must ensure that men are chosen who are appropriate to the provinces, especially those of the east. The subject of the ruler's relation to the law was a particularly well-worn one, definitively settled under Severus in favour of the emperor.[80]

What Domna sanctioned, then, was politically conservative. Did it embody warnings for contemporary politicians? It has been an irresistible temptation to scholars tormented by scarcity of evidence to find contemporary references in the *Life*. As a courtier Philostratus is unlikely to have made such allusions until after the death of the individuals involved, and then they are pointless, except as interesting historical parallels or as warnings. Although accepted villains such as Nero and Commodus had redeeming features in the eyes of Greeks, there is nothing to offend in the attitude that Apollonius takes towards previous rulers. Tiberius is alarming, Nero a bad egg with some good features (his plan to cut a canal across the Isthmus of Corinth, his liberation of Greece), Vespasian was acceptable, but for his return of Greeks to direct Roman rule, the reign of Titus good, Domitian a frightful tyrant; these conceptions had grown up long since.[81] J.-J. Flinterman's stringent examination of attempts to read specific contemporary references into the work reduces them to two: fratricide and a monarch's identification of himself with the Sun god. There is also the demand that Greeks should govern Greek-speaking provinces, Latin-speakers the western.[82] There is nothing systematic in these items. Not unnaturally Flinterman ends by acknowledging Philostratus' restricted field of vision with regard to socio-political developments, as compared with that of the senator and historian Dio.[83] Only her advice to Caracalla – reported by Dio – suggests that Domna was any more far-sighted.

Slightly more touchy in a work commissioned by and for an empress is Philostratus' evident conception of relations between philosophers and rulers (since philosophers cannot be rulers in an imperfect world, though rulers can be philosophers, as M. Aurelius had shown). The philosopher, inherently wise, is naturally the counsellor of the ruler, assuming that the ruler is a good one; famous examples such as that of Thrasea Paetus and the Helvidii Prisci from the reign of Nero and even of Vespasian, still more from that of Domitian, showed that the philosopher was implacably opposed to the tyrant. This explains the enhanced reputation of philosophers and the development, especially of Cynics and Neo-Pythagoreans, into gurus; Apollonius himself has superhuman qualities, which are not credited to any monarch that he encounters.[84] Whatever the brutal facts of his reign, there is no doubt that Severus was keen to appear as a 'good' ruler: so much is suggested by his assimilation of himself, first to Pertinax, then to M. Aurelius and his three predecessors. He may well have believed himself to be a good ruler too, one who, like Vespasian after the Year of the Four Emperors, had brought settled peace; his military campaigns against his rivals and the subsequent executions, as well as those carried out after the discovery of conspiracies, were forced upon him. Naturally he was deified by his sons. Moreover, the *Life of Apollonius* deals with events that took place a century or more before it was written. Shakespeare in 1606, the year after the Gunpowder Plot, was able to put on before King James VI and I a play that dealt with the political and moral ruin of a monarch, *King Lear*. As it had under the Roman Empire, the theme of monarchy preoccupied the thinking classes. Shakespeare was in no danger on that occasion: James did not imagine that he was vulnerable in the same way as Lear. However, as A. R. Birley reminds me, Ben Jonson got into trouble for *Sejanus his Fall* and Elizabeth I is supposed to have reacted emotionally to *Richard II*, set in the line of English kings, storming out with the words 'I am Richard!'

It is sensible then not to interpret features of the work as direct guides to contemporary politics: the restrictions of genre and the caution of the writer in the instability of the times make that as intellectually dangerous to the reader as it would have been physically dangerous to Philostratus.[85] Even more rash are the attempts that J.-J. Flinterman records to fit the work into Marxist ideological schemata.[86]

However, there is another level to the *Life* beyond its commonplace and jejune historical and political content: its religious and philosophical bent. It is possible to see Apollonius as a pagan parallel and rival of Christ (his biographer took pains to get him acquitted of any charge of magic).[87] That idea too should be treated cautiously. We are not dealing with the deliberate construction of a pagan rival to Christ,[88] rather with parallel developments in an age that was becoming increasingly anxious about the effectiveness of the distant emperor, the fate of individuals in a vast Empire, their physical, material, and moral welfare, and about the fate of that Empire itself. Under Marcus there had been incursions from beyond the Danube into central Greece, and the troops of L. Verus, returning from campaigns against the Parthians, had brought plague back with them. Saviour figures could arise in a variety of traditions. The saga of the pagan thaumaturge lacked the sternly monotheistic Jewish framework that made Christianity, and Christ, unique.

There is nothing about Christianity in Philostratus' *Life*, but it was familiar to Pliny and Tacitus; Domna must have known about it. Besides, the last notable attack on the Christians had been in 177 at Lugdunum, only just over a decade before Domna arrived there.[89] In spite of some martyrdoms under Severus there is no reason to believe that he held strong views on Christianity, and Domna may have felt anything between the kind of interest and even sympathy that Paul met with from Roman officials on his travels and the contempt that can be seen in Tacitus' account of the aftermath of the fire at Rome and in Pliny's letter to Trajan on the Christians of Bithynia-Pontus.[90] There is no sign either of interest in Judaism on Domna's part that would have pre-empted a move towards Christianity. Judaism had long attracted high-class Romans and, a generation after the fall of Jerusalem in 70 and the end of the Church there, could be seen as quite distinct from its offshoot. Now there was increasing hostility between Jews and gentile Christians. Neither is known to have provided Domna with an interlocutor.

Admittedly the Severan age was one of syncretism and experiment. Sex. Julius Africanus (*c.*160–240), a Christian of Jerusalem and Emmaus, wrote a *Chronographia* arguing that the world had half a millennium to run after the birth of Christ. In this syncretist atmosphere he enjoyed the favour of Elagabalus and Alexander Severus, securing help from the first for Emmaus and with it the title of Nicopolis, under the second installing the public library in the Pantheon at Rome, and dedicating his encyclopaedia, the *Cesti*, to the emperor. There is nothing to be said for the tale that Alexander had a collection of divine images including one of Christ; but there is no reason to doubt his mother's summons of Origen to her side nor the fact that she was addressed by the presbyter of Rome, Hippolytus.[91] But that was in the two generations that followed Domna's. We cannot make her a Jewish proselyte or a Christian convert.

R. Syme provocatively drew attention to the close proximity in the second century of Epicureans and Christians. 'Atheists both. . . . Both denied the gods, divination, the science of the Chaldaeans, and both asserted freedom of the will, the primacy of friendship, community of living, the practice of charity. Finally, they rejected distinctions of birth, wealth, or rank'.[92] In truth, however similar they may have seemed to outsiders, Christians and Epicureans were poles apart doctrinally: Epicurus' gods do not suffer or save. But the tenets and practices of both were alien to the interests of an empress (denying the science of the Chaldaeans; neglect of rank). Her interests, as far as we have been able to glimpse them, lay with the Platonists and Pythagoreans.

The poverty of contemporary reference in Philostratus' romanticized, even mythologized, biography makes J.-J. Flinterman see the author's relationship with his Severan patrons in purely literary terms. Scholars have played down the ideological content of the work altogether, and seen Philostratus as aiming, as a professional writer, to produce a well-rounded and entertaining piece of literature, in E. Bowie's words, rather than to further a propagandist interpretation of Apollonius as a Pythagorean sage.[93]

When Domna offered her commission, then, was it the sheer entertainment of Apollonius' occasionally picaresque adventures that drew her to the subject? There was probably more than that: triteness does not imply lack of sincerity. The account is allegedly a reworking of essays or a scrapbook written by Apollonius' disciple Damis of Nineveh, but even if that claim were accepted it need have no bearing on Domna's interest: the pedigree was less important than the tone. When the court was in the east, as it was from 213 until Domna's death, Domna was exposed to stories that magnified Apollonius' achievements and importance, even if she had not known them from her earliest childhood.[94] The commission suggests a woman who was attracted to guides to life, especially guides for rulers. She had come to power suddenly from the outer reaches of imperial society, and needed guidance then, as young women whose education may not have been taken as far as Domna's do when they marry into English royalty. On a mundane level, young Pompey the Great, coming to the consulship of 70 BC after years of fighting, had needed expert written advice from a constitutional expert, M. Terentius Varro, on the subject of senatorial procedure.[95] But Domna was past that stage. Her request to Philostratus seems to have come when the Severi had been in power for nearly a quarter of a century. After the death of her husband and the murder of her younger son an authoritative counsellor on a higher level, part-figment as he might be, would have been welcome.

8 Image and cult

Now comes a crucial part of any enquiry into Domna's life and significance as an historical figure. The question is how far she and her dynasty were instrumental in propelling Roman religion and in particular the imperial cult towards the oriental and the exotic. Such a Severan shift may be seen as a crucial part of a downturn in Roman political and cultural life for which the dynasty was responsible. These views were supported with material from the background of Severus himself as well as from that of Domna, suggesting that Severus came to know varieties of oriental cult when he was in command of a legion in northern Syria in 179.[1] Art too has been a field of contention centring on the conceptions of 'orientalization' and 'decline', as opposed to stasis, reaction, or development according to internal formal dynamics. As to religion, the idea of a Severan shift takes two forms: the first concerns the dynasty's introduction of exotic cults into the Roman pantheon, the second extravagant claims for the identity of the rulers as divine. The pervasive views of the early twentieth century have made scholars hypersensitive to special intensity and to anomalies in Severan religious ambitions, whether they took the form of introducing new deities associated or even identified with themselves, or of ratcheting up their own status in relation to the Graeco-Roman pantheon, both favouring the advance of tyranny. These two developments, and Domna's role in them, will be considered in turn.[2]

Something has already been said in the Introduction about the terms used in modern times for these discussions. Seeing an 'oriental' has always depended on taking some standpoint in the 'west'. Ever since the struggles of Greece and Persia in the fifth century BC there had been the temptation that still survives to identify the oriental with the despotic. For mainland Greeks, who had fought off the Persian monarchs Darius and Xerxes, their fellow Greek-speakers in Asia Minor were in danger of being softened by having been under the governance of Persia.[3] For Romans of the second century BC, mainland Greece itself seemed alien and, freed and then subjugated by Rome, decadent. In the Roman Empire the league of Greek cities that comprised the Roman province of Asia, now western Turkey, carefully entitled themselves 'the Greeks from Asia' ('*hoi apo tes Asias*

Hellenes').[4] Nineteenth- and early twentieth-century discussions also use the term 'Semitic', which belongs to race and language. What they had in mind was the Syrian, Palmyrene, Jewish, Punic, and Arab cultural influence exercised by peoples using those languages. Already in the early second century AD that influence was problematical for Romans, as Tacitus' description of Jewish customs shows, and Juvenal's distaste for the flowing of the Syrian Orontes into the Tiber.[5]

Roman religion ensured the success, even the survival, of the commonwealth by maintaining Rome's good relations with the gods. When Augustus came to power after two decades of civil war he reassuringly revived cults and rebuilt temples, eighty-two, he claims.[6] But the story of the Great Mother shows that Roman state religion was not exclusive. Already in the last decade of the third century a deity from Phrygia in Asia Minor had been brought to Rome, installed there, and naturalized: the Great Mother. It took more than two centuries for Romans to become accustomed to her priests, the castrated Galli, but by Herodian's time the Romans had a particular veneration for her, so he says.[7]

In a world-wide Empire syncretism and the rise of deities with universal appeal were only to be expected, especially when local and class dissatisfaction persisted or when the system was shaken: novel powers could rival or even outclass those of the well-established and too well-tried pantheon. Some were monotheistic, echoing and outdoing the one-man rule of the political structure. Judaism and Christianity awkwardly demanded the renunciation of traditional deities. The interest of Gentiles of high status in Judaism and the spread of Christianity, at first as a version of Judaism but after the fall of Jerusalem in 70 as an independent creed, are evidence of the search. In particular Christianity, in a class-structured world run by corrupt officials for a distant emperor, gave access on a basis of merit, effort, and belief and through an incorruptible intermediary to an all-powerful authority, infinitely superior to the fallible emperor.[8] Conversion to Judaism was discouraged by Domitian and Hadrian, and Christians were sporadically put to death on various pretexts; Severus forbade conversion to either cult, and Caracalla at the age of 7 is alleged to have seen a boy beaten for Judaizing.[9] Other new but non-exclusive cults offered the benefits of particular favour without demanding such sacrifices.

Among those, Mithraism and the once banned cult of Isis had been strong features of Commodus' reign, and the pretender Pescennius Niger had taken part in her rites. By extension the term 'oriental' may be held to include Egyptian influences; the capital of Egypt, Alexandria, was a city that was fiercely Greek, but even there, the religion and art of the hinterland had a life. In 69–70 Isis and Serapis served the interests of members of the Flavian dynasty, Vespasian and Domitian,[10] but their influence and the activities of their priests at Rome were problematical for the government. It was not until the reign of Commodus that Serapis, the protector of grain transports from Egypt, and so a deity of some importance to the people of Rome, appeared on official Roman coinage, as he did again under Caracalla.[11] The *Historia Augusta* claims that Caracalla 'brought' the cult to Rome, set up shrines to the deity throughout the city, and had the rites celebrated with greater pomp than ever before.[12] He may have shared popular enthusiasm for the cult, perhaps after his first visit to Egypt, or he was simply pampering the people of Rome. Alexander Severus, so gently handled in the fantasizing *Historia Augusta*, is credited with providing the shrine of Isis and Serapis with equipment, statues, slaves and ritual instruments.[13] The story then is one of increasing recognition over a long period of time, not one of a sudden Severan whim. Along with this goes the fact that F. Ghedini can categorically deny that there is any evidence for an assimilation of Domna to Isis, in particular that the coins displaying the nursing goddess and inscribed *SAECVLI FELICITAS* ('The Good Fortune of the Age') have any reference to Domna, beyond the fitness of such a reverse to a coin that showed a female on the obverse.[14]

Perhaps the most striking of new developments, and most relevant here, because of his position as the principal deity of Emesa and the one who came to envelop rivals in the region, is the cult of Sol, the Sun. That was no flash-in-the-pan of Elagabalus' reign. It too represents the search for an underlying single power, but the Sun was everywhere and made colonization easy; no startling conclusions can be drawn from his prominence under the first two Severi, most notably under Caracalla. In fact Sol had been celebrated in portraiture and on two coin types used under Commodus, without direct input from Syria. Rather he heralded a Golden Age. Commodus put his own head on the statue of Helios outside the Colosseum – but it had once borne Nero's. Earlier still there had been Sol Indiges, an Italic deity with a place in the Roman calendar, and Augustus founded a temple to Solar Apollo on the Palatine. An oriental Sol had a shrine established for him in AD 102 outside the Porta Portuensis, and Sol Invictus was flourishing by the mid-second century. In any case, the facts that Severus adopted a solar nimbus on his coin image and that Severan emperors were addressed as *invicti* are hardly decisive for any influence of Domna or Maesa in the advance of a Syrian god.[15]

What Commodus and the Severi after him did in the realm of religion, notably for the cult of Isis and Serapis, may very largely have been populist: they saw what the people wanted, and provided it. Severus tried to win over the inhabitants of Rome. 'In his reign we saw all kinds of shows in all the theatres at the same time, and night-long religious ceremonies performed in emulation of the Mysteries', writes Herodian of the Secular Games of 204.

Against the background of such popular novelties it is interesting to see Severus credited with the restoration of decaying Roman temples; an act that reassured the populace, as it had when Augustus performed it, and which had much wider implications for the future of the Roman state.[16] Accordingly, there was a contemporary revival in the cult of Vesta, a deity connected with *salus publica* (the security of the people), and Domna in particular is associated with Vesta-Mater. She probably rebuilt the temple burnt down in Commodus' reign, and Caracalla appears sacrificing in front of it in 214–15.[17] In Africa, too, the people were to know how the peace of the gods had been secured: on the Lepcis Arch, the vital *concordia* and *pietas* of the imperial family were embodied in the scene of sacrifice in front of a temple.[18]

As to the 'Imperial cult', the base from which it sprang feels unfamiliar to one brought up in the Judaeo–Christian tradition, because of Graeco-Roman conceptions of the relation between men and gods. Yahveh is different in kind from his creatures, and in Christianity there is only one being who is both God and man. Cicero hails a fellow senator who had helped him back from exile in 57 BC as 'parent, god, safety of our life'.[19] Virgil makes Tityrus in the *Eclogues*, restored to his plot of land by Octavian, say that the young Triumvir 'will always be a god in my eyes'; for Horace Augustus is an immanent deity.[20] To be sure, even for Christians there is little objectionable in one individual revering another metaphorically as a 'god' but Greeks and Romans did not see humans and gods as different in kind; gods were more intelligent, more powerful, and immortal. 'Heroes' such as Hercules and Aeneas, born of one divine and one human parent, show gods and men as members of the same species.

The all-powerful emperor was readily perceived as divine and, if he was held to deserve it, achieved full state cult after his death. Emperors who had ruled well were awarded divine honours, a temple and cult, by the Senate, with a priest and lower officials to serve it at state expense. This was what Augustus received in AD 14. His *virtus*, said Ovid, had made him part of the firmament.[21] Nero after a conspiracy in 65 was offered a temple by a senator and, realizing the implications, refused it. In the *Historia Augusta*, Severus encounters a black soldier near Hadrian's Wall. The Ethiopian approached him with a garland of cypress, dire omens that enraged Severus. The man's response was: 'You have conquered everything; now be a god in your victory'. As the Neronian senator also knew, deification followed death – both quite soon for Severus.[22]

Because of the gradations between gods and men there was a range of lesser honours, offered before the *post mortem* state cult, and provinces, cities, and individuals could offer their own forms of homage at any time they thought opportune. Some dedications did not treat the emperor as a deity but merely offered vows for his safety, or for his return from campaign, or simply celebrated him. More suggestive was the admission of a person's statue to a place within a divinity's temple, illustrating his association with the deity, and the construction of images of gods that bore the emperor's features – assimilating the two without identifying them outright.

All this was established long before Severus came to power. What part individual emperors played in setting up these cults is not always clear and in any case varied. We are well informed about Octavian's negotiations with the provincial city and tribal leagues of Asia and Bithynia, and Tiberius' and Claudius' modest deprecation of honours. Even at the lower level of homage, there were gradations available, and change took place over time. As Tacitus remarked, comparing the commemorative honours decreed by the Senate for Drusus Caesar in 23 with those that his brother Germanicus had received four years before, the latter were as usual more effusive than the earlier.[23] A gradual shift in tone was more important than changes in the deities most closely associated by the emperor with himself (Apollo with Augustus, Jupiter with Domitian); and in the language used by commoners in dealings with the imperial family, which would culminate in the courtly language of Christian Byzantium.

Deification eased relations between the emperor and his subjects: if he was more than human they were absolved from impossible competition with him. It was a way of coping with men of overwhelming power in a competitive society.[24] In the west it helped with its ceremonial to unify the all-important upper class behind Rome, most notably at Augustan Lugdunum and Claudian Camulodunum. Certainly Severus at Gorsium thought it worth reconstructing the temple of the imperial cult.[25] In Greek-speaking provinces where cities were used to negotiating with hellenistic monarchs and Roman proconsuls, there was no hesitation in offering the living Augustus and his successors cult and temples.

The lunches that emperors enjoyed were not free: cities and provinces that offered honours looked for returns in the form of privileges and benefactions. An emperor's reluctance to accept cult may have had more to do with his being unwilling to be trapped into obligations than with the proper modesty that was put forward as the reason. If cult were permitted, that imposed an obligation on him; to refuse it completely would be ungracious. The vital initiative came from below: the ruler accepted or modified what was offered. Paradigms are found early in their Principates in Octavian's negotiations of 29 BC, then in Tiberius' reaction to an offer of celebration of himself and members of his family by Gytheion in Laconia; finally and explicitly in Claudius' letter to the Alexandrians of 41, which methodically deals first with honours offered to him, then with their expectations of him.[26]

Elsewhere than in state-funded Roman religion, then, a person might well be deified before death. A woman's beneficence could also be acknowledged. The title *thea* (goddess) had long been conferred on empresses by Greek-speaking communities in the east. These early precedents have been noted: the coins of Pergamum devoted to Livia and the elder Julia, of Nicaea in Bithynia to Messalina, and of the attention paid a century later to Hadrian's wife Sabina; in fact the expression of devotion to these women has been said to exceed what is found for the Severan women.[27] The staple treatment of imperial ladies, their identification with local deities in the provinces, had begun under with Augustus' wife and daughter being taken in Greek-speaking areas as epiphanies of Ceres or Aphrodite, in Lycia the 'New' Ceres, the 'New' Aphrodite. They are not often found attributed to Domna, who

Figure 8.1 Domna and Luna.
AR (Double *denarius*). Obv. *IVLIA PIA FELIX AVGVSTA* (*JULIA DEVOTED AND FORTUNATE AUGUSTA*) Bust of Domna, hair with six ridges. Rev. *LVNA LVCIFERA* (*LUNA BRINGER OF LIGHT*) Luna draped, crescent on head, fold of drapery in circle round head, standing in *biga* of horses prancing l., leaning forward, reins in both hands. AD 211–17.

Source: *CREBM* 5, p. 431, no. 8.

in any case is often difficult to identify with certainty because her gentile name of Julia was shared by much earlier imperial women, notably the daughter and granddaughter of Augustus, his wife Livia after his death, other members of the first dynasty, and Titus' deified daughter; and it is hazardous to try to date an inscription from the style of the writing. As Kettenhofen points out, the difficulty itself is significant, because it serves to inhibit speculation about radical novelties under the Severi.[28] Province-wide as well as city cult of the empress in the east goes back to the earliest Julio-Claudian women. Priestesses of the imperial cult are common in Asia Minor, whether they are independent or the consorts of high priests.[29]

City cult for Domna is found at towns in Asia Minor such as Corycus in Cilicia and Termessus Major in Lycia-Pamphylia; each has a high priestess (*archiereia*). Perhaps Domna visited the cities on her travels, or a local family saw an opportunity of distinguishing one of its female members. But Termessus had already had a priestess of Domitian's wife Domitia Longina a century before, and then one jointly of the Augustae Plotina and Matidia; there was a longstanding tradition.[30] Domna is found as *thea* mainly in Lower Moesia, and six times in the city of Nicopolis ad Istrum, where the title recurs in the titulature of Mamaea. Here the signs of a local fashion are apparent: Commodus' wife Crispina had already enjoyed the title: loyalty to the Severan regime demanded that Domna and her successor receive no less.[31]

The strong claims made about the Severan ruler-cult, and its effects, in particular about Domna's part in it, have to be considered against this background of flexibility of thought, of variation through time and place. Again, various types of evidence have to be taken into account: the public writings of individual authors connected with a dynasty, using words carefully chosen; coins struck by central or municipal authorities, publicly funded temples; transactions recorded on inscriptions or papyri, too, and even ephemeral graffiti, have to be taken seriously, some because they involve expenditure, graffiti for their spontaneity. But the elaborately articulated formulations offer most information about the developed cult.

On the basis of such an inscription, it has been argued that at Athens – where she was also known as the 'New Roman Hera' – Domna was given offerings on 1 January each year, and more importantly that she was identified with Athena Polias ('Defender of the City') and a member of its pantheon.[32] An assimilation of Domna and Athena is suggested elsewhere by a helmeted bust from Salonica, of Pheidian inspiration, and by a coin of Gabala in Syria which shows Domna on the obverse, and Athena on the reverse, within a distyle temple, but there Athena is linked with Astarte.[33]

The stone is incomplete and the vital word mentioning the sacrifice that the polemarch is to offer her (*thuein*) is a restoration. Cooler judgments have been made: there is simply a reference to Domna, with her honorific titles; she is to have a golden statue in the Parthenon; offerings (*eisiteria*) are to be made to her and to Athena – who is thereby clearly shown to be distinct. In line 19 Domna is evidently '*synthronos*': the two females 'share a throne'. But that was not new: Livia and Julia Livilla, sister of Gaius Caligula, had shared temples or thrones with the same deity in Cyzicus and Pergamum.[34] As F. Ghedini remarks, the distinctions accorded Domna cunningly fit the possibility that as defender of the city she had played a part in improving its relations with Severus; her association with Athena was certainly appropriate for an empress who was *Mater Castrorum* and a devotee of philosophy. A. von Premerstein suggested that a mission of Philostratus brought about the cordial relations that led to the honours.[35]

Subtly lesser honours were available to Athenian notabilities. Regilla was the wife of the eminent second-century sophist Herodes Atticus. 'O Regilla', runs a Corinthian dedication, 'the city Council, as if hailing you Tyche, has set up the marble statue by her sanctuary'. A rich and influential woman in the aristocracy of Athens was seen as approaching the status of the Good Fortune of the city of Corinth.[36] Not being an empress, she did not quite reach the status of Domna and her predecessors.

Correspondingly, Regilla was not in such a good position to see that a city did indeed enjoy good fortune, which the title hinted was the function of the honorand. It had long been usual for empresses to be identified with the Good Fortune of a city, either expressly in inscriptions, as with Livia 'Tyche of the People and City' at Gytheion already in AD 15,[37] or implicitly, by showing her on coins with the attributes of the presiding deity, a cornucopia and turreted crown. This identification was made for Domna in Syria and possibly in Asia Minor, where Tyche held sway in part as a manifestation of imperial power. Her ties with Laodiceia in Syria were obvious: this was the city that Severus made a metropolis, capital of its province; and at Paltos in Coele Syria, when the image of Tyche was carried in processions she was seen as the empress.[38]

But Domna also enjoyed a unique distinction, that of being designated *Tyche tes oikoumenes*, the 'Good Fortune of the Inhabited World'. That came from the Council and People of the Istrians, and exemplifies the 'universalizing' tendencies that were already apparent in the Antonine title 'Lord' or 'Master' of the inhabited world.[39] Debarred by gender from formal power, though not from being a Latin *Domina* or (subsumed under the supremacy of Severus) a Greek *despotes*, Domna could become the world's presiding good fortune. Not the people of Rome, nor Italy, nor the citizen body, nor the Empire was the concern of the ruling dynasty, but the entire inhabited world or, in its extreme form, the universe. A related conception might be recognized in the phrase used of Domna in Africa: 'Julia Domna Augusta, goddess, Juno, presiding spirit of the world' ('. . . *Augustae deae Junoni orbis terrae*').[40] The extravagance was not a novelty. In the last years of the Republic the people of Carthaea on Ceos looked for salvation to Julius Caesar, 'God, ruler, and saviour of the inhabited world' ('*theon, autokratora, sotera tes oikoumenes*'), while Octavian after his victory over Antony's eastern empire was called 'Benefactor and saviour of the entire universe' ('*euergeten kai sotera tou sympantos kosmou*').[41] The same phrase that honoured Domna recurs at Istria in connection with Julia Maesa.[42] Kettenhofen suggested that the trigger for such effusiveness was a visit to the city by the imperial family when they were returning from the east in 202; it may be recalled too that the people of Istria were under constant threat in the second century from the incursions of tribes from beyond the Danube; their emperors needed to be masters of the entire world.[43]

In the west, as on the Arch of the *Argentarii*, the form of cultic reference in use there, to Domna's *numen* (in Gradel's words, '*numen* cult was merely a linguistic synonym for direct, godlike cult'), was adopted; so in Britain.[44] Italian towns had offered cult since the time of Livia. At Formiae there was a priestess of Augusta and the Fatherland (*Sacerdos Augustae et patriae*). The woman was wife of the regular consul of 199 and governor designate of Asia under Elagabalus. Presumably she was priestess of Domna or a later member of the dynasty in the city.[45]

In Rome itself, the orientalizing view of ruler cult under Severus and Domna has been given support by interpretations of religious practice in their time. An elaborate and finely documented study of some aspects of the imperial cult at Rome makes particular use of three monuments.[46] In one, 'the (Bacchic) sodalities . . . adorned with marble a shrine of the god Liber . . . and gave a mall and garden above the Nymphs which is the place called Memphis'. The religious sodality of Bacchus was thus involved in the construction of monuments in the imperial Gardens of Sallust, which had African associations to attract an 'African' emperor. So did the Septizonium, a three-storeyed portico with niches for fountains and, it has been suggested, symbols of the seven heavenly bodies, days of the week, which was set up by Severus at the south-eastern corner of the Palatine Hill, to face the Appian Way and allegedly to greet travellers from Africa.[47] The new buildings, where statues of Domna and Caracalla were placed, were established on sites granted by the imperial family and known as 'Memphis and the Nymphs' (Septizonium and Nymphaea were often associated). As to the name Memphis, Severus was a devotee of things Egyptian, and the Libyan Liber or Bacchus was rooted originally in Egyptian Memphis. Second, two freedmen of the Augusti 'made a cave and consecrated it' to Unconquerable Mithras; and finally a patron of the fishers and divers set up a flowery dedication to the god Caracalla (*deo*), for his birthday; it mentions all the Nymphs and Luna Noctiluca. The divine personages to be associated with the imperial family here were Mithras (his epithet associates him with the Sun) and the male and female lunar deities, Caracalla's particular patrons.[48]

This is an alluring web of ideas, but the point of the exposition is to show that these developments 'constituted a marked change in religious proclivities' and that the role of the imperial family in them was not passive and acquiescent.[49] Of course, the precedents that adulation of Commodus had already reached were hard to beat, and some of the evidence for positive imperial encouragement is hardly conclusive. Land was granted to the corporations, certainly, but they may have paid for it; any claim that the word *concessu* implies a free grant goes too far: the word implies 'permission' and suggests that the initiative came from below. The imperial presence on these sites could be due as much to the gratitude of the participants, who mention their own expenditure, as to any enthusiasm on the part of the rulers. The very diversity of the cults involved echoes the cosmopolitan nature of Rome. In particular the dedicators of the cave were imperial freedmen who may have been brought up in the imperial household, bought from another owner, or acquired fresh in the market: they will have had their own religious interests. Again a movement coming from below could be indicated. Research on 'oriental' religions under the Severi has been documented; they were burgeoning throughout the provinces, manifold amongst a variety of devotees.[50]

As to Egypt, Severus is said to have made out that he particularly enjoyed his visit because he was able to take part in the worship of Serapis, and it was while the family was at York that the Egyptian god made his appearance there, a slender fact which has given more ammunition to those who see orientalizing tendencies in the dynasty and who do not allow subjects much initiative.[51] There is a view that in the relief of the assembled deities on the pylon of the Lepcis Arch there is a double syncretism between Jupiter and Serapis and between that compound deity and Severus, although in general attempts to demonstrate an Egyptianizing of the iconography of Severus and Domna have not been successful.[52] Severus' personal interest in the cult of Serapis, as it is described in the context, looks a little like that of a tourist, part of seeing the curiosities that the country had to offer. One type of his statues sports four curls on the forehead in the manner of Serapis statues,[53] and may have been adopted during the Egyptian tour; but it was a style that had already been used for their portraits by private individuals of the Antonine age. Caracalla outdid his father (as in other matters): one of the reasons he gave for visiting Egypt in 215 was to sacrifice to Serapis, and he made his headquarters in the temple.[54]

Predominantly from the west, but from outside Rome, comes a group of documents that seem to establish Domna as the recipient of a new cult, that of the Dea Caelestis, the Goddess of Heaven first attested in Rome at the end of the first century AD. They are a central plank for those who treat Domna as an orientalizing factor. Carthage was a Roman colony, founded after the Romans had defeated and destroyed the Punic city in 146 BC. Her patron deity, identified with Juno, was lured away to Rome in the procedure called *evocatio* (summoning) – and restored thirteen years later when C. Gracchus founded his colony of Junonia there.[55] The cult remained embedded in the province as part of its Punic culture.[56] Domna was assimilated, it seems, to the Dea Syria, the Syrian goddess, and the Goddess of Heaven was the patron of Carthage who came originally from Syria and so, like Domna and the Severans, links Syria and north Africa. No wonder scholars have paid so much attention to the cult of the Dea Caelestis, claiming that the Semitic element in the Empire burst out 'in demonic form' when the triumph of Severus, the 'new Hannibal', was embodied in the form of his wife as the city goddess of Carthage.[57] In forming such theories early twentieth century scholars allowed their political views to play a part. The 'Orientalism' of Edward Said's French and British scholars, which aimed at control, was inverted, or rather bypassed, and Graeco-Roman fears were picked up and reflected.[58]

The theory was destroyed long ago.[59] The strongest evidence for the identification of empress and deity is the appearance of the latter on coins of 203–4, standing wearing a lofty headdress and carrying her emblems, sceptre and thunderbolt or tambourine, in front of a rock from which water bursts forth. There is no trace of Domna herself. Rather these coins commemorate a grant to Carthage by the rulers, probably of *ius Italicum*: the legend tells that we are dealing with *INDVLGENTIA* ('understanding generosity') towards Carthage, and it is paralleled by a contemporary type which commemorates *INDVLGENTIA* towards Italy, and accordingly displays the figure of Italy.[60]

Next in evidence came three inscriptions, the first from Carvoran on Hadrian's Wall.[61] It was a dedication in iambic verse to the Maiden of Heaven (Virgo Caelestis), made by M. Caecilius Donatianus, commanding officer of the garrison. The inscription speaks of the deity riding on a lion, as she does on coin reverses of Severus; she is Panthea with the attributes of the Magna Mater, Pax, Virtus, Ceres, and the Dea Syria. The dedicant, allegedly, uttered his words at a festival before an image of Domna, whose statues bear corn-ears, assimilating her to Ceres. The editors, citing the coin evidence, commented: 'This dedication to Virgo Caelestis is really to Julia Domna', and added that the accompanying statue was that of the empress with her divine accessories. Again, no word of her.[62] The statue was a private offering from a man whose name, both the *nomen*, derived from that of the Caecilii Metelli, conquerors and patrons in north Africa, and the participial *cognomen*, suggests African origin.[63] Even the date of the inscription is uncertain: the third century had been proposed; but a monument dedicated to the same goddess was erected at Carvoran by another commanding officer during the governorship of Sex. Calpurnius Agricola, 163–6, and this period should probably be preferred.[64]

More convincing at first sight was an inscription from the northern flank of the Capitol in Rome which mentions a priestess of the cult. By implication then it was maintained in a temple within the city boundary – near the temple of Juno Moneta – and so was a recognized cult within the Roman system.[65] But the inscription dates from 259 and, as Mundle points out, it is more likely, in view of what Dio and Herodian say about the occasion for the introduction of the cult within Rome,[66] that that particular step towards orientalization was taken by Domna's great-nephew Elagabalus, who installed the Emesene baetyl with Tanit Juno Caelestis in a Palatine Temple and renamed Jupiter Ultor as Jupiter Victor. Up to his time, as far as the evidence shows, the cult was a private one.[67]

Appropriately, then, comes a dedication from Moguntiacum, bearing titles of the period 214–17. It is not from the legionary headquarters, and is again the work of an individual, another officer, whose name is lost.[68] This monument does indeed seem to identify Domna with the Dea Caelestis. But the context is unclear and there is no evidence that the distant empress promoted the dedication. What then remains of the identification and the theory it supports? There is nothing to be said for the idea of active intervention by the family designed to promote the cult. This is an example of an individual expressing his loyalty in the way that came most naturally to him, in a familiar religious language. The weakness of the argument, based on a private dedication, is masked by careful research, and by presupposing Punic partisanship – which serves only to damage the argument further. Severus was a Roman senator whose standing depended on that, not on the memory of the Punic hero of the struggle between Rome and Carthage that ended a century and half before the Principate was founded.

But the line of thought that guided modern scholars was also open to loyal subjects of the Severi: a link between the Syrian goddess and the Syrian Empress by way of their common ties with north Africa, in Domna's case through Severus; it was taken by the officer at Moguntiacum, and would not have been unwelcome to the dynasty if drawn to their attention.

As an appendix to this identification with the Dea Caelestis it is worth considering the fact that Domna may have been identified with the city goddess of Carthage under her Roman name of Juno. She was no mean deity, as Virgil's *Aeneid* tells. However, the evidence is not strong: E. Kettenhofen found only one possible identification, in an inscription from Ksar Toual Zammel by a dedicant who may be a relative of Severus, as his *nomen* suggests: Q. Fulvius Dida Bibulianus to Juno the Queen Julia Domna: 'Junoni Reginae Juliae Domnae'.[69] Furthermore, identification may not have been what the dedicant intended: the words of the inscription are disordered and an 'and' may have dropped out between the names of goddess and empress.

Orientalization has been detected in the style and appearance of Domna, for example, on the Arch of the *Argentarii*. She is shown in a prominent position at a Roman sacrifice, which is unwonted for a woman, as it was unusual for a woman to take part in the public processions such as that shown on the Lepcis Arch.[70] Domna is presented in a style that F. Ghedini can compare with that of a monument from Dura Europus in which Conon is shown sacrificing with his daughter Bithnanaia, placed in a position – immobile and her bust encapsulated in a veil – which also recalls that monument. Moreover, the gesture of the raised right hand, to be seen in a second century AD statue of Sanatruces, monarch of Hatra, may also be traced back to oriental roots in a seal of Hammurabi, though it is found in Greek monuments and belongs not only to the deity but also to the worshipper. In connection with the Roman imperial family it is first found on a coin of Geta from 200–2. As to the caduceus that Domna is apparently

Figure 8.2 Caracalla; Harmony of solar and lunar rulers.
AV. Obv. *ANTONINVS PIVS AVG PON(tifex) TR(ibunicia) P(otestate) IIII*. Bust of Caracalla, laureate, draped, cuirassed, r. Rev. *CONCORDIAE AETER NAE (TO EVERLASTING HARMONY)* Busts (jugate), r., of Severus, radiate, draped, and Domna, wearing *stephane*, draped, on crescent. AD 201.

Source: *CREBM* 5, p. 204, no. 260.

holding, which has been taken as a sign of her status as *Mater Castrorum*, like the sceptre borne by Faustina (II),[71] it is a complex symbol with Egyptian associations, which also belongs to the Punic Tanit but in the Graeco-Roman world serves to invoke peace, including peace between gods and men (*pax deorum*). Ghedini exploits the comparison with Bithnanaia still further when she suggests that the Domna of the Arch recalled the experience of Domna and her sister Maesa when they assisted at their father's service to the Solar god of Emesa. Only the severe dress of Domna belongs to the Roman matron, with her lunate diadem going back to Livia. The oriental elements in Domna's presentation on the Arch of the *Argentarii* and on those in the Forum and in Lepcis she tracks down to placards that Severus had painted in the east to publicize his victories.[72]

On the Arch at Lepcis, on the other hand, the empress's figure recalls Greek models, and Domna may have selected one that goes back to the Venus Genetrix of Arcesilaus, commissioned by Julius Caesar for the deity's Roman temple. At the scene of sacrifice on the north-eastern panel of the attic she is conventionally shown under the protection of Juno, while, more boldly, the goddess's peacock accompanies her on the scene of the assembled gods. Assimilation of Empress and Queen of the gods is in order: in the east Livia had already been called 'the New Hera', and the association of empress and goddess had been resumed with Sabina, perhaps, as Ghedini suggests, because of the equation of Trajan with Jupiter. It may have continued with Plautilla, Mamaea, and Sohaemias.[73]

One may wonder all the same how much was due to Domna's own selection. Greek and oriental elements in representations of her are part of a language familiar to artists, and which they may even have employed without the idea of creating a new effect. Rather the conclusion reached long ago about the Arch of the *Argentarii*, that it was an amalgam of diverse traditions, drawn from different regions, remains suggestive. The artists followed the bent they knew. Accordingly on the political front, whatever Domna's dress and role on the arches, it would be mistaken to see in them the beginning of a series of 'reforms' that would lead to the intrusion of Domna's sister and niece in the Senate and to Sohaemias' creation of a women's mock Senate, the *senaculum*.[74]

So far individual monuments have been considered, but overall production may prove illuminating and less liable to mislead. It is from the aggregated evidence of inscriptions and coins (particularly significant because of their official status, especially when they are the work of central government), that the overall standing of Domna in the galaxy of Roman imperial deities can be gauged. Domna's contemporaries and the historians have surprisingly little to tell on the subject. Apart from attention given to Serapis, it was only when the innovations of Elagabalus took Rome and Italy by surprise that there was direct comment on the imperial cult of the Severan age, and that suggests that it had remained on conventional lines. From coins and inscriptions can be assessed not only Domna's own and her husband's ambitions, but also the response of constituencies throughout the Empire.

Coins and inscriptions devoted to Domna have been called 'innumerable'.[75] The quantity, exceeding those of any other Roman empress, has fuelled the suspicions of scholars who see in her an ambitious alien. This begs the question of her ability to control the output of inscriptions from communities and individuals all over the Roman world, and the minting of coins in provincial cities, some theoretically independent (*civitates liberae*). The quantity of tributes to Domna alone or included in those devoted to her husband and sons or to the entire family certainly shows her perceived importance in politics and social life. But taken with the others they bear witness to publicized relief and a sense of confidence: the Roman world was going to survive, even though on Commodus' death it had been shaken by civil wars in a way unknown since AD 68–9, and for longer. In the earliest period of Severus' Principate the inhabitants of areas within his control would have been keen to demonstrate loyalty; in the first two years the Empire east of the Bosporus was added, with further manifestations to be expected; finally the liberation of Gaul and Britain from Clodius Albinus would have allowed those provinces too to show their delight.

Occasions for setting up inscriptions were diverse, and the forms the monuments took almost equally so: statue bases with the imperial names in the accusative case (the dedicator erected the images) or in the dative (the monument was dedicated to the emperor and his family), the commemoration of benefactions such as buildings; the fulfilling of vows for the safety of the rulers (*pro salute*). Even if all had survived, the complex motives that led to their creation could not be exhaustively explained, nor the way their incidence varies from one period and region to another. Financial means, the availability of suitable stone, local culture, personal motives, fashion and rivalry, the nearness of the imperial family, all played their part. Dedicants have one thing in common: willingness to spend money, state, community, or private, on demonstrating loyalty to members of the dynasty.

A thorough survey of the epigraphic material yields information that is unexpected at first sight.[76] There were only three dedications for the safety of Domna alone, without reference to any particular deity, compared with sixty-five for her and other members of her family: usually the empress appears with her husband and sons, or with Caracalla alone. But this is not so surprising: she travelled with them and cities, military units, and individuals they encountered wanted to encompass the entire family in their devotion. Such figures put her importance to the public into perspective. Kettenhofen points out that the shared stones are almost equally divided between Severus and Caracalla, although the father reigned three times as long. The increased striking rate may reflect the enhanced prestige of the widowed empress in the regime of an inexperienced Princeps.

The most striking geographical feature of the distribution of inscriptions set up for members of the imperial family is that there were fewer from Syria and the Orient generally than might have been expected. If her own constituency failed to notice its native princess, that is a disappointing result for those who see the empress as a force for oriental advancement. Among communities that are represented are Dura, perhaps in gratitude for the grant of colonial status, and Gerasa, possibly as a result of the imperial family's stay there.[77]

Emesa itself has nothing to show, which would be remarkable if the haul of inscriptions in general from the over-built site were richer; but easterners, even Emesenes, have their say elsewhere: at El Kantara, C. Julius Aelurio, centurion of the Third, Augustan, Legion and commander of a group of Emesene troops, is one of those dedicants, about ninety instances over all, who invoked a deity to protect the health of the imperial family, in this case Hercules Sanctus. The dedicant in 214 of another inscription of this type, for Caracalla and Domna, was Aelius Surus ('Syrian'), councillor of the colony of Bassiana, east of Sirmium, which derives its name from Caracalla's original *cognomen*. Other monuments give similar evidence of the devotion of individual Syrians: the Aurelii Claudii at Napoca offered a stele, to the Syrian goddess for their safety, also in 214, and in two inscriptions from Heliopolis a *speculator* of the Third, Gallic, Legion, stationed at Raphaneae, offered his dedication 'to the gods of Heliopolis', Jupiter, Venus, and Mercury, for the same purpose. Only one such inscription is devoted to the safety of Julia Domna alone.[78] Far in the west, in Tarraconensian Spain, a Claudius Marinus, whose *cognomen* might be connected with Semitic words for 'king', offered prayers for her.[79] One or two exceptional inscriptions seem to indicate gratitude for help received from the empress. So perhaps with the building inscription from Pergamum erected by L. Didius Marinus, procurator of the province of Asia. But this highly placed official is the man who very probably married Cornificia, daughter of Marcus Aurelius; his debt may be guessed.[80]

As a warning against overemphasizing Syrian protégés, the number of north Africans, especially from Lepcis, may be considered, who offered dedications to the family.[81] Africa also predominates in vows for the safety of the Severi. At Lambaesis, where the Third Legion, Augusta, was stationed, M. Ulpius Optatus made his offering on behalf of Caracalla and his mother. This officer is allowably a fellow countryman of Domna's, despite the characteristically African form of his *cognomen*. Among the other communities Thuburbo and Thugga offered several collective vows.[82]

The sites of cities, which abounded more than anywhere else in the provinces of western Asia Minor, have yielded up most dedications. Not surprisingly, the hellenized and articulate provinces of Asia and Bithynia are notably well represented among those honouring the imperial family, as by Nicomedia, which had been granted its second neocorate by Severus.[83]

Although the Danubian provinces of Upper and Lower Moesia were not well urbanized, they still have a number of dedications to show, concentrated in certain places. Like Asia Minor, this region was a tramping ground of the court as it made its way from one end of the Empire to the other. So the College of Shippers on the Danube honoured Domna with a dedication at Axiopolis, and Nicopolis ad Istrum was notably productive; it is said to offer as many dedications as Rome itself.[84] This good showing is not due, as one might have expected, to the zeal of the many troops stationed in the Balkans. Among the bodies of troops dedications seem fewer than might have been expected, given the stress laid by Severus and Caracalla and by historians on their role as soldiers and their dependence on the army.[85] On the other hand, Kettenhofen draws attention to the high number of inscriptions for which individuals were responsible.[86] Severus' decisive victories made such demonstrations seem well worth while to ambitious or nervous officials.[87] It is not surprising to find a comparative dearth of dedicatory inscriptions in the west. There were disparities in local practice, and after the bloody defeat of Clodius Albinus the new masters of the world passed though his Gallic base only on their way to and from Britain.

A thorough examination of the epigraphic documents takes their variety into full account, and the conclusion to be drawn is that there was nothing out of the ordinary: provincial 'epiphany' inscriptions, in which the honorand is described as 'the New' manifestation of a deity, are not enough to make an altered constitutional or religious position for Domna.[88] The dedications made by loyal subjects empire-wide are commonplace, time-honoured, and conventional.

The evidence of coins is split between government-controlled issues from mints at Rome and in the provinces, and those that were put out by provincial communities for their own use. The difficulty of interpreting the numismatic evidence and its links with other forms of representation has been noted, and a sober verdict, delivered more than a century ago, has been refined more recently in a study that illuminatingly, if a little too sharply, divides the period of Domna's 'reign' into five periods: civil wars (to 199), establishment of the dynasty (to 203), ascendancy of Plautianus and its aftermath (to 208), the end of Severus' reign and the joint rule of her sons (to 212), and Caracalla's sole rule. So in the second phase three areas are stressed: motherhood with types of Venus Genetrix, Mater Deum, and Ceres Frugifera; virtues are represented by *PVDICITIA* and *PIETAS* (*AVGVSTA* and *PVBLICA*). There was also a focus on individual family members, especially the heirs.[89] It is a valuable analysis, as long as connotations beyond the confines of each category are not forgotten, most obviously, as we shall see, those of the bringer of grain, Ceres. There is agreement that coin types, like the titulature, stress Domna's role as wife and mother, despite the part she played in politics.[90] One might say that her part in politics was defined by her role as wife and mother, real and metaphorical.[91]

It is worth noting that numismatic studies have adhered to the view of the coinage as propagandist. Another view, that the ideological content was intended by mintmasters and designers to suit the emperor, would not damage the exposition, but on the contrary would support it. As it is, there is

Figure 8.3 Caracalla 'Germanicus'; Luna.
AE. Obv. *M. AVRELIUS ANTONINVS PIVS AVG GERM(anicus)* Bust of Caracalla, r., bearded, draped, laureate, and cuirassed. Rev. *P(ontifex) M(aximus) TR(ibunicia) P(otestate) XX IMP III COS IIII P(ater) P(atriae)* (in exergue) *S(enatus) C(onsulto)* (*BY DECREE OF THE SENATE*) Luna draped, crescent on head, fold of drapery in circle round head, standing in *biga* of horses prancing l., leaning forward, reins in both hands (as on Fig. 8.1). AD 217.

Source: *CREBM* 5, p. 492, no. 306.

some wavering as to how far Domna herself controlled types and so was responsible for the muted issues of the period of her eclipse and Plautianus' ascendancy. The alternative view avoids that difficulty.[92]

In the wider context of the Roman coinage, sporadic and unremarkable identifications with convenient female abstractions, almost divinities in themselves (*FECVNDITAS, PROVIDENTIA*),[93] which had no life or personality but served to embody desirable qualities and attainments, were being made long before Domna's time. In particular, there is nothing unusual about the designs on her early Roman coins, showing the qualities that lead to pleasing accompaniments of the regime, such as *SAECVLI FELICITAS* ('The Good Fortune of the Age'), or its results: *BONVS EVENTVS* ('The Happy Outcome') and *AETERNITAS* ('Immortality'). It is arguable that Severus chose older and more traditional types because he was an outsider; people would not discern any break with the past.

In particular S. Lusnia allows only one type of the Roman coinage that assimilates or associates Domna with a divinity, Magna Mater, and she does not even here commit herself to assimilation, though she holds in general that the empress is associated with the divine elements of Severan rule.[94]

It is no surprise then to find the *Mater Castrorum* as Victoria, an expression of the *virtus* and *felicitas* of the Roman people, both in the solemn procession shown on the Arch of Lepcis, on a relief in Warsaw in which she is crowning Caracalla with laurel, and on a cameo in Kassel, where she is seated on captured military gear, sporting a hairstyle that belongs to her youth; this was something that an officer stationed on the Rhine evidently ordered on his own account. Long ago Livia, wife of Augustus, mother of Tiberius, and grandmother of his heirs, had been portrayed as decoration on swords on the northern frontiers, but the type on the cameo is normally used for Roma and Victoria, and the assimilation is virtually confined to Domna.[95]

Ceres had more personality and had long been a favourite deity with empresses on their coins: the food supply was always in the minds of Mediterranean man. Domna's association with her hardly calls for comment, but for a remarkable marble statue from Ostia, in which a veiled Domna holds corn ears and poppy heads, It belongs to a type that at Rome goes back to the Flavians and is taken to be either a flattering court portrait, probably, to judge by the idealization of the features, posthumous, or a product of Ostian interest in the deity and her produce, which also preoccupied the rulers.[96]

The presence of the Phrygian deity of universal fecundity, Cybele, in her chariot on coin reverses of Domna looks suggestive, and there can be little doubt of the assimilation of the Mother of the Gods and the *MATER AVGVSTORVM*. Again it was earlier than Domna. One precedent seems to have been Livia, but Sabina, the Faustinas and Lucilla gave Cybele further attention. She was the most familiar and Romanized of the eastern goddesses associated with fecundity. She cannot serve as evidence of orientalization, for she was not oriental enough, especially after her four centuries at Rome; Phrygia was too far west, Phrygian was an Indo-European language, and Phrygians too familiar from Homer onward as allies of the Trojans, ancestors of the Romans. As such they were useful to the Julio-Claudian and Antonine dynasties, and so to the Severi.[97]

What emerges from examining Severan ruler cult is principally how important it remains to distinguish private from official initiatives.[98] The constructions of private individuals and groups, the officer at Moguntiacum, the imperial freedmen, and the trade association at Rome, are distinct from items for which the central government was fully responsible, and even from the activities of provincial cities such as Athens. At the same time allowance has to be made both for private dedicators second-guessing what might be acceptable to their masters and for sensitivity on the part of rulers to their subjects' thinking. The passion of a private individual might lead to the idea of constructing a shrine, as it did with Cicero in 45 BC when his daughter Tullia died.[99] A city expressed its devotion by collective resolutions, more thought out and self-seeking, for they might lead to the erection of statues or more expensively to the foundation of games or a shrine. The precedent that the resolutions set could commit the community to making equally expensive offerings to later *principes*. An official state cult proper should be manned, maintained and housed at state expense, sanctioned and regulated by decree of the Senate. What would have been significant for Domna and for imperial policy would have been the adoption of an 'oriental' cult associated with the empress as an officially recognized and financed cult of the Roman people, celebrated in the capital of the Empire, preferably on the Capitol itself. That was what Elagabalus imposed.

Hardly less important, the earlier Severan age does indeed mark some change in the practices and language of the people, as well as in the expectations of the emperor and his family. Reference to the divine spirit and majesty of the emperors (*numen maiestasque*) now became 'obligatory'[100] – in a social rather than a legal sense. This was an early stage in the progress towards the bombastic language conventional in the Late Empire. As we have seen from the ecstatic Roman corporation of fishers and divers, individuals and private societies were allowed their own expressions of devotion. 'The Goddess of Night has become a light', it exclaimed when Caracalla returned to Rome on his father's death in 211, referring to his relations with the deity that Caracalla most revered, the Moon. Literary flights at a higher level, such as that made by Pseudo-Oppian with 'The Assyrian goddess of Cythera (that is, Aphrodite) and Selene, the Moon goddess that never wanes' (*Assyrie Kythereia kai ou leipousa Selene*) must be taken for what they are: literary conceits. The Syrian poet identifies the Emperor's mother with the two most important deities of his and her homeland, the Dea Syria. Her cult had been embedded in lands outside Syria, even in Rome, since the time of Nero, who took an ephemeral interest in it. Both these deities in their many variants represented not only the fecundity that guaranteed the welfare of the Empire's millions but that which had given the Emperor to the world. The Moon in particular (*LVNA LVCIFERA* under Domna) had a history on Roman coin reverses connected with imperial women from Faustina (I) onwards (*DIANA LVCIFERA, IVNO LVCINA*), again attached to the notion of fecundity.[101]

Nonetheless, Severus and his wife, and Caracalla, remained close to the original installation of the cult of the personality under Augustus, if we leave aside the advance that shocked contemporaries in Caligula, who in private cult identified himself with Jupiter and insisted on the erection of his statue in the Temple at Jerusalem, and take on board Domitian, who encouraged his officials to address him as 'god and lord'. Only the first title was abandoned in the sequel. 'Dominus' had a civil use as a form of address: 'Sir', and was regularly use by Pliny when he addressed Trajan. Its Greek equivalent *despotes* did not have that dimension. Under Severus the ruler became *dominus noster* (our Lord), which, as G. Bersanetti points out, was not demanded by them but conferred by their subjects.[102]

Moreover, the Severan dynasty came to power by violence and Severus kept his position by the same means. His alleged advice to Caracalla, to look to the army and ignore the rest,[103] fits Caracalla's own preoccupation with fighting and his characterization as an uncouth brute. There may be a contrast to be drawn here with the conduct of Commodus, who made peace with his opponents on the Danube and after that occupied himself at Rome and with his own image. The extravagance of Commodus – though assassinated emperors are subject to unfavourable reporting – seems to have gone beyond any claims of Severus and Caracalla. For Commodus divinity was a substitute for proven merit. He made himself out a second Hercules, going about with lionskin and club, as sculptures, notably the bust in the Palazzo dei Conservatori, show. Towards the end of his reign Commodus programmatically associated himself with a series of other deities led by Hercules. It is not all identification: Commodus also represented himself as under the protection of these deities, and that was nothing new. Interest in the hero went back, according to C. R. Whittaker, to Mark Antony, Caligula, Nero and Domitian. None was a reputable precedent, but then there was Trajan.[104] Unless this was what Whittaker calls 'religious infatuation' it looks as if Commodus was, desperately perhaps, struggling to carry himself beyond the danger that the feuds of his courtiers were bringing on him.

Lines taken by Severus provided an example for later emperors. In the coinage the new dynasty, working to perpetuate itself, insisted on the family and the dynastic principle, as had, for example, Vespasian in displaying his sons. This example, it has been shown, was followed in turn by Philip the Arabian.[105] What sort of a lead did Domna provide for her female successors? Her sister Maesa's honours were modest, as one might expect for a mere grandmother of emperors: the reverses of the Roman coinage have only one novelty: some bear the legend *IVNO CONSERVATRIX* ('Juno the Preserver'), which occurs on reverses of Mamaea and of Elagabalus' first wife Julia Paula.[106] This last item suggests that there was no intention of identifying the woman with the deity, though Maesa might be seen as having contributed to the survival and accession of Severus Alexander. Rather the deity has them under her protection. In the provinces Maesa is shown as the motherly Demeter, bringer of the harvest, on a coin of Amastris in Pontus, an identification already known for Livia under Tiberius.[107] And she is 'Diva Julia' at Tutugi in Spain.[108] Domna established precedents in her titulature, as we shall see, but Maesa did not or could not develop them. That was left to her 'reigning' daughters.[109]

As to her daughter Sohaemias, the mother of Elagabalus, there have been attempts to see her too identified with Juno Regina and Caelestis. The basis is an inscription from Deir-el-Kalaa in Syria which has been interpreted as referring to the paying of a vow in Latin to Jupiter Optimus Maximus Balmarcos and Juno Regina and Juno Sima and 'C(aelestis) S(ohaemias)' and in Greek to the sacred god Bal and the goddess Hera and the goddess Sima and the younger Hera (*Neotera Hera*). Admittedly Venus Caelestis and Juno Regina appear on the Roman reverses of Sohaemias, but that does little more than make the spectator associate the empress with the named deity.[110] Whatever the letters *CS* mean, there is nothing more here than a local initiative involving a local cult of Hera.

Maintaining the public–private distinction confirms the need to distinguish the kinds of evidence, sculpture, inscriptions and coins. Centrally produced coins in particular expose an official view, which subjects were expected to accept; inscriptions and sculpture may reflect that too, but they can also reflect the dedicant's individuality; they may be cut as official records for central government or local authority or, as we have noticed above, at the wish of an individual or a private corporation. The coins show conservatism in the selection of types, and continuity with previous regimes. Further, and more significantly, the deities selected by private dedicants for comparison, assimilation, or even identification with members of the imperial family have often looked appropriate for the particular dedicant – the gods of his native land. And that prompts the question whether the impulse towards 'orientalism' imputed to the Severi is not rather the visible effect of changes in the composition of the articulate strata of the Empire, or at least in their beliefs. The change was coming from below. Naturally that cannot have been a one-way process: the effect on the authority of the views of its audience also needs to be taken into account, and beliefs of the people that came to be reflected back by the ruling dynasty.

9 Aftermath

Domna's ashes were given a strange resting place. They were taken back to Rome, no doubt very quietly, and placed in the Mausoleum of Augustus,[1] a compromise that kept her out of the current dynastic arrangements: Septimius Severus had usurped the ancestry of Commodus, which went back to Hadrian, whose tomb was the present Castel Sant'Angelo on the Tiber. That was where Severus and eventually Caracalla were buried, like their 'adopted' forebears the Antonines, including Commodus.[2] Elagabalus came to power in June 218, when Macrinus was defeated in battle on the territory of Antioch.[3] His grandmother Maesa, now herself Augusta,[4] naturally ordered the remains of her sister to be reinterred in Hadrian's mausoleum, along with those of Geta.[5] Not that the older alternative was dishonourable: it was a mark of distinction when Nerva was installed in it in 98, for the preceding and now disgraced Flavian dynasty had made its own mausoleum elsewhere.[6] Now another Julia was interred in the Augustan Mausoleum, not perhaps for her name, but to show that she was of the past.

Consecration followed. Perhaps already under Macrinus, in a conciliatory gesture to supporters of the past regime, especially in the east, Domna became Diva Julia (Pia, Domna or Augusta), after the precedent of so many deceased empresses and female relatives of the ruler, from Livia onwards. It was a regular concomitant of being 'Augusta'.[7] Domna was still to add her mite of legitimacy to the Severan dynasty when it was revived by her great-nephew Elagabalus; and her sister Julia Maesa might hope to benefit from the precedent. Coins show '*CONSECRATIO* by decree of the Senate', and they are echoed under Alexander Severus, alongside consecration issues of Maesa and Caracalla.[8] It was the least that could be done for one who had achieved greater prominence than all the imperial women in the preceding century, from Trajan's modest Plotina onwards.

What deification meant, and how far it guaranteed the survival of Domna's memory, is another matter. A temple with a corps of priests to celebrate the cult would represent the full set of honours. In fact, there was a whole range which at its lower end, as for Nero's deified infant daughter and Domitian's infant son, would be no more than the grant by the Senate of status and title; the boy's deification is known only from his appearance on coins.[9] The last *divus* to attain a temple was M. Aurelius; Antoninus Pius and his wife Faustina (I) had to share one.[10] Evidently Caracalla, dealing with his father, avoided the expense. The elevation of women connected to the emperor entailed fewer practical consequences than that of a deceased emperor. It could be done with dispatch and take place even before the funeral ceremony, as it did with Trajan's sister Marciana Augusta in 112 and with Faustina (I) in 140. There could always be extras, such as the arch that Sabina, unusually for a woman, seems to have been awarded in 136, which shows her apotheosis on one of its reliefs. Faustina (II) had received a temple where she died in Asia Minor; the place was renamed Faustinopolis after her, but according to the *Historia Augusta* she lost it at the hands of Caracalla, and Elagabalus found a better use for it, dedicating it to his own god. Some women were enrolled in the list of *divi* who were to be celebrated by troops throughout the Empire; the list survives in the third century papyrus, the *Feriale Duranum*, from the fortress at Dura-Europus on the Euphrates.[11] Domna's deification, for all its utilitarian purpose for Caracalla's Severan heir Elagabalus, who claimed to be his son, and for the cousin who succeeded him, seems even so to have been only titular, hence both discreet and inexpensive.

Macrinus' reign was brief and troubled, although he tried to make it more stable by raising his son Diadumenian to the rank of Caesar, with the resonant *cognomen* Antoninus.[12] Renewed hostilities and negotiations with the Parthians made it necessary to him to return to Mesopotamia in the

Figure 9.1 Macrinus' Liberality.
AV. Obv. *IMP C(aesar) M OPELL SEV(erus) MACRINVS AVG* Bust of Macrinus, radiate, draped, cuirassed, r. Rev. *LIBERALITAS AVG* Macrinus and Diadumenian, both togate, seated l. on platform, extending r. hands and holding rolls in l. hands at sides; on r., officer standing, on l. Liberalitas, as with Pertinax on Fig. 3.1; at foot of platform, citizens standing. AD 217–18.

Source: *CREBM* 5, p. 506, no. 71.

summer of 217. The following winter gave him a breathing space in Antioch, where he tried to win over the population by giving them a *congiarium*, and on the conclusion of peace he was able to announce a 'Parthian victory' at the beginning of 218.[13] By delaying, however, he had encouraged his detractors in Rome, who were demonstrating against him in the theatre in the late summer of 217. There was also hostility in the cities of Asia Minor: Pergamum, recently honoured by Caracalla, was offering him insults.[14]

In mid-May 218 mutiny broke out among the troops at Raphaneae, near Emesa, and Macrinus was overwhelmed; his reversal of Caracalla's pay rise was probably a major cause.[15] When he moved to Apameia to appeal to the Second, Parthian, Legion he found that they were also disloyal and there was nothing for him to do but flee back to Antioch and then into Anatolia, easy prey for the followers of Elagabalus and fulfilling the oracle that was delivered to him, so we are told, when he visited infallible Zeus Belus at Apameia. His son was killed in flight to the Parthians.[16]

So successful had Severus and his wife been in their aim of establishing their dynasty, and so successful Caracalla in winning the loyalty of the army for it, that when Caracalla was assassinated no claim to rule (donatives apart) was greater than membership of it. That appeal gave direction to the first outbreak against Macrinus and the later defections, though he might have survived if he had conducted a really successful campaign against Parthia and had not altered the terms on which men were to be admitted to the army: existing soldiers thought that their own terms would be the next to change. His coin reverse proclaiming *FIDES MILITVM* ('The Loyalty of the Troops') betrays his unease. Some centurions were loyal, but could not stand against the rank and file.[17]

Domna's sister Maesa had two daughters by her husband Julius Avitus of Emesa, Sohaemias and Mamaea. Sohaemias' husband was likewise a Syrian, Sex. Varius Marcellus from Apameia, who had risen from equestrian service to the Senate; but their son, properly named Varius Avitus, undertook a priesthood at Emesa which was probably hereditary. His connection with the important Syrian deity may have helped to win him the support of soldiery stationed in the east, or recruited there, especially the Third, Gallica, Legion, whose home was close to Emesa at Raphaneae.[18]

So, with the help of a leading member of the aristocracy of Emesa, Eutychianus, and a Gannys, perhaps the boy's guardian,[19] Caracalla's adolescent first-cousin-once-removed, Varius Avitus, became another Antoninus, a Caracalla *redivivus*, though not before Macrinus' Praetorian Prefect had executed Mamaea's daughter and son-in-law.[20] To strengthen Elagabalus' claim it was given out, whether by Maesa or, more plausibly by Eutychianus, as Dio claims, that he was the fruit of an affair between his mother Sohaemias and the late emperor.[21] In 204, the probable year of Elagabalus' birth, Sohaemias was at Rome taking part as leading equestrian lady in the Secular Games. Not surprisingly Elagabalus' coin portraits display the resemblance to Caracalla that Dio and Herodian mention.[22]

Dio and Herodian diverge in their accounts of the rebellion.[23] If Dio is right, in contrast to Herodian, who assigns Maesa a leading role, to attribute the elevation of Elagabalus to Eutychianus and Gannys, acting with the support of a few soldiers, freedmen, and Emesene councillors, without the participation or even the knowledge of the surviving imperial women, and taking Elagabalus to the troops, it sidelines them immediately; and that has some consequences for our view of their significance in the reign that followed, wealthy as Maesa was. There may rather have been an alliance between the women, who must have feared for their boys, and the men who were best able to act for Elagabalus, few though they may have been at the beginning. Certainly Macrinus is said to have 'declared war' on the women as well as the rebels under arms.[24] Any alliance between Elagabalus' supporters began to break up when it succeeded: Gannys had proved a successful commander and was an associate in government, but he was executed on the triumphant journey to Rome.[25] Elagabalus had other allies to please, notably the legionary prefect of the the Second, Parthica, P. Valerius Comazon, who secured control of the Orontes valley and was rewarded with the Prefecture of the Guard. Comazon was powerful and is accused by Dio of causing the death of the senator Claudius Attalus; but he survived the fall of Elagabalus. A lesser equestrian figure, whose name is mostly lost from the stone that records his career, passed from a secretarial post at court to a legionary legateship, perhaps of that of XVI Flavia Firma at Samosata; he held a suffect consulship in the years 217–18, but fell back into the equestrian order, only to be recognized as a 'companion' (*comes*) of Elagabalus and to hold the Prefectures of Grain and the Praetorian Guard in 220–2. Unlike Comazon, he did not live through the next change of emperors.[26]

Caracalla had made no provision for the succession, and we have no idea what Domna's wishes would have been, failing a productive marriage on his part. The lack of preparation was why, when the upheaval came in 217–18, the child Elagabalus and his supporters fatally had little to commend him but his kinship with Caracalla, who may already have been deified by Macrinus in a conciliatory gesture, and whose official nomenclature Elagabalus adapted.[27] His only other asset, in default of training for rulership, was his priesthood, which went back through Maesa and Domna's father to earlier generations of the family. And that post, as much as oriental religious fanaticism, may help to explain why Elagabalus brought the cult to Rome and gave it such prominence. The god of stone was all he had. In the east Caracalla's heir was acceptable to the armies, the priest of Elagabal welcome in the Levant. At Rome matters were more complicated. Caracalla was anathema to many senators while to the common people he was still loved, and the man who engineered his assassination correspondingly loathed. They would not accept Macrinus and shouted to make Jupiter their emperor. Elagabalus or his advisers were to cut that knot. Orders were sent ahead that the representation of the new emperor's deity was to be set up in the Senate House and shown veneration.[28] Attempting to extend his existing authority, perhaps even to provide the exhibition that westerners expected,[29] Elagabalus transported the black stone to Rome with him, arriving there in July 219.[30] In Rome he established temples for the deity, one on the Palatine, the other suburban.

Even that went beyond what Severus and Domna would have countenanced, but some time after he arrived Elagabalus went further, ordering the new deity to take precedence over all others, including Jupiter. If this was not opportunism on his part, there must have been some development in his thinking. That is shown by Dio's account: the priesthood to which he was elected, presumably by the Senate, and the circumcision he is said to have undergone in connection with it, are placed after his arrival in Rome. His original, local, priesthood went back to the period before his elevation to the Principate.[31] The new cult was to subsume other, traditional, practices in an all-embracing syncretism: it was to include their emblems, from the Palladium that Aeneas had brought from Troy, the ancient Salian shields, and the Vestal fire, to the representation of the Great Mother, whose rites he celebrated. 'All gods were the servants of his god'.[32] So Elagabalus caused outrage by finally *substituting* his god for Jupiter Optimus Maximus and imposing his own local practices.[33] His own supremacy was mirrored in heaven, and the syncretism that his system involved was symbolized by his symbolic marriage in 221 to the Vestal Virgin Aquilia Severa and Athena's to Elagabal.[34] The emperor defeated his own ends: he had to divorce the war goddess and Aquilia and offer the deity of the black stone another consort: the venerable Caelestis of Carthage (Tanit), who was likewise brought to Rome.[35] These measures were as harshly judged as Elagabalus' advisers and servants, who were made out to be as depraved as Elagabalus himself, and not chosen for their intellectual or moral endowments.[36]

The reign has had few defenders and would have been the despair of the cautious Julia Domna that we have come to know,[37] but Elagabalus had no trumps to play: descent from Caracalla was no recommendation to the Senate in any case. He took another card, but it was ill chosen. He alienated his peers with high expenditure on displays of power, as Caracalla had done with his costly wars. Domna with her years of experience at the centre would have been a better adviser for him in addition to Maesa, whose power is agreed by the sources, than his mother, the novice Sohaemias. Yet ancient claims that Sohaemias and Maesa ran Elagabalus' regime while he devoted himself to his deity are now treated with caution: at Rome politics and religion were all part of the same fabric, and Elagabal's supremacy tore the fabric of Roman religion.[38] Strategic political positions might have been subject to the influence of the women, but disagreements are reported, and it may have been neglect of Maesa's views, as well as of other factors for stability, that led to Elagabalus' downfall.[39] Maesa can be presented as an advocate of Roman traditionalism. If that is right, it throws an unusual light on stereotypes of female power. Certainly in the sources Maesa is made to try to restrain Elagabalus' myriad extravagances.[40]

Figure 9.2 Julia Maesa and fecundity.
AR. Obv. *IVLIA MAESA AVG* Bust of Maesa, draped, head bare, r.; hairs in vertical waves and fastened in queue and small bun at back; one ridge. Rev. *FECVNDI TAS AVG* Fecundity, draped, standing front, head l., extending r. hand downward and holding cornucopia in l. hand – fold of drapery over l. arm; at feet, l., child, draped, standing front, head r., holding up r. hand. AD 218–23.

Source: *CREBM* 5, p. 539, no. 63.

Sohaemias, on the other hand, according to the *Historia Augusta*, sat on the consuls' benches (*subsellia*) in the very Senate house, the first woman to do so. That would be a public action, and so likely to be true, if the writer of the *Historia* had not been so much inclined to give free rein to his imagination. If it is true it shows how little Sohaemias trusted Elagabalus' other advisers. We are also told, again as a novelty, that Elagabalus would take Maesa into the House – to lend himself greater authority.[41] The story that the same reign saw a *senaculum*, a pseudo-Senate on the Quirinal Hill consisting of women and presided over by Sohaemias, might be a flight of fancy on the part of the author, but he does not allow it any real importance: it dealt merely with 'absurd' matters of female etiquette. The writer may be influenced in his handling of Sohaemias by dislike of later empresses and their preeminence.[42]

Judgments of ancient writers on the excesses of Sohaemias are not borne out by her public face in inscriptions and other monuments, where nothing 'un-Roman' has been detected.[43] Naturally she had not been 'Augusta' under Severus. When her son came to power the obvious title for her, following the example of Julia Domna, was 'Augusta, mother of our Augustus', as she is described in an inscription set up by the Third, Augustan, Legion in Africa, while Maesa was 'Mother of the Camps and of the Senate and Grandmother of our Augustus'. Whether Sohaemias was *Mater Castrorum*, or not, it seems that she never attained Domna's distinction as *Mater Senatus*.[44]

As to the adoption by Elagabalus of his cousin as a safety device of Maesa's we again have the slender authority of the *Historia Augusta*. Dio says simply that Maesa and Sohaemias were present when Elagabalus on 26 June 221 (perhaps the exact anniversary of the day on which Augustus had adopted Tiberius) adopted as his heir his 13- or even 12-year-old cousin Gessius Bassianus Alexianus,[45] who had taken the toga of manhood the same day. Elagabalus on the Quirinal Hill was following Severus' approved example with Caracalla in advancing his heir to the name and rank of a 'Caesar'.[46] In accordance with the rules of adoption and to associate the new heir more closely with the dynasty and its claims to roots in that of the Antonines, he now became Marcus Aurelius Alexander.[47]

The new prop to the regime was also a potential rival, and one who in turn felt threatened; their mothers certainly shared these fears. It was this escalating rivalry and the favour shown to Alexander by the military that led to the Praetorian uprising of 222 in which Elagabalus and his mother were murdered, along with the urban and praetorian prefects. Sohaemias was with her son 'as Augusta and as his mother', says Herodian. The title Augusta had a life of its own and its possessor a twofold status.[48] Maesa did not live long after the change; Herodian overestimates the length of the period, and so her importance.[49]

The return to a style of governance closer to that of Domna's heyday would have been welcome to her. Yet however sharp the ideological change between the two regimes, there was continuity between the reigns of Caracalla, Elagabalus, and Alexander, if only because of the habit and inertia that R. Syme has stressed. Some shifts of 'policy' resulted from attempts of weak regimes to stay in power.[50] Specifically, half the governors of Elagabalus' regime had held office already under Caracalla. Of the Augustae Maesa and Mamaea are likely to have enjoyed a dominant influence, for they overlapped the reigns of Elagabalus and Alexander. There are also officials whose appointment may have been secured by Domna's succcessors: for Sohaemias Aur. Eubulus of Emesa, a financial controller (*procurator a rationibus*) who was killed with his master, and M. Flavius Vitellius Seleucus, *ordinarius* consul of 221, the year after Comazon, and probably a Syrian.[51]

The new M. Aurelius Severus Alexander, one part of whose final imperial name was blamelessly hellenic, while another pointedly recalled the founder of the dynasty, continued it for another thirteen years, and, in contrast with Elagabalus, is eulogized by the ancient sources, largely on moral grounds: Alexander is presented as sober, economical, sound on taxation, righteous, respectful of the Senate and of traditional religion, and anxious to be taken for a genuine Roman rather than a Syrian; Elagabalus' eunuchs were dismissed.[52] Moreover, he is alleged to have appointed two jurists of distinction, Ulpian and then Paul, to be Prefects of the Guard. Ulpian was killed by his own unruly troops.[53] The gesture toward syncretism that the *Historia Augusta* guilefully attributes to Alexander is that of keeping a chapel containing the images of superior deified emperors, Apollonius of Tyana, Christ, Abraham, and Orpheus, as well as his own ancestors.[54]

According to Herodian, Alexander was entirely under the thumb of his mother and grandmother; and the wording of an inscription from Djemila is consistent with this, though it does nothing to confirm it. It describes him as 'Son of Julia Mamaea Augusta, grandson of Julia Maesa Augusta'.[55] This use of the metronymic, although it also occurs for Domna with Geta and for Faustina (II) with Annius Verus, younger son of M. Aurelius, is a curious echo of the attempt that we have already noticed to confer the title 'son of Julia' on Tiberius. It also suggests his adolescent status.[56] With his youth and inexperience Alexander was likely to be under someone's thumb. Although Mamaea is not prominent in the epigraphic record of the reign, it was then that an empress may have attained the status of a *de facto* co-ruler, or one effectively even above that level. She is not allowed an important role in the reign of Alexander as portrayed by the *Historia Augusta*, because it idealizes him. More instructive are the coins on which the Emperor is shown reviewing the city troops, with the legend *ADLOCVTIO* ('Address to the Troops'), with mother and son facing each other on the obverse.[57] Allegedly she both found Alexander's wife Barbia Orbiana for him and then had her exiled to Africa.[58] It was Mamaea's powerful position that made it easier for Herodian to blame her for Alexander's military failures. first against the formidable Sassanid Persians, who had supplanted the Parthians as the great rival to Rome in the east, then against the Germans, and so for their ultimate downfall. She made him behave like a coward.[59] Greed was another of her alleged failings. It probably reflects soldiers' discontent with their pay. Alexander and his mother were killed on 21 March 235 when they were about to buy off the Germans instead of fighting them.[60] The pretext reported for the assassination of Alexander and Mamaea was that he was a 'child'; hence her responsibility for his decision not to fight.[61] He and his predecessor were extremely young, and that had allowed Maesa, Sohaemias, and Mamaea public dominance. Domna had hardly enjoyed such standing, even under Caracalla, for he was a full 23 when he came to sole power, Sohaemias was a widow, and Alexander's father too was dead, probably killed by an officer of Macrinus in 218, like his daughter and son-in-law.[62] Mamaea's high profile and real power have nothing to do with the development of any orientalizing monarchy under the Severan women. It was due to the age of the emperors. The fact that, unlike Agrippina, Mamaea kept her influence until the end may be due to her or Alexander's personality – he had no achievements of his own on which to base his authority – or to a want of forceful or clever advisers like Nero's friends Burrus and Seneca who might have weaned him away from her.

Mamaea was routinely Augusta on her son's accession and perhaps *Mater Castrorum* with it, certainly before the death of her mother Maesa – which shows the latter's relative lack of prominence. Like Domna, Mamaea was to extend the title to cover 'the Senate and her Native Land', and like Domna she had her name on milestones alongside that of the emperor; their subjects referred to them both as 'our lords'.[63] Unofficially, Mamaea equalled Domna in titulature, becoming by 227 'Mother of the Human Race', as well as of the Camps, the Senate, and her Native Land. The phrase *despoina tes oikoumenes*, 'Mistress of the Inhabited World', was also applied to her, and it is not new either: Domna had enjoyed it before, and in conjunction with Severus.[64] The related title *Tyche tes oikoumenes*, 'Good Fortune of the Inhabited World', is another example of the universalizing tendency. It has been thought that Mamaea was being attributed the honours of Cybele, the Phrygian goddess: there will have been an association between them in people's minds, and that this was so is suggested by three votive dedications made to the Magna Mater on behalf of Mamaea; but it was an association that distinguished the two personalities involved.[65]

Naturally Mamaea achieved the same variety of honour and homage as her great predecessor – dedications, honorific inscriptions and votives, vows for the safety of the honorand[66] – even though the commemorations were far fewer in number than Domna had had, and largely the work of comparatively humble officials or of private individuals. The governor of Britain who was responsible for one was a rarity; freedmen are prominent. Two violent changes of regime within five years must have made dedicants less bold than those had been who spent money on in inscriptions and statues under Severus in the confidence that the existing regime would last; and the offerings are local rather than province-wide in significance.[67] The distribution is interesting. The Balkans, Moesia, and Thrace are still prominent, with Nicopolis ad Istrum and now Tomis playing their part, and produced one-third of the dedications; but only a few come from Africa, a province

Figure 9.3 Elagabalus and the troops.
AV. Obv. *IMP P CAES M AVR AN TONINVS AVG* Bust of Elagabalus, laureate, draped, cuirassed, r. Rev. *FIDES EXERCITVS* (*LOYALTY OF THE ARMY*) Loyalty, draped, seated l. on throne, holding eagle on extended r. hand and vertical standard in l.; in front of her, l., standard erect in ground. AD 218–22.
Source: *CREBM* 5, p. 531, no. 10.

Domna had visited and which had had a special reason for honouring Severus and his family. More surprisingly there is a dearth of dedications from Syria, where Mamaea might have expected to be honoured.[68]

The reverses of the Roman coinage after Domna can mostly be traced back through Severan precedents to the Antonine age: *IVNO CONSERVATRIX*, a counterpart of the familiar Jupiter Conservator, emerges into prominence under Maesa. *ABVNDANTIA AVG* or *TEMPORVM* ('Augustan Plenty'; 'The Plenty of the Times') was a novelty, provoked perhaps by the need to reassure the populace that supplies, especially of grain, would not fall short, or that they were being restored; *VENVS FELIX* went back through Domna.[69] The provincial coinages reveal an association with Athena, Artemis, and Cybele, Isis at Aegae and Alexandria, Mithras at Trapezus, Serapis at Magnesia ad Sipylum, all of which can be presented as conservative, and avoiding the innovating extravagance that scholars have seen as streaming in with oriental ideas.[70] Those in the Empire who placated Mamaea's *numen*, called her *thea*, and provided the services of high priestesses were doing nothing new. The importance to the prestige of local families of such well-established offices, and hence the tendency to continue them from one reign to another, should be taken into account.[71]

Mamaea's old all-embracing maternal title took on a distinctively Christian colouring when Galla Placidia interested herself in warring sects of the Church and earned praise as 'Mother of the eternal, true-thinking, and Christian Empire'.[72] This intellectual, philosophical input that came from the Christianizing of the Empire was a development of earlier spheres of religious interest for the Augustae. Although there may have been no more fundamental independence for women, it probably led to a broadening of their room to manoeuvre.[73]

The third century has been parcelled up as an age of crisis, the reasons self-evident: internal disorder and brigandage, defeat and invasion on all sides, a quick succession of brutal soldier emperors, put forward by their troops and slaughtered if they were unwilling, rising costs, especially of army pay,[74] rampant inflation of the currency, demoralization of the provincial ruling classes, the weakening of culture. The word 'crisis' is objectionable, for it implies brisk change for better or worse after a turning point, and this 'crisis' conventionally lasted until the accession in 284 of Diocletian, one of the brutal soldiers, and his establishment of the tetrarchy, which formally divided the responsibilities of Empire between two Augusti and their two Caesars. When it began is less clear, a common problem with attempts to chop history up into periods. It depends on which particular thread is being followed, economic, military, political, or cultural; the moment selected depends on the criteria of the commentators and their point of view. The death of Alexander Severus in 235 was followed by the first of the soldier emperors. At the other extreme, for Cassius Dio, the end of M. Aurelius' reign and the accession of Commodus marked the beginning of an age of iron and rust.[75] Dio was a senator and too close for his own comfort to autocratic and rapacious emperors and to a court convulsed under the weak Commodus by struggles between a series of servants, including freedmen, trusted by him – Saoterus, Perennis, and Cleander – and the aristocrats bent on removing them and reconstructing power for themselves at the centre of the Empire. These struggles, as well as the mere passing of time, gradually eliminated the friends of the respected M. Aurelius. Certainly, as Herodian recounts, Commodus' reign already saw a threatening rebellion on the Rhine, in Gaul, affecting Spain and Italy, led by the deserter Maternus, and the revolt of Bulla.[76] There was unrest in the Empire, and rebels and deserters were encouraged by the campaigns of the early 190s.[77] Even before that, on the military front, there had been invasions in the reign of M. Aurelius that broke into mainland Greece and Italy. The *Historia Augusta*, for what that is worth, seems to take a different turning point from Dio's, the death of Severus: his sons did no good, and the Roman Empire became something for brigands to plunder.[78]

Herodian has been given credit by G. Alföldy for recognizing symptomatic changes that were taking place under the Severi and that were to lead to the 'crisis', while Dio, whenever he was writing the programmatic speech that he puts into the mouth of Maecenas, evidently still believed that the age of the Antonines could be restored.[79] For Herodian, in Alföldy's view, Severus was the first of the soldier emperors of the mid-third century. Herodian understood the significance of the deterioration of relations between military and civil authorities and of Severus' grants of privileges to the soldiery; of strains in society due to alterations in the ruling class (vehemently stressed for the reign of Elagabalus); and of the movements of the Danubian peoples, underestimated by Dio. He thought that the auctioning of the Empire to Julianus was first time the solders' characters began to be corrupted and that Severus undermined discipline by offering the troops easy conditions, leading them astray into luxury. His fantasy of a plan to divide the Empire west and east between Caracalla and Geta foreshadowed what was to happen under the Tetrarchy.[80]

At Emesa the priestly office did not come to an end with Elagabalus; it meant too much to the city from the religious and the financial point of view for that. Besides, local communities had to look after themselves, poised as they were between Persian and Roman power. The rebellion late in the reign of Philip (I) the Arabian (244–9) of a significantly named Iotapianus, who claimed kinship with Alexander Severus, shows old structures still functioning as the central power declined. Iotapianus is 'King of Syria' perhaps of Cappadocia too.[81]

Whether a relative of Domna's carried on the priesthood or it was taken over by a new family, there was still a leader to champion local interests and drum up local resistance in the Orontes valley in the face of Persians invading under Sapor I. The Persians captured Antioch (253) and advanced to Arethusa but no further. The opposition they met was enough, and Sapor withdrew his troops beyond the Euphrates. The thirteenth *Sibylline Oracle*

Figure 9.4 Sohaemias and Venus Caelestis.
AR. Obv. *IVLIA SOAEMIAS AVG*. Bust of Sohaemias, draped, head bare, r., hair waved vertically and knotted in queue and small bun at back. Rev. *VENVS CAELESTIS* Venus, draped, standing front, head l., holding apple up in r. hand and vertical sceptre in l. – fold of drapery over l. arm; star in field. AD 218–22.

Source: *CREBM* 5, p. 536, no. 45.

tells of a priest in the lead, 'sent from the sun, appearing from Syria. . . . The city of the sun will arise, and around her the Persians will endure the terrible threats of Phoenicians.' The priest of Aphrodite who is said to have repulsed the Persians was a Sampsigeramus.[82]

Emesene coins now show a pretender called L. Julius Aurelius Sulpicius Severus Uranius Antoninus, along with the name of the city and a representation of the black stone in the temple. This in the view of many scholars is the Sampsigeramus who saved Emesa, and he went on to declare himself emperor, bolstering his status as a champion of the Empire against invasion. The support from elements of the Syrian legions that he probably enjoyed may have been due to the connection he claimed with the Emesene dynasty. Uranius' rule came to an end when the Emperor Valerian arrived in the east.[83]

Most prominent of the contemporary dynasties there was that of Odenathus of Palmyra which also ended in a declaration of Roman legitimacy – since no help came from Rome – and in the reign of his widow Zenobia.[84] Even the 'legitimate' emperor, Aurelian, struggling with the Persian forces, recognized the divine figure that appeared to him as the Sun god of Emesa; when he occupied the city in 272, he is said to have built a new temple for the deity and even to have established one at Rome; coins proclaimed Sol Invictus as 'Lord of the Roman Empire'. I. Gradel sees in this, and in Elagabalus' earlier installation of his god at Rome above Jupiter, dissatisfaction in the governing elite with the state cult in its established form, though Elagabalus' need to insist on his own legitimacy may also have been significant.[85] Whatever the perceived readiness for reform, Aurelian's was ephemeral, and Jove was re-established by Diocletian; it was with Constantine's recognition of Christianity that innovation triumphed.

Emesa figures as the background to the deaths of two notable men of the age: Odenathus was assassinated in 266 or 267 as he celebrated a festival there, and it was the scene in 273 of the execution of the polymath Cassius Longinus, perhaps a native of the place, who had encouraged the defection of Zenobia. But it passed its heyday with the downfall of the caravan city Palmyra.[86] It is a plausible view that its importance and economic success rose and fell along with Palmyrene; after 235 it could expect little imperial patronage.[87] The pretender Uranius Antoninus put a camel on the reverse of his coinage, whether as a symbol of commerce or simply a reference to his territorial power base is unknown.[88] The historian Ammianus Marcellinus, a native of Antioch writing in the later fourth century, included Emesa in his excursus on the eastern province with Seleuceia, Tyre, Sidon, Berytus and Damascus as one of the great and fair cities of Phoenice, a region full of delights and loveliness.[89] But his contemporary Libanius, also of Antioch, took a closer look. Emesa was in decline, 'no longer a city, though it continues to send ambassadors and crowns to the emperors, knowing its poverty but ashamed to fall from the number of cities, even though its affairs have dismissed it long since'. Worse was to come: the century and a half after 491 produced only half as many coins as the same period before, though a hundred years after Libanius the walnut trees of Mount Lebanon were being cropped by a village that still made Homs its market centre.[90] Nevertheless it survived to become a Monophysite community of Syria adhering to the doctrine that Christ's nature was single and divine. Alienated from the dominant Catholic Orthodoxy of Constantinople, it welcomed the defeat of the Byzantine Emperor Heraclius in 636 and the coming of Islamic rule: 'We like you and your rule and justice better than the oppression and tyranny under which we have been living'.[91] Homs did indeed benefit from the rise of the inland communities, as against the coastal cities, when they ceased to be part of a Mediterranean Empire after the Arab conquest that was to give rise to such fear and awe in western observers.[92] Under Arab rule Emesa became the centre of a province (*jund*). Yet it remained a strongly Christian city, for it was the scene of violent disturbances in 855, when discrimination against Jews and Christians was introduced, and the Christian population was still large in the twentieth century. It is not completely surprising in view of that strong Christian presence that Homs kept a reputation in early modern Syria as a centre of conservative fanaticism, but no connection can be made between that fact and the once powerful life of Emesa as a 'sanctuary-city'.[93] In modern times its fertile plain came to be a centre of cotton cultivation, and the city was industrialized. But Roman columns and Christian relics are still to be seen in the Great Mosque of Homs, which may occupy the site of the old temple.[94]

It is legitimate to ask the question, even if no sure answer can be given, about Domna's perspective on her own age. The ancient habit of viewing humanity as having deteriorated from golden beginnings into men of silver or iron provided her with one framework, and historians' schematization of history into a series of world empires, of which Rome's was the last, offered another view.[95] But the historians' framework was philosophical and theoretical, and however Dio adapted the cliché the decline from gold had taken place long since. Was the Roman Empire now thought to be anywhere near its end? Severan ideology could not allow that. On the contrary, the establishment of the new dynasty was to guarantee continued Roman success. And it was believed: emissions of local coinage and the cutting of inscriptions by communities and individuals is testimony. Domna was under an obligation to believe the doctrine. Her menfolk conducted successful campaigns along familiar lines and without catastrophe in the Near East, north Africa, Britain, and Germany. Until the death of Caracalla she had no reason to believe that her dynasty might not continue indefinitely. She was aware of the shortage of funds for these campaigns. That had been a preoccupation of emperors since Augustus, but the expenditure of Severus and even more of Caracalla on the army on which they depended was a notorious and hated feature of their regime, and another area in which Caracalla outdid his father.[96] It was the very failure of the Severan dynasty to survive that led to the political upheavals of the third century. Those upheavals went along with, but did not cause, military failure, economic problems, and 'one of the most difficult periods for Latin authors',[97] all commonly lumped together as the 'Third Century Crisis'. Until 235, despite inevitable changes in the personnel of the imperial regime, especially with the rise and fall of Macrinus, the continuity noticed above helped to keep government and public opinion, locally at any rate, on an even keel. Most of the unpleasant effects were felt locally, at Rome or in the east.

In relation to her predecessors as 'First Lady', Domna may seem to have enjoyed as great a degree of prestige and honour as any of them, and in her titulature she exceeded what Faustina (II) had enjoyed. Indeed a scholar concerned in particular with the physical manifestations of Domna's power, insists on its intensity: she is shown taking part in public ceremonies both religous and political. It is a bust of Domna that is the largest extant representation of a woman from the ancient world.[98] Yet there is a strong contrast between spectator and leading actor to be drawn. Domna is presented as a spectator at these ceremonies; when she does take a leading role, as at the Secular Games, it is only at the head of the rest of the women. On the coins, the types associated with Domna go back to those of the Antonine women (not surprisingly, when the dynasty strenuously laid claim to descent from theirs). The old female deities and abstractions continued. Only in the provinces could a development be found, with Domna's presentation as Juno alongside Severus as Jupiter-Serapis at Lepcis. With the empress's association in the provinces with such traditional deities as Juno, Athena, and Victoria closes the first phase of her 'reign'; in its second, during the reign of Caracalla, nothing more significant can be found, demolishing the idea of any progress in this direction that was encouraged from above. Interest in oriental cults, notably in the army, was spontaneous, part of a developing mysticism. They functioned without the imperial family, which had repeatedly been proven human, weak, and fallible.

Correspondingly, although she was involved in crises of state, Domna cannot be seen engineering the events of her own time; perhaps with the exception of the fall of Plautianus, there was none in which Domna played a decisive and active role. In this respect she may already have been outstripped by Agrippina the Younger a century and a half before. Even if it is not true that Agrippina murdered her husband Claudius, her adroitness on the day of his death helped secure the Principate for Nero alone, and succeeded in affecting Nero's behaviour during the first five years of his Principate to a degree that is measurable from the fact that he had to have her assassinated. A similar story is told of Livia, that she murdered Augustus, but few are credulous enough to believe it. Much more plausible is the story of Plotina's bringing about, or making up, the adoption of Hadrian on the deathbed of Trajan.[99] Domna failed to protect one of her sons against the other, and the rest of her tenure of her position was, if not well-defined, perfectly conventional: the important thing was she existed as a mother figure. Vows recorded on inscriptions for the safety of Domna's sister Maesa and her niece Sohaemias do not show their domination of Elagabalus' new regime;[100] it was simply that their, and his, membership of Domna's dynasty was important for his legitimacy.

Figure 9.5 Alexander Severus and Liberalitas.
AV. Obv. *IMP C(aesar) MAVR(elius) SEV(erus) ALEXANDER AVG* Bust r. laureate, draped, cuirassed. Rev. *LIBERALITAS AVGVSTI* Liberality standing front, head, l., holding abacus in r. hand and cornucopia in l.; fold of drapery over l. arm. April AD 222.

Source: *CREBM* 6, p. 115, no. 1.

There can be no final revelatory twist. All through this book Domna's position has been plotted by invoking points of reference from other epochs – mainly three. First the role of Livia, the originator; then that of Agrippina, who realized the possibilities; finally that of Theodora, who belonged to an age of entrenched and remote majesty and by force of personality carried the empress's power a stage further towards recognition. The qualities of the sources have something to do with this apparent progress. But so have the achievements of these women. Equally interesting are the gaps, when the issue of female power fades. In this perspective Domna in many ways recalls Livia more than Agrippina the Younger or Theodora. The youth of Caracalla's successors extended the power of Domna's kinswomen in another way, and because of Elagabalus' ideological needs made it look as if they were contributing to a cultural transformation of the Empire and its government. But that was an illusion: the Principate, plastic as it was, was going under pressure through one of its many mutations.

The reputation that Domna left behind her was important for the development of empresses' positions in the future. But Domna could not be seen alone: she would also be judged with hindsight, in the light of the regimes of her female relations. They have been seen by M. Clauss as opening up a way to the accepted influence of women in the Christian Empire, though with a very different dynamic under the influence of the new religion.[101] That may overestimate their importance, for they were not held up as models: rather, gender roles had shifted in the society of the first two centuries of the Principate and opportunities for women to play leading parts remained, to be exploited through a new ideology. Domna's contemporary Cassius Dio was still too close to the court and the scene of action not to remain subject to prejudices. At any rate he considered Domna preferable to Caracalla and Plautianus.[102] By the time the next writers emerge in the fourth century she had become part of the Severan legend, responsible for the excesses of her son, and a precedent for the later over-powerful Severan empresses, Maesa and Sohaemias. After the murder of Alexander Severus in 235 there was hardly an opportunity for dynastic development, and nobody had an interest in claiming legitimate descent from the Severans, or in rescuing their reputation.

Domna's life can be divided into neat segments, girlhood as the daughter of a aristocratic family; early married life; the anxious period of Severus' bid for power; the secure end of his reign, when Domna was empress at his side, interrupted by the enmity of Plautianus; and the period of her widowhood. However, the insidious real change, and a fatal turn for the worse, came as the central period developed, the Severan regime became entrenched, and her sons grew to manhood and rivalry. Caracalla demanded power, and Geta would not be outdone. Her unease may have begun from Geta's elevation to Caesar, and as the feud developed and the outcome became predictable and was finally realized, there was no way back to human happiness. On the most basic level there was fear. The death of Commodus and the ensuing brutal struggle brought her and her family irrevocably into danger, even if Severus was not directly involved; there was no mercy for the woman who had taken part in the plot, Commodus' mistress Marcia, and daughters of M. Aurelius had fallen victim too. Domna's own life was in danger between her husband's bid for power in 193 and his final success in 197, when the wives of his rival were killed. The ascendancy of Plautianus, when Severus was in his fifties and ailing, was another danger. Since the Flavians the imperial women had been secure; even Domitia Longina, the widow of the assassinated Domitian, had been allowed to live in retirement. Later, for the six years when Caracalla was alone in power, Domna would have feared, not the emperor himself, perhaps, but what would happen if he fell without leaving an heir of his body, or at least one who respected his mother. Domna's life as empress was remarkable for its progresses through the provinces, each city making her arrival and that of the emperor an occasion for ostentatious rejoicing, while grand celebrations at Rome were designed to raise the morale of the city population and to display the security of the dynasty. Inwardly it was a never-ending anxiety for that security, and of efforts to protect it. Dio uses Domna as a warning against overestimating the importance of worldly success: looking at her reminds the student that the successful are not to be congratulated unless they can take real pleasure in life, unalloyed and untrammelled.[103] How much either outward pomp or intellectual interests assuaged her fear and grief cannot be told.

So much for Domna's personal story. We can go on to assess the merits of the three other 'stories' that surround her. First, the descent of Domna's immediate family from the first-century rulers of Emesa. Whether it was literal truth or a half-truth based on collateral descent or a distant connection or an outright fabrication, it was useful to her and made it easier for fellow provincials, not least fellow Syrians, to accept her supremacy. Despite doubts based on the lack of direct evidence it has not been disproved.

Next, Domna's power. This must be seen against the background of the power of the dynasty as a whole. Perceptions of the emperor had developed since the time of Augustus. Minimalist conceptions based on constitutional grants, such as Augustan senators might have cherished, faded very early. The emperor, along with his co-rulers, was supreme lord of the world, a conception was fully accepted under M. Aurelius and the Severi. What power Domna had depended on Septimius Severus. She was certainly an important figure in focusing the loyalties of the armies and especially of the eastern part of the Empire, where Severus was confronted by the Parthians as well as by his rival Niger. Severus committed brutal murders and acts of tyranny, responses to fear and intended to intimidate. There is no sign that Domna tried to intervene. Her own effect on internal politics was limited: she was unable to prevent the murder of one son by the other, or to deter Caracalla from actions that contributed to his own death. Her influence is best seen in the deference that was demanded and obtained for her, and

Figure 9.6 Julia Mamaea and Juno the Preserver.
AV. Obv. *IVLIA MAMAEA AVG* Bust of Mamaea, draped, bare-headed, r. Rev. *IVNO CONSERVATRIX* Juno veiled, draped, standing front, head l., holding patera in extended r. hand and vertical sceptre in l.; to l., peacock standing front, body inclined l., head turned back to catch drops from patera. AD 222.

Source: *CREBM* 6, p. 119, no. 43.

in practice in the traditional role of supporting friends in their official careers and as courtiers, with expectation that they would support her in return if she needed it. Dio, outliving her by a dozen years or more, significantly remained hostile to Domna, a woman of power, and the kinswoman of others.[104] He had time to build up a perspective on her life, but may well have fostered existing prejudices under the influence of the shocks that the Senate had taken under Elagabalus. According to Dio, Caracalla inherited his villainy from the Syrian side of his ancestry,[105] but such stereotypical prejudices of Greek-speakers from western Asia Minor are interesting only for the light they shed on the author. Repeatedly the precedent of Livia has seemed relevant. Domna did not wield the power of the younger Agrippina, because her husband was in control through his troops, while Agrippina's had never succeeded in asserting his authority in that way.

Finally, orientalizing in religion and culture and in the Roman state. It is not necessary to deploy that charge against the regime, however repugnant it appears. As to religion, the traditional cults persisted, while the Arch of Septimius Severus gives rise to a different view of artistic development: 'The destruction of the ancient, humanistic attitude still preserved in the Antonine style is evident . . . and with it the generation of a new style, consistent with the changing requirements of an impersonal, monolithic society'.[106] Severus would have admitted to demanding discipline and obedience in army, people, and Senate. But it would have astonished husband and wife alike to be told of the charge of orientalism. Nothing can be found in state cults up to the reign of Elagabalus that could fit this word. More than a century ago, it was insisted that Domna was receiving 'no unusual divine honour'.[107]

The degree of attention throughout the Empire was another matter: it is accounted for by the crisis that initiated the reigns of Severus, and the length of imperial journeys round the Empire. They were offered private cult and other forms of homage according to the varied traditions of their multicultural subjects, who themselves were engaged in coping, in religious terms, with social, political, and economic changes. This is a vital point that must be attended to in assessing changes imputed to the Severi: a single striking case serves to make it: the dedication to Sol Elagabal made at Intercisa by the Emesene cohort stationed there, celebrating imperial visits – in their own way.[108] In her personal interests and studies, Domna betrays nothing that was particularly 'eastern' in character. Her closest associates came from reputable cities of mainland Greece, the Aegean and western Asia Minor, Philostratus was a native of Athens, with family on Lemnos; Antipater came from the Phrygian city of Hierapolis. Any idea that her 'circle' was a response to the advance of Christianity is not well supported.[109] She shared her interests with the intellectuals of her age, and the imperial family responded to its religious enthusiasms. If who we are is determined partly by where we come from, where we are, and what we choose to be, Domna had a wide choice: Syrian princess, cultured Greek lady, but above all Roman empress weighed down with the traditions of that position.

Where then is the historian to stand? In aristocratic Rome before the introduction of the cult of Cybele in the second Punic war? In the second century BC, just before the influx of teachers and philosophers from the Greek east? In the first and early second centuries AD, when Jewish proselytism and the influence of devotees of Isis were a source of fear? Commerce, the influx of teachers, sophists, and philosophers, the institution of slavery and the emancipation in Rome and Italy of household slaves, many of them Greek-speakers, were enriching the society and culture of Rome and rousing suspicion and dislike among insecure conservatives three centuries before Domna's birth. The 'orientalizing' portrait had its origin in nineteenth century German scholarship, which reflects nationalistic views of the Reich and of possible threats to its development and a related ideology of exclusion, sexist, racist, and specifically anti-Semitic. The acceptance of the portrait among English-speaking scholars, beneficiaries of an Empire based on the exploitation of lesser breeds and unconscious of where they were standing, was only to be expected.[110]

Glossary of ancient terms

(Plurals in parentheses)

a cubiculo slave or freedman in charge of (the emperor's) private quarters; chamberlain

advocatus (***advocati***) *fisci* lawyer employed to defend the interests of the imperial treasury

a libellis secretary dealing with petitions to the emperor

alimenta (plural) provisions, sustenance

argentarius (***-arii***) dealer in silver; banker

auctoritas respect, influence that enables a person to get others to obey, even without having the official authority to order them to do so

aureus (***aurei***) gold piece, worth 10,000 sesterces

caduceus winged staff with two serpents, usually carried by the god Mercury

cognitio judicial enquiry conducted on the initiative of the Senate or by a magistrate in virtue of his *imperium*

cognomen (***cognomina***) surname assigned to individuals for personal peculiarities or achievements (e.g. 'Strabo', 'squinting', 'Parthicus', 'victorious over the Parthians'); often hereditary and distinguishing one branch of a clan from another (e.g. Cornelii Lentuli, Cornelii Scipiones)

comes (***comites***) companion (on an expedition); origin of the title 'Count'

congiarium (***congiaria***) a gift, nominally of oil but in the imperial age of money, made occasionally by the emperor, notably on his accession, to the populace of Rome and sometimes to that of other cities

consilium plan; advice; board of advisers, especially *consilium principis*, that of the emperor

Constitutio Antoniniana ordinance granting Roman citizenship made by Caracalla to all free subjects of the Empire

curator (***civitatis***) (***curatores***) official given a charge by the emperor, often of a community, with special reference to its financial affairs

decennalia festivities celebrating ten years of an emperor's reign

denarius (***denarii***) silver coin, worth four sesterces, standard currency throughout the Empire

dies imperii day on which an emperor counted himself as having come to power

diploma (***diplomata***) pair of tablets folded over, especially certificates of honourable discharge given to auxiliary troops and Praetorian guardsmen

duovir (***duoviri***) one of the two supreme magistrates in a Roman colony or *municipium*

eques (***equites***) 'knight', member of the upper class who was not a member of the Senate, possessor of property worth 400,000 sesterces

eques singularis (***equites singulares***) cavalryman selected for duty as bodyguard, orderly, etc.

fanum (***fana***) shrine

fasces (plural) bunch of rods carried before magistrates, embodying their power to punish (consuls had twelve, praetors six, and so on)

flamen (***flamines***) one of a group of prestigious priests at Rome or in Italian or provincial cities with constitutions based on that of Rome

gens (***gentes***) clan; section of Roman society bearing the same *nomen* or *gentilicium* (*gentilicia*), clan name

imperium (***imperia***) power of command granted by assembly of Roman People; primary power of emperors, whose English title is derived from ***imperator***, commander; the Roman Empire, sphere of command of the Roman People

ius Italicum privilege granted to favoured provincial cities, giving their territory the same status as Italian land and so exempting it from tax paid by provincials

latus clavus broad purple stripe on the tunic of senators and young men who aspired to membership of the Senate; worn by permission of the emperor after Augustus and Tiberius

legatus (***legati***) legate (a) subordinate officer of an emperor or a proconsul, in charge of a legion or a province; *legatus iuridicus*, one concerned especially with the administration of justice; (b) ambassador

ludus (***ludi***) games; *ludi saeculares*: Secular Games, held once a century or once every hundred and ten years

municipium (***municipia***) the second highest class of a Roman city, inferior to a colony

neocory, neocorate (***neocories, -ates; Greek neokoria*** (*-ai*) wardenship of temple; title awarded to communities responsible for building and maintaining a temple, usually of the imperial cult

nomen (***nomina***) name, see *gens*

numen (***numina***) divine spirit or will, godhead (literally, 'nod of the head')

officina (***officinae***) workshop, especially of the mint

opus reticulatum 'net-work', brickwork in a diamond pattern

patrician, patricius (***patricii***) member of the original ruling aristocratic families at Rome, or of one later elevated to that status

patrimonium property inherited by one emperor from another

***phylarch*, Greek *phylarchos* (*-oi*)** tribal leader, sheikh

***polemarch*, Greek *polemarchos* (*-oi*)** 'war-commander', one of a college of leading magistrates at Athens

***praenomen* (*praenomina*)** forename given to boys soon after birth, e.g., Publius, Lucius

***primipilaris* (*primipilares*)** centurion commanding the first century of the first cohort of a legion, leading centurion

potentia power not sanctioned by law or custom; often excessive power

***potestas* (*potestates*)** power officially granted (to carry out certain actions)

***procurator* (*procuratores*)** agent in charge of estates or business affairs; if acting for the emperor (*procurator Augusti*), normally of equestrian rank and, in imperial provinces, in charge of taxation as well as estates

proskynesis (Latin *adoratio*) Greek name for obeisance to or prostration before the emperor, a Persian and Byzantine practice also offered to divinities and so taken to imply that the person honoured was more than human

res privata private property (of the emperors); privy purse

***saeculum* (*saecula*)** age, century

***sella curulis* (*sellae curules*)** curule chair, a folding stool of ivory, on which consuls, praetors, and some aediles might sit as a sign of their authority

senaculum place where the Senate meets, often to discuss matters with persons outside the Senate

***sestertius* (*sestertii*)** sesterce, bronze coin and unit of currency

***speculator* (*speculatores*)** military scout; spy

***stator praetorianus* (*statores praetoriani*)** member of a special corps attached to the Praetorian Guard

***subsellium* (*subsellia*)** bench (in theatre, Senate or court)

***sufes* (*sufetes*)** one of the supreme magistrates in a Punic town

***tabularius* (*tabularii*)** messenger who carries letters

toga virilis toga of manhood, garment formally assumed by Roman male citizens when they had reached puberty

tria nomina the 'three names', *praenomen*, *nomen*, and *cognomen*, making up a Roman name (such as Lucius Septimius Severus) that only Roman citizens were allowed to use

***vexillum* (*vexilla*)** banner of an army unit

vicennalia festivities celebrating twenty years of an emperor's reign

vigintivirate*, *vigintiviratus set of twenty junior magistracies, divided into four groups carrying different prestige, held at the beginning of a would-be senator's career,

virtus 'manliness', merit, especially courage

Notes

Introduction

1 She figured as a secondary character in BBC *Timewatch*'s programme of April 2006 on the succession of Caracalla and Geta at Eboracum in 211 and the discovery there of decapitated bodies which may be those of executed courtiers. (I owe this information to the kindness of Professor A. R. Birley.)

2 Individuals in history: L. N. Tolstoy (1957 [1869]) *War and Peace*, tr. R. Edmonds, Harmondsworth, 2, 1425.

3 This story of the deleterious effect of Domna and her dynasty was initiated by the eminent late nineteenth-century student of ancient religion and social history, A. von Domaszewski, and it remains influential: Domaszewski (1895; 1909). For Gibbon too, however, cited by Birley (1999: 197), Septimius Severus was 'the principal author of the decline'. See further Chapter 8, on cult. Distinguished followers included Hasebroek (1921); F. Altheim (1952) *Niedergang der Alten Welt: Eine Untersuchung der Ursachen*, Frankfurt on Main, 2, 255–66. Shahid (1984: 42), on the basis of nomenclature, speaks of 'this imperial Arab matriarchy'. The stereotypical oriental woman emerges in casual phrases: e.g. Ghedini (1984: 10): 'La syriaca, con l'astuzia typical de l'orientale' ('The Syrian woman, with the astuteness typical of the oriental').

4 It was a conventional interpretation of mid-sixth century Byzantine foreign policy that 'Justinian was dazzled by his conquests in the West . . . whereas Theodora believed that the sinews of the empire were in the east', an idea rebutted in Evans (2002: 105).

5 'Orientalism' (of western intellectuals): Said (1995: 2f.). Criticisms: Said (1995: 329–54).

6 The first story is common currency: Millar (1993: 119f.); bibliography for the second and third is surveyed by Ghedini (1984: 187), singling out Williams (1902) for its more balanced view, the radical work of Mundle (1961) and the scrupulous documentation of Kettenhofen (1979: 173 for misguided attention).

7 Beauty: Vict. *Caes.* 21.3, explaining Caracalla's incest with her, naturally says that he was 'forma captus', 'unable to resist her beauty'. *HA Car.* 10.2 describes her as 'very beautiful'. Birley (1999: 76); E. Gibbon (1900–2) *The Decline and Fall of the Roman Empire*, rev. J. B. Bury, London, 1, 127. (Domna died at about 47 years of age.)

8 Representation on the Arch of the *Argentarii*: Williams (1902: 280). For the bust in the Vatican, Ingresso Superiore, see W. Helbig (1963) *Führer durch die öffentlichen Sammlungen klass. Altertümer in Rom*, ed. 4 by H. Speier, Tübingen, 5 no. 5.

9 Hair: Ghedini (1984: 28), citing for Crispina K. Fittschen (1982) *Die Bildnistypen der Faustina minor und die Fecunditas Augustae*. Abh. der Akad. der Wiss. in Göttingen, Phil.-Hist. Kl. 126, Göttingen, 82–8; bibl. 44 n. 16. Variants classified; 89 and 110 n. 339. Baharal (1992: 114) places the characteristic Domna hairstyle after 211. Hair pieces: Ghedini (1984: 44 n. 14), citing Parlasca (1970: bibl. 129 n. 43), and Tertullian, *Women's Dress* 2.7; cf. Clement of Alexandria, *Paedagogus* 3.11. Side loops: Ghedini (1984: Figs. 2; 5–7). Baharal (1992: 110) notes wigs as allegedly characteristic of Assyrian women – and that sculptured wigs appear earlier in Roman portraiture (114). Cf. also Galen, *On the Compounding of Drugs* 1, Kühn 12, 434.

10 Domna as the Venus de Milo: P. Herminius (2001) 'De Mythistorico "Veneris Meliae" artificio eiusque auctore reperto', *Vox Latina*, 37: 331–53, no. 145.

11 Panthea's charms: Lucian *Portraits*.

12 Portraits of Domna: Ghedini (1984: figures); Meischner (1964: plates); Fittschen and Zanker (1983: 27–30, nos. 28–31, Plates 38–40).

13 A face written on: Ghedini (1984: xi).

14 Renunciation of pork: Her. 5.6.9.

15 Historians' difficulties: W. Eck, in Temporini (2002: 105f.); Kettenhofen (1979: 3).

16 The name of Caracalla: Ghedini (1984: 17 n. 33).

17 This point was made by Martijn Icks: John of Antioch in the heading of his account was an exception.

1 The woman of Emesa

1 Syria: Jones (1971: 226, map); the chapter on Syria is indispensable; so too is *Naval Intelligence* (1943). For applications of the names 'Syria' and 'Syrians', see Hitti (1951: 57f.).

2 Geographers: Horden and Purcell (2000: 53) cite al-Muqadassi, with strictures on generalizations.

3 International route: Hitti (1951: 60). Economic life of Syria: Butcher (2003: 135–79).

4 Situation and naming of Emesa, see E. Merkel, in Altheim and Stiehl (1964: 139–48). Olive presses: Chad (1972: 38). Fertile plain: *Naval Intelligence* (1943: 27; 213). Seasonal migration ibid: 270f.) Homs receives about 29 cm. rain a year (405), but there are canals from the river. Coins: Chad (1972: 27), citing H. Seyrig, *Ant. Syr.* 5 (1958) 50f. Dalmatian merchant: *IGLS* 2394.

5 Fluctuating boundary: Hitti (1951: 238).

6 Obscurity of Emesene history: Seyrig (1959a: 184f.). Outline: Butcher (2003: 91–3).

7 'Antiquity' of Emesa: Sullivan (1990: 62).

8 Emesa's situation: Horden and Purcell (2000: 240f., Map 15).

9 Hellenization: Jones (1971: 244). Arethusa: Appian, *Syrian Wars*, 57. Hamath: Jos. *Ant.* 1.138.

10 Revolt of Maccabees: E. Schürer (1973) *The History of the Jewish People in the Age of Jesus Christ (175 BC–AD 135)*, ed. 2 by G. Vermes and F. Millar, Edinburgh, 137–73. Early rulers of Emesa: 1. *Maccabees* 11.39 ('Simalcue the Arabian'); Diod. Sic. 33.4a (Iamblichus); Jos. *Ant.* 13.131 (Malchus).

11 Sampsigeramus: Diod. Sic. 40.1a–b. Pompey: Cic. *Att.* 2.16.2. Annexation: Justin, *Epitome of Trogus*, 40.2.2, with Altheim and Stiehl (1964: 162f.); Chad (1972: 33–8), reviewed by Röllig (1973–4: 283–5) and Sullivan (1990: 63f.; 198f.).

12 Pompey's arrangements: Jones (1971: 260–2). The dynasty: Sullivan (1977a).

Arethusa's era: (Sullivan 1977a: 201f., with n. 13). Arethusa well governed: Strabo, *Geography*, 16, 753.

13 Cicero in Cilicia: Cic. *Fam.* 15.1.2. For the possibility that Cicero took a messenger for the ruler, or that there was joint rule, see Sullivan (1990: 200).

14 Emesene territory: Strabo, *Geography*, 16, 753. Iamblichus at Alexandria: Jos. *War* 1. 187f; Jos. *Ant.* 14.128f.; cf. [Caesar] *Alexandrian War* 1.1: 26.

15 Caesarian and Triumviral Emesa: Chad (1972: 41–5). Caecilius Bassus governor of Syria: Dio 47.27.1; Strabo, *Geography*, 16, 753.

16 Iamblichus killed: Dio 50.13.7.

17 Alexander (*PIR*^{2} A 497): Plut. *Ant.* 66.8 (Alexas). Deposed: 72.3f. Jos. *War* 1, 393; Dio 51.2.2.

18 Iamblichus II (*PIR*^{2} I 7) restored to Emesa, without Arethusa: Jos. *Ant.* 19.338; 20.139; Jos. *War* 7.226; Dio 54.9.2; Chad (1972: 47) puts the restoration in 27.

19 Palmyra inscription: Cantineau (1931: 139, no. 18). Sampsigeramus II (*PIR*^{2} I 541) was still in office in 44: Jos. *Ant.* 19.338. The relationship between Iamblichus II and Sampsigeramus II is unclear: Sullivan (1977a: 212). By 52 Azizus had taken over: 20.139.

20 Sampsigeramus as intermediary: Seyrig (1959a: 185). For Palmyra, see Drijvers (1977: 837–63).

21 'Great kings' at Heliopolis: *ILS* 89 58; *IGLS* 2760. Togidubnus: Smallwood, *G-N* 197, with J. Bogaers (1979) *Britannia* 10: 243–54.

22 Sohaemus: *PIR*^{2} I 582. Emesa: Jos. *Ant.* 20.158. Sophene: Tac. *Ann.* 13.7.1; see Chad (1972: 70); Barrett (1977). Arca: *HA Alex.* 1.2.

23 Jewish rebellion: Jos. *War* 2.481; 483; 501. Vespasian: Tac. *Hist.* 2.81.1; 5.1.2.

24 Sohaemus against Antiochus IV: Jos. *War* 7.219; 226.

25 Azizus: *PIR*^{2} A 1693. Agrippa II: see Jones (1938: 216–61). Drusilla: *PIR*^{2} D 195. The marriage: Jos. *Ant.* 20.139. For these connections, see Sullivan (1990, Stemma 6).

26 Aristobulus: *PIR*^{2} A 1051. Drusilla: *PIR*^{2} D 195. Iotape (IV): Jos. *Ant.* 18.135 with *PIR*^{2} I 45; Sullivan (1990: 297, with Stemma 5).

27 Julia Mamaea and her husband: Seyrig (1959b). Sullivan (1990: 327) admits that the ties with the later family are 'difficult to discern'. A Sohaemus received the kingdom of the Ituraean Arabs from Caligula in 38: Dio 59.12.2.

28 Agrippa's conference: Jos. *Ant.* 19.338.

29 Population of Antioch: *OCD*^{3} 107. Chad (1972: 9), speaking of Emesa as the capital of Syria-Phoenice, thinks of 250,000 there; he notes not more than 2000 in 1785.

30 Increasing wealth of Emesa: Chad (1972: 157f.). Jewels: Seyrig (1958, with colour plate and Plates 25–8). Dyke: Seyrig (1959a: 189, n. 30). The first-century dam on the Orontes enlarged the lake and aided irrigation: Butcher (2003: 140; 163).

31 Phylarch: Cic. *Fam.* 15.1.2; Strabo, *Geography*, 16, 753. Arabs: Dio 50.13.7.

32 Emesenes as tent-dwellers: Millar (1993: 302f.), insisting on the difficulties of assessment caused by lack of evidence.

33 City features: Pausanias, *Guide to Greece*, 10.4; Millar (1993: 256) for criteria. Languages in Syria: Butcher (2003: 283–9).

34 'Arabs': Dio 50.13.7. Emesa's varying name: I. Benzinger 5 (1905) *RE* 5: 2496f. ('Dionysius' in Stephanus Byzantius is not from Halicarnassus). Pliny *NH* 5.81, but 'Emisa' in Ptolemy, *Geography*, 5.14.15. Kuwait: Chad (1972: 56).

35 Categories of Syrian cities: *Naval Intelligence* (1943: 112). Citadel: ibid: 213. Leather working was a significant twentieth-century industry: ibid: 215. Wells: ibid: 355.

36 Survival of names: Jones (1971: 228f.).
37 Building by Herod the Great and Agrippa I: Jones (1938: 78; 98f; 105–10; 211–13). Emesa built up: Liebeschuetz (2001: 56).
38 'Kingdom based on a city': Sullivan (1990: 62).
39 Coining: Head, *HN*[2] 780. A Domitianic issue is rejected: Dieudonné (1906: 133 n. 1); Seyrig *Ant. syr.* 5 (1958), 204 n. 1; it is not included in A. Burnett et al. (1999) *Roman Provincial Coinage* 2, London.
40 Councillors: Dio 78(79). 31.3.
41 Greek inscriptions: Isaac (1990: 226); see *IGLS* 1998–2710, inscriptions from the Emesene district.
42 Palmyrene and Parthian culture and dress: Seyrig (1950); Seyrig (1959a: 190f.).
43 Impossible visit by Antoninus Pius: Chad (1972: 112, but cf. 113).
44 Territory: see map in Seyrig (1959a: 188); Millar (1993: 34), citing *AE* 1939, 180; 300.
45 Arethusa under Emesene control: Strabo, *Geography*, 16, 753. Liberation by Pompey: Jos. *War* 1.156; Jos. *Ant.* 14.75.
46 Wealth of Commagene: when Antiochus IV was restored by Caligula after exile from 18–37, he was granted 100 *HS* m., about 5 *HS* m. each year: Suet. *Cal.* 16.3.
47 Intercisa unit: Cohors milliaria Antoniniana Hemesenorum c. R sagittariorum: *AE* 1910, 141; cf. *CIL* 3, 3328 and 10318 ('*domo Hemesa*'), with C. Cichorius (1901) *RE*, 295; Chad (1972: 125). Local deities: cf. Deus Azizus in *AE* 1910, 142. Title: Fitz (1972) and J. Fitz (1983) *Honorific Titles of Roman Military Units in the Third Century*, Budapest, 257. J. Spaul (2000) *Cohors*, BAR Intern. 841, ed. 2, Oxford, 411–14 (summary of evidence with comments). A *numerus Emesenorum* in Numidia with Caracalla: *AE* 1926, 145, with H. T. Rowell (1937) *RE* 17: 1333f.
48 Emesa annexed soon after 92: so, apparently, M. P. Charlesworth, *CAH* 11, 40; 72–8: S. Schwartz (1990) *Josephus and Judaean Politics*, Columbia Studies in the Classical Tradition 18, Leiden, 116 n. 31, with geographical detail. Not long after 72: Kennedy (1996: 731); Isaac (1990: 40) is cautious; so Sullivan (1977a: 218); cf. Chad (1972: 77f.; 109–11, cf. 114) (without a monarch until annexation by Pius), citing A. Piganiol (1962) *Histoire de Rome*, ed. 5, Paris, 373f. for the view that it remained autonomous from Trajan to Pius; Röllig (1973–4: 285) rebuts a Commodan date.
49 Priestly position: Chad (1972: 74). Second-century connections: Chad (1972: 92–9). Sohaemus son of Diodorus as priest for life at Abila of Lysanias in 166–7: Chad (1972: 123f.), citing R. Mouterde (1951–2) *Mélanges de l'Université Saint-Joseph 29*, 78f. But the name could be a coincidence.
50 Priestly powers: Strabo, *Geography*, 12, 535 (Comana in Cappadocia, with priest and king); p. 537 (Venasa in Cappadocia, worth 25 talents a year); pp. 556–9 (Comana in Pontus).
51 Silas: according to Chad (1972: 92), this was a common name in central Syria, but borne by a dynast of Lysias near Apameia who had been deposed by Pompey: Jos. *Ant.* 14.40. Towers imported into Rome by Elagabalus: Her. 5.6.9, *HA Elag.* 33.6, with J.-M. Lassère (1975) *REA* 77: 131–6.
52 Citizenship: Chad (1972: 58) suggests Caesar as the donor to Iamblichus I; so Braund (1984: 44).
53 Minervinus: J. Lauffray (1944–5) *Bulletin du Musée de Beyrouth* 7, 68, no. 5.
54 Sohaemus and Sampsigeramus: *IGLS* 2216. Sohaemus: *PIR* S 546. For other possible members see the series *IGLS* 2212–14; 2917. A Iotape died in 108 (*IGLS* 2215), and a Iulius Alexander of Emesa, killed by Commodus (*PIR*[2] I 135). T. Flavius Sampsigeramus of *IGLS* 2217, also dead in 108, looks from his *nomen* like an outsider.

55 Ti. Balbillus: *ILS* 4329–31 (AD 199); 1346 (201), from Rome.

56 Sohaemis: Dio 78(79).30.2; Her. 5.3.3; cf. Wuthnow (1930: 110). Symiamira: *HA Elag.* and *HA Macr.* 9.4. Symiasera: Eutropius, *Brevarium* 8.22.

57 The intellectual Iamblichi: respectively E. L. Bowie and D. J. O'Meara, *OCD*[3] 742f. The *Babylonica*: Photius, *Bibliotheca*, ed. Budé (1960), 2, p. 40.

58 Name Iamblichus: Chad (1972: 143), citing *IGLS* 2144; 2320; 2339; 2435 (AD 133 to the Christian period).

59 Home at Emesa: *HA Macr.* 9.1. Chad (1972), in text and in 'Tableau', p. 167, unequivocally lassoos his *dramatis personae*, 157 BC to fourth century AD, for the ruling dynasty. Millar (1993: 119f.) points out that the claim of continuity 'masks profound problems.'

60 Bassianus: [*Epit. Caes.*] 21.1 (Caracalla); 23.2 (Domna's father). Her. 5.3.2–6 (Alexander as Bassianus Alexianus) refers to the cult as 'Phoenician', and Heliodorus, author of the novel *Aethiopica*, calls himself (10.41) a Phoenician of Emesa (i.e. as the people called themselves, a Canaanite); he was taking a liberty with a famous name, which originally applied only to the coastal area containing Tyre and Sidon and western Palestine but later was extended to Palestine and a large part of Syria.

61 'Basus': *CIL* 3, 7751 and 783, with Birley (1999: 223) citing Domaszewski (1909: 209–11) with Chad (1972: 126). Bassus (cf. I. Kajanto (1965) *The Latin Cognomina*, Helsinki) was widely distributed: Wuthnow (1930: 34f.). C. Julius Quadratus Bassus: see below note 81. The adjectival form is interesting; 'Bas(s)us' would have suggested that the holder was permanently a priest; 'Bassianus' implies that the holder had a connection with the priesthood, or, if he took the name late in life, that he was a former priest.

62 Bassiani: *ILS* 8914.

63 Domaszewski (1909: 212f.), on exile at Athens. Quarrel: *HA Sev.* 3.7; hence the Roman citizenship conferred on Athenians also by Caracalla: *IG* 3, 1177, with P. Wolters (1903) *MDAI(A)* 28: 294, on the contrast with confederate Sparta.

64 Emesene cult: J.-P. Rey-Coquais, *PD*, *s.v.* Emesa, with bibl. Black stone: Damascius (1971) *Life of Isidore* in Photius, *Bibliotheca*, 6, Budé, Paris, pp. 42f.; H. Lammens (1919) *Le Culte des bètyles et les processions religieuses chez les Arabes pré-islamiques*, Cairo (*n.v.*). Temple: Her. 5.3.4f.; Avienus, *Descriptio Orbis Terrae*, 1083–90 (mid-fourth century), insisting on its height, and so suggesting that it stood on the later fortress mound. Date: Chad (1972: 123): coins of M. Aurelius show only the stone; the temple may be as late as Severus. Coins of Domna and Caracalla: Dieudonné (1906: 140–5). Betyls: Lightfoot (2003: 546 n. 20). For the siting of the temple at Emesa, see King (2002) and Young (2003).

65 Wide range of cults: Chad (1972: 131–51), citing A. Caquot (1970) *Les Sémites occidentaux* in *Histoire des Religions* 1, *Encyclopédie de la Pléiade* 29, Paris, 339f. ('chaos' at Palmyra and Dura-Europus). Syrian religion: Butcher (2003: 335–71).

66 Chaldaean influence: Chad (1972: 111; 113), noting Iamblichus' *Babylonica* (see above, note 57).

67 Dioscuri: Chad (1972: 139f.; 144). Emesene monument: S. Abdul-Hak and A. Abdul-Hak (1951) *Catalogue illustré du Département des Antiquités greco-romaines au Musée de Damas* 1, Damascus, 80, no. 9, carrying the eagle of Shams. Aziz: *Ant. syr.* 1, 99; 4, 132.

68 Triad at Hatra: A. Caquot (1952) *Syria* 29, 104; 114–17. Elagabalus: Seyrig (1971: 345f.). Triads at Palmyra, with Bel and Baalshamin, both with Aglibol: Butcher (2003: 346).

69 Arab Sun god: Altheim and Stiehl (1966), 3, 125–35. Allât at Emesa: *IGLS*

2571n.; note Minervinus (see above, note 53). The temple in Damascius (see above, note 64) is dedicated to 'Athena'. Chad (1972: 149f.), also shows a bas-relief from Homs in the Musée du Cinquantenaire, Brussels (Athena-Allât, Aglibol, Simia) and one from Khirket Ouadi Souâne in D. Schlumberger, *La Palmyrène du nord-ouest*, Pl. 31, no. 1 (Allât, Shams).

70 Origins of pantheon: Chad (1972: 151).

71 Sun cult at Palmyra: Seyrig (1959) *Syria* 36: 58–60; (H)eliogabalus: *Chronographi Minores, Mon. Germ. Ant., Auct. Antiquissimi* 9, 74; Vict. *Caes*. 23.1; [*Epit. Caes*.] 23.1.

72 Derivation of 'Elagabal': Altheim and Stiehl (1966), 3, 128f.; Millar (1993: 301): 'LH'GBL. Her. 5.3.2–5 calls the language Phoenician, on which see Millar (1993: 305f.) and note 60 above. Swain (1999: 182 n. 81) finds the development less problematical: GBL producing the sense 'creator'.

73 Iamblichus and variants: Wuthnow (1930: 56). Meaning: *IGLS* 2144n.

74 Distribution of 'Sampsigeramus': Wuthnow (1930: 105). Meaning: Hitti (1951: 308 n. 1): Aramaic for 'may the Sun god strengthen'; cf. Chad (1972: 135–7), rejecting the variants presented at *IGLS* 2212 n.: 'Shams a décidé'.

75 Aziz: Wuthnow (1930: 13) (distribution); Chad (1972: 139f.) cites J. Février (1931) *La Religion des Palmyréniens*, Paris, 16–33; *IGLS* 2218.

76 Sohaemus (Suhaym): Chad (1972: 141f.).

77 Coins: Head, *HN*^{2} 780f.; *BMC Galatia* 237–41.

78 Elagabal at Nazala (Quaryaten): Starcky (1975–6). Butcher (2003: 343f.) sees Shamash, the Semitic Sun god, grafted on to a local deity at Emesa. Quotation from Millar (1987: 129).

79 Trade route and Indian plant: Millar (1993: 309).

80 Origin of Emesan prosperity and Elagabal: Seyrig (1959a); cf. Millar (1987: 129).

81 Gaii Iulii in the dynastic family: see above, notes 51f. Governors of Syria called Julius (drawn to my attention by A. R. Birley): *PIR*^{2} I 507 (Antius Quadratus, 104–6), 508 (Quadratus Bassus, 115–17), 573f. (Severi, *c*.132 and 156–9), 618 (Verus, 163–6). *Tria nomina*: Chad (1972: 121 n. 1) on *IGLS* 2359 *bis* and 2361.

82 Plebeian family (*ek demotikou genous*): Dio 78(79). 24.1; *HA Alex*. 5.4 calls her a noblewoman (*nobilis mulier*). See Millar (1964, 166) on Dio's interest in the official standing of the family.

83 It is interesting to note the Sohaemus, of royal ancestry, imposed on Armenia in L. Verus' war of 162–6, after having been adlected into the Senate and reaching the consulate: Photius, *Bibliotheca*, ed. Budé, 1960, 2, p. 40; Dio 71.3.1[1]; Fronto, *Letters to Verus* 2.1.15; *PIR* S 546; Halfmann (1979, 45; 175f. no. 96).

84 Integration and participation in imperial service: Millar (1993: 304).

85 Dedication of Avitus: *AE* 1963 (for Alexianus, see Chapter 2, note 1). Millar (1993: 304) compares the dedication from the tell of Emesa itself by Maidouas son of Golasos 'to the Sun God Elagabalus': Moussli (1983: 257–9 no. 2).

86 Origin of 'Domna': Birley (1999: 72; 222), following Kettenhofen (1979: 76f.) and Shahid (1984: 41f.). Semitic names at Emesa: Nitta (1989: bibl. 286 n. 15). A Sarra is commemorated with her daughters Domna, Sarra and Melcha at Deir-Cheraf, near Sebastyeh: *CIJ* 2, 1169.

87 Name 'Maesa': Wuthnow (1930: 69). Birley (1999: 222), following Shahid (1984) and Hitti (1951: 343 n. 3), implausibly takes it for the feminine version of Maesius, an ancient Roman name.

88 A Sohaemus at Augustan Petra: Jos. *War* 1.574. Connotation: Birley (1999: 222). Mamaea: Wuthnow (1930: 71), and cf. the tetrarchy Mammisea on Pliny's list, *NH* 5.81. Women's names: Rey-Coquais (1977: 177).

89 'Domna' as an honorific title: Kettenhofen (1979: 77): *CIL* 3, 7520 ('Iuliae Dominae Matri castrorum'); 8, 24031 ('Iuliae domine Aug.'); 24091 and 13, 5085 (both 'Dominae Aug.').

90 'Exceptional opulence': Seyrig (1959a: 184f.).

91 Consequences of divorce: Treggiari (1991: 466–9).

92 An inheritance for Domna? Cervidius Scaevola in *Dig.* 32.38.4 (Antonine), cf. 93 *pr.* See Birley (1999: 72; 223) and Zwalve (2001), who argues powerfully for our Domna (the only person known of that name): he had a Syrian-sounding name and would belong to the same generation as the Jewish princess Drusilla's son, who died in the eruption of Vesuvius at Pompeii, 79; the Emesene king took part in the siege of Jerusalem and a kinsman might have served as *primuspilus* (as Ovid's friend: *Ex Ponto* 4.7.49) Vestalis, son of the prince M. Julius Cottius (I owe these references to the kindness of A. R. Birley). It would not have required particular courage to decide against Domna if the case arose before her husband's accession. But cf. *PIR*[2] I 662.

93 Severus' property in 191: *HA Sev.* 2.5 (A. R. Birley drew my attention to the implication of this passage as emended by Mason Hammond 1940). Statue of Septimia Polla: *IRT* 607, with Birley (1999: 214) following Duncan-Jones (1982: 68 and 94).

94 Empresses' patrimony? Temporini (2002: 235), citing *Dig.* 31.1.56f. on the failure of bequests to the deceased Plotina and Faustina.

95 Livia's buildings: Barrett (2002: 199f.); cf. Tac. *Ann.* 3.64.2, allegedly resented by Tiberius, and for the building issue, 3.72.

96 Domna's date of birth: Ghedini (1984: 5) and Kienast (1996: 167) suggest *c.*170. Age of Roman girls at marriage: B. D. Shaw (1977) *JRS* 77: 30–46. Birthday between 25 June and 25 Jan.: Premerstein (1913: 257 n. 2; 259); *Fer. Dur.* 313–16 hazards 25 Sept.; P. Herz (1978) *ANRW* 2.16.2, 1183 n. 343 cautiously proposes Oct.–Dec.; Kettenhofen (1979: 83) notes too the slip in *PIR*[2] I 663, p. 313 (close to the beginning of the Athenian year).

97 Domna the younger sister: Birley (1971: 297); *contra*, Hitti (1951: 343), also commending Maesa's superior ability.

98 Romanization: B. W. Winter (2003) *Roman Wives, Roman Widows: The Appearance of New Women and the Pauline Communities*, Grand Rapids, MI 32–8, invokes S. Alcock (1993) Graecia Capta: *The Landscapes of Roman Greece*, Cambridge; M. C. Hoff and S. I. Rotroff (1997) *The Romanization of Athens: Proceedings of an International Conference*, Oxbow Monographs 94, Oxford; R. Lawrence and J. Berry, eds. (1998) *Cultural Identity in the Roman Empire*, London; G. Woolf (1998) *Becoming Roman: The Origins of Provincial Civilization in Gaul*, Cambridge; C. Ando (2000) *Imperial Ideology and Provincial Loyalty in the Roman Empire*, Berkeley, CA. On east and west specifically in Syria, see Butcher (2003: 15–17 (identities are projected on to the past) and 270–80).

99 Arab expansion: Chad (1972: 17–24).

100 Language at Palmyra: J. F. Matthews (1984) 'The Customs Law of Palmyra: Evidence for Economic History in a City of the Roman East', *JRS* 74: 157–80, at 164; Cantineau (1931: 139–41, no. 18).

101 Scepticism due to lack of evidence: Millar (1987: 129), the editors (p. x) inclined to demur. Hitti (1951: 417) simplistically describes the impact of hellenistic culture on Syria as 'skin deep, affecting a crust of intelligentsia in urban settlements'. Hellenization: Millar (1983); Bowersock (1990: 29–40), stressing the strength of the tradition; Lightfoot (2003: 72–83).

102 Nomenclature: Nitta (1989: 302) speaks of 'sparse hellenization'.

103 Alien languages in court: Ulpian in *Dig.* 45.1.1.6.

104 Western building technique: H. Dodge (1987) 'Brick Construction in Roman Greece and Asia Minor', in S. Macready and F. H. Thompson, eds., *Roman Architecture in the Greek World*, London, 106–16.
105 Pyramidal monuments: Chad (1972: 89f., 91–3), citing E. Will (1949) 'La Tour funéraire de la Syrie', *Syria* 26: 273 (five all-told); Butcher (2003: 298f., Fig. 131). Cf. also the Mausoleum at Halicarnassus and monuments constructed for the family of Jonathan by the Jews (Jos. *Ant.* 13.211).
106 Thugga monument: MacKendrick (1980: 25, with Fig. 1.9) and giving the stylistic verdict.
107 Iranian influence? Seyrig (1937: 7f.); Seyrig (1959a: 191).
108 Sober assessment of the development of Palmyra, part of the Roman world by the second century (*boule* and *demos* by 74, visit of Hadrian, stationing of auxiliaries after Verus' Parthian expedition): O. Hekster and T. Kaizer (2004) 'Mark Antony and the Raid on Palmyra: Reflections on Appian, *Civil Wars* V, 9', *Lat.* 63: 70–80, esp. 79f.
109 Posidonius: Strabo, *Geography*, 16, 753.
110 Apollodorus: *PIR*² A 922.
111 Josephus' and Justus' Greek: Jos. *War* 1.3. Justus: Jos. *Life* 40.
112 Language and awareness of being Greek: Isoc. *Pan.* 50. Apollonius: Flinterman (1995: 89–127 and 233f.). Languages: Phil. *Apoll.* 1.19.
113 Domna's dress: Ghedini (1984: 34–7, Fig. 1 and Pl. B), postulating sketches made in the east for Severus' Parthian triumph. Syrian dress: Butcher (2003: 327–31).
114 Lucian: Rochette (1997: 243).
115 Alexander Severus: Her. 5.7.5.
116 Domna writing Latin: Dio 77(78).18.2.
117 Latin in Britain: Dio 76(77).16.5.

2 Marriage

1 Avitus husband of Maesa: *PIR*² I 190, citing Her. 5.7.3; Dio 78(79). 30.2. Alexianus the priest I 192, with *AE* 1921, 64=1963, 42=1979, 450, and Radnóti (1961); Pflaum (1979); Halfmann (1982; rapid success of C. Alexianus under Severus, and check to his career). The two identified: Bowersock (1983: 117); Leunissen 1989, esp. 379, with consulship about 200; Birley (1999: 223 no. 45), cf. *PIR*² I 192, based on Pflaum (1962), making him first cousin to Maesa's husband; Birley (1971: 298f.). He may have been a kinsman of his wife: the prince of Arethusa and Emesa executed by Augustus was an Alexander (*PIR*² A 497); Birley (1971: 298) recalls C. Julius Alexio of Emesa in the first century AD. For the most recent examination of Avitus' career, see Birley (2005: 200; 225f.; 314).
2 Marriages: Birley (1999: 221–4). Sohaemias' children: *ILS* 478. For a most recent examination of Marcellus' career, see Birley (2005: 181; 226; 299; 313f.).
3 Date of Severus' birth: Dio 76(77). 17.4, implying 145; *HA Sev.* 1.3 (146). See Birley (1970: 65–7); Birley (1999: 220), with bibliography, esp. Guey (1956), for 145.
4 Berenice: B. W. Jones (1984) *The Emperor Titus*, London, 59–63; 91–3.
5 Pompeianus: *PIR*² C 973. Avidius: *PIR*² A 1402. Antioch: *HA Avid.* 9.1. Greek-speaking senators: Hammond (1957) gives an idea of the proportion (more than half provincial senators eastern under M. Aurelius). As to consulars, see Leunissen (1989: 74–87), with only slow changes, and Asia Minor and Africa doing best under Severus.
6 'Syrian' knavery of Caracalla: Dio 77(78).6.1[A]; 10.2; E. Cary's Loeb rendering,

'craftiness', neglects the active component of an adjective that means 'do-everything'. 'Syrian' effrontery (*tolmema*): Dio 78(79). 39.4.

7 Earrings: Petronius, *Satyricon* 102.14; Juvenal, *Satires* 1.104. See the warrior mask from Homs, now in Damascus, illustrated in Seyrig (1952: Pl. 27 no. 6); Chad (1972: 55).

8 Gallic contribution: Tac. *Ann.* 11.23.6.

9 Juvenal's prejudice: Juvenal, *Satires* 3.60–2: 'Non possum ferre, Quirites, Graecam urbem'.

10 African senators: Hammond (1957) (one-third the provincials African under M. Aurelius); Pelletier (1964) (great advance over Gaul under Severi); Birley (1999: 19; 24f.) (the men and their background).

11 First consul from Africa: Q. Aurelius Pactumeius Fronto of Cirta: *ILS* 1001; *PIR*[2] P 38.

12 Urbicus: Birley (1999: 24f.).

13 Agricola and Severus' brother: Birley (1999: 34). Younger or elder: Birley (1999: 218).

14 Salvius Julianus: Birley (1999: 25; 40f.).

15 Cornelius Fronto: *PIR*[2] C 1364.

16 Africa and advocates: Juvenal, *Satires*, 7.148f.

17 Petronius: *PIR*[2] P 288.

18 Severus' kinsman: *HA Sev.* 1.2 has great-uncles (*patrui magni*). Severus' father: Birley (1999: 213f. no. 20); stemma 216f. Consuls: P. Septimius Aper (214 no. 15) and C. Septimius Severus (219 no. 25), sons of the Lepcitane magnate C. Claudius Septimius Aper (214 no. 16).

19 Lepcis/Leptis: I follow Birley (1971: 20, n. 1) (cf. Birley 1999: 19) in preferring the former; cf. *IRT* p. 73. Early history and Libyan name LPQY: Birley (1999: 2f.).

20 Tribute: [Caesar] *War in Africa* 97.

21 Lepcis' status: Aurigemma (1950); Guey (1953: 351–8).

22 Neo-Punic: *IRT* 10–13. It continued in Tripolitania until the end of Roman rule, at Lepcis down to Domitian: Millar (1968: 132f.). Oea: Sicinius Pudens, cited by Birley (1999: 26) (Apuleius, *Apologia* 98).

23 Severus as 'African': contending views: see Birley (1971: 2–4), with Domaszewski (1909) and Hasebroek (1921) in one corner and Platnauer (1918) in the other; further bibl. Ghedini (1984: 9, n. 75).

24 Intermarriage: Birley (1999: 220).

25 Severus' Italianized forebear: Statius, *Silvae* 4 *pr.*: 'one of the most cultivated members of the second order in the state'; 4.5. 33–40. The comment of Broughton (1929: 132) lacks nuance.

26 *Nomen* Septimius: Birley (1999: 219): in (Neo)Punic the word *sufetim* and the name Septimius, especially in the vocative, might both have been written as PT.M.

27 Gallicus: PIR 2 R 248; Birley (1999: 16; 18f.). Statius, *Silvae* 1.4.

28 'Punic Sulla': *HA Nig.* 6.4; Miller (1939: 23f.).

29 Severus' tastes and appearance: *HA Sev.* 19.7–9. As to beans (*leguminis*) and height, A. R. Birley draws attention to Syme (1968: 201):

> What might be this vegetable, identity of which is taken for granted? Not obvious to everybody, at least in later ages. One might have suspected garlic – Severus was cruel and insensitive. Perhaps the leek. . . . Better . . . the chick-pea. . . . Not so. It is invention. The next sentence describes the physique of Severus. He was 'ingens'. That is false. Cassius Dio contradicts: he was short and sturdy [76(77).16.1].

30 Severus' deficient education: Dio 76(77).16.1.
31 Severus' voice: *HA Sev.* 19.9. Punic: [*Epit. Caes.*] 20.8. Latin and Greek: Dio 76(77).17.2; *HA Sev.* 1.4. Philosophy: 18.5. Literature and success: 18.11. See Hammond (1940); Barnes (1967).
32 African accent: *HA Sev.* 18.9; see Birley (1999: 35) (provincial, not foreign) and p. 42. Sabine vowels: Suet. *Vesp.* 22. Hadrian: *HA Hadr.* 3.1.
33 Narbonensis Italian: Pliny *NH* 3.31.
34 Julianus' mother: *HA Jul.* 1.2.
35 Public speech and departure for Rome: *HA Sev.* 1.5.
36 Severus' sister: *HA Sev.* 15. Latin forgotten: Birley (1999: 131f.; 213f.). Sceptical: Hasebroek (1921: 116).
37 Husbands educating wives: Pliny *Ep.* 1.16.6.
38 Severus not a military tribune: see *HA Sev.* 2.3, against Eutropius, *Breviarium* 8.18, who also makes him a Treasury advocate, with Birley (1999: 39f.).
39 Snakes and ladders in dim senatorial careers: *ILS* 915; Birley (1999: 50) notes that Sardinia's Punic legacy may have interested Severus.
40 Lepcis arch: *AE* 1967, 536.
41 Support from M. Aurelius: Birley (1971: 90) on *HA Sev.* 3.1, against Hasebroek (1921: 8).
42 Command of IV Scythica: *HA Sev.* 3.6; see Birley (1999: 58).
43 Age of iron and rust: Dio 71(72). 36.4, cf. Her. 1.1.4; for Commodus' reign in Herodian, see Zimmermann (1999: 43–150). Golden age: Millar (1964: 122f.), followed by Hekster (2002: 98), on '*Saeculum felix*' ('Fortunate age').
44 Condianus: Dio 72(73).6.1–7.2.; *HA Comm.* 4.9, with Grosso (1964: 158f.) and Birley (1999: 61f., 73). Athens: *HA Sev.* 3.7.
45 Pertinax's restoration: *HA Pert.* 3.3–5.
46 Penalties for celibacy: Suet. *Aug.* 34; *Tituli Ulpiani* 14, cited by Treggiari (1991: 73f.): no grace period was allowed men.
47 Paccia: *PIR*[2] P 20. Marriage: *HA Sev.* 3.2; cf. 14.4.
48 Daughters: Birley (1999: 225), on *HA Sev.* 8.1, citing Hasebroek (1921: 49).
49 Paccia ignored in autobiography: *HA Sev.* 3.2. Monuments to Paccia and Severus' family: *ILS* 440; *IRT* 410–23.
50 Marriage and horoscope: *HA Sev.* 3.9, cf. *HA Geta* 3.1. Friends: *HA Sev.* 3.9. Sceptical: Syme (1976: 300), adding the plebeian origin as another item to be deleted after Severus became emperor.
51 Domna's name: Birley (1999: 75f.). Hitti (1951: 307) thinks that the oracle of Bel at Apamea foretold Domna's greatness.
52 Meeting of Severus and Domna: Kettenhofen (1979: 59), with n. 387 discussing the source.
53 Severus' career: *HA Sev.* 2.2–4.7.
54 Maternianus: Dio 78(79).4. Earlier fatal horoscopes and consultations: e.g. Tac. *Ann.* 2.30 (Libo Drusus); 16.41 (P. Anteius).
55 Superstition: Birley (1999: 41f.), citing Cramer (1954: 208–17); cf. Dio 74(75).3.1 and 3; Her. 4.12.3f.; *HA Sev.* 1.7–10; *HA Geta* 2.6, where it is attributed to men from north Africa. Hasebroek (1921: 7) uses *HA Sev.* 2.8f. (AD 173) to show a preoccupation going back to early years in Africa. Astrologer: *HA Nig.* 9.6. Niger: *RIC* 4.1, p. 30, no. 44a and 44b.
56 Egyptian ban: J. Rea (1977) *ZPE* 27: 151–6.
57 Severus' response to Dio's treatise: Dio 72(73).23.1f.
58 Autobiography: Her. 2.9.4. 'Poor stuff': R. G. Lewis (1993) 'Imperial Autobiography, Augustus to Hadrian', *ANRW* 2.34.1, Berlin, 629–706, at 706. The evidence, besides *HA Sev.* 3.2, is *HA Nig.* 4.7; 5.1; *HA Alb.* 7.1; 10.1; 11.4; Her. 2.9.3. Omens: Dio 74(75), 3.
59 Tarraco: *HA Sev.* 3.4.

60 Oracle of Bel twice consulted: Dio 78(79).8.5f.; first it quoted Homer *Iliad* 2.478f., a flattering description of Agamemnon, later Euripides, *Phoenissae* 20. Balty (1981: 6) dates the first visit to 180. Imperious deity: Balty (1981: 10 n. 34); 'Fortunae rector': *CIL* 12, 1277.

61 Charge of consulting seers: *HA Sev.* 4.3.

62 Faustina preparing the nuptial chamber: Dio 74(75).3.1.

63 Dowry rules: J. F. Gardner (1986) *Women in Roman Law and Society*, London, 97–109, esp. 102.

64 Epithalamium: *Pan. Lat.* VII (6), with R. Rees (2002) *Layers of Loyalty in Latin Panegyric,* AD *289–307*, Oxford, 168.

65 Leap in the dark: Ghedini (1984: 16, n. 3). Hadrian and Domna: ibid. xii.

66 Date of marriage: *HA Sev.* 3.9; Dio 78(79).6.5; Röllig (1973–4: 175); Ghedini (1984: 4 and 16, n. 22) (185 or 187). Governor forbidden to leave province (*exire provinciam*): Cicero, *Against Piso* 50.

67 Birth of Caracalla: Dio 78(79).6.5 (4 April 188); cf. *HA Sev.*3.9; *HA Car.* 9.1 and Eutropius, *Breviarium* 8.20.2 (died at 43!); [*Epit. Caes.*] 21.7 (about 30); Hasebroek (1921: 12). Year: Hammond (1940: 161f.) and (definitive) Alföldy (1996), explaining (31 n. 58) how 186 (favoured by Ghedini 1984: 5f.) came to be implied; 186 makes it necessary to take Domna as Caracalla's stepmother.

68 Christian milk: Tertullian, *To Scapula* 4.6 (with Severus saving Christians of senatorial rank 4.7), so taken by Frend (1965: 324). Metaphorical '*lac*': *TLL* 7.2, 818 at C 2 b. Lugdunum Martyrs: Eusebius, *The History of the Church* 5.1–3, with Frend (1965: 1–30). Alternative explanation: H. U. Instinsky (1963) *Die alte Kirche und das Heil des Staates*, Munich, 75f., n. 27; Birley (1999: 154), and 'Attitudes to the State in the Latin Apologists', in *L'Apologétique chrétienne gréco-latine à l'Epoque prénicénienne*, Entretiens sur l'Ant. class. 51, Geneva, 249–89, at 258 n. 22. It is also implausible to bring *HA Car.* 1.6, on the 7-year-old Caracalla's indignation at the beating of a friend for Jewish (i.e. Christian?) sympathies in connection with this passage.

69 Maternus: Her. 1.10, sceptically examined by Hekster (2002: 64–7); *HA Comm.* 16.2; *HA Nig.* 3.4. See also Alföldy (1989: 69–80) and Zimmermann (1999: 63–6; 85–112) for comprehensive deconstruction.

70 Sicily: *HA Sev.* 4.2.

71 The date of Geta's birth, 27 May (189), according to *HA Geta* 3.1, was long accepted; independent, authentic evidence points to another date, as shown by Barnes (1968a: 522–5), 7 March, followed by Birley (1999: 218). Cf. *HA Sev.* 4.2 (Rome, accepted by Balsdon 1962: 151); Whittaker *ad* Her. 3.10.1, suggests that he was born in Sicily, but the birth date was well before the start of the proconsular office.

72 Stepmother: *HA Sev.* 20.2; *HA Car.* 10.1; *HA Geta* 3.3; 7.3; Vict. *Caes.* 21.3; [Epit. Caes] 21.5; Orosius, *History against the Pagans* 7.18.2; *contra* [Oppian] *Cynegetica* 1.4; Phil. *Soph.* 622; *CREBM* 5, lxxxvi (both sons on coins). Incest: see Chapter 6.

73 *Praenomen*: Bleckmann (2002: 270). See also Birley (1999: 218), suggesting that the change may have been due to an attempt to avoid confusion with his uncle, and was reversed after the uncle's death.

74 Sight of Rome: Amm. Marc. 16.10.13–15.

75 *Synkletikos/hypatikos*: e.g. *IGR* 3, 95, a woman from Pontus; C. Roueché (1993) *Performers and Partisans at Aphrodisias in the Roman and Late Roman Periods*, *JRS* Monographs 6, London, 179, no. 56.

76 Maesa: Her. 5.3.2; 8.3. Bassianus: Williams (1902: 260), citing the Arval Acts of 213, where Gessius Bassianus presides (*CIL* 6, 2086).

77 Harmony (*CONCORDIAE AETERNAE*) rev.: *RIC* 4.1, 162, no. 522: Severus radiate, Domna on crescent, jugate.
78 Nero's heterosexuality: E. Champlin (2003) *Nero*, Cambridge, MA, 162–7.
79 Cornificia: *HA Pert.* 13.8.
80 Charges against Domna: *HA Sev.* 18.8, where D. Magie blames Plautianus, citing Dio 75(76).15.6; 78(79).24.1.
81 Twenty-five consuls in 190: Dio 72(73).12.4. A. R. Birley suggests that it was a scheme of Cleander's for making money.
82 Consulship: Leunissen (1989: 132).
83 Estate: *HA Sev.* 4.5f.
84 Ostrich: Dio 72(73). 21.1–3. See Hekster (2002: 154f.).
85 Alexander: Dio 72(73).14.1–3; *HA Comm.* 8.3, with Grosso (1964: 322–6), noting the broken-backed narrative (Rome, then Syria), and Birley (1999: 223).
86 Laetus: *PIR*[2] A 358; *AE* 1949, 38, with Birley (1969: 252f.); Birley (1999: 82).
87 Visit to Africa: *HA Comm.* 9.1.
88 Commodus' last appointments: Birley (1999: 83–8). Julianus and Laetus: *HA Jul.* 6.2. Albinus' career: Alföldy (1968); see also Birley (2005: 174–80).
89 Severus not a candidate for Empire: Hammond (1940: 164). Severus implicated in a widespread plot: Domaszewski (1898); Càssola (1965: 474f.).
90 The murder: Dio 72(73). 22.1–6; Her. 1.16f.; *HA Comm.* 17.3; Vict. *Caes.* 17.8f.; see Birley (1999: 87f.).

3 Domna on her travels

1 Domna at Rome in 193: Ghedini (1984: 6). Wives and mistresses from Commodus to Julianus: see Chapter 4.
2 Pertinax's involvement: *HA Pert.* 4.4; in Her. 2.1.3f. the plotters think of him after the murder; cf. Dio 73(74) 1.1f. (ambiguous).
3 Reign of Pertinax: Dio 73(74).1–10; *HA Pert.* 4–15. Julianus: Dio 73(74). 11–17.6; Her. 2.6.4–5.14; *HA Jul.* 2–8. Unpopularity and assassination: Dio 73(74). 9.1–10.3; Her. 2.4f.; *HA Pert.* 10.8–11.13; 15.6f. (inconsistent dating). Pertinax's murder: Dio 73(74). 9f.; *HA Pert.* 10.8–11.13. Caretaker: Champlin (1979), but see Zimmermann (1999: 159–64): Herodian's version as a worthless reworking (to fit his preconceived ideas etc.) of Dio 73(74).3.3 (Pompeianus and M'. Glabrio in positions of honour on either side of the imperial chair).
4 Severus' dream: Dio 74(75).3.3; Her. 2.9.5f.
5 Laetus suspect: Dio 73(74).8.1; *HA Pert.* 10.8.
6 Niger's military success: Dio 72(73).8.1. Roman support: Dio 73(74).13.5; Her. 2.7.2–6; *HA Nig.* 2.2f.; 3.1.
7 Julianus' fear of Niger: *HA Jul.* 5.1; *HA Nig.* 2.4.
8 Albinus of Hadrumetum (*HA Alb.* 1.3; 4.1) was a kinsman of Niger's principal supporter Asellius Aemilianus (Dio 74[75].6.2), though not of Niger himself: Albinus' little son 'Pescennius' in *HA Alb.* 7.5 is an invention; and Hadrumetum was the home town of Didius Julianus' mother (see Chapter 2, note 34). On Albinus' family, with its connections with D. Clodius Albinus, see Chausson (2002: 860f.). On the pre-193 careers of Niger and Albinus, cf. remarks in Birley (2005: 178–9). After 193: Schumacher (2003).
9 Candidates of 193: Dio 73(74).14.3–5.
10 Moesian legions in 69: Suet. *Vesp.* 6.2.
11 Events of 69: K. Wellesley (2000) *The Year of the Four Emperors*, ed. 3, London.
12 Consultation and legionary histories: Birley (1999: 97; 158).

13 Severus' coup: *HA Sev.* 4–6, the date confirmed by the *Fer. Dur.* 2.3, 100f. Fall of Julianus: *HA Jul.* 5–8.

14 Geta's position: Leunissen (1989: 250). Supporters rewarded: Whittaker *ad* Her. 2.9.12; legions *ad* 10.1. Pudens (suff. AD 194; legate of Lower Germany 197–8): There is now evidence that Pudens' predecessor was still governor of Pannonia Inferior in August 192: cf. Birley (2005: 186–8, esp. 187 n. 20), with further refs.

15 Attempts on Severus: Dio 73(74).16.5–17.1; *HA Sev.* 5.8; 7.4; *HA Nig.* 2.6. *HA Jul.* 5.8. Severus' attempt on Albinus: Her. 3.5.2–8; *HA Alb.* 8.

16 Division of Empire proposed: *HA Jul.* 6.9.; *HA Sev.* 5.7f.

17 Interamna: *HA Sev.* 6.2.

18 Avenging Pertinax: *HA Sev.* 5.4; Birley (1999: 97; 105; 199f.).

19 'Pius': Birley (1999: 200). Taking Pertinax's name: *HA Sev.* 7.9 (later regretted). Date of 'Pius' (regularly from 195): A. Magioncalda (1991) *Lo sviluppo della titolatura imperiale da Aug. a Giustiniano attraverso le testimonianze epigrafiche*, Turin, 49. For the iconography of Pertinax, Severus and his rivals, leading back to that of the Antonines, see Balty (1964).

20 '*Pertinax*' and '*severus*': *HA Sev.* 14.13.

21 Severus in Rome in person: Her. 2.12.2.

22 Julianus' Praetorians: Dio 73(74).17.2.

23 Promise not to execute senators: Dio 74(75).2.1–3. Decorations: 4. Ups and downs in relations with the populace: Sünskes Thompson (1990: 104–12). Largesses: ibid. 104–6.

24 Niger's claim: *HA Sev.* 6.7.

25 Albinus Caesar: Dio 73(74).15.1; Her. 2.15.2–4; *HA Alb.* 1.2; 3.4 (where the offer is genuine); *ILS* 414f. See on Albinus and the years 193–7 Schumacher (2003) and Birley (2005: 174–80). Schumacher (2003: 368f.) pointedly contrasts Albinus with C. Liciniuus Mucianus, Vespasian's potential rival who had nonetheless accepted him: Tac. *Hist.* 2.77.1.

26 Byzantium besieged: Dio 74(75).10.1–13.6.

27 Change in the Guard: Dio 74(75).1.1f.; 2.4–6. Legionary recruitment: G. Webster (1996) *The Roman Imperial Army of the First and Second Centuries* AD, ed. 3, London, 108.

28 Life of Prime Minister's spouse: C. Blair and C. Haste (2004) *The Goldfish Bowl: Married to the Prime Minister*, London, esp. 263–81.

29 'Funeral' of Pertinax: Dio 74(75).4.1–5.5; *HA Pert.* 15.1–5; *HA Sev.* 7.8f. Headgear: Ghedini (1984: 28 and Pl. 1). Resemblance between this and the headgear of Batnanaia at Dura Europus seems to be exaggerated by Haynes and Hirst (1939: 18f.), based on F. Cumont (1926) *Fouilles de Doura Europos*, Paris, *Atlas* XXXVf.

30 Severus' day: Dio 76(77). 17.1–3. Murder of Plautianus: see Chapter 5.

31 Commodus' hostages: Her. 3.2.4.

32 Securing sons: Birley (1999: 97) suggests Fabius Cilo as the agent.

33 Niger's children, and those of his ally Asellius Aemilianus: Her. 3.2.3–5; 3.5.6 (Niger's generals); *HA Sev.* 6.10f.; 8.11; 9.2; 10.1; *HA Nig.* 6.1f.

34 Time taken for news to arrive from the east: EJ^2 69 yields 21 Feb. to 2 April in AD 4. Campaign against Niger: Dio 74(75).6.1–8.3; Her. 3.1–4.6; *HA Nig.* 5.2–6.1.

35 Departure from Rome; Geta's offer: *HA Sev.* 8.8 and 10.

36 Perinthus: Halfmann (1986: 219), citing Schönert (1965: 20; 172f., nos. 461 and 463); cf. E. Hohl (1924) *Bursians Jahresbericht* 200: 202.

37 Dating of Niger's defeat: Birley (1999: 112f., with n. 13); Magie (1950: 1540) and Halfmann (1986: 219) assign Issus to May; similarly Whittaker *ad* Her. 3.4.2.

38 Murder of Vitellius' son: Tac. *Hist.* 4.80.1; Suet. *Vit.* 18.

39 Fate of individuals: Barnes (1968b).

40 Inter-city feuds: Nicaea and Nicomedia: Her. 3.2.9; 3.3; Laodiceia and Antioch, Tyre, and Berytus: 3.3–5. Rewards and punishments: Downey (1961: 239–42); Ziegler (1978), with Antioch a restored city 197–8, when Laodiceia obtained its colonial status Birley (1999: 114f.). Antioch: Her. 3.6.9; *HA Sev.* 9.4f. Others: 5 and 7. Rewards: Ulpian in *Dig.* 50.15.1. Byzantium was also punished eventually: Her. 3.6.9.

41 Province of Phoenice: E. S. Bouchier (1906) *Syria as a Roman Province*, Oxford, 93n. Boundaries: Butcher (2003: 84f.): starting between Paltus and Balaneae-Leucas, they ran inland north of Raphanea and south of Arethusa to include Palmyra, but not Dura Europus.

42 Severan coins from Emesa, 193–6: *CREBM* cxvii–xxi; D. R. Walker (1978) *The Metrology of the Roman Silver Coinage 3. From Pertinax to Uranius Antoninus*, *BAR* Suppl. 40, Oxford, 14f.; Birley (1999: 246, n. 12) ('dubious'); dating from the advance of Severus' army: Rubin (1980: 205); Walker (1978: 60f.). Emesa a colony with *ius Italicum*: Ulpian in *Dig.* 50.15.1.4; Paulus at 1; 8.6. Coins have *EMISON (sic) KOLONIAS* and *METR(OPOLEOS) KOL(ONIAS) EMISO(N): BMC Galatia* 238–40, nos. 9–21. Centuriation: W. J. Van Liere (1958–9) 'Ager Centuriatus of the Roman Colonia of Emesa (Homs)', *Annales Archéologiques de Syrie* 8–9: 55–8 (maps); *Barrington* 68 C4 shows an area about 10 km. square to the north-east of the city.

43 Celebrations of Severan passage: cf. the boycott at Anazarbus by the philosopher Agesilaus, father of Oppian: *PIR*^{2} A 457.

44 Burdensome imperial transits: Millar (1977: 28–39) (balanced view). Domitian and Trajan: Pliny *Pan.* 20. *SEG* 37, 1186, from Tacina, is a letter of Caracalla on soldiers' misconduct. Billeting: e.g. R. Rees (2004) *Diocletian and the Tetrarchy*, Edinburgh, 48, on *P. Beatty Panopolis* 1.53–9; 167–79; 221–4; 249–51; 332–7. Bunting, etc.: *Pan. Lat.* 5 (8). 8.4, tr. Rees 138. *Adventus*: S. G. MacCormack (1972) 'Change and Continuity in Late Antiquity: the Ceremony of *Adventus*', *Hist.* 21: 721–52; A. R. Birley has kindly drawn my attention to J. Lehnen (1996) *Adventus Principis: Untersuchungen zu Sinngehalt u. Zeremoniell der Kaiserankunft in den Städten des Imperium Romanum*, Prismata 7, Frankfurt (dynastic aspect 254f.).

45 Winsome sons: the Berlin tondo, Berlin, Staatliche Museen. Preussischer Kulturbesitz, Antikensammlung, Inv. 3139, with Neugebauer (1936). Geta's portrait survives on coins.

46 *Expeditio Asiana* ('Expedition into Asia'): *ILS* 1140; Dio 75. 1–3; *HA Sev.* 9.9–11. Byzantium: Dio 74(75). 14.1; with Hasebroek (1921: 79f.). A fine pair of dedications was made to Severus and Domna at Bostra in that year: Fiaccadori (1999).

47 Tracking the expedition: a soldier of X Gemina dying en route in Ancyra in early September 195: *AE* 1941, 166.

48 Domna as '*Mater Castrorum*': *PIR*^{2} I 663 (pp. 313f.), dated in *BGU* 2, 362, 13, xi., l.16f.; *CIL* 12, 4345; 14, 120; Instinsky (1942: 200–3); Kettenhofen (1979: 79–81), variants 230 n. 39. Symbiosis: Montalbò (1999: 346).

49 An 'un-Roman' title: Domaszewski (1909: 72); *contra*, Instinsky (1942: 200–3), following Alföldi (1934: 69). Fink et al., *Fer. Dur.* 175, suggest that the title carried with it a military cult and Whittaker *ad* Her. 3.5.1, that it coincides with one of Severus' salutations as *imperator*. First epigraphic attestation: Kettenhofen (1979: 81) (year ending 9 Dec. 195; *CIL* 8, 26498, with Clodius Albinus as Caesar); thenceforward the title appears on two-thirds of inscriptions that mention her and on 90 per cent of those set up in her

honour. Significance of *Parthicus Arabicus* and *Parthicus Adiabenicus*: Birley (1999: 116).

50 Caligula 'Father of the Armies': Suet. *Cal.* 22.1, with Wardle (1994) *ad loc.* noting Tac. *Ann.* 2.55.5.

51 Faustina's title of 174 or 175: Dio 71(72).10.5, noted by Instinsky (1942: 201f.); see also Kettenhofen (1979: 230 n. 43); it coincided with Marcus' seventh salutation as *Imperator* on his victory over the Quadi.

52 Domna portrayed on military equipment: Ghedini (1984: 18 n. 48). Portraits: *Fer. Dur.*, 174 n. 807. Helmet: M. Rostovtzeff and P. V. C. Baur (1931) *The Excavations at Dura-Europus: Preliminary Report of Second Season*, New Haven, CT, 2, 183, with Plate 23 (Berlin Museum, Sammlung Lipperheide 86). Predecessors: B. Severy (2003) *Augustus and the Family at the Birth of the Roman Empire*, New York, 86f.

53 Crispina as *Mater Castrorum*: *CIL* 8, 22689.

54 Pertinax's name omitted from coins (198): *CREBM* 5, cxxx. Abolition of Pertinax's games: *HA Pert.* 15.5.

55 M. Aurelius Antoninus: Her. 3.10.5; Birley (1999: 117). It appears 195–6, after Severus began referring to himself as 'son of Marcus'.

56 Antonine and Severan portraiture, esp. in connection with Domna's hairstyle: Baharal (1992). Lusnia (1995) also stresses links with Faustina in the first and second phases of her coinage (down to 202), listing other qualities shared with Antonine women from Faustina to Crispina: *Hilaritas*, *Laetitia*, *Pudicitia* and *Pietas*.

57 Joke on Severus' parentage: Dio 76(77).9.3f.; *PIR*[2] P 537.

58 Deified M. Ulpius Traianus: *CREBM* 3, 100f., nos. 498–508.

59 Albinus Caesar: Her. 3.5.2. Its possibilities: Schumacher (2003: 368). Albinus had proconsular *imperium*, but not tribunician power (363).

60 Albinus supported by senators: Her. 3.5.2; *HA Alb.* 12.1; cf. 9.6; 13.3.

61 Caracalla Caesar: *HA Sev.* 14.3 (recognition by Senate). Caracalla is in 'hopes of empire' in Severus' letter to Aezani (late 195), *ILS* 8809: see Birley (1999: 119f.; 215), citing the inscription of Szentendre (Soproni 1980), which he dates to June or July 195, and Mastino (1981: 15 and 28f.), citing *AE* 1971, 28, has M. Aurelius Antoninus Caesar on 29 June 196; Whittaker *ad* Her. 3.5.7. Caracalla's 'Antoninus Caesar' obverses (196–?): *RIC* 4.1, 212f. See Schumacher (2003: 366) (Caesar on his birthday, 4 Apr. 196).

62 Geta Antoninus: *HA Sev.* 10.5; 19.2; *HA Car.* 1.1.; *HA Geta* 1.1; 5.3; but cf. *HA Diad.* 6.9.

63 Domna inciting Severus against rivals: *HA Alb.* 3.5.

64 Dedication to Divus Commodus, brother of Severus (Thugga): *AE* 1951, 75; cf. Dio 75(76). 7.4; *HA Comm.* 17.11f.; *HA Sev.* 10.3; 11.3f.; 12.8; 19.3; Vict. *Caes.* 20.30; *CIL* 8, 9317 (195!). Further documentation: Birley (1999 247 n. 24); Hekster (2002: 189–91), with nn. 135 and 138. Senate's view: *HA Comm.* 19.2.

65 Fathers deified: Her. 4.2.1.

66 Favour to Albinus: *HA Sev.* 11.3. Severus' anger: 12.3.

67 Dating of military *diplomata*: S. Dušanić (2003) 'The Imperial Propaganda of Significant Day-dates: Two Notes in Military History', in J. J. Wilkes, ed., *Documenting the Roman Army: Essays in Honour of M. Roxan*, *BICS* Suppl. 81, London, 89–100, at 96. Dušanić also notes the use of 7 Jan., when Augustus first assumed the *fasces*, to date *diplomata* of city troops and *equites singulares* after 207 or 210.

68 News of Albinus' proclamation: *HA Sev.* 10.1.

69 Imperial party in Rome: *CREBM* 5, xcii and 148 no. 603: *PROFECTIO AV* ('The Emperor's Departure'). Severus' dedication: *ILS* 418; A. R. Birley draws

attention to the propaganda value of this; cf. Alföldy (1996: 34 n. 71) and refs. in *CIL* 6.8.2, p. 4309 *ad* 6, 954.

70 Alpine passes blocked: Her. 3.6.10.

71 Children among the soldiery: B. Rawson (2003: 65).

72 Fabius Cilo: *PIR*^{2} F 27.

73 War with Albinus and his fate: Dio 75(76).4.1–7.3; Her. 3.7.7; 8.1; *HA Sev.* 11.9; *HA Alb.* 8.4–9.4f.

74 Aftermath of victory: Dio 75(76).7.4–8.5; *HA Sev.* 12–14. 1; *HA Alb.* 12.3f. Severus' executions of senators: Leunissen (1989: 400–2). Caligula's lecture: Dio 59.16.1–7.

75 Geta's ambitions: Birley (1999: 122), based on *HA Sev.* 10.3–6.

76 Vespasian's sons: Tac. *Hist.* 2.77.1.

77 Stability is rightly stressed by Lusnia (1995: 130). 'Security': *RIC* 4.1, 212, no. 2; cf. 314, no. 4 (Geta, *c*.198–200); 'Unceasing hope': 212, no. 5. Claudius: *RIC* 1^2, 128–30, nos. 99 and 115. Vespasian's sons too were associated with *Spes* ('Hope'): *RIC* 2, 63, no. 396. Cf. M. E. Clark (1983) 'Spes in the Early Imperial Cult: "The Hope of Augustus"', *Numen* 30: 80–105. In 20 it was already associated with the emperor's heir: W. Eck et al., eds. (1996) *Das Senatus Consultum de Cn. Pisone patre*, *Vestigia* 48, Munich, 46, l.129.

78 Claudius' triumph: B. Rawson (2003: 315). M. Aurelius: *HA M. Aur.* 12.10.

79 *Princeps iuventutis*: *RIC* 4.1, 244 no. 140 (201–6), cf. 316, 15 (Geta, 200–2). 'Deinde future senum': Ovid, *Art of Love* 194. Nero: *RIC* 1^2, 125 nos. 75, 78f. Domitian: 2, 41, no. 233.

80 'Designated': *CIL* 8, 14394. 'Destined': *ILS* 442; 446f.; *RIC* 4.1, 212 no. 6 (?196–8); *CIL* 8 5699f.; *part(i)c(i)pi*: *AE* 1889, 86.

81 Cn. Cornelius Cinna, *cos* AD 5: Sen. *Clem.* 1.9.6; Dio 55.14–22, with Barrett (2002: 131–4) and Swan (2004: 151f.), on 16.1:

> Dio has Livia elevate this motif (advice from a woman) to a doctrine on the . . . consort who, having an equal stake in the emperor's fortunes . . . and a share in ruling . . . gives the honest counsel that only one whose salvation is inextricably linked to his can.

Claudius and women: Suet. *Claud.* 26–9; Dio 60.8.4f.

82 Livia as political support: *Das Senatus Consultum de Cn. Pisone patre* (above note 77) 46, l.116f.; Vell. Pat. 2.130.5.

83 Parthian war: Dio 75 (76).9.1–12.5; Her. 3.9; *HA Sev.* 15f. *CIL* 6, 225; 227; 738; 31322: safe return of the 'Divine House'.

84 Voyage east: *HA Sev.* 15.2; Birley (1999: 129).

85 Province of Mesopotamia: *ILS* 1331, 8847; 9148.

86 Arch (*ILS* 425: *imperium . . . propagatum*): Brilliant (1967); Rubin (1975: 425–31) (panels facing the Capitol showing Hatra: Severus represented himself as fully victorious). Coins: *RIC* 4.1, 68f. Celebration: *Fer. Dur.* Col. 1, l.14; 28 Jan.; it was J. Guey (1948) *REA* 50: 60–70, who pointed out the significance of 28 Jan. 98 and 198.

87 Caracalla Augustus: Her. 3.9.1 (antedating); *HA Sev.* 16.3; 18.9f. So in *ILS* 2485, of 3 May 198; autumn 197 suggested by Kienast (1996: 162).

88 Geta Caesar: Her. 3.9.2 (antedating); *HA Sev.* 16.4.

89 Severus' visit to Apameia: Dio 78(79).8.6. Heliopolis: *IGLS* 6, 2765.

90 Imperial women on coins: Barrett (2002: 300–2); N. Kokkinos (1992) *Antonia Augusta: Portrait of a Great Roman Lady*, London, 87–104, and the discussions in Temporini (2002).

91 Athenian honours: *AE* 1920, 53, with Oliver (1940) and Kettenhofen (1979: 109); see also Chapter 8. Athens: *HA Sev.* 3.7.

92 Livia and Samos: J. M. Reynolds (1982) *Aphrodisias and Rome*, *JRS* Monograph 1, London, 104–13, no. 13; Barrett (2002: 331f.).

93 The account of the voyage is abbreviated by *HA Sev*. 17.1–4: R. Syme (1979) *RP* 2, Oxford, 652. Chronological problems and stress on Severus' judicial activity: Hannestad (1944). Arrival not before March or April 199: N. Lewis (1979) *Hist*. 28, 253f.; Halfmann (1986: 220); Birley (1999: 250 n. 13). Stay: Dio 75(76). 13.1f.; Williams (1902: 267f.); Hasebroek (1921: 124; 170).

94 Ban on divination: see Chapter 2, note 56.

95 Reforms and prosperity: *SB* 7696, 82–6; 100–5; *Apokrimata*.

96 Council: *HA Sev*. 17.2; cf. Claudius to the Alexandrians, Smallwood, *G-N* 370, ll. 66–72.

97 Severus and Alexander: Rubin (1975: 438f.), citing Dio 75(76).13.2.

98 Severus' enjoyment of antiquities: Dio 75.13.2; *HA Sev*. 17.4.

99 Julia Balbilla: Hemelrijk (1999: 164–70). Forebear of Ti. Julius Balbillus, late second century priest of Sol Elagabalus: *ILS* 1346; 4329–31.

100 Antiochus IV: see Chapter 1. Ti. Claudius Balbillus: *PIR*[2] C 813; Pflaum (1960–1: 34–41, no. 15).

101 Plautianus in Egypt: Dio 75(76).14.2–5, with Birley (1999: 137). In Greek he was Severus' *oikeios*, probably *familiaris*, a good friend: *Cologne Papyri* 123 in *Apokrimata* ll. 47f. His rise, with allusion to sexual relations with Severus: Her. 3.10.6. D. Van Berchem (1937) *Mémoires de la Société nationales des Antiquitaires de France*, Ser. 8, Vol. 10, 188, connected his power with the development of the military supply system called *annona*; more plausibly it is connected with the political needs of the emperor.

102 Return by ship after Nile cruise: *CIG* 5973; Halfmann (1986: 220f.).

103 Caracalla *pater patriae*: *CIL* 8, 6037 (200); accepted by Kienast (1996: 182), but cf. P. v. Rohden (1896) *RE* 2: 2438, citing *ILS* 459 of 205 (all three rulers), and Mastino (1981: 102) ('reinciso'). *Toga virilis*: Her. 3.10.1; *HA Sev*. 16.8.

104 Reconstructing the imperial route: Birley (1999: 143); Halfmann (1979: 218f. and 221, bibl.); cf. Fitz (1972: 89), citing *Cod. Iust*. 2.31 (32). 2 for Severus at Sirmium in mid-March, but this evidence is invalid: Grosso (1968: 38); Birley (1971: 214 n. 2). *Decennalia*: Dio 76(77).1.1.

105 Setting out for Africa in 202 or 203: Halfmann (1986: 222); 202; Birley (1999: 146–54). For the view of H. Mattingly *BMC* 5, clix, that there was a visit to Africa in 207, based on the galley that appears on coins of 206–8 and on references to Africa personified (255†; 346 no. 847; 348f. †*‡; 352 no. 859), see Ghedini (1984: 88f., with bibl. nn. 330–7), and Halfmann (1986: 222): Her. 3.13.1 has Severus in the country in Italy. Travel in Africa: *IRT* 292, from Lepcis, prays for the return of the imperial family 'to their city'; see Birley (1999: 153); *AE* 1954, 153 (Timgad); 1957, 123; *CIL* 8, 2557 (Lambaesis). Stay at Lambaesis, 203: Halfmann (1986: 222).

106 Plautianus' career: Grosso (1968) and see Chapter 5.

107 *Ius Italicum*: *Dig*. 50.15.8.11. Building at Lepcis during Severus' stay: Procopius, *On Buildings* 6.4.5. See R. Tomlinson (1992) *From Mycenae to Constantinople: The Evolution of the Ancient City*, London, 191–6 (bibl. 230).

108 Lepcis arch: Townsend (1938); Ghedini (1984: 57–110, bibl. nn. 3–9).

109 Lepcis style: Tomlinson (1992: 198: see note 107), after Ward-Perkins (1948; 1951). A. R. Birley (1992) *University of London Archaeology Bulletin* 29: 46 conjectures that the procurator (and acting proconsul) (P. Aelius) Hilarianus, who sentenced Perpetua and others to death at Carthage on Geta's birthday, 7 March 203 (Musurillo 1972: 125), and who was evidently from Aphrodisias (*CIG* 2792), might have been specially appointed to his procuratorial post with instructions to supervise his fellow Aphrodisian craftsmen.

110 World-wide talents assembled: Phil. *Soph*. 601.

111 Advance in Africa: Birley (1999: 153); cf. *HA Sev.* 18.3.
112 'Safe return': Halfmann (1986: 222) refers the return 'to their city' (*in urbem suam*') of the Lepcitane *IRT* 292 to Rome rather than Lepcis (so *AE* 1968, 8).
113 Return to Rome: *AE* 1935, 157 ('for their return', by *equites singulares*), with Grosso (1968: 40–3).
114 Arch: Brilliant (1967). *ILS* 425, with '*rem publicam restitutam*', probably going back to the Augustan age: '*Laudatio Tyriae*', EJ 357 l.25,
115 Games: Dio 76(77).1.4f.
116 Secular Games: Her. 3.8.10. Calculations: Pighi (1965: 26–9); sources: 95–100; 137–9; text: 140–75; chorus: 222–8. Septimius/*septimus* (seventh) is a point made by Birley (1971: 224). Last celebration: G.-B. Pighi (1975) *DE* 4.4. 2112, with sources.
117 Domna at Secular Games: Williams (1902: 273); Pighi (1965) III 9 and 65f.; IV 9; V^a 52 and 83 (pp. 149, 155 and 168); Sohaemias V^a 26 (p. 158). Whittaker *ad* Her. 3.8.10 denies Livia a role. Arch: Ghedini (1984: esp. 135).
118 Severus' absence: Birley (1999: 169).
119 Women abroad: developments and hostility: Halfmann (1986: 90–2) noting Cic. *Phil.* 5.22; 13.18, and referring to A. J. Marshall (1975) 'Roman Women and the Provinces', *Ancient Society* 6: 109–27 and T. Raepsaet-Charlier (1982) 'Epouses et familles de magistrats dans les provinces romaines aux deux premiers siècles de l'Empire', *Hist.* 31: 56–69 (with catalogue). For Fulvia see E. Hemelrijk (2004) *CQ* 54: 192f. (bibl.).
120 Agrippina's role with the army: Tac. *Ann.* 1, 40f. (14); 69 (15). Quarrels of Plancina and Agrippina: Tac. *Ann.* 2.55.5.
121 Drusus and Livilla: Tac. *Ann.* 3.34.11–13. Julia the Elder treated with insufficient care at Ilium: Nicolaus of Damascus *FGrH* 2 A no. 90 Fr. 134. Gaius: Dio 55.10.18.
122 Modesty: Sen. *Dial.* 12.19.6.
123 Pertinax's mother in Germany: *HA Pert.* 2.3.
124 Trajan's entourage: Halfmann (1986: 91); Temporini (2002: 202f.).
125 Pompeianus commander: PIR^2 C 973; Pflaum (1961: 31–4).
126 Commodus in the north: Birley (1987: 174).
127 Marcus' journey to the east: Temporini (2002: 251). Commodus: Dio 71(72). 22.2; *HA Comm.* 22; 12.3.
128 Halala-Faustinopolis: see *PE s.v.*
129 Assembly on the Danube: Temporini (2002: 253).
130 Recognition of wives: Halfmann (1986: 92); *ILS* 427 and 2186 for Domna; 505 for Philip the Arabian and Otacilia Severa, *AE* 1981, 134, for Gordian III and Sabina Tranquillina.
131 Imperial ancestry of Domna and Faustina (II): Whittaker *ad* Her. 1.7.4.

4 Empress

1 'Empresses': Temporini (2002: 9).
2 '*Ornatus*' of imperial brides: Claudian, *Epithalamium for Honorius* 13f.
3 *Proskynesis*: Alföldi (1934: 45–62); Theodora: Procopius, *Secret History* 30.23. Empresses cannot have been ignored: Procopius must be referring to obligatory obeisance.
4 Exemption from the laws: Ulpian in *Dig.* 1.3.31.
5 '*Lex de imperio Vespasiani*': *MW* 1, 16–21. M. Aurelius *despotes*: *IGR* 4, 579; Severus and his family: *IGR* 3, 1533f.; 4, 878, with Ghedini (1984: 144). Severus' attempts to acquire *auctoritas*: Moran (1999). Procopius, *Secret History* 30.26, claims that Justinian required that form of address. *Kosmokrator*: *SB* 4275.

6 Coping with autocrats: Price (1984: 23–52).
7 Lucilla's honours: Her. 1.8.4; C. R. Whittaker notes the *vexilla* of 2.3.2 and 8.6 and the *fasces* of 7.6.2. Torch, see his n. on 2.3.2, citing T. Mommsen (1887) *Römisches Staatsrecht* 1.1[3], Berlin, 423f.; Alföldi (1934: 111–18).
8 Exclusion of women: Ulpian in *Dig.* 50.17 (*De diversis regulis iuris antiqui*). 2.
9 Intimidation: *Dig.* 40.9.9.
10 Publicity: *Consolation to Livia* 351f.
11 Requests to Hadrian: Dio 69.10, 3a; Smallwood, *N-H* 114, both cited by Temporini (2002: 212f.).
12 Trajan's women: Pliny, *Pan.* 83.5–84.8.
13 M. Aurelius' wife: *Meditations* 1.7, cited by Temporini (2002: 252).
14 Nero's *imperium*: Tac. *Ann.* 14.17.6; Valentinian III: M. Clauss, in Temporini (2002: 389) on *Chron. Gall. A. DXI*, in *MGH Auct. Ant.* 9.1 (*Chron. Minora* 1) p. 663.
15 Agrippina *socia imperii*: Tac. *Ann.* 12.37.6. Maria: Claudian, *Epithalamium for Honorius* 277, noted by M. Clauss, in Temporini (2002: 375).
16 Female co-rulers: Swan (2004: 151), on Dio 55.14.3.
17 Domna's normal position: *AE* 1977, 535, probably before AD 202; but cf. *CIL* 6, 225 (after Geta).
18 Amazons: Suet. *Cal.* 25.3; *HA Comm.* 11.9; *CREBM* 4, clxxxii.
19 Cloak: M. Clauss, in Temporini (2002: 370, with Fig. 51), and H. Leppin, in Temporini (2002: 476).
20 Attempted management of Commodus by the *consilium*: C. R. Whittaker *ad* Her. 1.5.1.
21 Berenice: Quintilian 4.1.19. Claudius' *matronae*: Smallwood, *G-N* 436, l.9.
22 Ambassadors: Tac. *Ann.* 13.5.3; cf. Dio 60(61).33.7; 61.3.4.
23 Constantia at trials: Amm. Marc. 14.9.3, cited by M. Clauss, in Temporini (2002: 360).
24 Agrippina's curtain: Tac. *Ann.* 13.5.2.
25 Marcia in the Senate: *HA Pert.* 5.2.
26 Portraits in Senate: M. Clauss, in Temporini (2002: 370f.; 403).
27 Women's right to feast: cf. Dio 49, 15.1 and 18.6. Tiberius: 55.2.4; 8.2 (Dio notes Livia's *separate* feast for senators' wives; this could be a dig against the Severan women); 57.12.5 (Tiberius prevented Livia giving a mixed feast).
28 Livia's scheming: Tac. *Ann.* 1.3–7.
29 Tiberius' views: Tac. *Ann.* 1.14.3, with Purcell (1986).
30 Senators on Livia: Vell. Pat. 2.130.5; W. Eck et al., eds. (1996) *Das Senatus Consultum de Cn. Pisone patre*, *Vestigia* 48, Munich, 46f., ll.115–18.
31 Skill with dreams: *HA Geta* 1.5.
32 Palatium: E. Papi in Steinby, *Lexicon* 4, 27–38.
33 Building 200–4: Papi, in Steinby, *Lexicon* 4, 32 (the family in residence). Vastness of Palace: Her. 4.1.2. See Millar (1977: 18–24).
34 Livia's levées: Dio 57.12.2, with Barrett (2002: 165).
35 Agrippina sent away: Tac. *Ann.* 13.18.5.
36 Domna's separate receptions under Caracalla: Dio 77(78).18g.3. *HA Alex.* 25.10, (fictionally) has Alexander Severus banning women of ill repute.
37 Theodora: Temporini (2002: 475, Fig. 58).
38 Theodora informed of papal election: M. Clauss, in Temporini (2002: 459).
39 Irene and Theophanou: H. Leppin, in Temporini (2002: 491f.; 494).
40 'Reigning empress': *CREBM* 5, clxxxvi; cxcv.
41 Agrippina's two lictors: Tac. *Ann.* 13.2.6; cf. 1.14.3 (Livia).
42 Vesta temple: see Chapter 8, note 17.

43 Arval prayers for Livia AD 27 (Henzen, *AA*, xxxviii); offerings to Domna's 'Juno' 213–14 (cxcviiif; cci).
44 Deification of Antonia: Levick (1990: 45). Domitillae: H. Castritius, in Temporini (2002: 170–4).
45 '*Iuliae filius*': Tac. *Ann.* 1.14.1–3.
46 'Son(s) of Domna': *CIL* 8, 9035 (Geta), cf. 9237; *CIG* 1075. Verus: *CIL* 8, 11323, cited by Bleckmann (2002: 271).
47 Praise for the source of Caracalla: Henzen AA, cxcvii = Scheid (1998a: no. 99., ll. 17–19): '*Iuliae Aug(ustae), matri Aug(usti) feliciter! Ex te, Aug(usta), Aug(ustum) videmus! D(i) t(e) s(ervent) in perpetuo, Aug(usta), Aug(uste)!*'
48 Cognates: e.g., Gaius in *Dig.* 38.8.2.
49 Importance of the people: Whittaker (1964).
50 'Augusta': Lusnia (1995: 120f.) notes coins with *IVLIA DOMNA AVG*. in 194–5 (the opening of her coinage), passing to *IVLIA AVG* on the model of Livia, 195–211. Coins of Paltos in Syria in 194 have *AUGOUSTA DOMNA*: Meyer-Zwiffelhoffer (1994: 100).
51 Pertinax's refusal of titles: Dio 73(74).7.1f. *HA Pert.* 5.4; cf. 6.9. They were honoured in Egypt: Birley (1999: 92) on *BGU* 646 = *Sel. Pap.* 222; and cf. *ILS* 410.
52 Julianus' Augustae: *HA Jul.* 3.4f.; 4.5. Julianus emancipated his daughter, but on his death she lost property and title, receiving only his body: 8.9f.
53 Livia, and early history of 'Augusta': Barrett (2002: 322–5); M. B. Florey (1988 [1997]) 'The Meaning of *Augusta* in the Julio-Claudian Period', *AJAH* 13: 113–38, at 113, overstresses the (contingent) qualification of motherhood; cf. Ghedini (1984: 8).
54 Nero's baby: Tac. *Ann.* 15.23.1.
55 Nero's conferment of 'Augusta': W. Eck, in Temporini (2002: 163); Poppaea's successor Statilia Messalina: Florey (1988: 126) (see note 53).
56 Trajan's women as Augustae: Pliny, *Pan.* 84.6.
57 Faustina (II): Raepsaet-Charlier (1987: 80, no. 63).
58 Variety: Benario (1958b: 67).
59 Coins without 'Augusta': Williams (1902: 261) (omitted in error, *CREBM* 5, 102, nos. 412 and 414). 'Augusta' and its implications: Kettenhofen (1979: 78f.). Replaced by 'Dom(i)na'? Omitted after death when 'Diva' is used: *AE* 1899, 56; 1910, 125. Coinage of 193: *CREBM* 5, p. 27f.
60 'Julia Augusta': PIR^2 I 663, p. 312. This can cause confusion between the two: *ibid.* pp. 313 and 415, also on 'diva Iulia' and 'Iulia Augusta': *IGR* 4, 180; *AE* 1953, 178; L. Robert, *REG* 63 (1951) 205 no. 44.
61 'Julia': Dio 74(75).3.1, etc.; Maesa is 'the sister of Julia Augusta': 78(79). 30.2f.
62 Severus' early coin types: *CREBM* 5, 20–4; 27f.; 38, with Birley (1999: 106).
63 Types of portrait: Fittschen (1978: 39).
64 *AETERNITAS: RIC* 4.1, 166, 539–41; *FELICITAS*: 115 no. 181.
65 *SECVRITAS*: Williams (1902: 279).
66 Bleckmann (2002: 339).
67 *HILARITAS*: *RIC* 4, 168 nos. 556–8; 208 no. 855 (cf. 74. noting a connection with the festival of Cybele). *FORTVNA FELIX*: 167 no. 552; 208 no. 854; cf. 234 no. 154 (Caracalla).
68 Three Graces: W. Eck, in Temporini (2002: 110 with Fig. 12), on *RIC* 1^2, 110 no. 33.
69 Elder Agrippina: *RTC* 1^2, 108 nos. 7 and 13. *Carpentum*: 112 no. 55.
70 Agrippina's obverse: *RIC* 1^2, 150 no. 1; jugate busts: no. 6f. Significance of nominative: W. Eck, in Temporini (2002: 151, with Fig. 15).
71 'Münzrecht': M. Clauss, in Temporini (2002: 459). 'Sharing fully in mint

privileges and even in the giving of donatives': *RIC* 4.1, 89, based on 273 no. 383B (*MONETA*, the Mint); cf. *CREBM* 5, clxix, on *AEQVITAS PVBLICA*, 'Fair dealing by the State', of 211. Lusnia (1995: 137), is uncertain if Domna had any real say about the types representing her or if she would have had the power to organize the programme. Against: W. Kaczanowicz (2001) *Antiquitas* 25: 34f. Theodora: the explanation that she had not borne Justinian a child, and that it was a right accorded to mothers, is unconvincing.

72 Livia as builder: Purcell (1986: 88–90); Portico: Dio 54.23.5f.; 55.8.2; cf. Suet. *Aug*. 29.4. Domna's structures: Williams (1902: 275) on *CIL* 6, 997.

73 Oath by Caligula's sisters: Suet. *Cal*. 15.3.

74 Lagina milestone: *CIL* 3, 482.

75 Numbers of milestones with Domna's name: Kettenhofen (1979: 97), noting the matronymic in Caracalla's titulature in the African milestones *CIL* 8, 10340 and 22403.

76 Fortuna Redux: see Williams (1902: 279). Victory: *CIG* 3956b, 4701b, and '*Ob vict. Germ.*', *ILS* 433; '*Pro salute victoria et reditu*' (of the three Augusti and of Domna, mother of the two Augusti) in *Arval Acts* of 6 October 213 (Henzen cxcvii); *CIL* 3, 138 (Baalbek, for the victories of Caracalla and Domna); *RIB* 590 (for the victory of Caracalla and Domna).

77 Syene inscription ('*sub imperio*', with Severus and his sons and Domna in the genitive case, and with officials involved): Williams (1902: 271) on *CIL* 3, 75; cf. *IGR* 1, 380.

78 Alimentary schemes: G. D. Woolf (1990) 'Food, Poverty and Patronage: The Significance of the Epigraphy of the Roman Alimentary Schemes in Early Imperial Italy', *PBSR* 196–228 ('theatre'); Rawson (2003: 59–64).

79 M. Aurelius' scheme: *HA M. Aur*. 7.8. Reliefs: W. Helbig (1963–72) *Führer durch die öffentlichen Sammlungen klassischer Altertümer in Rom*, ed. 4, by W. Ameling et al., Tübingen, pp. 199f., no. 3234.

80 *Alimenta*: *RIC* 4, 204 no. 827.

81 Domitia Longina: B. Levick (2003) *Hommages à C. Deroux. 3. Histoire et Epigraphie, Droit*, Collection Latomus 270, Brussels, 250–70.

82 Plotina's management: Birley (1997a: 77). Accomplice: Dio 69.1.2.

83 Faustina (II) as kingmaker: Dio 71(72). 22.3f.; *HA M. Aur*. 24.6; *HA Avid*. 7.1–3; cf. 9.5–11.8.

84 Lucilla's plot: Dio 72(73).4.4–6; Her. 1.6.4; 8.3–8; *HA M. Aur*. 20.6f.; *HA Comm*. 4.1–4. Modern analyses: Grosso (1964: 145–64); Càssola (1965) *PP* 20: 452; Birley (1999: 60f.); Hekster (2002: 52–5) (senatorial involvement).

85 Cleander: A. Stein, *PIR*[2] A 1481; *AE* 1952.6, showed Commodus calling Cleander his *tropheus*; cf. Pflaum (1960–1: 465, no. 180 *bis*, Mantissa add., 1007f.). As A. R. Birley points out, the evidence allows Cleander the title 'Guard prefect with the anomalous title *a pugione*'; cf. Grosso (1964: 116ff.) Fall: Dio 72(73). 13.1; Her. 1.13.1–4; *HA Comm*. 7.1.

86 Marcia (Aurelia Ceionia Demetrias: *ILS* 406) on her knees: Her. 1.16.4.

87 M. Falkender (1983) *Downing Street in Perspective*, London, 88; 96f.; 101–3; R. Taylor (1664) *The Court and Kitchen of Elizabeth Commonly called Joan Cromwell*, London, repr. Cambridge, 1983, 39. Bad advisers: Hekster (2002: 69) on freedmen.

88 Plautianus' accusations: Dio 75(76). 15.6f. See Chapter 5.

89 Domna's conversation in Britain: Dio 76(77). 16.5. Moralizing 'prudery': Ghedini (1984: 23 n. 99).

90 Domna urging war against Albinus: see Chapter 3.

91 Marinus: *PIR*[2] D 71. Cornificia: Pflaum (1961: 36f.). But see Birley (2005: 327f.), with doubts on Marinus' eastern origin, and citing B. Salway, in Cooley (2000: 149) for doubts on the marriage to Cornificia.

92 Greek-speaking consulars, including from Syria Alexianus; L. Aurellius Commodus Pompeianus (Antioch), *ord.* 209; Pompeianus, suff. ?212; ?Iul. Ant. Seleucus, suff. before 218–221; ?M. Flavius Vitellius Seleucus; Claudius Pompeianus (Antioch), ord. 231; L. Ti. Claudius Aurelius Quintianus (Antioch), ord. 235: Leunissen (1989: 366–70).

93 Avidius: *PIR*[2] A 1402. Pompeianus: C 973.

94 Avitus: see Chapter 2, note 1. Equestrian born, so not the son of C. Iulius Avitus, *cos.* 149 (Pflaum 1962: 95). Check to his career: Halfmann (1982). Another sufferer: Ti. Claudius Candidus of Cirta, who had fought against Niger: A. von Domaszewski (1905) *MDAI(R)* 20: 159; Leunissen (1989: 97; 153 n. 106).

95 Death of Avitus: Dio 78(79).30.2.4.

96 Caracalla's dispositions: Halfmann (1982: 225); Birley (1999: 221f., no. 36). Caracalla allowed Mamaea to retain her rank as the wife of an ex-consul when she married him: Ulpian in *Dig.*1.9.12.1.

97 Rehabilitation of Marcellus: Halfmann (1982: 224f.).

98 Marcellus' career: Dio 78(79).30.2; *ILS* 474.8; Whittaker *ad* Her. 5.3.3. Birley (1999: 224, no. 50) accepts Halfmann (1982: 226); cf. Pflaum (1960–1, 2, 638–42, no. 237); Corbier (1974: 437–48; 703f.); Birley (1981: 296–8); B. E. Thomasson (1996) *Fasti Africani*, Stockholm, 179f., dates the Numidian post to the last years of Caracalla's reign. A. R. Birley has noted another reason for following Halfmann's dating: he became Prefect of the Military Treasury precisely to look after the extra revenue from the *vicesima hereditatium*, that had become the *decima hereditatium* (see Chapter 6, note 59).

99 Absentee prefects: Halfmann (1982: 228f.).

100 Papinian removed: Dio 77(78).1.1; 4.1[a]. Salway (1997: 152) traces a tendency for Guard Prefects to be paired military men and jurists back to the fall of Plautianus, with Ulpian, jurist and sole prefect, murdered by his soldiers.

101 Consolidating loyalty in Numidia: Halfmann (1982: 233), citing Fitz (1977: 547–50).

102 Domna's mediation: Dio 77(78). 2.2.

103 Asper's origin: Halfmann (1979: 200, no. 134); Halfmann (1982: 232, with n. 58). Inscription from Heliopolis: Barbieri (1952: 72, no. 295). Fall: Dio 77(78).5.3.

5 Plautianus and the struggle for the succession

1 Marriage council: Tac. *Ann.* 12.1.

2 Plautianus in 193: *HA Sev.* 6.10; 15.4. Rise: Dio 75(76).14.1–16.5; Her. 3.10.6 (with Zimmermann 1999: 195). Kinship: Her. 3.10.6; Ghedini (1984: 9, with bibl. n. 74). Tenure of office: Grosso (1968: 17f.). *Clarissimus*: *ILS* 2185 of 9 June 197; *Cologne Papyri* 123 in *Apokrimata*, l.47f. of 14 March 200, shows him as prefect, not necessarily without a colleague. Prefect of the Watch: Grosso (1968: 14f.) on *CIL* 14, 4380. Disgrace: Dio 73(74). 15.4 (the name of the person involved is uncertain). Relationship to Severus: Chausson (2002).

3 Sejanus: Levick (1976: 158–78) (bibl. 2000). Portraits: Suet. *Tib.* 65.1.

4 Sejanus and Plautianus' power: Dio 58.14.1. Cf. Hasebroek (1921: 131): 'Es is der Geist des Orients, der sich in der Stellung dieses Allgewaltigen dem legitimen Herrscher und seine Hofe gegenüber offenbart'. Athenian statue: J. H. Oliver (1941) *Hesperia* 10: 85–90, no. 37.

5 Plautilla: *PIR*[2] F 564. Marriage and celebrations, before 28 Aug.: Dio 75(76). 14.5; 15.2; 76(77). 1.1–3; Her. 3.10.5 and 7f.; *HA Sev.* 14.8.

6 Caracalla's hatred of Plautianus: *HA Car.* 2.7. Plautianus' hopes: Dio 76(77). 4.5.

7 Caracalla and his wife: Her. 3.10.8; cf. Dio 76(77).2.5–3.1. Child: Gagé (1934: 40–65), followed by Haynes and Hirst (1939: 5), deploying the vague 'hopes' in Pighi I 22f. (p. 142); cf. *CREBM* 5, cliv; A. Stein, *PIR*² F 564, was rightly sceptical.
8 *Concordia*: Levick (1978). Caracalla and Plautilla: *RIC* 4.1, 231 no. 123 (*FELIX*).
9 The Augusta: Dio 77(78).2.6. Augg.; *AE* 1977, 705; *AE* 1914, 177 is particularly flowery (201–2 from Thugga), showing Plautianus as kinsman of Domna's menfolk.
10 Accusations against Domna: Dio 75(76). 15.6. His segregation of his wife (7) is readily understandable.
11 Hostility between Domna and Plautianus: Dio 75(76).15.6f.; 76(77).4.4f., with de Regibus 1946,142f. *PVDICITIA*, according to Lusnia (1995: 126f.), like *PIETAS AVGVSTA* and the numismatic stress on domestic harmony, was intended to reassure the public; it had been used for Faustina (II), Lucilla and Crispina. Agony: Dio 79(80). 24.1. Coin reverses: Lusnia (1995: 130f.) (three types *p.a.*, only two new).
12 Dio 75(76).15.2[a] ('fourth Caesar'); 76(77). 5.3f. (attendant senators); Her. 3.10.6–11.3. Integrated: *AE* 1944, 74. *Comes*: *ILS* 456.
13 Tiberius' fear: Suet. *Tib.* 65.2.
14 Mullet and bedside episodes: Dio 75(76).15.3f.
15 Plautianus'ascendancy: Dio 75(76).14.1–76(77). 2; Birley (1999: 161–3).
16 Severus' wish to be survived by Plautianus: Dio 75(76).15.2.
17 Saturninus: Dio 75(76).14.2; *PIR*² A 403.
18 Plautianus' title: Dio 75(76). 14.1, cf. *CIL* 6, 225f., where he is placed after Domna.
19 Slip: Dio 75(76).15.7. Plautianus' wife was perhaps Hortensia: Birley (1999: 225 no. 53), adducing the name of their son C. Fulvius Plautius Hortensianus, *PIR*² F 555.
20 'Grand Cameo': Temporini (2002: 95, Fig. 10). *Domus*: F. Millar (1993) *JRS* 83: 1–17; B. Severy (2003) *Augustus and the Family at the Birth of the Roman Empire*, New York, 214–19 (Ovid); Smallwood, *G-N* 197 (Flavian Britain); *RIB* 1700 (Severan Vindolanda); Severan frequency: Hekster (2002: 194, with n. 162).
21 Arch of the *Argentarii*: Pallottino (1946); Ghedini (1984: 27–53, with Pl. 1 and bibl. n. 1); Claridge (1998: 259, Figs. 123f.), noting like Haynes and Hirst (1939: 13) that the structure is a gate(way). The busy monument, originally 6.9 m. high. was faced in tough Travertine below, Proconnesian above. Coarelli (1986: 324f.) is damning: '*horror vacui*'; '*resultati mediocri*'.
22 *CIL* 6, 1035; reread by Ghedini (1984: 27f.), insisting (29) on the semi-official nature of the document. Privilege: Haynes and Hirst (1939: 9).
23 Domna and the Games: Ghedini (1984: 42); see Chapter 3; and for details of the relief, see Chapter 8, note 72.
24 Incarnation of the dynasty: Ghedini (1984: 76). Date of the Arch: 88–90, with notes 328–37 for bibl. 207 is proposed by Hill (1964: 6 and 34).
25 Domna and Severus on the Lepcis Arch: Ghedini (1984: 61f.), with Fig. 2 for the sacrificial scene of the north-east attic panel. Even in the *Concordia Augustorum* scene, of the south-west attic (Fig. 5) where she is to one side, she is in a divine (and military) context (64). Comparison with Ara Pacis: 66.
26 Plautianus mocked: Dio 76(77).2.3.
27 Dio 75(76).15.4 (in Asia en route for the east); 16.2 (within a year of his fall); *HA Sev.* 14.7. Grosso (1968: 35) detects a temporary loss of power in 199 for which Domna was responsible; Whittaker *ad* Her. 3.11.3 (the final decline).

28 Statues removed; punishment of Racius (Dio on the jury): Dio 75(76). 16.2f.; *HS Sev*. 14.5. See Crook (1955: 81) and Millar (1964: 17).
29 Death of P. Geta: Dio 76(77).2.4.
30 Herodian's account, Her. 3.11.1–12, 12; attacked by Hohl (1956), but cf. Whittaker *ad* Her. 3.11.1.
31 Senate's reaction: Dio 76(77).5.1–6.1; Her. 3.15.4 (Geta).
32 Exile and death of Plautilla and Plautus: Dio 76(77).6.3; 77(78).1.1; Her. 3.13.2.
33 Dio 76(77).3.1–6.3.
34 Fall of Marcellus and Caecina: Levick (1999: 192–5). Titus the forger: Suet. *Tit*. 3.2. Perhaps Euodus was the scribe.
35 Plautianus a nuisance: Her. 3.11.3. Claudius' technique: Levick (1990: 58f.).
36 Domna's joy: Dio 76.4.4f. Ghedini (1984: 11) suggests that she played an active part.
37 Officers: Birley (1971: 234) on Dio 76(77).3.2 and Her. 3.11.4.
38 Two prefects: Her. 3.13.1. Second wife: *HA Car*. 8.2. Severus': Stein in *PIR*^{2} A 388 (Whittaker on Her. 3.13.1 has Papinian a favourite of Domna); Papinian's: Kettenhofen (1979: 61f. with n. 412) (T. Honoré, *OCD*^{3} 21, also regards Papinian as of African origin).
39 Coinage after 205: Lusnia (1995: 131f.).
40 Ephesus inscription: *CIL* 3, 427 = *CIG* 2971, noted by Williams (1902: 274). Apronianus as governor of Asia (*PIR*^{2} P 842) may have been involved in this scheme (Dio 76(77).7.3–5 (Quintillus); 8.1–9.2 (Apronianus). Plot of 208: *CIL* 8, 1628 (Sicca Veneria).
41 Cornificia's husband: *AE* 1954, 171; *ILS* 1396. Vibia's: *CIL* 15, 7402, with Pflaum (1961: 38f.).
42 *Spes*: see Chapter 4, note 77. 'Mater Caesaris': Kettenhofen (1979: 83f.). Antoninus: *HA Sev*. 10.6.
43 '*Mater Augusti et Caesaris*': *CIL* 8, 17872 (cf. 18253). Rubin (1975: 434) has 197. Kettenhofen (1979: 84) remarks on the unsurprisingly high numbers from Severus' native Africa, especially Proconsularis; Moesia is also particularly well represented.
44 '*Mater Augustorum*': Kettenhofen (1979: 85f.). Premature use: *IRT* 37; 397; 402f.; *CIL* 6, 226.3, 154 has '*castrorum liberorumque*', 'of the camps and of her offspring'; cf. 13.6542f. (Kettenhofen 1979: 234 n. 78)
45 Infants on throne: *RIC* 3, 271, nos. 709–12; 346 nos. 1665f.; *HA Comm*. 1.10.
46 Commodus Augustus, 27 Nov. 176: Hekster (2002: 38).
47 Harem: Domaszewski (1895: 72), though aware of the abortive Livian precedent. Honours to mothers: Ghedini (1984: 8).
48 Ghedini (1984: 8), citing *RIC* 1, 154 (index).
49 *Destinatus*: Kettenhofen (1979: 83f.), with n. 81; Hasebroek (1921: 192): 9 June to 28 Aug.; Fitz (1967–8): 4 April; Mastino (1981: 29, list 84): 19 Feb. to 4/7 May. *Destinatio*: Cf. EJ^2 94a, l.6, etc.
50 Succession plans: Whittaker *ad* Her. 3.10.1 and 14, 2, citing *CREBM* 5, cxxxix and cliif.
51 Aezani and Caracalla: *ILS* 8805.
52 Three-year interval: noted by Alföldy (1996: 35), inferring Severus' preference for Caracalla. Advancement of Augustus' and Tiberius' pairs of sons: Levick (1976: 40f.); 48. A. R. Birley draws attention to Hadrian's insistence on Antoninus adopting Marcus and Lucius, maybe influenced by his *imitatio Augusti*.
53 Geta's advance: usually taken to be 209, e.g. Kettenhofen (1979: 85); G. Di Vita-Evrard's (1987) redating of *IG* II/III 1077, in *Praktika tou 8 diethnous*

synedriou ellenikes kai latinikes epigraphikes 1982 II, Athens, 144, to the end of 210, is rejected by Birley (1999: 274), citing an official document: M. Roxan (1994) *Roman Military Diplomas 1985–1993*, London, no. 191.

54 Geta's nomenclature: Birley (1999: 160 f.; 218, no. 22). Geta, 'nobilissimus Caesar', probably took the *toga virilis* in 204 (*HA Sev.* 14.8; 202 according to Whittaker *ad* Her. 3.10.1). His *praenomen* fluctuated between Publius and Lucius. From his first consulship, 205, he was Publius. Birley plausibly suggests that Geta had taken to Lucius when his brother became M. Aurelius Antoninus, also avoiding confusion with Severus' brother P. Geta (no. 21), who died in 205.

55 Geta Pontifex Maximus: *CIL* 8, 9035.

56 Real sons as successors: *HA Sev.* 20.1f.

57 Dual Principate: E. Kornemann (1930) *Doppelprinzipat u. Reichsteilung im Imperium Romanum*, Leipzig (extreme). Augustus: Levick (1976: 29f. and 236 n. 57). Tatius: Livy 1.10–14.3,

58 Final step in preparations: Birley (1999: 187).

59 Saving Geta: Whittaker *ad* Her. 3.15.6.

60 Fortune: *HA Sev.* 23.5–7.

61 Domna's role: Williams (1902: 281), based on *HA Geta* 5. Cf. Kettenhofen (1979: 85; 234 n. 94).

62 Rival debauchery: Dio 76(77).7.1–3 (Caracalla favoured the Blues: 77(78). 10.1); Her. 3.10.3f.; 13.2–6; repeated 4.4.2.

63 British expedition: Dio 76(77).11–16; Her. 3.14f. Motive: Birley (1999: 174) (glory of conquest). Sons: Dio 76(77).11.1; Her. 3.13.2. For the sources *in extenso*, see Birley (2005: 180–208).

64 Severus' gout: *HA Sev.* 16.6; 18.9; 23.3; *HA Car.* 11.3. 'Grand climacteric': Gell. 15.7.

65 Situation in Britain: Birley (1999: 170–3). Conquest of Scotland: Dio 76(77) 13.1.

66 Road repairs: U. Schillinger-Häfele, *MZ* 73–4 (1978–9) 367. Philostratus: Phil. *Apoll.* 5.2. Campaigns: Her. 3.14.

67 Assassination attempt and council: Dio 76(77).14.3–7. M. Heil (2003) *Britannia* 34: 268ff., plausibly interprets a papyrus as evidence for the title Britannicus being assumed on 31 March 210; this probably followed the negotiations with the enemy, during which Caracalla's attack took place; cf. Birley (2005: 202). Travel deleterious: Syme, *RP* 5 (Oxford, 1988) 451 (British examples n. 63).

68 Hand-shaking on the south-west panel of the attic of the Lepcis Arch: Ghedini (1984: 63f. and Fig. 5).

69 Argentocoxus: Dio 76(77).16.5. Date of Eboracum's colonial status: Birley (2005: 12f., 333).

70 Death of Severus: Dio 76(77).15.2; 17.4; Her. 3.14.2; *HA Sev.* 23.2–7.

71 Deaths of Euodus, etc.: Dio 77(78).1.1. The discovery of decapitated bodies at York, probably victims of Caracalla's purge (BBC *Timewatch*, April 2006), is so interpreted by A. R. Birley. Attitude of army: Her. 3.15.5. Temporary reconciliation: Dio 77(78).1.1; Birley (1999: 188).

72 Caracalla and Moon: see Chapter 8, notes 46, 48, 101. See Alföldy (1996: 35f.), with reference to Caracalla's later coinage.

73 Aquae Vescinae: *AE* 1914, 217.

74 Fatal discord between heirs: Tac. *Ann.* 1.4.5.

6 The reign of Caracalla

1 Livia as a factor for continuity: Temporini (2002: 80). Kettenhofen (1979: 16–19) has a valuable section on Domna's power under Caracalla; bibliography n. 73.
2 Caracalla's dislike of advisers: Dio 77(78).11.5.
3 Severus' deification: *HA Sev.* 19.5. Coinage of 211: Hill (1978).
4 Caracalla's *dies imperii*: *Fer. Dur.* p. 82. Whittaker's tentative suggestion *ad* Her. 3.15.3, that Caracalla accepted a formal renewal from the Senate, is not to be maintained.
5 Fate of Severus' corpse: Dio 76(77).15.3f.; Her. 3.15.7 (alabaster); 4.1.3; *HA Sev.* 24.2, offering a golden urn or (implausibly) an uncremated body in a coffin.
6 Feuding: Her. 3.15.4f.; 4.1.2 and 5. Journey: *HA Sev.* 24.1f. For the downfall of Geta in the ancient sources, see Alföldy (1989: 179–216).
7 Coinage of Caracalla: *RIC* 4.1, 286 no. 452; Geta: 338 no. 164f.
8 Division of Empire: Her. 4.3.5–9. derided by Kettenhofen (1979: 21, and 242 n. 165), cf. Alföldy (1989: 189–92 and 213f.); Birley (1999: 256 n. 2); accepted by L. Perret (1992) 'La succession de Septime-Sévère et le projet de partager de l'Empire', *Rev. des Et. hist.* 88: 445–58 (*n.v.*); Crook (1955: 81f.); C. Turton (1974) *The Syrian Princesses*, London, 99 (*n.v.*) and others cited by Marasco (1996: 123 n. 22). Bibliography and further on division: Zimmermann (1999: 204 n. 264f.); Herodian on Caracalla and Geta: 203–14.
9 Advantages of undivided Empire: *Pan. Lat.* 10.2, 11.2, tr. R. Rees (2004) *Diocletian and the Tetrarchy*, Edinburgh, 130.
10 Domna hostile to Caracalla: Dio 78(79).23.1; 24.1 (*aei dia telous dia phthonou echousa*).
11 Domna as Jocasta: Her. 4.9.3 (the Alexandrians).
12 The Emperors at Rome: Her. 4.1.2–5. Alföldy (1996) has Caracalla in Rome for his birthday.
13 Emperors at apotheosis of Severus: Her. 4.2.
14 Contrasting characters: Her. 4.3, 2–4; cf. 3.10.3f.; cf. *HA Geta* 4f.
15 Caracalla as intellectual: Meckler (1999); Whittaker *ad* Her. 3.10.4 and 4.3.2, citing Dio 77(78). 11.3 (philosophy); 13.7 (music); 78(79). 8.4 (cites Euripides); Phil. *Soph.* 626f. (enthusiasm for Heliodorus the Arab sophist); *AE* 1933, p. 76. Composition: Th. Wiegand (1932) 'Zweiter Bericht über die Ausgrabungen in Pergamon 1928–32: Das Asklepieion', *Abhandlung. der Preuss. Akad. der Wiss.*, 1932, Phil.-hist. Kl., Berlin, 53, no. 6; A. Wilhelm (1933) *Sitzungsb Berlin. Akad.* Phil.-hist.-Kl., Berlin, 836–46.
16 Murder of Geta and massacre of his followers: Dio 77 (78). 2–4.1; 12.4f.; Her. 4.4.3. Poisoning: Her. 4.2; *HA Car.* 2.5. See Alföldy (1989: 193–7); Sünskes Thompson (1990: 61–5).
17 Date of murder: Barnes (1968a: 522–5); Barnes (1971: 264f.), emending the *Chronogr. of 354* (*MGH auct. ant.* 9 p. 147) to give Geta a reign of *m(enses) X d(ies) XXII* (10 months, 22 days) until 26 Dec. Halfmann (1982: 230 n. 49) prefers XV (19 Dec.); after the Saturnalia (17–23 Dec.): Dio 77(78). 2.1. A few coins show Geta in his fourth year of tribunician power (10 Dec. onwards): *RIC* 4.1, 327 nos. 93A; 341, nos. 179–81. Dio 77(78). 2.5 implies 26 Feb.
18 Domna wounded like Aphrodite: Ghedini (1984: 21 n. 102) on Homer, *Iliad* 5, 314–17, and citing Nau (1968) (who deplores the neglect of female figures in historiography). Hostility to the dynasty may account for the humour.
19 Planned assassination: *HA Car.* 2.5.
20 Murder by centurions: Dio 77(78). 2.3; by Caracalla: Her. 4.4.3. Marasco (1996) regards ancient myth as the source of Herodian's invention, but there is obvious drama in his version.

21 Nero to the Senate: Tac. *Ann.* 13.17.5.
22 Caracalla and the military: Alföldy (1989: 197–203; 214–16). Gifts to Praetorians and army pay rise: Dio 77(78). 3.1f.; Her. 4.4.7, with Whittaker *ad loc.* Alban legion: *HA Car.* 2.7f.; *HA Geta* 6.1f. Scepticism: Alföldy (1989: 200f.).
23 Caracalla in the Senate: Alföldy (1989: 203–11); Dio 77(78). 3.3; Her. 4.5.1–7; *HA Car.* 2.9–11; *HA Geta* 6.5.
24 Danger of Domna: *HA Car.* 3.3; *HA Geta* 7.3.
25 Geta's burial: Dio 78(79). 24.3.
26 Scrap: cf. E. Gibbon (1900) *The History of the Decline and Fall of the Roman Empire*, ed. J. B. Bury, London, 1, 132f.
27 Massacre: Dio 77(78). 4.1–6.1; Her. 4.5.6–6.5 9 (booing; soldiers); 4.9.2 (procurator); *HA Car.* 3.4–4.8; 5.1 (governor of Narbonensis); *HA Geta* 6.6f. Papinian's death: *HA Sev.* 21.8; *HA Car.* 4.1f.; 8.1–9; *HA Geta* 6.3; Vict. *Caes.* 20.33f. exonerates Caracalla; cf. Bird (1984: 136, n. 23). The name of C. Septimius (Severus) Aper is confirmed by P. Holder, ed. (2006) *Roman Military Diplomas 5*, *BICS* suppl. 88, London, no. 454; or *Der Neue Pauly*, 11, col. 435 (I owe these refs. to the kindness of A. R. Birley); cf. Birley (1999: 274). He notes that the governor of Britain, C. Julius Marcus, had a great many dedications to Caracalla and Domna set up, but his name was deleted systematically: Birley (2005: 203–8). Cornificia: Dio 77(78) 16.6[a]. 'Laenus' of Dio 77(78). 5.4 may be 'Laetus' of *HA Car.* 3.4, forced to suicide. Caracalla's relations with the populace: Sünskes Thompson (1990: 112–18), with largesses 112f.
28 Attempt on Cilo and involvement of Asper: Dietz (1983) on *HA Car.* 4.5f.; *HA Geta* 6.4.
29 Mourning banned: Dio 77(78). 2.6.
30 Avitus and Marcellus against Geta: Halfmann (1982).
31 Martialis' flaminate: Williams (1902: 281), citing *CIL* 8, 4196f.
32 Six fragments of monuments to Geta at Athens: *Hesp.* 3 (1934) 76, no. 75; 15 (1946) 237 no. 70. At Timgad Geta's name was struck out and replaced with that of Domna: *CIL* 8, 17871.
33 Severus on Caracalla's position: '*Hate kai autokratoros ontos*': Dio 76(77). 14.6.
34 Livia's new status: Barrett (2002: 144f.; 148; 151–9; 170) (official position): *contra*, Temporini (2002: 77).
35 Domna advising: cf. Dio 77(78).10.4 (finance). Williams (1902: 291) justly speaks of a limited effect; cf. Bowersock (1969: 109). Lusnia (1995: 121 and 137), regarding this period as Domna's greatest, notes the comparative modesty and safe imagery of its coin types.
36 Elagabalus at Thyatira: *IGR* 4, 1287. Maesa with Domna: Dio 78(79).30.3; perhaps it was from Domna's Antiochene residence that she was expelled by Macrinus: Her. 5.3.2; *HA Macr.* 9.1. Kienast (1996: 181) has her at Rome when Caracalla was assassinated.
37 *Mater Castrorum*: see Chapter 3, note 48f. '*Mater Aug./imp.*', etc.: *IRT* 404. '*Mater Castrorum et senatus et patriae*': *CIL* 6, 1035 (204). See Kettenhofen (1979: 86–97). The date of Domna's extended titles is discussed by Kettenhofen (1979: 86) and by Dietz (1983: 383f.), reviewing previous work, in connection with *AE* 1965, 338. Kettenhofen too favours the period of Caracalla and Geta's joint rule, citing the coin evidence (Hill 1978). *Mater/parens patriae*, proposed for Livia in 14: Tac. *Ann.* 1.14.1; Suet *Tib.* 50.3; Dio 57.12.4; 58.2.3, and which appear on coins of Lepcis (*RPC* 1 209, no. 849f.), see Barrett (2002: 156f.) and Kettenhofen (1979: 85).
38 'Mother of the Roman People': *CIL* 6, 419=30763; *IGR* 1, 577, with Ghedini (1984: 23 n. 122).

39 Claudius proposed as 'Father of the Senate': Tac. *Ann.* 11.25.7 (perhaps ironically). Commodus: *CREBM* 4, 730 nos. 222–5; 812 no. 604. Ghedini (1984: 13), drawing attention to Pliny, *Pan.* 1.1 and 2.3, reveals the latent power.

40 Domna as '*Mater Patriae*': See Kettenhofen (1979: 86) and Dietz (1983: 383f.) (reviewing earlier theories). Benario (1958b), followed by Lusnia (1995: 134), argues for an earlier date, and Kettenhofen allows that there are inscriptions that support his view, especially from Africa; *AE* 1965, 338, is an example, and *CIL* 3, 419 = 30763, like *ILS* 426, if genuine and in pristine condition. Kettenhofen (1979) rebuts the view in *PIR*^{2} J 663, p. 313, that the recut *CIL* 6, 1035, is evidence of Domna's possessing the title under Severus. Coins bearing it belong to 211 and later; *CREBM* 5^2, 432 no. 11f.; 469 no. 213f.; 432 nos. 11, 11A, 12. Ghedini (1984: 13) favours an earlier date, but with a change of political climate that brought them into general use only later. Trajan '*Optimus*': F. A. Lepper (1948) *Trajan's Parthian War*, Oxford, 35.

41 Titles shared with Plautilla: Kettenhofen (1979: 240, n. 136); *AE* 1968, 590; 1977, 705: plain 'Augg.'

42 Maesa and Mamaea: Ghedini (1984: 14, with n. 120), accepting Benario (1959: 11); but cf. Kettenhofen (1979: 145f.; 152); Mamaea 159.

43 Orientalization: Hasebroek (1921: 92), but cf. Instinsky (1942: 204–7).

44 Anomalous titulature: on *CIL* 8, 23405, Domna is '*Mater Augustorum et castrorum et patriae*' (if the restoration is correct); on 23750 she is '*Mater Augusti, mater castrorum [. . .]totiusque divinae domus*' ('of the entire divine house').

45 Caracalla *pius felix* (to honour Commodus: Hasebroek 1921: 91): Mastino (1981: 91–7); Van't Dack (1991: 329). *Pia Felix*: date: Kettenhofen (1979: 237, n. 97; 242 n. 167); 211/12 Baharal (1992); Ghedini (1984: 13), citing *RIC* 4.1, 63, 272–5, and 310–13. Henzen, *AA cxcvii* = *ILS* 451, l.25 shows it in use in 213.

46 *Felicitas*: Cicero, *The Imperium of Cn. Pompeius* 28.

47 *Pietas*: coins: Crawford, *RRC* nos. 308; 450; 477; 516. Tiberius: Suet. *Tib.* 17.2. Matidia: *RIC* 2, 301 no. 759. Caracalla: e.g. 4.1, 220 nos. 52–5a.

48 Commodus' tombstone: *ILS* 401.

49 Provincials' attitudes: Hekster (2002: 94f.).

50 Domna's receptions: Dio 77(78).18.2f. Philiscus' appointment from her, through the emperor: *par'autes dia tou basileos*: Phil. *Soph.* 622; see Chapter 7. Justinian acknowledged consulting Theodora: *Nov.* 8.1; she also entertained embassies: Procopius, *Secret History* 30.24.

51 Praetorian Guard: Dio 78(79).23.2.

52 Correspondence and responses: Dio 77(78).10, 4.

53 Vitellius transferring bureaux to *equites*: Tac. *Hist.* 1.58; *ILS* 1447=MW 338.

54 Domna's official functions: Kettenhofen (1979: 17) against the over-precise *PIR*^{2} J 662 (p. 315); Ghedini (1984: 23 n. 127) is undecided.

55 Letter to Ephesus: *AE* 1966, 430 = *I. Ephesos* 2, 212 (l.11); 'Benefits' (*euergesion*, l.10, opposed to *epidemias*): Robert and Robert (1967) with praise at 61f. So Lifshitz (1970), also noting the city's educational role (cf. Thucydides 2, 41, Pericles on Athens) and, in an attractive but not binding suggestion, making her understand the Greek *ergasterion* ('workshop', l.13) as a translation of the Latin *officina* (Cicero, *Orator* 3.12). Further references: Hemelrijk (1999, 356 n. 83).

56 Overestimate of Domna's position: e.g. Van Berchem (1974: 305) ('elle administrait l'Empire'); Lusnia (1995: 137), following H. Mattingly in

CREBM 5, clxix: by the last phase of her coinage she was to all intents and purposes running the Empire. *Contra*, Kettenhofen (1979: 18) on Dmeir (Syria) inscription: Roussel and De Visscher (1942–3); *SEG* 37, 1186, from Tacina, is a letter of Caracalla concerning misconduct of soldiers. Bleckmann (2002: 277) is also sceptical.

57 Increasing devotion to Domna: Bleckmann (2002: 276).

58 Severus' injunction: Dio 76(77).15.2. Caracalla's costly wars and dependence on army: Dio 77(78).10.1 and 4.

59 Advice (on expenditure): Dio 77(78).10.4; (unsuccessful): 18.1f. *Constitutio*: Grant (1996: 46). Varius Marcellus and the revenues: see Chapter 4, note 98.

60 Breakthrough for women: W. Eck, in Temporini (2002: 103).

61 Domna used for dating: Williams (1902: 292), citing *CIL* 8, 2369f.

62 Domna's hostility to Caracalla: see above, note 10. Geta's personality: see note 14.

63 Caracalla's date of birth: see Chapter 2, note 67. Stepmother: see Chapter 2, note 72.

64 Incest (and 'marriage'): Her. 4.9.2f.; *HA Sev*. 21, 7; *HA Car*. 10.3f.; Eutropius, *Brevarium* 8.20, identical with Eusebius-Jerome, *Chronicon* 216, 18f. Helm and [*Epit. Caes.*] 21.5; cf. Vict. *Caes*. 21.3; Orosius, *History against the Pagans* 7.18.2; *Chronogr. of 354* (*Chron. Min*. 1, 147). Given its wide coverage, Kettenhofen (1979: 60), probably rightly, ascribes the story to the *Kaisergeschichte*. Victor, like *HA Car*. 10.2, blames Domna. The notion of Domna as stepmother has the same source (Bird 1984, 136, n. 23) or, less plausibly, Marius Maximus (Syme 1968: 91; Syme 1971: 123). Fraternal feuding as the explanation: Whittaker *ad* Her. 3.10.5.

65 'Jocasta': Her. 4.9.3, with Whittaker *ad loc*.

66 Incest story: Marasco (1996: 127 n. 50), refuting the idea of Plautianus as source. The dating of any putative wedding (*HA Car*. 10.4 and *HA Sev*. 21.7) makes it unlikely. Penella (1980) rightly saw two hostile traditions (against mother and son) converging; cf. Domna's adulteries in *HA Sev*. 18.8. Whether Marasco is right to date the beginning of the story before the death of Geta is unclear, and one of his reasons for ascribing the story to Egypt is unconvincing. It is that the Egyptians (and Ptolemies) were used to intercourse and marriage between brother and sister; but we are dealing with a different relationship, and if they were so used to it why should it be bruited as a scandal? Marasco's subsidiary supports (the devotion of Caracalla to Isis and Serapis and interest in things Egyptian, linking him with Caligula, whose relations with all his sisters was suspect) are peripheral. See also Rubin (1980: 173–6) and Zimmermann (1999: 206 n. 276) with further refs.

67 Dio and the incest story: Marasco (1996: 119 n. 1) rightly rejects the view that excerptors and epitomators of Dio excised the story from his narrative: Dio claimed, 77(78).16.1–2[2] and 4, that Caracalla became impotent.

68 Various versions: Penella (1980: 382 n. 1) noted Victor's friendly attitude towards Caracalla, and suggests, implausibly, that the sexual factor may have been intended to mitigate the fratricide or account for the rivalry.

69 Rumour's function: P. A. Lienhardt (1975) 'The Interpretation of Rumour', in J. H. M. Beattie and R. G. Lienhardt, eds., *Studies in Social Anthropology: Essays in Memory of E. E. Evans-Pritchard*, Oxford, 105–31.

70 Alexandria: see Marasco (1996). Alexandrian ribaldry: H. Musurillo (1954) *The Acts of the Pagan Martyrs* (Acta Alexandrinorum), Oxford, 19 no. IV, l.50f. Claudius the cast-off son of a Jewess: Suet. *Vesp*. 19.2: Vespasian a 'fish-finger monger'.

71 Faustina's misconduct: *HA M. Aur*. 19.7–11.

72 Persian incest: Plut. *Artax*. 23.5, cited by Marasco (1996: 103, n. 62).

73 Semiramis: Dio 78(79).23.3. Her death: Justin 1.2.10; Orosius, *History against the Pagans* 1.4.7f.

74 Caracalla as father of Elagabalus: Dio 78(79).33.3f.; Her. 5.3.10; Eutropius, *Brevarium* 8.22; *HA Macr.* 9.4; *HA Elag.* 2.1.

75 Plan to murder Domna: *HA Car.* 3.3; *HA Geta* 7.3 (stepmother in each case). The assimilation with Nero was noticed by Hohl (1950: 15f., n. 11) and accepted by Penella (1980: 383), who suggested that the scandal-mongering writer Marius Maximus may have been responsible, if not the author of *HA* himself; no matter that Maximus was a contemporary of Caracalla's, as long as he survived him and could publish with impunity. For explicit comparisons of 'bad' emperors with earlier paradigms, Penella (1980: 384) cites *HA Commodus* 19.2: he was 'more savage than Domitian, more debauched than Nero'.

76 Caracalla in the north: Dio 77(78).13.3–15.7; Her. 4.7.2–7; Vict. *Caes.* 21.2; *HA Car.* 5.1–7. At (?) Carnuntum 5 Dec. 212: *Cod. Iust.* 4.29.1. German campaign: *ILS* 1159; into the Agri Decumates by 11 Aug. 'German victory': Henzen, *AA* cxcvii, ll. 20–5; *CIL* 8, 4202. Alamanni not distinguished from Germani at this time: Alföldy (1989: 406–18, esp. 410). 'Showing the flag': T. S. Burns (2003) *Rome and the Barbarians, 100* BC–AD *400*, Baltimore, MD, 277–9, with n. 17.

77 Caracalla's conscience: Her. 4.7.1. His account was accepted in the later, Latin, sources: [*Epit. Caes.*] 21.3.

78 Support of army: Her. 4.7.4–7.

79 Domna in Germany: Williams (1902: 288) arguing plausibly but not quite conclusively from the Acts of the Arval Brothers 'her' German victory; so Ghedini (1984: 14, with n. 123), bibl., including M. Christol (1975) *BJ* 175: 128–39, esp. 135f.

80 Domna crowning Caracalla: Ghedini (1984: 113–19), Fig. 12f.), citing Charles-Picard (1966: esp. 606f.). Agrippina and Nero at Aphrodisias: *JRS* 77 (1987, Pl. XXIV). *CIL* 9.4637 looks to be dedicated to Domna and Victoria (but may be garbled).

81 Sojourn in Rome unlikely (*contra*, Whittaker *ad* Her. 4.8.1): Halfmann (1986: 226); the slight evidence for it is Dio 77(78).16.1 (his dealings with the Vestals) and *Cod. Iust.* 7.16.2 (a rescript dated from Rome). *Antonine Itinerary*: Van Berchem (1937) *Mém. Soc. nat. Ant.* 8–10, 117–202. Balkan stay: Halfmann (1986: 226), citing *AE* 1973, 437, for a visit to Gorsium and J. Fitz (1961) 'Il Soggiorno di Caracalla in Pannonia nel 214', *Accad. d'Ungheria in Roma, Quad. di Docum*, 2: 5ff.; Fitz (1972: 91–6); Erdélyi and Fülep (1954: 323 no. 326). Whittaker *ad* Her. 4.8.3, stresses 'important work' in Dacia. Date of winter spent at Nicomedia: Scheid (1998b).

82 Parthian campaigns: Her. 4.10–13. Preparations: Whittaker *ad* Her. 4.10.1. Caracalla as Alexander: Her. 4.8.1–3, with Whittaker *ad loc.*

83 Marriage proposal: Dio 78(79).1.1; Her. 4.10.1–11.7.

84 Olympias: Nau (1968: 49f., Pl. 4.1); Kettenhofen (1979: 126f.); Ghedini (1984: 152–4).

85 Perinthus: Halfmann (1986: 227), with Schönert (1965: 192, nos. 570–6).

86 Shipwreck: Dio 77(78).16.7; Henzen, *AA* cc, l.8f.; 86, with, as Williams (1902: 290) pointed out, sacrifice to 'Iunoni Juliae Augustae', her Juno.

87 Achilles' tomb: Herod. 4.8.4; Phil. *Apoll.* 4.11.

88 Thyatira and other possible halts: Halfmann (1986: 228). Statues at Pergamum: Habicht (1969: 33–8, nos. 12–16). Neocorate: *IGR* 4, 451.

89 Route through Asia Minor: Halfmann (1986: 227f.), rebutting the view of B. Levick (1969) in J. Bibauw, ed., *Hommages à M. Renard* 2, Collection Latomus 102, Brussels, 426–46, that he followed the route of Alexander the

Great, and citing *I. Prusias* 6 (mentioning 'the sacred passings through', l.15) and 9 ('towards the east', l.11).

90 Thyatira's assize district: *IGR* 4, 1287. Profitability: Dio of Prusa 35.15f.

91 Caracalla's patience: inscription of Dmeir: Roussel and De Visscher (1942–3), with Crook (1955: 82–4; 142).

92 At Antioch (immediately after arrival in east?): Dio 77.20.1; Her. 4.8.6; colonial status: *Dig.* 50.15.8.5, with Ziegler (1978) for the vicissitudes of Antioch and Laodiceia. Laodiceia: Halfmann (1986: 224). Pelusium donkeys: *P.Oxy.* 3602–5.

93 Roman reverses: *CREBM* 5, 487, no. 286 (before 10 Dec. 215). Disorders involving a pro-Getan faction: C. R. Whittaker *ad* Her. 4.9.2.

94 Stay in Egypt: Dio 77(78).22.2–23.4; Her. 4.8.6–9.8; *HA Car.* 6.2f.; J. Chronology: J. Rea *ad P.Oxy.* 3602–5. Halfmann (1986: 225 and 229). J. Schwartz (1959) *CE* 34: 120–3, who on *P.Strassb.* 245 argues for Caracalla contemplating a return visit; amended by J. E. G. Whitehorne (1982) *CE* 57: 132–5, thinking of a tour up-country. Massacre: Dio 77.22f; Her. 4.9.3–8, with C. R. Whittaker *ad loc.*; *HA Car.* 6.3. Interpretation and dating: Sünskes Thompson (1990: 159–66). Noting affection for Geta and suggesting that the disaster has been exaggerated in ancient writing: Buraselis (1995). Earlier restiveness: H. Musurillo, ed. (1954) *The Acts of the Pagan Martyrs* (Acta Alexandrinorum), Oxford, 229–32 with *cognitio* held by Caracalla. Danger to Romans: Bruun (1995).

95 Parthian campaigns: Dio 78(79).1.1–3.3; Her. 4.11.2–9. Winter at Edessa: Dio 78(79).5.4; *HA Car.* 6.6, with Halfmann (1986: 229f.) discounting the letter as December of some year between 213 and 217 and restored as being 'from Antioch', where 'from Alexandria' might be possible, though with a line slightly longer than its neighbours (J. Robert and L. Robert (1954) *La Carie: Histoire et Géographie historique* 2, Paris, 274 no. 149).

96 Caracalla 'mad' (from 212): Dio 77(78). 15.2–7; [*Epit. Caes.*] 21.3.

97 Caracalla's grant of citizenship: Dio 77(78).9.5; Ulpian in *Dig.* 50.5.17; P. Giessen 40 with Sherwin-White (1973: 279–87). Date: Gilliam (1965: 212); cf. Millar (1962: 214). As A. R. Birley reminds me, not all scholars have agreed that the papyrus refers to the *Constitutio*: Wolff (1976: 193–209) is against, Kuhlmann (1994: 217–39, bibl. 217) more favourable.

98 Cost of troops: e.g. Dio 77(78).10.1; cf. 12.6.

99 Eastern expedition: Dio 77(78).19.1f.; 78(79). 1.1–9.3; it would have been the occasion for Caracalla to make Emesa the capital of 'Phoenicia Libanensis', recorded in 265 by Mal. 296.

100 Maternianus' and Julianus' letters: Dio 78(79).4. Letter passed to Macrinus: Her. 4.12.6f.

101 Superstition: see Chapter 2.

102 Assassination of Caracalla: Dio 78(79).5 (8 Apr. 5.5 and implied 11.6); *HA Car.* 6.6–7.2 (6 Apr.). Covert: Her. 4.12f.; *HA Macr.* 4.7. Conspirators: Whittaker *ad* Her. 4.14.2. Mattingly (1953: 262–4) is inclined to exonerate Macrinus.

103 Macrinus chosen: Dio 78(79).11.4–6. Parthians: Her. 4.14.1. Macrinus' reign: Dio 78(79) 12.1 – 41.4; *HA Macr.* 2–15.1.

104 News of Caracalla's death: Dio 78(79). 23.1. Ashes sent to Rome: Dio 78(79). 9.1; *HA Car.* 9.1 and 12; *HA Macr.* 5.2.

105 Death of Maternianus: Dio 78(79).15.3.

106 Caracalla loved by troops: Dio 78(79).17.4. Sharing hardships: 13.1; Her. 4.7.5–7. Praetorians with Caracalla: Millar (1993: 146).

107 Macrinus' nomenclature: *HA Macr.* 2.1, wrongly adding Antoninus; 5.7.

108 Macrinus' survival in 205: Dio 78(79).11.2. Procurator: Pflaum (1960–1: 667 no. 248).
109 Reign of Macrinus: Dio 78(79).12–40.2; Her. 4.14.2–5.4.11, with Zimmermann (1999: 214–21); Whittaker *ad* 4.15.5 on the chronology of relations with Parthia; Mattingly (1953: 965–9).
110 Macrinus' reception by Senate: Dio 78(79).20.2; *HA Macr*. 2.3f.; 7.1.
111 Could Domna have saved Caracalla?: Ghedini (1984: 14f.).
112 Maesa' money: Her. 5.3.2; 4.1; 8.3. Maternianus: *PIR*[2] F 317.
113 Death of Domitia Lepida: Tac. *Ann*. 12.64f.
114 Domna's suicide: Her. 4.13.8. Attempted: Dio 78(79).23.1.
115 Murder of predecessor's women: Lactantius, *Deaths of Persecutors*, 51.
116 Abuse, and Macrinus' reaction: Dio 78(79).23.1f.
117 Diadumenian's nomenclature: Dio 78(79).19.1f.; *HA Macr*. 7.5; *PIR*[2] O 107, p. 444.
118 Positive message (*chresta tina*): Dio 78(79).23.2.
119 Hopes of continuing in power: Dio 78(79).23.2f.
120 Suicide: Dio 78(79).23.6; Her. 4.13.8.
121 Domna's aim sole rule (*autarchese*): Dio 78(79).23.3; rebutted by Ghedini (1984: 24 n. 137).
122 Domitia Longina: B. Levick (2002) 'Corbulo's Daughter', *Greece and Rome* 49: 199–211.
123 Ordered to leave Antioch: Dio 78(79).23.4–6. Maesa ordered to Emesa: Her. 5.3.2.
124 Self-command: so Ghedini (1984: 15). Whittaker *ad* Her. 4.13.8 notes that the verb *apokarterein* can denote hanging as well as starvation, and Marasco (1996) again invokes the literary precedent of Jocasta. But hanging was not a Roman method.
125 The interval between Caracalla's death and Domna's is not allowed by Kienast (1996: 167).

7 Cultural activities

1 Domna as an educated woman: Hemelrijk (1999) is fundamental. A. R. Birley has drawn my attention to the later women. Philostratus: see Bibliography, p. 219.
2 Evidence for education: Hemelrijk (1999: 92–6).
3 Tiberius' education: Dio 55.9.5.
4 Husbands as educators: Levick (2002: 141f.).
5 Domna's study of rhetoric: Hemelrijk (1999: 25, with n. 38).
6 Mamaea and education: Her. 5.7.5. Hostile to philosophy: *HA Alex*. 14.5. Alexander's sister: *HA Two Maximins* 29.3. A. R. Birley notes that *HA Alex*. is almost undiluted fiction, as is most of *HA Max*., not least 'Theoclia': cf. Syme (1968: 168n., 172n.).
7 An early date for the second sophistic 'movement': Winter (2002: xi and *passim*.)
8 'Fixation on the past': Flinterman (1995: 49–51), discussing Bowie (1970: 6).
9 Sophists on embassies: e.g. Phil. *Soph*. 601. Listed: Bowie (1982: 55–7). Qualities required: Plut. *Mor*. 805B (*Political Precepts* 10.9); Flinterman (1995: 34f.), on Bowersock (1969), who stresses the socio-political aspect: professional status gave rise to sophists' political role; Bowie (1982), however, plausibly regards sophists as well-to-do city men, some of whom preferred an intellectual life to a political one.
10 Trajan and Dio: Phil. *Soph*. 488.
11 Adrian of Tyre: Phil. *Soph*. 589.

12 'Second Sophistic': Phil. *Soph*. 481.
13 Pius not a sophist: M. Aurelius, *Meditations* 6.30.2.
14 Plato's mistrust of sophists: *Gorgias* 463B; 501B; Isidore of Pelusium, *Epistle* 2, 42 in *PG* 78, 484. Sophistic is firmly confined by Brunt (1994).
15 Development of Dio of Prusa: C. P. Jones (1978) *The Roman World of Dio Chrysostom*, Cambridge, MA, 9–12.
16 Euphrates: Pliny *Ep*. 1.10, with Sherwin-White's n. Artemidorus: Pliny *Ep*. 3.11. Advisers: E. D. Rawson (1989: 253) notes that philosophers 'have a tradition behind them which sets them somewhat apart'.
17 Sages: Flinterman (1995: 2; 193) traces the idea to Neo-Platonic pseud-epigraphic *hypomnemata*.
18 Ti. Claudius Atticus Herodes: *PIR*[2] C 802.
19 Appearance important: Winter (2002: 114), citing Phil. *Soph*. 536.
20 Proteus: Phil. *Apoll*. 1.4, discussed by Flinterman (1995: 52f.).
21 Sophists' activities: Flinterman (1995: 29–51). Distinguished from rhetors: Bowersock (1969: 14). Fees: Winter (2002: 49), citing Phil. *Soph*. 494.
22 Comparison with male senators taking to philosophy: Hemelrijk (1999: 127). Philosophy a manoeuvre: Ghedini (1984: 10).
23 Bibl. of Romans and philosophers: B. Rawson (2003: 153 n. 16).
24 Gathering of savants: Phil. *Soph*. 601, with Birley (1999: 150f.).
25 Hoplite general: Flinterman (1995: 16, n. 71). Post held in absence: Anderson (1986: 6, and 19 n. 35); *contra*, Flinterman (1995: 19).
26 Chronology of career: Flinterman (1995: 19–21), followed by Hemelrijk (1999: 123), assigning Athenian functions to the period 200/21–205/6.
27 Philostratus and Ocean tides: Phil. *Apoll*. 5.2, with Flinterman (1995: 24).
28 Imperial family at Tyana: Münscher (1907: 484f.).
29 Philostratus' friend Gordian: Phil. *Soph*. 480, with Bowersock (1969: 6–8), favouring Gordian I and referring to the number of governorships held by him (perhaps taking him to Syria): Her. 7.5.2; Barnes (1968b) argues in favour of II: if the dedication is to I it dates the work to 237/8, when he was proconsul of Africa (or to 221/2, when he could have been consul not long after being proconsul of Achaea). II would imply *c*.230, when he was proconsul of Achaea; the dedicatee was a descendant of the sophist Herodes Atticus, which Barnes denies for I. Barnes considers three possibilities for the meeting of Philostratus and Gordian II at Daphne: Gordian was commander of the Fourth, Scythian, Legion; he was in the entourage of Caracalla; he was with his father as legate to the governor of Coele Syria. For the Anatolian origins of the Gordians, see A. R. Birley (1966) 'The Origins of Gordian I', in *Britain and Rome: Essays Presented to E. Birley*, Kendal, 56f. On Gordian I and II, see Birley (2005: 338–41).
30 Philostratus' satisfactions: Anderson (1986: 5f.).
31 *Letter* to Domna: Phil. *Ep*. 73.
32 The *Letter* inauthentic: Bowersock (1969: 104), listing defenders n. 2; add C. P. Jones (1972) *Plutarch and Rome*, ed. 2, Oxford, 131f.; Anderson (1977); Penella (1979); Hemelrijk (1999: 305 n. 121). Kettenhofen (1979: 15) also regards the *Letter* as inauthentic.
33 Philostratus claiming influence: Phil. *Ep*. 72; Flinterman (1997: 86).
34 'Philosopher', *kuklos*: Phil. *Soph*. 622; Phil. *Apoll*. 1.3 ('*tou peri auten kuklou*'; 'of the circle round her)'; cf. Dio 75(76).15.1; 77(79). 18.3.
35 Sabina's friends: Hemelrijk (1999: 119), based on *HA Hadr*. 11.3.
36 Philosophers and the great: Lucian, *Paid Companions*, 36. Rusticus: Plutarch, *On Inquisitiveness* 15; *Mor*. 522D–E.
37 Doubts expressed by F. Solmsen (1920) *RE* 20.1, 137 ('eine gewisse Dosis Phantasie'); Bowersock (1969: 103–9), with 102 n. 1 for modern proponents,

noting (n. 5) Platnauer (1918: 128) for Messalina. Also sceptical: Barnes (1968b: 595); Anderson (1986: 4f.); Flinterman (1995: 22). Not all recent views are unfavourable: 'Intellectual': Ghedini (1984: 11); criticism of Bowersock's view: 187. Shotter (2003: 385): 'Under their influence [the matriarchs'] there was an extraordinary outpouring of largely Greek writing'; Dio and Herodian are mentioned. Balanced accounts: Hemelrijk (1999: 122–6), especially persuasive on the nature of the 'circle', and Birley (1999: 168).

38 Aspasia: Flinterman (1997: 82–5).

39 Lucian, *Portraits* 3–8.

40 Bowersock (1969: 103) on V. Duruy (1879) *Histoire des Romains et des peuples soumis à leur domination* 6, Paris, 91f; earlier bibl. Ghedini (1984: 192 n. 1).

41 Learned gathering: Münscher (1907: 477). Philiscus: Phil. *Soph.* 622. Bowersock (1969: 103 n. 4) notes a procuratorship in Thessaly.

42 Antipater: Phil. *Soph.* 607; R. Heberdey et al., eds. (1912) *Forschungen in Ephesos* 2: *Das Theater*, Österreichische Archäologische Institut (ÖAI), Vienna, 125f., no. 26. with Bowersock (1969: 4f.).

43 Oppian: for writers so named see Bibliography, p. 218.

44 Aelian: Phil. *Soph.* 624f.

45 The historical existence of Sammonicus (*HA Car.* 4.4; *HA Geta* 5.6; *HA Alex.* 30.2; *HA Gordian* 18.2; Macrobius, *Saturnalia* 3.9.6) has been questioned: Bowersock (1969: 107); Champlin (1981) picks out literary and political threads, Greek and African, contributing to Sammonicus' downfall. Galen: Swain (1996: 366–72). If Galen died in 199, he hardly had time to settle in to membership, but Hemelrijk (1999: 305 n. 120) accepts the view that he survived for another decade, even to 215. Hair dye passage: *On the Compounding of Drugs* 1, Kühn 12, 434f.

46 Historians as members: Münscher (1907: 477). Millar (1964: 19f.) notes Dio's respectful attitude to Apollonius of Tyana in 67.18.1f., as opposed to 77(78). 18.4, written after Domna's death; it reflects her regard for the sage.

47 Whittaker *ad* Her. 1.16.3. Philostratus on Domitian's murder: Phil. *Apoll.* 8.25–27; Dio's version (67.15.6–16.7) differs. Discussion: F. Grosso (1954) *Acme* 7: 495–505; Millar (1964: 20).

48 Platnauer (1918: 144f.). Bowersock (1969: 102 n. 1) singles out ('especially egregious') the list of J. Bidez (1939) *CAH* 12: 613f.

49 Hermocrates: Phil. *Soph.* 608–12, dying before the age of 30; Münscher (1907: 475f.); possibly present in R. Heberdey et al., eds. (1912) *Forschungen in Ephesos* 2: *Das Theater*, ÖAI, Vienna, 125f., no. 26, but in an uncertain role.

50 Diogenes Laertius 3.47 (Plato); 10.29 (Epicurus). Arria: Galen, *To Piso, on Antidotes to Venom* 2, Kühn 14.218f. Hemelrijk (1999: 304 n. 119) points out that an intended dedication to Domna may have been omitted on her death, but that this is unlikely, since any deferential title of address is wanting.

51 Geta's qualities and favour with Domna: see Chapter 6.

52 Pro-Getan 'circle': Whittaker *ad* Her. 3.15.6. Antipater: Phil. *Soph.* 607. Philostratus: Phil. *Ep.* 72. Sammonicus: *HA Car.* 4.4; *HA Geta* 5.6 (Geta's favourite reading), with Champlin (1981) and Birley (1999: 207). Quadratus: *PIR*[2] A 1244; F. Jacoby (1926) *FrGHist* 4, 2C, Berlin, no. 97, 2A pp. 337–50; comm. 2C pp. 301–3.

53 Unknowns: Kettenhofen (1979: 15).

54 Mobility: Bowersock (1969: 109).

55 Tiberius' reading: Suet. *Tib.* 70.3.

56 Capital: F. G. B. Millar (1977) *The Emperor in the Roman World*, London, 39.

57 Origen: Eusebius, *Church History* 6.21.3f.; Orosius, *Against the Pagans* 7.18.7. See Downey (1961: 305f.); Bowersock (1969: 108); Whittaker *ad* Her. 6.6.4; Hemelrijk (1999: 126).

58 Papinian and Antipater: Bowersock (1969: 106), rebutting the idea of relationship between Domna and the lawyer, refers to W. Kunkel (1967) *Herkunft und soziale Stellung der römischen Juristen*, Forsch. zum röm. Recht 4, ed. 2, Graz, 224–9.

59 Gap: Dio 75(76). 15.7, with Bowersock (1969: 106).

60 Zenobia's court: Stoneman (1992: 129–32).

61 Receiving all the most eminent men and discussing philosophy with them: Dio 77(78). 18.3: *espazeto . . . pantas tous protous . . . kai meta touton eti mallon ephilosophei*.

62 Hirelings: Lucian, *On the Hired Friends of the Powerful*, alluded to by Bowersock (1969: 109).

63 Philiscus' appointment: Phil. *Soph*. 622, with Flinterman (1995: 22). Plotina: *ILS* 7784 (further refs. *PIR*[3] P 679); Oliver, *Gk. Const.* no. 73.

64 'Tes philosophou', Phil. *Soph*. 622. Limitations for women: Levick (2002).

65 Plato: De Lacy (1974).

66 Apameia: Balty (1981: 11f.), citing Porphyry, *Life of Plotinus* 2f. for Numenius' heirs, Libanius, *Orations* 52.21 for Jamblichus, and 48.14 for the devotion of the upper class to the oracular Zeus, and Theodoret, *Church History* 5.21.7–10 and 14f. for the temple as a centre of resistance to Christianity, destroyed 386. Antioch: *Acts* 11.26.

67 Phil. *Apoll*. 1.3: '*kai gar tous rhetorikous pantas logous epaeinei kai espazeto*'.

68 Julia Cornelia Paula wife of Elagabalus: *PIR*[2] I 660 (cautious on relationship).

69 Oriental influence: Ghedini (1984: 11).

70 Severus' astrology: see Chapter 2. Thrasyllus: Cramer (1954: 92–108); G. J. Toomer in *OCD*[3] 343.

71 Disputants, including 'Geometricians': Flinterman (1995: 23f. and 66), against Münscher (1907: 477), and others he cites (n. 111), noting *Dig*. 50.13.1.1; *Cod. Just*. 9.18.2; as in 1997: 78, he stresses the Pythagorean connection; so Burkert (1972: 54); Kettenhofen (1979: 16) notes the broad *theia*, matters of religion, as an interest. Disputes: Phil. *Ep*. 73.

72 Pythagoreanism: H. Thesleff (1961) *An Introduction to the Pythagorean Writings of the Hellenistic Period*, Åbo, Sweden; W. Burkert (1972) *Lore and Science in Ancient Pythagoreanism*, Cambridge, MA; D. R. Fideler, ed. (1987) *The Pythagorean Sourcebook and Library*, Grand Rapids, MI.

73 Literary aspect of philosophy: Flinterman (1995: 32).

74 Phil. *Apoll*. 1.3 ('*tous rhetorikous pantas logous*'); Phil. *Ep*. 73 (Aeschines' 'style'); see Penella (1979: 162 with n. 13).

75 Plato's style imitated: Phil. *Soph*. 486f., with De Lacy (1974: 6). Affected by Gorgias: Isidore of Pelusium, *Epistle* 2, 42 in *PG* 78, 484. Penella (1979: 163) notes sophistical elements attributed to Apollonius by Philostratus.

76 Interest in Plato's content: De Lacy (1974: 7).

77 Birley (1999: 168).

78 Commission: Phil. *Apoll*. 1.3. 'A wise man', etc.: Phil. *Apoll*. 1.28. Hellenism: Swain (1999: 195).

79 Dates of *Apoll*.: Flinterman (1995: 25 and 66).

80 Analysis of the advice by Flinterman (1995: 208–13). Liberality: Phil. *Apoll*. 1.38; other merits, including control of sons and freedmen 5.36. The ruler and the laws: Flinterman cites (n. 444) Pliny *Pan*. 65.1; *Dig*. 32.23; *Inst. Just*. 2.17.8, where Severus and Caracalla declare that they live by the laws; *CJ* 6.23.3.

81 Previous emperors: Flinterman (1995: 156; 168f.).

82 Contemporary references: Flinterman (1995: 217–30). Fratricide: Phil. *Apoll.* 1.28; 6.32. Sun god: 3.28. He uses these references as evidence for publication after Elagabalus' death in 222. Proconsulships: 5.36. Flinterman (1995: 123f. and 226f.) connects the complaint about proconsulship (5.36) with a decline in the proportion of easterners governing Asia (Leunissen 1989: 83f.; 88f.: twenty-one proconsuls, of whom twelve are certainly westerners and six more may be).

83 Restricted field: Flinterman (1995: 228f.; 240). He observes (227) that in Phil. *Soph.* 625 Philostratus evidently approves of the murder of Elagabalus.

84 Development of gurus: Flinterman (1995: 87; 171; 179f.). He suggests (237f.) that the source of Philostratus' conception was a Neo-Pythagorean text passing as memoirs of a disciple of Apollonius. Superhuman qualities: 188.

85 Flinterman (1995: 218f.) rightly rejects any idea that Philostratus was used against Plautianus. So at 219f., the suggestion of Lenz (1964) that Phil. *Apoll.* 8.7 represents an attempt by Domna to influence Caracalla.

86 Marxist interpretation: E. M. Schtajermann (1964) *Die Krise der Sklavenrhalterordnung im Westen des röm. Reiches*, Berlin, 253–91, discussed by Flinterman (1995: 221f.). (Domna represents an intelligentsia connected with the municipal aristocracy which, with cities declining, resented its dependence on the provincial aristocracy; the bureaucracy offered them a way out. To Caracalla the sophists were objectionable.)

87 Magic: Flinterman (1995: 60 and 231) points out superhuman attributes: he was a son of Zeus (Phil. *Apoll.* 1.6; cf. 1.19; 2.17). A similar charge against Jesus was debated between the Platonist Celsus, writing *c*.176. and Origen, *Against Celsus*, *c*.249. Shotter (2003) regards Phil. *Apoll.* as a 'sanitization' of Christianity.

88 W. Schmid and O. Stahlin in W. von Christ (1924) *Geschichte der griechischer Literatur*, Handb. der Altertumswiss. 7.2.2, ed. 6, Munich, 776, considered that Domna wished Apollonius to be presented as a counterpart to Christ.

89 Lugdunum episode: Eusebius, *History of Church* 5.1.3–2.8 (Musurillo 1972: xxii; 62–85); Frend (1965: 1–30). Severan policy: Covolo in Covolo and Rinaldi (1999: 189–92).

90 Views of Christians: Tac. *Ann.* 15.44; Pliny *Ep.* 10.96f.

91 Africanus: F. L. Cross, rev. E. A. Livingstone, eds. (1997) *The Oxford Dictionary of the Christian Church*, ed. 3, Oxford, 913. Alexander's collection: *HA Alex.* 29.2, with Syme 1968, 138: 'some to this day take it for authentic history'. Hippolytus: Hemelrijk (1999: 306 n. 127), citing M. Richard (1963) *SO* 38: 79f.

92 Epicureans and Christians: R. Syme (1988) *RP* 5: 577.

93 Entertainment: Bowie (1978: 1666).

94 Damis: Phil. *Apoll.* 1.3, with Bowie (1978: 1653–71), who has no truck with 'Damis': his prominence is owed to the existence of a loyal follower of Severus, T. Flavius Damianus, *PIR*[2] F 253; Flinterman (1995: 79–88) takes the source more seriously (85) as a pseudepigraphic Pythagorean work of the late second or early third century.

95 Pompey's request: Aulus Gellius, *Attic Nights* 14.7.2f.

8 Image and cult

1 'Orientalism': Domaszewski (1909: 198).

2 Cult offered Domna: Kettenhofen (1979: 98–112). For the imperial cult in Asia Minor, Price (1980) and (1984) are indispensable.

3 Tyranny and luxury: E. Hall (1989) *Inventing the Barbarian: Greek Self-Definition through Tragedy*, Oxford, 56–100. Aeschylus' *Persae* and Euripides' *Bacchae* are discussed by Said (1995: 56f.).

4 'The Greeks from Asia': *SB* 1.4224.
5 Orontes in Italy: Juvenal, *Satires* 3.62.
6 Temples built by Augustus: *RG* 20.4.
7 Magna Mater: Her. 1.11. See Alföldy (1989: 366f.), noting loose usage. Earlier history: F. R. Walton and J. Scheid in *OCD*[3] 416f. (bibl.).
8 Guarantees of safety: Arrian, *Discourses of Epictetus* 4.1.91–8.
9 Status of Judaism: E. M. Smallwood (1976) *The Jews under Roman Rule from Pompey to Diocletian: A Study in Political Relations* Studies in Judaism in Late Antiquity 20, Leiden, corr. repr. 1981; E. S. Gruen (2002) *Diaspora: Jews amidst Greeks and Romans*, Cambridge, MA, esp. 15–53. Christianity: Frend (1965). Severus: *HA Sev*. 17.1. Caracalla: *HA Car*. 1.6.
10 Isis: R. E. Witt (1971) *Isis in the Graeco-Roman World*, London, 222–42. Domitian and Isis: Suet. *Dom*. 1.2. Vespasian and Serapis: Tac. *Hist*. 4.81. Note Otho's celebration of the rites: Suet. *Otho* 12.1.
11 Serapis on Commodus' coinage: Ghedini (1984: 84), with n. 281, citing *CREBM* 4, 756 nos. 359–61, etc., and for Caracalla 5, 464 no. 189f. Protector: Hekster (2002: 110). According to *HA Comm*. 9.4–6 and *HA Car*. 9.11, he practised the cult, shaved his head, and carried a statue of Anubis; cf. 16.4; *HA Nig*. 6.8f.
12 Caracalla and Serapis: *HA Car*. 9.10; he also interested himself in Mithraism: *HA Car*. 9.9.
13 Isis and Serapis: *HA Alex*. 16.8.
14 Domna and Isis: *RIC* 4.1.170, no. 577, etc., with Ghedini (1984: 155f.), discussing McCann (1968: 57) (Severus' early association with Serapis).
15 Sol taking over Levantine cults: Seyrig (1963: 18). Sol at Rome: Indiges: K. Latte (1960) *Römische Religionsgeschichte*, Handb. der Altertumswiss. 5.4, Munich, 232 n. 1; Alföldy (1989: 368, with n. 81). Oriental Sol: 349f. (*CIL* 6, 31034). *Indiges*: Halsberghe (1972: 26–9). Early second century AD: *RIC* 2, Index 3; Commodus: Hekster (2002: 99f.; 116; 178). Colossus' head: Her. 1.15.9, cf. Suet. *Nero* 31.1. Caracalla: Whittaker *ad* Her. 5.5.5, citing *CREBM* 5.465 no. 195, with Dio 77(78).10.3, and 486 no. 283. He associates the radiate lion of *RIC* 4.1, 252 no. 273, etc., with Caracalla's visit to Emesa in 215; Aguado Garcia (2001). Alexander: *CREBM* 6.30. Synopsis of development, mentioning the Empresses: R. Lim (2003) in G. Woolf, ed., *Cambridge Illustrated History of Roman World*, Cambridge, 283; Stoneman (1992: 145) cites Cicero, *Dream of Scipio* 4. Caracalla *invictus*: Mastino (1981: 97).
16 Temple restoration: *HA Sev*. 23.1. Severus as *restitutor*: Alföldy (1989: 354).
17 Vesta: Koch (1958) *RE* 8A: 1759; 1768f. Temple rebuilt: Williams (1902: 275); *TDAR* 557–9; *PDAR* 2, 505–9; R. T. Scott in Steinby, *Lexicon* 5, 125–8. Cf. *RIC* 4.1, 171 nos. 584–7A, etc. Caracalla: *RIC* 4.1.247, nos. 249f.; 251f., nos. 271f.
18 Pylon relief of sacrificial scene: Ghedini (1984: 80 and Fig. 10). Domna as Concordia gets a sceptical reception: ibid. 140–2.
19 A senator as god: Cicero, *On his Return, to the Citizens*. 11: '*parens deus salus nostrae vitae*'.
20 Augustus' divinity: Virgil, *Eclogue* 1.7; Horace, *Odes* 2.12.49–52; 3.5.2f.
21 Augustus deified: Tac. *Ann*. 1.10.8; Ovid, *Poems from Pontus* 4.8.63,
22 Nero's temple: Tac. *Ann*. 15.74.3. Ethiopian: *HA Sev*. 22.4f., keeping the MSS text; cf. Birley (2005: 199f.).
23 Inflation of honours: Tac. *Ann*. 4.9.2.
24 Competition with the great: Gradel (2002: 102); Ghedini (1984: 124).
25 Gorsium temple reconstructed: J. Fitz (1972) *Acta Arch. Debr*. 24: 38–41, citing *CIL* 3, 3342. Plan: *Gorsium-Herculia*, ed. 6, Székesfehérvár, 1996, 45.

26 Octavian's response to cult: Dio 51.20. 6f.; Tiberius': EJ^2 102; Claudius': Smallwood, *G-N* 370.

27 Extravagance of precedents: Kettenhofen (1979: 118f.), with *BMC Mysia* 139, no. 248f. (Livia and Julia); *Pontus* 154 no. 14; (Messalina) *IGR* 3.663; 4, 1492 and 1595 (Sabina), all from Anatolia.

28 Problems caused by inscriptions of 'Dea/Thea Julia' alone; W. H. Buckler (1914) *Rev. de Phil.* 38: 211–14. Thus Kettenhofen (1979: 113f.) ascribes *AE* 1953, 178, to Livia or Augustus' daughter, and *CIG* 2815, a *thea Julia nea Demeter* from Aphrodisias, to the reign of Tiberius; examples from Anatolia, 115–18 (*non liquet* on a *Hestia, nea Demeter* from Lampsacus, *IGR* 4, 180, there ascribed to Livia).

29 Parian priestess of Agrippina the Younger: *IG* 12, 5, 275, cited by Kettenhofen (1979: 122).

30 Cults of Domna in Asia Minor: F. Taeger (1957–60) *Charisma*: *Stud. zur Gesch. des antik. Herrscherkultes*, Stuttgart, 2 411, draws attention to Domna as *thea* where no such status is ascribed to her menfolk *IGR* 1, 575–8, Nicopolis); it was surely a substitute for official titles. Termessus: *TAM* 3.1.97 and 99. Domitia Longina: 83; Plotina and Matidia: 98. Possible reasons for cult and high priestess on Cyprus: Mitford (1950: 81f., no. 44).

31 Title *Thea*: see Kettenhofen (1979: 106f.). Crispina: *IGBulg*. 613. Mamaea: *AE* 1951, 9.

32 Domna and Athena: *IG* II/III^2 1076; the most valuable documentation of Domna's cult in Greece: Kettenhofen (1979: 111); Premerstein (1913); Oliver (1940) and *Hesp.* 10 (1941) 84f.; cf. L. Robert (1946–7) *REG* 59/60 323f.; Ghedini (1984: 128–31), with n. 67 (bibl.), is cautious.

33 Salonica bust: Ghedini (1984: 128f. and Fig. 14), citing S. Pelekides (1924–5 [1927]) *Arch. Deltion* 9: 121–44; G. Despinis (1975) *Akrolitha. Arch. Deltion.* Publ. 21, Athens, 11–16. Gabala coin: Ghedini (1984: 132), citing *BMC Galatia*, etc., 245 no. 10 (for Astarte see xvi), and comparing a coin of Laodiceia ad Mare, 258 no. 81, which has a bust of Domna within the shrine (but she is *AVG. DOMNA TYCHE METROPOLEOS*).

34 Athena and Livia: *IGR* 4. 144; Julia Livilla: 4.464.

35 Rôle of Apollonius (196 or 197): Premerstein (1913: 254; 263f.; 270).

36 Regilla at Corinth: J. H. Kent (1966) *Corinth* 8.3: *The Inscriptions 1926–1950*, Princeton, NJ, 59 no. 128, cited by Winter (2002: 134f.).

37 Livia as Tyche: EJ^2 102.

38 Domna as Tyche: Kettenhofen (1979: 108), citing *BMC Lydia*, 259f. nos. 147f., 150, for Sardes; *BMC Galatia*, etc., 245 no. 13 for Gabala in Coele Syria, and 258 no. 81 for Laodiceia; cf. Ghedini (1984: 142f.), rightly rejecting the Gabala reverse and noting that the identification is attested only for Livia and Domna. Paltos taking up Laodiceia's theme: Meyer-Zwiffelhoffer (1994: 95–8) (until the death of Geta). Perhaps at Dura-Europus: M. Rostovtzeff and P. V. C. Baur (1931) *The Excavations at Dura-Europus: Preliminary Report of Second Season*, New Haven, CT, 2, 183.

39 'Tyche of the World': V. Parvân (1916) *Histria* 4, *Aula Academiei Române* 2.38, Bucharest, 644–6, no. 34; Ghedini (1984: 143f.), citing the masculine titles, dates to 214.

40 Domna as Juno: *IRT* 291.

41 Extravagant honours not novel: Kettenhofen (1979: 248 n. 249), citing *IG* 12.5, 557; *IGR* 3, 719.

42 Maesa honoured like Domna: Pârvan (1916: 654 no. 37).

43 Visit to Nicopolis: Kettenhofen (1979: 248, n. 242).

44 *Numen*: *RIB* 976 of AD 213 (Longtown); the concept: Gradel (2002: 234–50

at 248). With Venus in a Puteolan *templum* construction of 211–17: *Not. d. Scavi* 1954, 285.

45 Priestess at Formiae: *AE* 1971, 79; Kettenhofen (1979: 104f.), accepts Domna as the recipient. The priestess' husband M. Aufidius Fronto: Dio 72(79). 22.5.

46 Imperial cult at Rome: Palmer (1978), on *ILS* 3361 (Bacchic sodalities); *AE* 1926, 116 (the freedmen; there is no mention of Domna in this inscription); and *CIL* 6, 1080 = 31236 and p. 3777 (fishers and divers; dated to 204 by Palmer (1978), to 211 by Alföldy (1996)); elaborate commentary, 1099–13. Palmer (1978) notes the appearance of Diana or Luna Lucifera on the coins of Domna and Plautilla: *CREBM* 5, 237 no. 420f.; 307 no. 765†; 311 no. 782; 430–2 nos. 1–4; 7f.; 10; cf. *ILS* 3247. See also Ghedini (1984: 7); Lusnia (1995: 123).

47 Septizonium (-zodium, -solium): *HA Sev.* 19.5; 24.3–5, with *TDAR* 473–5; Benario (1958a: 717); *PDAR* 2, 302–5; G. Pisani Sartorio in Steinby, *Lexicon* 4, 269–72, Figs. 123–6.

48 Connexions between Domna and her menfolk and Sol Aeternus and Luna in *CIL* 2, 259 (Olisipo) were noted by Williams (1902: 299f.).

49 'Change': Palmer (1978: 1086); 'acquiescent': 1120.

50 'Oriental' religions: Walser (1975: 646f.).

51 Serapis cult: *HA Sev.* 17.7. Caracalla: *CREBM* cxcixf.: 'Part of that advance of eastern cults to full imperial status that had begun as early as Commodus . . . and of that excessive interest in religion that marked Caracalla's later years'. York: Shotter (2003: 242). Serapis in Britain: *RIB* 658 (by Cl. Hieronymianus, legionary legate of VI Victrix, probably from the Greek-speaking part of the Empire: Birley 1981: 265).

52 Severan iconography: McCann (1968: 109–17) (assimilation in portraiture of Severus); Turcan (1978: 1036f.) (caution on assimilation); 1059f. (Severus' portraits show no intentional resemblance to Serapis). Jupiter-Serapis-Severus on the Lepcis arch: Ghedini (1984: 82f., with Fig. 11).

53 Serapis type: Fittschen (1978: 28), comparing coin types of 200 on. Private use: 35.

54 Caracalla and Serapis: Dio 77(78).23.2; Her. 4.8.6. Temple: *HA Car.* 9f. *IGR* 1, 1063 (Alexandria) describes Caracalla as 'philosarapis'. *CIL* 6, 570 indicates a temple at Rome (Regio VI) constructed by Caracalla; *IG* 14, 1024 is dedication at Rome for the safety of the 'Great' Caracalla to the 'Great' Helios Serapis (Benario 1958a: 719).

55 *Evocatio*: *HA Macr.* 3.9, with Ghedini (1984: 174, n. 270). See Kettenhofen (1979: 101–3), on *AE* 1949, 109, cf. *IRT* 291.

56 Dea Caelestis in north Africa: Mundle (1961: 236) notes the temple from Lambaesis begun by the legate of Numidia Lepidus Tertullus, evidently, from his *cognomen*, an African (Leglay 1956: 300–7 = *AE* 1957, 123, of 203?), and the Antonine dedication from Sabratha (*IRT* 2).

57 Significance of Caelestis: Domaszewski (1909): 'mit dämonischer Gewalt'. He also invokes the Punic triad called upon by Dido in Virgil, *Aeneid* 4.58 (including Ceres *legifera* – bringer of law, whom he identifies with the Virgo), and Hannibal's treaty with Philip V in Polybius 7.9. Severus is the new Hannibal because he restored Hannibal's grave (Th. Wiegand (1902) *MDAI(A)* 27: 321f. on Tzetzes, *Chiliades* 1, 798–805). See Ghedini (1984: 144–51); for Rome she cites M. Guarducci (1946–8) 'Nuovi Documenti del Culto di Caelestis a Roma', *Bull. Com.* 72: 11–25. A main plank in orientalizing platform: 144.

58 Political prejudices influencing scholarship: J. Elsner (2004) 'Late Antique Art: the Problem of the Concept and the Cumulative Aesthetic', in S. Swain and

M. Edwards, eds., *Approaching Late Antiquity: The Transformation from Early to Late Empire*, Oxford, 271–309, at 275f., on J. Strzygowski (1901) *Orient oder Rom. Beiträge zur Geschichte des spätantiken und frühchristlichen Kunst*, Leipzig, 'Hellas suffocating in the embrace of the orient', and his opponent A. Riegl (1901) *Spätrömische Kunstindustrie*, Vienna. It is noteworthy that Said (1995: 18f.) excludes German scholarship from the scope of his study, concentrating on the imperial ambitions of France, England and the United States: 'Orientalism was fundamentally a political doctrine willed over the Orient, because the Orient was weaker than the West'.

59 Caelestis and Domna: Mundle (1961). Kettenhofen (1979: 98–101) concurred with Mundle (1961), pointing out that few of Domna's inscriptions (460 known at the time) mentioned the Dea Caelestis, and that in the temple dedication she is disjoined from her. There is a cult at Lambaesis, but not connected with Domna (Leglay 1956: 304, citing the undated *CIL* 8, 2592). *IRT* 291 (*Dea Juno orbis terrae*) is a private cult; Venus Caelestis of *AE* 1956, 144, is uncertain.

60 *Ius Italicum*: Ulpian in *Dig*. 50.15.8.11, with Hasebroek (1921: 134). *INDVLGENTIA AVGG IN CARTH*: *CREBM* 5, 208f. nos. 279–82; 218 nos. 333–8; 248 no. 466*; 332 no. 825*; 334f. nos. 830–2; 343 no. 845*; *IN ITALIAM*: 209 no. 282*; 218 no. 339.

61 Carvoran inscription: *RIB* 1791.

62 Scepticism on Domna and Caelestis: Toutain (1943: 308) described the identification as 'pure hypothèse, sinon même fantaisie'.

63 Donatus African: I. Kajanto (1965) *The Latin Cognomina*, Helsinki, 20.

64 Carvoran inscription third century: E. Hübner, *CIL* 7, 759. Dedication by prefect of the First Cohort of Hamians: *RIB* 1792. Hamii of Epiphania: Birley (1999: 152; 185). In Britain: P. A. Holder (1982) *The Roman Army in Britain*, London, 117.

65 Priestess of Dea Virgo Caelestis at Rome: *ILS* 4438.

66 Elagabalus and Dea Caelestis: Dio 79(80).12.1; Her. 5.6.4f. So Ghedini (1984: 145, with n. 276); see Chapter 9.

67 Caelestis a private cult: Ghedini (1984: 146–8) is unwilling with K. Kraft (1952–3) 'Der goldene Kranz Caesars, etc.', *JNG* 3–4, repr. Darmstadt, 1969, 84–91, to associate Severus and Domna (as Tanit-Caelestis) with the Marlborough Cameo, of uncertain date and authenticity.

68 Moguntiacum dedication: *CIL* 13, 6671, dedication to '[*Juliae Augustae*] *Caelesti Deae* [*matri imperato*]*ris Caesaris* . . .' by a soldier of Legio XXII Antoniniana Primigenia (214–17) is a private initiative. See Toutain (1943–5) and Mundle (1961: 231f.).

69 *Junoni Reginae Juliae Domnae*: L. Déroche, *MEFRA* 60 (1948) 72–83 = *AE* 1949, 109, with Kettenhofen (1979: 102f.).

70 Women in processions: Ghedini (1984: 71, and Fig. 8), on the south-east panel of the attic, citing the parallel of Messalina (Suet. *Claud*. 17.3).

71 *Mater Castrorum*: see Chapter 3, note 48f.

72 Oriental parallel: Ghedini (1984: 30) (against the 'African' interpretation of the frontal posture in Charles-Picard 1962) on F. Cumont (1926) *Fouilles de Doura-Europos: Texte*. Haut.-Comm. en Syrie, Service des Ant., Bibl Arch. et hist. 9, Paris, 41–51 (sacrifice; Bithnanaia, with Pl. 35). R. hand: Ghedini (1984: 33f., with nn.) associating it with the worship of Sol; Sanatruces' statue in Baghdad, illustrated in Chad (1972: 87). Coin of Geta: *RIC* 4.1.317 no. 21. Caduceus: Ghedini (1984: 38–41). Emesa recalled: Ghedini (1984: 35f.). Placards: Ghedini (1984: 37), citing Her. 3.9.12.

73 Domna and Venus Genetrix: Ghedini (1984: 58, with n. 15 and Fig. 2); Juno: Ghedini (1984: 62f.; 85 and Fig. 11; 125–8); here Ghedini cites epigraphic

evidence for the assimilation of Domna and Juno; *IRT* 291 and *AE* 1949, 109 from Tunisia (the texts have been subjects of discussion); Greek evidence for Domna as the Nea Hera (*IGR* 4.881 and 3.856 from Tacina and Corycus respectively). Livia: *IGR* 4.319. Sabina and Juno: *RIC* 2, 386 no. 394f.; 477 no. 1028, with Ghedini (1984: 127f.) and Kettenhofen (1979: 119); Mamaea: Kettenhofen (1979: 165) with n. 716. Ghedini eliminates many gems from consideration.

74 Amalgam: Charles-Picard (1962: 1258f.). 'Reforms': Ghedini (1984: 43), on *HA Elag.* 4.1–4; 12.3.

75 Innumerable references: *PIR*[2] I 663, p. 312, sending readers to the indexes of *CIL* 3 (Balkans and eastern provinces), 6 (Rome) and 8 (north Africa). See lists in Kettenhofen (1979: 199–209).

76 Survey of monuments: Kettenhofen (1979: 128–35). Total: 135. Offered for the safety of Domna alone: *AE* 1911, 5 (by L. Didius Marinus); *CIL* 3, 121, with p. 790 (from Kanawat); R. Cagnat, *Syria* 5 (1924) 112 (from Soueida, Jebel Druse).

77 Little material from Syria: see Kettenhofen (1979: 132 and 142f.) noting *CIL* 3, 6714 (Chabinas, from four cities of Commagene); *AE* 1950, 230 (Berytus colony). Dura: *SEG* 7, 332 (Dura, from the city council); 816 (Gerasa, from the city); *AE* 1973, 552 (Bostra, the city).

78 Numbers and examples of dedications: Kettenhofen (1979: 138f.): Aelurio: *AE* 1933, 45; Surus: *AE* 1968, 430; Aurelii Claudii: *AE* 1960, 226; Baalbek: *CIL* 3, 138 = *IGLS* 2711f.; cf. the honorific inscriptions from Palmyra set up by a priest of Bel, *IGR* 3, 1533f. Rome: *CIL* 6, 1070 ('*salvis dominis nostris*'). Domna alone: *CIL* 6, 786.

79 Claudius Marinus: *CIL* 2, 2529.

80 Didius Marinus: Pflaum (1960–1: 765–9, no. 295); Syme (1971: 152); Kettenhofen (1979: 129), citing *AE* 1933, 282, and on the name 263 n. 418.

81 Warning against overestimating Syrian material: Kettenhofen (1979: 263 n. 420). African dedicators (130): the procurator M. Julius Punicus of *IRT* 392, 422, 434 and 403, and Pflaum (1960–1: 653f. no. 244); the procurator D. Clodius Galba of Pflaum (1960–1: 655 no. 244 *bis*) (possibly a relative of Albinus spared by Severus: Birley 1969: 267). Possible Lepcitanes: *IRT* 390 with 402, 419 and 433, like the centurion Messius Atticus of *IRT* 408 with 438f. Sufetula: the *curator* P. Aelius Rusticus of *ILAfr.* 130f. Relations between Severus and Africa: Heywood (1940) and (1962); cf. Kettenhofen (1979: 245 n. 211).

82 Vows: Kettenhofen (1979: 136f.). Optatus: *AE* 1926, 145. For Ostia he names Cn. M. Marcius Rustius Rufinus, Prefect of the Watch 205–7, *CIL* 14, 4386; L. Petersen, *PIR*[2] M 246, does not accept that he became Prefect of the Guard. *AE* 1952, 218, from Ephesus, presents a procurator of the inheritance tax, M. Romanius Juventinus, probably a connection of Romanius Montanus, procurator of a troop of gladiators who also made a dedication to Domna (C. Habicht (1969) *Die Altertümer v. Pergamon.* 8.3. *Die Inschr. des Asklepieion*, Berlin, 37 n. 16).

83 Contribution of Nicomedia: *IGR* 3, 6, noted by Kettenhofen (1979: 134.

84 Contribution of Axiopolis: *CIL* 3, 7485, with Kettenhofen (1979: 131); Nicopolis: 132f.

85 Dedications by the military: Kettenhofen (1979: 131), including dedications from I Minervia at Bonna to Diva Julia, *AE* 1910, 125; to Julia Augusta from Cohors I Britannica in Dacia, *AE* 1929, 1; Cohors V Lingonum at Porolissum, 1958, 232; Cohors XXIV voluntaria Antoniniana c. R. (of volunteer Roman citizens) at Murrhardt in Upper Germany, 1895, 33 (= *CIL* 13, 6531; '*devota numini eius*'); from Cohors I Aelia Hispanorum at Longtown, *RIB* 976; from

the slaves of the camp treasury at Lambaesis, *AE* 1914, 38. Further dedications: Birley (2005: 204; 206).

86 Williams (1902: 305) notes that dedications by communities and troops were made directly to the imperial family, others (less bold, perhaps) to deities on their behalf.

87 Kettenhofen (1979: 134) draws attention to *IGR* 4, 698 (Synnada), set up in the proconsulship of Q. Tineius Sacerdos, consul with Elagabalus in 219; *ILS* 9464: Q. Licinius Nepos, proconsul of Asia (Priene); *CIL* 3, 1685f., with Dio 78(79). 22.2–4 and Birley (1999: 195): Q. Anicius Faustus, the African then governor of Upper Moesia.

88 Significance of the documents: Kettenhofen (1979: 120–2; 172–4).

89 Ghedini (1984: 124); Williams (1902: 301); Lusnia (1995: 120f.). Second phase 125f.

90 Importance of motherhood: Hemelrijk (1999: 145), citing Lusnia (1995) and N. B. Kampen (1991) 'Between Public and Private: Women as Historical Subjects in Roman Art', in S. Pomeroy, ed., *Women's History and Ancient History*, Chapel Hill, NC, 218–48. Lusnia (1995: 122, n. 11) draws attention to the '*Fecunditas*' of Faustina (II) in 152 on the birth of her sixth child.

91 *MATER DEVM* reverses and enthusiasm for the identification of Severus and Domna with Serapis and Isis led Frend (1965: 327 with n. 194) into attributing the title 'Mother of the Gods' to Domna and so making her identical with Cybele; rebutted by Ghedini (1984: 23 n. 122) and see note 97 below.

92 'Propaganda': Lusnia (1995: 120 n. 4, bibl.). Alternative view: Levick (1982). Control by Domna: Lusnia notes that Hill (1979) assumes that the *officina* of Albinus was assigned to her, with coins issued 'under her authority' henceforward. It is hard to think of anything more than informal consultation. See Chapter 4.

93 Abstractions are found in the epigraphic evidence: '*Evidente inlustrique providentia*': *CIL* 3, 427 = *CIG* 2971; cf. *CIL* 8, 1628 (dedication to Jupiter *Conservator*).

94 Assimilation or association of *Mater Augustorum* with the Magna Mater towards the end of Severus' reign: Lusnia (1995: 132f., with n. 53), rejecting the dating of Hill (1979: 40) to 205; she notes (125f.) that Mater Deum appears first on reverses of the Deified Faustina (I) in 141–2, then became standard down to Lucilla. 'Divine elements': Lusnia (1995: 138). Conservatism: Lusnia (1995: 139).

95 Victoria: Kettenhofen (1979: 125). South-east panel of the Lepcis Arch: Ghedini (1984: 70, with Fig. 8); Warsaw: 113–19, with Figs. 12f., of unknown provenance; for precedent Ghedini cites Trajan's Arch at Beneventum. Cameo: Möbius (1948–9) *Arch. Anz.* 63–4: 102–12; Ghedini (1984: 132–5 with Fig. 16). For Roma and Victoria depicted on piles of weapons, Ghedini cites T. Hölscher (1967) *Victoria Romana: Arch. Untersuch. zur Gesch. u. Wesenart d. röm. Siegesgöttin v, den Anfängen bis zum Ende des 3 Jhs. n. Chr.*, Mainz, 126f., and R. Mellor (1981) 'The goddess Roma', *ANRW* 2.17.2, 1011–17.

96 Ceres: R. Calza (1978) *Scavi di Ostia* 9: *I ritratti* 2, Rome, 50f., no. 63; Kettenhofen (1979: 125f.); Ghedini (1984: 135f. with Fig. 17), cautious on other claimed representations, with nn. 144f. for Livia as the subject, and 154 for other women. Kettenhofen (1979: 126f.) also notes a possible Omphale in the Vatican and cameos that may identify Domna with Tanit and Olympias.

97 Domna and Cybele: Kettenhofen (1979: 123f., with n. 371); there is little epigraphic attestation for the connection (n. 375); Ghedini (1984: 136–9, with Fig. 22), citing *RIC* 4.1, 168 nos. 564–6, 207–9 nos. 841 and 861, and 210 no. 882; Lusnia (1995: 125). Livian precedent: P. Lambrechts (1952) 'Livia-

Cybèle', *La Nouvelle Clio* 5 (1952) 251–601 (*n.v.*): Diva Faustina (I): *RIC* 3, 165 no. 1145; 1150; Faustina (II); 270 no. 704–6; 346 no. 1663f.; 353 no. 1753.

98 Distinction of public and private: Gradel (2002: 9–13), citing Festus 284L.

99 Tullia's *fanum*: Cic. *Att.* 12.18.1; 21.2; 36.1.

100 *Numen* and *maiestas*: Alföldy (1996, 31 n. 57), on *ILS* 2157 of 210, where Cohors V of the Watch is '*devota*' to the imperial *numen* and *maiestas*, and other Roman inscriptions. So Kettenhofen (1979: 246 n. 220).

101 Luna and fecundity: [Oppian,] *Hunting with Dogs* 4–7, with Kádár (1966); Kettenhofen (1979: 127f.). Spread of Dea Syria cult: Ghedini (1984: 149–51), citing *CIL* 6, 399, Suet. *Nero* 56 and *RIC* 4.1, 273 no. 379, etc., for *LVNA LVCIFERA*; nn. 349–53 for earlier 'lunar' types. (She takes Domna's appearance in the garb of Artemis on a coin of Argos as a local phenomenon: 151f.)

102 Caligula and cult: Gradel (2002: 140–62); Domitian: *dominus et deus*, Suet. *Dom.* 13.2; Pliny *Ep.* 10, uses *domine* to Trajan. '*Dominus noster*': Bersanetti (1946: 43).

103 Care for the army: Dio 76(77). 15.2.

104 Commodus 'had yet to establish his authority' in 180: Hekster (2002: 198): cf. Dio 73(74).4.2f. with Birley (1999: 85–7). Hercules and emperors: Dio 59.26.7 (Caligula); 63.20.5 (Nero); Martial 9.64; Pliny *Pan.* 14.5 (Domitian); Dio of Prusa, *On Kingship* 1.56–84 (Trajan). Antony and Nero: E. Champlin (2003) *Nero*, Cambridge, MA, 135f.; 172f. Commodus: Hekster (2002: 117–29), and see index there; C. R. Whittaker *ad* Her. 1.14.8 f., where '*mania*' is ascribed to him; see also Dio 72(73).15 (titles), and *HA Comm.* 8.5–9 (*Romanus Hercules*); 9.4–6 (cult of Isis; rites of Mithra brutalized); 11.8f. (*Amazonius*); 14.3 (Commodan golden age); 15.6 (Roman people *Commodianus*); *HA Diad.* 7.3. Whittaker cites the Commodan coinage, *CREBM* 4, clxvii–clxx; clxxviii; clxxxii, for Sol, Minerva Augusta, Jupiter Conservator/Defensor salutis Augusti, Magna Mater, Isis and Serapis. Severus and Hercules: Hekster (2002: 191–3).

105 Severus' example followed: W. Kaczanowicz (1996) *Notae Numismaticae* 1, 82–5, citing T. Kotula (1987) *Septymiusz Sewerus*, Wroclaw, 54–60.

106 *IVNO CONSERVATRIX*: Kettenhofen (1979: 149), on *CREBM* 5, 377 no. 297.

107 Maesa as Demeter: Kettenhofen (1979) on *BMC Pontus* 89, no. 34; Livia: n. 26,

108 'Diva Julia Aug. (Maesa)': *AE* 1917, 9.

109 *Mater Castrorum*: Kettenhofen (1979: 146); list of inscriptions mentioning her 310.

110 Sohaemias as Caelestis: Kettenhofen (1979: 155f.), discussing *IGR* 3, 1079, as interpreted by Ronzevalle (1903: 44–7). Juno Regina on the coinage: *CREBM* 5, xxxiii.

9 Aftermath

1 Interment in tomb of C. and L. Caesar: Dio 78(79).24.3.

2 Castel Sant'Angelo Severus' tomb: Her. 3.15.8; 4.1.4; *HA Sev.* 19.3; 24.2; cf. *HA Geta* 7.2, with topographical slip. Commodus: *HA Comm.* 17.4. Caracalla: *HA Car.* 9.12; *HA Macr.* 5.2f.

3 Defeat of Macrinus at Immae 35 km. east of Antioch: Millar (1993: 146).

4 Maesa Augusta: Kettenhofen (1979: 144f.): there is no evidence for the title before 14 July 218, *CIL* 6, 2104, l. 23; Domaszewski (1909: 216) held that it was conferred by Caracalla.

5 Interment: Dio 78(79).24.3, with Her. 4.13.8.
6 Nerva's burial: *PIR*[2] C 1227 (p. 294).
7 Augustae deified: H. Castritius, in Temporini (2002: 169).
8 Date of consecration: Ghedini (1984: 158–60), rejecting Mommsen, *St.* 2, 833, n. 3 (deification by Alexander Severus and Maesa). Williams (1902: 296) has Macrinus deifying Caracalla; so Gilliam (1969: 286). Kettenhofen (1979: 105f.) reviews inscriptions on which Domna is *Diva*, including *AE* 1899, 56, decurions of Gilli in Africa Proconsularis, dating from 229; *CIL* 8, 26225; 13, 12042 (leg. I Minervia at Bonna); see Gilliam (1969) (Domna replaced Sabina or Faustina (II)); Fejfer (1992) (*non liquet*). Coins: *RIC* 4.1.275 no. 396; 313 no. 609; memorial issues 4.2.127 no. 715f.
9 Nero's daughter: Raepsaet-Charlier (1987: 213); Domitian's son: *PIR*[2] D 181, p. 58.
10 M. Aurelius' temple: Gradel (2002: 355).
11 Deification of Marciana and Faustina (I): Gradel (2002: 301f.). Sabina's honours: Gradel (2002: 306). Faustina's temple: *HA Marc.* 26.9; *HA Car.* 11.6f.; *HA Elag.* 1.5f. Matidia and Marciana in the *FD*: Gradel (2002: 348).
12 Diadumenianus Caesar: Dio 78(79).19.1; Antoninus: Dio 78(79).19.1 and 37.6 (omitted); *HA Car.* 8.10; *HA Macr.* 1.5; 2.5; 5.1; *HA Diad.* 1.1.
13 See Mattingly (1953). Macrinus in Mesopotamia: Dio 78(79).26.2–27.2; Her. 4.15; *HA Macr.* 2.2; 8; 12.6. Victory: *CREBM* 5, ccxxi; 522f. nos. 129f., 130*, 135 etc. Winter at Antioch: Her. 5.2.3.
14 Pergamene hostility: Dio 78(79).20.4; cf. Chapter 6, note 88.
15 Discontent at Rome: Dio 78(79).20.1; see Sünskes Thompson (1990: 118–22). Fall of Macrinus: Dio 78(79).31–40; Her. 5.3.6–4.1; *HA Macr.* 8.3f.; 10; 15.1. Loss of pay: Dio 78(79).12.7, 28.2f.
16 Raphaneae mutiny: Dio 78(79).31.4. Macrinus at Antioch: Her. 5.4.1; *HA Macr.* 8.4 and 10. Journey to Apameia and return to Antioch: Dio 78(79). 34.1[2]; 5.78(79). 40.2. Oracle of Zeus: Dio 78(79).40.4. For this deity see Chapter 2, note 60. Fall of Macrinus: *HA Macr.* 8.3. Death of Diadumenianus: Dio 78(79).40.5; *HA Macr.* 10.3.
17 Macrinus and soldiers' conditions: Dio 78(79). 28f. Centurions: 32.4. *FIDES*: *CREBM* 5, 494 no. 1; 497 nos. 13–15; 505 nos. 64f. Sedition: Sünskes Thompson (1990: 68–73).
18 Martijn Icks warns against assuming that the priesthood was certainly hereditary, and notes that Elagabalus was not known by that name during his lifetime, so that cannot have been an attraction to the troops. Raphaneae legion: Her. 5.3.9; Bleckmann (2002: 282).
19 Eutychianus' identity and role are disputed (Xiph. 344.22, cf. Dio 78(79). 31.1 has him a freedman); Kettenhofen (1979: 26f. and 29–32) on grounds of age denies his identity with Comazon (below, note 26). Gannys is called Elagabalus' *tropheus*, 'nurse' and *prostates* by Dio 79(80).39.4. '*Prostates*' is used for the Latin *tutor*, legal guardian, by Plut., *Numa* 10.
20 Execution of Mamaea's daughter: Dio 78(79).31.4.
21 Elagabalus' birth: Dio 78(79), 31, 3; 32.2; Her. 5.3.10; 4.3; *HA Car.* 9.2; *HA Macr.* 9.4; 15.2; *HA Elag.* 1.4. Epigraphic acknowledgment at Thyatira: *IGR* 4, 1287.
22 Resemblance to Caracalla and its effect: Dio 78(79).32.3; Her. 5.4.4. Sohaemias in Rome: Pighi (1965: 158) noted by Whittaker *ad* Her. 5.3.10.
23 Divergence of Dio and Herodian on fall of Macrinus: Kettenhofen (1979: 23–8). Transition to Elagabalus: Zimmermann (1999: 222–32); bibliography: 222 n. 357.
24 Women ignorant of the revolt: Dio 78(79).31.4. Maesa's role: Her. 5.3.3;

initiative: 10f.; wealth: 3.2 and 11; *HA Macr.* 9.1 and 5. Few supporters: Dio 78(79).31.3 (garbled). War declared on the women: Dio 78(79).38.1.

25 Gannys' role and death: Dio 78(79).38.3; 79(80).3.1; 6.1.

26 Role of Comazon: Syme (1971: 141) plausibly ascribes the former camp prefect (Dio 79(80) 4.1f.) a leading position on the conspiracy; see also Pflaum (1960–1: 752–6 no. 290). Execution of Attalus: Dio 79(80).3.5 (perhaps the same man as in Chapter 3, note 39). Comazon and —-tus: Salway (1997).

27 Caracalla deified: *HA Car.* 11.5; *HA Macr.* 5.9. Martijn Icks warns that circumspection is necessary on deification by Macrinus. (In any case ceremonies may have taken place with the armies that would not have been sanctioned by the Senate.) Elagabalus became M. Aurellius (so spelt after the *Constitutio Antoniniana* vulgarized 'Aurelius') Antoninus, and 'divi Magni Antonini filius', 'son of the deified Antoninus the Great': *HA Macr.* 7.6.

28 People's hatred of Macrinus: Dio 78(79). 20.1–3. Representation in the Senate House: Her. 5.5.6.

29 Exhibitions expected: Lightfoot (2003: 509).

30 Elagabalus' route: A. Dupont Sommer and L. Robert (1964) *La Déesse de Hiérapolis Castabala (Cilicia)*, Bibl. arch. et hist. de l'Inst. français d'arch. d'Istanbul 16, Paris, 80–2.

31 Superiority of Elagabal: 7; dated to 220 in *CREBM* 5, ccxxviii; ccxxxvii–ix. Priesthood and circumcision: Dio 79(80).11. Previous life as priest: Her. 5.3.3. and 6–8, with Whittaker *ad locc.*

32 Cult of Elagabalus at Rome: *HA Elag.* 3.3–5; 6.6–7.5.

33 Substitution of Elagabalus' cult: Whittaker *ad* Her. 5.5.5 and 5.8, and noting Dio 79.11.1 and *HA Elag.* 3.4.; 6.7; 7.4, with *CREBM* 5, 564f., 569, and 571.

34 Elagabalus' marriage to Aquilia: Dio 79.9.3f.; Her. 5.6.2; *HA Elag.* 6.6 (vicissitudes in their union: *PIR*[2] I 648). Elagabalus 'married' his deity first to Pallas Athena, then to the Punic Urania, the Astroarche of the Phoenicians, a Moon goddess: Her. 5.6.3–5.

35 Caelestis: Dio 79(80).12.1; Her. 5.6.4f. The Venus Caelestis reverse of the hybrid *CREBM* 5, ccxxxvii belongs to Sohaemias.

36 Elagabalus' advisers, etc.: Dio 80.16.1–6 (the chamberlain Aur. Zoticus); *HA Elag.* 15.1.

37 Elagabalus traduced: Salway (1997: 131–3; 148).

38 Rule by Sohaemias: Bleckmann (2002: 285). Kettenhofen (1979: 33–7) is essential. Maesa's power: Whittaker *ad* Her. 5.5.5, citing Dio 79(80).17.2; *HA Elag.* 12.3; *CREBM* ccxxxiiif. Significance of Elagabalus' regime: Gradel (2002: 351). Reception of his deity: O. Hekster (2003) in L. de Blois et al. (eds) *The Representation and Perception of Roman Imperial Power*, Amsterdam, 33. Moods of populace: Sünskes Thompson (1990: 122–5), with largesses 122f.

39 Disagreements in the ruling clique: Kettenhofen (1979: 34). Positions: Her. 5.5.1.

40 Maesa a restraining influence: Her. 5.5.5; 7.1f.; 8.3f.; *HA Elag.* 31.4.

41 *Subsellia*: *HA Elag.* 4.1; cf. 18.3; Dio (79(80).17.2. Kettenhofen (1979: 67f.) draws attention to similar stories about manipulation of the Senate by Galla Placidia. Maesa: *HA Elag.* 12.3.

42 Senate of women: *HA Elag.* 4.3; *HA M. Aur.* 49.6. J. Straub (1966) *Historia Augusta Colloquium* 1, *Antiquitas* 4, Bonn, 221–40, gives it a run, but cf. Kettenhofen (1979: 68f.) and Wallinger (1990: 99–103). Bibl. by F. Coarelli in Steinby, *Lexicon* 4, 265.

43 Sohaemias' monuments: Kettenhofen (1979: 151f.); cf. Benario (1959: 11f.).

44 Sohaemias' titles: Volubilis: *AE* 1936, 39; not *Augusta* under Severus: *IGR* 1, 402. In *CIL* 8, 2564, Sohaemias is *Aug. Mater Augusti nostri*, Maesa *Mater*

Castrorum et Senatus and *Avia Augusti nostri*; in *AE* 1955, 260, Sohaemias is Mother of the Camps. She rose higher for Histria as 'Tyche of the inhabited world': V. Parvân (1916) *Histria* 4, *Anal. Academiei Române* 2.38, Bucharest, 653, no. 37. For Domna as *Mater Castrorum*, see Chapter 3, note 49; *mater senatus*: see Chapter 6, note 37.

45 Alexander Severus adopted: Dio 79(80).17.2 (name Bassianus; 78(79).30.3); Her. 5.3.3; 7.1–4 (Alexianos); *HA Elag.* 5.1.

46 Alexander's advance to Caesar: Bleckmann (2002: 289) citing a military diploma; M. Roxan and P. A. Holder (2003) *Roman Military Diplomas IV*, Institute of Classical Studies, School of Advanced Study, London, 572, no. 307, for M. Aurelius Alexander's new title of *Caesar imperi(i) et sacerdo(tis)*, 'Caesar of the Empire and of the Priest' (sc. of Elagabalus' deity); or rather, as A. R. Birley suggests, comparing *RIB* 1465, *sacerdo(tii)*, 'of the priesthood'.

47 Alexander's changes of name: Birley (1999: 221 no. 34).

48 Plot against Alexander: Her. 5.8.2f.; *HA Elag.* 13–17.3; *HA Alex.* 2.4. Assassination of Elagabalus and Sohaemias: Dio 79.21.1; Her. 5.8.8. Military unrest under Elagabalus: Sünskes Thompson (1990: 75–8).

49 Death and deification of Maesa (Nov. 224 to Aug. 226: *FD* 22 and 113f.): Her. 6.1.4; *RIC* 4.2.127 nos. 712–4.

50 Weak regimes: Millar (1964: 104), for Alexander citing *P.Fayum* 20. For Alexander and the populace of Rome, see Sünskes Thompson (1990: 125–9), with largesses 125–7.

51 Continuity: C. R. Whittaker *ad* Her. 6.1.3. For the 'symbolic dichotomy' of Elagabalus and Alexander in the *HA*, see Chastagnol (1994: xli); 'Struggle over *paideia*': Zimmermann (1999: 232–51). Effect of bureaucracy: Syme (1971: 146). Appointments: Kettenhofen (1979: 42). Eubulus: Dio 79(80).21.1. Seleucus: Leunissen (1989: 368).

52 Reign of Alexander: Her. 6.; *HA Elag.* 35.2 (*optimus*, 'the best'). Nature of biography: Kettenhofen (1979: 69–73); according to Birley (1999: 206), it is 'one of the major sources of misinformation, still often disseminated, on the third century'. Repudiation of Syrian influence: *HA Alex.* 28.7; 44.3; 64.3.

53 Prefects: Dio 80.1; 2.2; *HA Alex.* 26.5; cf. *HA Nig.* 7.4; *HA Elag.* 16.2. Paul: *PIR*[2] I 453. I 453. The evidence for Paul being Guard Prefect is suspect: Syme (1979) *RP* 2: 794–8; Syme (1984) *RP* 3: 1399–1401; Syme (1971: 147f.). For the date of Ulpian's murder (223 not 228), cf. Syme (1971: 34f., 153) and *RP* 3: 1403.

54 Chapel: *HA Alex.* 29.2. In a forthcoming paper ('Rewriting second- and third-century history in late antique Rome: the *Historia Augusta*', given at the FIEC Conference, Ouro Preto, Brazil, August 2004), which he kindly allowed me to read, A. R. Birley notes that the author wants to show a 'good' pagan emperor tolerant of religions as Christian emperors were not.

55 Alexander dominated by women: Her. 6.1.1, with Whittaker noting *AE* 1912, 155.

56 Alexander Mamaeae: *HA Alex.* 3.1; 5.2, etc.; Bleckmann (2002: 291). He did everything in accordance with her advice: 60.2; 61.2–7; 66.2. For Tiberius, Geta, and other earlier examples, see Chapter 4, notes 45–7.

57 Addressing the troops: *CREBM* 6, 187 no. 733. Unruly soldiers under Severus Alexander: Sünskes Thompson (1990: 80–91).

58 Barbia Orbiana: Her. 6.1.9f.

59 Mamaea's womanish influence: Her. 6.5.8f.

60 Mamaea's greed: Her. 6.1.8; 9.4 and 8, with Whittaker *ad* 6.8.8. on the problem of army pay. Downfall: Her. 6.8f.

61 Death of Alexander: Her. 6.9.1–8; *HA Alex.* 59.6–8. Mamaea blamed: *HA Alex.* 63.5. Her greed: 14.7; Her. 6.1.8.

62 Sohaemias a widow: *ILS* 478. Marcianus' death: Dio 78(79).33.2–34.1[2].

63 Inscriptions referring to Mamaea: Kettenhofen (1979: 156–71). She was not *Augusta* before 222 (Zonaras (Dio) in Boissevain 3, 477 no. 2 (Dio 80, Loeb ed, p. 488)); *contra* Benario (1959: 13), but his support, *AE* 1933, 281 from Pergamum, has been reinterpreted by Habicht (1969: 35 no. 14). *Mater Castrorum* with *Augusta* before Maesa's death: *AE* 1967, 573; and *senatus et patriae* from 227: 1942–3, 7. *Mater Castrorum* was part of her official titulature: *IGR* 1, 1143 (Antinoupolis) and 1437 (Tomis); the expanded title is not invariably used. Mamaea on milestones: *IGBulg.* 1827 (Hadrianopolis, Thrace); *SEG* 12, 517 (Anazarbus, Cilicia).

64 Mamaea perhaps 'Mistress of the Inhabited World' on Balkan inscriptions: *CIL* 3, 7970. Severus and Domna: *IGR* 4, 878 (Ilias). Maesa: see above note 44.

65 Mamaea and Magna Mater: Bleckmann (2002: 292), citing *CIL* 2, 3413 (Carthage); cf. Williams (1904: 94): Cybele and Mamaea. Unofficial: Kettenhofen (1979: 161). Votives for Mamaea to Magna Mater, noted by Kettenhofen (1979: 171): *CIL* 8, 19981; *AE* 1919, 60; *ILAlg.* 1, 1983.

66 M. Aurelius Heraclitus was centurion of the *Statores Praetoriani*, dedicating to Jupiter Optimus Maximus for the safety of Alexander and Mamaea: see Fitz (1972: 223 n. 3).

67 List of monuments for Mamaea: Kettenhofen (1979: 311–14). Ribchester in Britain: *RIB* 587 from a centurion and local commandant. Freedmen: Kettenhofen (1979: 166f.) notes *AE* 1914, 80, by Glycerinus, an imperial freedman at Laodiceia Combusta; *CIL* 2, 2664, by M. Titius Rufus, a soldier of the Seventh, Gemina, Legion in Spain, dedicating 'numini maiestatique eius', 'to her divine spirit and majesty'; *AE* 1893, 72, by Polychronius, an imperial freedman; *IGR* 3, 354: Aurelius Attalianus priest of the Augusti to Alexander and Mamaea; more significant are inscriptions involving auxiliary units, *CIL* 3, 797f., dedicated by the legate of Dacia, Iasdius Domitianus, at Alsó-Ilosva, cf. *AE* 1950, 16=1969/70, 546, at Cumidava. Another unit at Ulciscia Castra dedicated *CIL* 3, 3638f. So *AE* 1893, 37, from the *Exploratio Halicensis* at Kastell Feldberg; *CIL* 2, 3733, from veterans at Valencia; *AE* 1927, 75, from Traianopolis; *IGR* 1, 1437, from the council and people of Tomis.

68 Distribution of monuments: Kettenhofen (1979: 169f.): *IGR* 3, 806, honorific from the council and people of Side in Pamphylia (Domna has also been proposed); 354, for the safety of Alexander and Mamaea and their house from a high priest at Sagalassus, and 1, 1143, from the council of Antinoöpolis in Egypt. *SEG* 3, 537 = Merlat (1951: 11–13 no. 8), from Augusta Traiana, is the work of Aurelius Sabinus 'Syrus' (name, nationality, or both?), a wine merchant and priest of Jupiter Dolichenus. Dolichenus is also mentioned in an inscription from Zugmantel set up by a prefect of the First Cohort of Treverans, Merlat 327–31, no. 338 = Schwertheim (1974: 64f., no. 56c). Cf. *AE* 1940, 148, to Malagbelus for the safety of the imperial couple, from a troop of Palmyrenes at Messad in Algeria, and *CIL* 3, 7955, to the same Syrian deity at Sarmizegethusa from Primitivus, freedman and *tabularius* in Dacia Apulensis. Jews too might take part, praying to Deus Aeternus: *AE* 1966, 302 (Intercisa).

69 Novelties and precedents: Kettenhofen (1979: 165); *IVNO CONSERVATRIX*: *CREBM* 5, 435 (Domna); 540n. and 577 no. 297 (Maesa) 555 no. 176‡ (Paula); 6, 119 nos. 42–54 (Mamaea). *CONSERVATOR*: 3, 323 no. 527* (Hadrian). *ABVNDANTIA*: *CREBM* 5, 559f. nos. 189–94 (Elagabalus); 6, 172f. nos. 591–4 (Alexander); *TEMPORVM*: 174f., nos. 610*f. (Mamaea, bronze medallion). *VENVS FELIX*: 132f. nos. 188–203 (Mamaea), cf. 5, 167f. nos. 85–90 (Domna); 4, 407 nos. 169f.; 537 nos. 957–9; 543f. nos. 1002f.;

656 no. 1592* (Faustina(II)); 696 nos. 47–51; 767 nos. 424f.; 769 nos. 440f. (Crispina). Note a winged Mamaea: *CREBM* 6, 165 no. 537.

70 Streaming in of oriental ideas: Herzog in his *RE* articles, citing Domaszewski (*Domna* 929); criticized by Kettenhofen (1979: 175).

71 Homage to Mamaea: Kettenhofen (1979: 163–6): *numen*: *RIB* 919, from a vexillation of German Marsaci; cf. 976 to Domna. *thea*: *AE* 1951, 9 (Nicopolis ad Istrum, where there were precedents). (High) Priestess; *TAM* 3, 1, 78 (from the time of Elagabalus or Alexander). *AE* 1971, 430, l. 11, from Beroea (the emperor also honoured, at a gladiatorial show).

72 Galla Placidia: St. Peter Chrysologus, *Sermon* 30 in *PL* 52.556f., cited by M. Clauss, in Temporini (2002: 387).

73 New expanded role for Christian empresses: H. Leppin, in Temporini (2002: 488f.).

74 Army costs: Whittaker *ad* Her. 4.4.7.

75 Age of rust: Dio 71(72).36.4.

76 Rebellion under Commodus: see Chapter 2, note 69. Bulla: Dio 76(77).10.

77 Rebellions: *ILS* 1153. For Pescennius Niger and millenary beliefs in the east at the time of Commodus' death see Alföldy (1989: 128–38).

78 Severus' death a turning point: *HA Sev.* 19.6.

79 'Crisis': Alföldy (1989: 319–24). Herodian's awareness of crisis: 273–94. Herodian's insight: 274, citing Maecenas' speech, Dio 52.14–40. For the date of Dio's composition, Alföldy proposes 222, Millar (1964: 102–4), 214. Her. 1.1.4–6 contrasts the first two hundred years of the Principate and the catastrophic sixty that followed.

80 Dio underestimates Danubian movements: Millar (1964: 171). Corruption: Her. 2.6.14, with Whittaker's comment; 3.8.4f. Division of Empire: Her. 4.3.5f. See Chapter 6.

81 Iotapianus: Vict. *Caes.* 29.2, with A. Stein (1916) *RE* 9.2: 2004f.; Chad (1972: 162), citing for the period 253–70 A. Alföldi (1937) *Berytus* 4: 41–68; Alföldi (1938) *Berytus* 5: 47–91; R. Mowat (1912) *RN* Sér. 4, Vol. 16: 193–7.

82 Capture of Antioch: *Oracula Sibyllina* 13, 150–4; Mal. 296f. (Sampsigeramus). *IGLS* 1799–1801 illustrates the plight of the region in 252–3, and a hero's efforts on its behalf.

83 Uranius Antoninus: Seyrig (1958); Chad (1972: 162), citing Mal. 296f. Bowersock (1993: 128), with n. 24 for the significance of the name Uranius (? 'heaven-sent'); Isaac (1990: 227f.) follows Baldus (1971: 236–50), who concludes that the usurper dropped 'Sampsigeramus' in favour of 'Uranius Severus Antoninus'.

84 Zenobia: Isaac (1990); Stoneman (1992).

85 Emesan deity appears to Aurelian: *HA Aur.* 25.3 and 5; Odenathus and Longinus (Zosimus 1.56): cf. Hitti (1951: 303; 395; 399f.). Domaszewski (1909: 205 n. 1) pointed out that Aurelian's deity at Rome was not specifically Emesene, but a Sun god *tout court*. Aurelian and Sun gods: Stoneman (1992: 183–7). Appetite for 'reform': Gradel (2002: 352).

86 End of Palmyrene prosperity: Seyrig (1950: 1).

87 Palmyrene connection: Millar (1993: 301), citing Seyrig (1959a), and 309.

88 Significance of camel: Chad (1972: 167), citing Seyrig, *Ant. syr.* 6, 71f, 'simple chameau de caravane'; but cf. Baldus (1971: 59f.).

89 Emesa on a par with other cities: Amm. Marc. 14.8.9. Avienus' *Description of the World* (mid-fourth century, but based on the Hadrianic Dionysius Periegetes), still refers at 3. 1086 and 1090 to its 'lofty refulgent pediments' and to 'the pediments of its lofty temple vying with the summits of Mt. Lebanon'.

90 Emesene decline: Libanius, *Orations* 27.42; *Letters* 846. Coins: Liebeschuetz (2001: 24). Market centre: Theodoret, *A History of the Monks of Syria* 17.2f. D. Kruger (1996) *Simeon the Holy Fool: Leontius' Life and the Late Antique City*, Berkeley, CA, 7 and 21, points out that the 'Emesa' of this text owes more to Cyprus than to Syria.

91 Response to Islam: *Naval Intelligence* (1943: 127); cf. Said (1995: 59). Basis of Arab success, including Monophysite dissent: T. E. Gregory (2005) *A History of Byzantium*, Malden, MA, 161–70.

92 Homs' advantage: Liebeschuetz (2001: 56).

93 Nearly 16 per cent of Christians in Homs: *Naval Intelligence* (1943: 213).

94 *Jund* centre at Homs: Hitti (1951: 484); riot: 544; mosque: 511. Cotton and industrialization: Chad (1972: 9). Islamic Homs: King (2002–4).

95 Schematization of history: J. S. Swain (1940) 'The Theory of the Four Monarchies: Opposition History under the Roman Empire', *CP* 35: 1–21.

96 Severi and the army: Domaszewski (1904: 639 n. 4).

97 Third century writers: G. B. Conte (1987) *Latin Literature: A History*, tr. J. B. Solodow, Baltimore, MD, 621.

98 Domna's power: Ghedini (1984: 188–92), cautiously expressed. Coins: 189. Largest portrait (0.75 m.): Williams (1902: 281) (Vatican, Ingresso Superiore, W. Helbig (1963) *Führer durch die öffentlichen Sammlungen klass. Altertümer in Rom* 1, ed. 4 by H. Speier, Tübingen, l5 no. 5.

99 Agrippina's alleged poisoning of Claudius: W. Eck, in Temporini (2002: 150f.). Livia's of Augustus: Barrett (2002: 242–6). Plotina: Birley (1997a: 77).

100 'The ladies . . . dominated the new regime': Salway (1997: 131 n. 17), based on *ILS* 470.

101 Severans as forerunners: M. Clauss, in Temporini (2002: 439).

102 Dio's view of Domna: Hemelrijk (1999: 306 n. 130); see Penella (1980) for the implausible view that the unfavourable attitude of the *HA* was due to the influence of Plautianus.

103 Human happiness ('*hedone tis . . . tou biou kai alethes kai akeratos kai eutychia kai akraiphnes kai diarkes*'): Dio 79(80).24.2.

104 Hostility to Domna: Kettenhofen (1979: 10–13).

105 Syrian villainy: see Chapter 2, note 6.

106 Religious survival: Alföldy (1989: 372). Severan style: Brilliant (1967: 32).

107 No unusual divine honours to Domna: Williams (1902: 303).

108 Emesene cohort at Intercisa: *ILS* 9155; *AE* 1910, 141; cf. Chapter 6, note 81.

109 Nature of the 'circle': see Chapter 7.

110 English imperialism: note the language used of Indians in authority: M. L. S. Bennett (1995) *The Ilberts in India 1882–1886: An Imperial Miniature*, London. Reception of Rome in 'multicultural' Britain: E. Dench (2005) *Romulus' Asylum: Roman Identities from the Age of Alexander to the Age of Hadrian*, Oxford, 1–35.

Bibliography

Ancient works on the period (see *OCD*^{3} and Birley 1999: 203–8)

Aurelius Victor, Sextus, *De Caesaribus* (*On the Caesars*), tr. with introduction and commentary by H. Bird (1994) Translated Texts for Historians 17, Liverpool; see Bird (1984). These moralizing biographies, modelled on those of Suetonius, the work of a pagan senator, came out probably in about AD 360. The author claimed familiarity with Severus' autobiography (20.22) and was a source of *HA Severus* 17–19.

Cassius Dio, Lucius, *History of Rome*, Books 73–80 (ed. and tr. E. Cary and H. B. Foster, Loeb ed., vol. 9, 1927). Dio, from Nicaea in Bithynia, born about AD 164 or 165 into a senatorial family, was suffect consul *c.*205–6 and consul for the second time in 229 with Severus Alexander as colleague. On his own account (72(73).23) he wrote a monograph on the portents that led Severus to hope for the Principate. When this was well received by the emperor, he was inspired to write on the civil strife that followed the murder of Commodus. The favourable reception of this too encouraged Dio to go on to the whole of Roman history, correcting partisan views expressed in his earlier work (Rubin 1980: 41f.). He claims to have spent ten years researching and twelve in writing it, concluding with his own retirement in 229 (80.5.2f.). Differing interpretations of this, with starting points varying between 194 and 212, have been reviewed by C. L. Murison (1999) *Rebellion and Reconstruction: Galba to Domitian. An Historical Commentary on Cassius Dio's Roman History Books 64–67*, American Philological Association Monograph 37, Atlanta, GA, 8–10 arguing for 202–23, when Books 1–76 came out, the rest being posthumous or post-Severan, and by Swan (2004: 1–3; 28–36; 378–80), with AD 200–22 for an *editio princeps* of Books 1–76 and ?230 for a revision and Books 77–80. All views accept that Dio finished his work after Domna's death; hence fluctuating opinions are to be expected. Barnes (1984: 253), with a late date, argues for a greater contribution than has been thought from Dio's own reflection and experience. Certainly he was well placed to write as a contemporary senator who governed provinces, was on the emperors' council (Crook 1955: 157), and was with Caracalla in Bithynia. He was correspondingly liable to prejudice (73(74).12.2 reveals debts to Pertinax and prosecutions of Didius Julianus). The Severan portion, apart from the years 217–18, survives only in Byzantine excerpts and epitomes and the book division is uncertain (Murison 1999: 1–5).

Digest, the compilation of Roman law ordered by Justinian (527–64): see Th. Mommsen, aided by P. Krueger, ed., translated by A. Watson (*c.*1985) *The Digest of Justinian*, 4 vols., Philadelphia, PA. It contains material from the reigns of Severus and Caracalla, as well as excerpts from legal works by contemporary lawyers, such as Ulpian.

Diogenes Laertius compiled lives of philosophers (ed. and tr. R. D. Hicks, Loeb ed., 2 vols., 1925), probably in the first half of the third century. See H. S. Long, rev. R. W. Sharples, in *OCD*³ (1996) 474f. (bibl.).

Epitome on the Caesars 21–3. Purporting to be an epitome of the monograph of Aurelius Victor, the work, dating to the end of the fourth century, is independent, though drawn from a related source. Edited with intro., notes and French translation by M. Festy (2002) *Pseudo-Aurélius Victor, Abrégé des Césars*, Budé, Paris.

Eutropius, *Summary History of Rome since the Beginning*, tr., introd., notes and commentary by H. Bird (1993) *Eutropius: Breviarium*. Translated Texts for Historians 14, Liverpool. The ten-book work of this Gallic courtier of the Emperors Julian and Valens was written in about 369 and carried Roman history down to the death of Jovian (364).

Galen of Pergamum, celebrated physician, son of an architect and a voluminous writer, lived from 139 at least to 199, to 216 at latest, serving the court from M. Aurelius' reign onwards. He was considered a philosopher as much as a physician, one with particular veneration for Plato. See L. Edelstein (1996) rev. V. Nutton, in *OCD*³ 621f. (bibl.).

Herodian, *History of the Empire after Marcus* (ed. and tr. with full nn., C. R. Whittaker, Loeb ed., 2 vols., 1969–70); see Alföldy (1971b = 1989: 240–72). For Herodian's life and status, see Zimmermann (1999: 302–19). Born *c.*178, he was a native of western Asia Minor or of Antioch in Syria, perhaps a freedman, was a subordinate official at Rome in the early third century, and wrote his moralizing and rhetorical eight-book history for a readership in the eastern half of the Empire, ending with the accession of Gordian III (238), in the mid-third century. It depends in part on Cassius Dio (how much is disputed), and develops the role of mediator that Dio ascribes to Domna. Kettenhofen (1979: 3) accepts that the work is 'an historical novel'; similarly Alföldy (1989: 70) with n. 8; he and Birley (1999: 204) offer lists of prosecuting and (fewer) defending counsel (Bowersock 1975 finds merit in his account of Elagabalus), and Zimmermann (1999: 1–16) supplies analysis of discussions. Herodian is seductive to a biographer of Emesene empresses, for he 'preferred heroines' (Birley 1999). Zimmermann (1999: 17–41) has valuable insights, explaining why Herodian invented or distorted things and the aims of the work.

Historia Augusta (*Augustan History*; the title was given by I. Casaubon in 1603 to a work also but misleadingly called '*Scriptores Historiae Augustae*'); ed. and tr. D. M. Magie, Loeb ed., 3 vols., 1921–32; tr. with introduction (Birley 1976); tr. into French with introduction including the history of the controversy over authorship (Chastagnol 1994; see Syme 1971). This set of biographies of emperors and usurpers 117–284, with a gap from 244 to 260, the only continuous source for the history of the second and third century, is modelled on the work of Suetonius and purports to be by six authors writing in the reigns of Diocletian and Constantine (284–337); probably they are by a single author writing under Theodosius (379–95): the *HA* was used by Symmachus (340–402). The author becomes less and less anchored to the evidence available to him (for which see Barnes 1978): the lives of Hadrian, Pius, M. Aurelius and Septimius Severus (which depend partly on Eutropius and Aurelius Victor respectively, as well as on Marius Maximus: Birley 1999: 206), are considered comparatively reliable; Birley describes the *Niger*, *Albinus* and *Geta* as 'mainly pure fiction', though, like the *Macrinus*, *Diadumenianus*, *Elagabalus* and *Severus Alexander* ('one of the major sources of misinformation . . . on the third century'), they include authentic material from the source of the *Severus*. Barnes (1968a: 523) holds that the *Caracalla* has an 'excellent' third-century biography behind it. The worthlessness of the *Geta* was shown by Hasebroek (1916); cf. Kettenhofen (1979: 62) with examples. The bent of the work is pro-senatorial and hostile to hereditary monarchy and to military intervention in politics. For its account of Domna, see Wallinger (1990: 82–90). For use of Marius Maximus, Dio, Herodian, and Latin Epitomators, see Chastagnol (1994: xli and lix–lxxii).

Jerome (St., Eusebius Hieronymus) *c.*347–420, besides translating Scripture into Latin, translated and expanded the early fourth-century *Chronicle* of world history by Eusebius of Caesareia, R. Helm, ed. (1956, 1984) *Die Chronik des Hieronymus*, Berlin.

Kaisergeschichte, a putative 'Imperial History' of the first half of the fourth century covering the period from the second to the fourth century, postulated by A. Enmann (1884) *Philologus* Suppl. 4.3: 337–501, to account for resemblances between compilers such as Aurelius Victor, his 'epitomator', Eutropius, and Orosius. The author seems to have drawn on Marius Maximus. See Barnes (1978: 91–7).

John Malalas of Antioch, *c.*480–570, wrote an imaginative world history, *Chronographia*, with special stress on his native city: *The Chronicle of John Malalas*, tr. E. Jeffreys et al. (1986) Byzantina Australiensia 4, Melbourne, in eighteen books extending beyond 563.

(L.) Marius Maximus (Perpetuus Aurelianus) (*PIR*² M 308; fragments in H. Peter (1967) *Historicorum Romanorum Reliquiae* 2, ed. 2, Stuttgart, 121–9, was a senator and general contemporary with Severus who began his career in about 178, was governor of Syria, Africa, and Asia, and was Prefect of the City in 217–18 and consul for the second time in 223. Marius' antecedents (African, perhaps from Thugga, with father rising to an equestrian procuratorship) are set out in Birley (1999: 205), more fully in Birley (1997b) 'Marius Maximus the Consular Biographer', *ANRW* 2.34.3: 2678–757. His popular biographies (Nerva to Elagabalus) continued Suetonius. They were organized by category and included documents and scandalous material. They were drawn on (or referred) to twenty-six times in the *HA* and may lie behind the biographies up to the *Elagabalus*, of which he has been thought to be the main source (Kettenhofen 1979: 57f.); other scholars minimize Marius' contribution and postulate an unknown writer 'Ignotus'; see Birley (1999) for protagonists. Marius was also used by the author of the *Kaisergeschichte* (*q.v.*) and the *Epitome de Caesaribus* and, as Birley points out, he and Dio could have known each other's work

[Oppian,] *Hunting with Dogs* (*Cynegetica*, ed. and tr. by A. W. Mair, Loeb ed., 1928). Four books in hexameters dedicated to Caracalla by a poet who calls himself a Syrian from Apameia. The authentic Oppian was author of the work on fishing, *Halieutica*. See Bowersock (1969: 108), citing R. Keydell (1939) *RE* 18.1: 698–708.

Orosius, *Histories against the Pagans* (*Adversus Paganos*, ed. M.-P. Arnaud Lindet, Budé ed., 1990–1). Seven books written with the encouragement of St. Augustine by a Spanish presbyter in Africa. They proceed from the Creation to AD 417 and were intended to show that Christianity had not, as pagans argued, brought disaster to the world.

Papinian (Aemilius Papinianus), a highly regarded jurist, of African or Syrian origin, perhaps a relative of Domna; assessor to the Praetorian Prefect, then *a libellis*, was Praetorian Prefect from 205 to 211; he was murdered in 212. He wrote *Quaestiones* (*Problems*) and *Digesta responsa* (*Ordered Opinions*). See T. Honoré in OCD^3 (1996) 21.

Paulus (Julius Paulus), jurist; he was assessor to Papinian and member of the imperial advisory council. His output included seventy-eight books on the praetor's edict, twenty-six of *Quaestiones* and twenty-three of *Responsa*. See Syme (1971: 147–50; 156f.); Syme (1984) *RP* 3: 790–804; 1393–414; T. Honoré in OCD^3 (1996) 786f.

(L. Flavius) Philostratus, b. 164–74. Sophist and Athenian magistrate; his father and great-nephew were also sophists (see OCD^3 (1996) 1171), and his family had members in the third century Senate. Philostratus was encouraged by Domna to write the hagiographic *Life of Apollonius of Tyana* (*Ta es ton Tyanea Apollonion*), ed. and tr. F. C. Conybeare, Loeb ed., 2 vols., 1912). Written in the second or third decades of the third century, it contains factual material but is not concerned with historical truth. Other works include *Lives of the Sophists* (*Bioi sophiston*, ed. and tr. W. Cave Wright, Loeb ed., 1921) which is basic for the understanding of the 'Second Sophistic'. See Chapter 8.

Tertullian (Q. Septimius Florens Tertullianus), *c*.160 to after 212; his last securely datable work is the *Ad Scapulam* of that year. He came from Carthage, the son of a centurion, and was a rigorist apologist for Christianity and writer on ethics. Editions: W. H. C. Frend, rev. M. J. Edwards, OCD^3 (1996) 1487f. See Barnes (1971), disputing the story that he was a centurion's son.

Ulpian (Domitius Ulpianus), jurist from Tyre, was *a libellis* from 205 onwards; he composed more than two hundred books under Caracalla. After service as Prefect of the grain supply in 222 he became Prefect of the Praetorian Guard, but was assassinated the following year. He wrote on the Praetor's Edict, and on the duties of proconsuls. See T. Honoré in OCD^3 (1996) 483.

Xiphilinus, John, a monk, native of Trapezus, between 1071 and 1078 compiled abridged excerpts of Dio's history. See P. A. Brunt, (1980) *Classical Quarterly* 30: 488–92.

Zonaras, Johannes, in the earlier twelfth century was commander of the Guard and imperial secretary, then a historian writing in exile. He wrote a universal history from the Creation to 1118. The historians from whom he took excerpts included Dio and Xiphilinus.

Zosimus, an *advocatus fisci* of uncertain identity, early in the sixth century wrote a pagan Greek *New History* (*Historia nova*) of the Roman Empire from Augustus to 410, the first three centuries in Book 1. See F. Paschoud (1975) *Cinq Etudes sur Zosimus*, Paris.

Modern works

Aguado Garcia, P. (2001) 'El Culto al *Sol Invictus* en la Época de Caracalla', *Hispania Antiqua* 25: 295–304.

Alföldi, A. (1934) 'Die Ausgestaltung des monarchischen Zeremoniells am römischen Kaiserhofe', *MDAI(R)I* 49: 3–118.

—- (1935) *Insignien und tracht der römischen Kaiser. MDAI(R)* 50: 3–171.

Alföldy, G. (1968) 'Herkunft und Laufbahn des Clodius Albinus in der Historia Augusta', *Historiae-Augustae-Colloquium Bonn 1966/67*, Bonn, 19–38.

—— (1971a) 'Zeitgeschichte und Kriesenempfindung bei Herodian', *Hermes* 99: 429–49 (= 1989, 273–94).

—— (1971b) 'Herodians Person', *Ancient Society* 2: 204–31 (= 1989, 240–72)

—— (1974) 'The Crisis of the Third Century as Seen by Contemporaries', *Greek, Roman, and Byzantine Studies* 15: 89–111 (= 1989, 319–24).

—— (1989) *Die Krise des römischen Reiches. Geschichte, Geschichtsschreibung und Geschichtsbetrachtung*. Ausgewählte Beiträge. Heidelberger althist. Beiträge und epigr. Stud. 5, Stuttgart.

—— (1996) 'Nox dea fit lux! Caracallas Geburtstag', in G. Bonamente and M. Mayer, eds., *Historiae Augustae Colloquium Barcinonense 1993. Hist.-Aug. Coll.* NS 4, Bari, 9–36.

Altheim, F. and Stiehl, R. (1964–9) *Die Araber in der alten Welt*, 5 vols., Berlin.

Anderson, G. (1977) 'Putting Pressure on Plutarch: Philostratus *Ep.* 73', *CP* 72: 43–5.

—— (1986) *Philostratus: Biography and Belles-Lettres in the Third Century AD*, London.

—— (1993) *The Second Sophistic: A Cultural Phenomenon in the Roman Empire*, London.

Aurigemma, S. (1950) 'L'avo paterno, una zia, ed altri congiunti dell' imperatore Severo', *Quaderni di Archeologia della Libia* 1: 59–77.

Baharal, D. (1992) 'The Portraits of Julia Domna from the Years 193–211 AD and the Dynastic Propaganda of L. Septimius Severus', *Lat.* 51: 110–18.

Baldus, H. R. (1971) *Uranius Antoninus: Münzprägung und Geschichte*, Antiquitas 3.11, Bonn.

Balsdon, J. P. V. D. (1962) *Roman Women, their History and Habits*, London.

Balty, J. (1964) 'Les premiers portraits de Septime Sévère: problèmes de méthode', *Lat.* 23: 56–63.

—— (1981) 'L'Oracle d'Apamée', *Antiquité classique* 50: 5–14.

Barbieri, G. (1952) *L'Albo senatorio da Settimio Severo a Carino, 193–285*. Stud. pubbl. dall'ist. Ital per la Storia ant. 6, Rome.

Barnes, T. D. (1967) 'The Family and Career of Septimius Severus', *Hist.* 16: 87–107.

—— (1968a) 'Pre-Decian *acta martyrum*', *Journal of Theological Studies* NS 19: 509–31.

—— (1968b) 'Philostratus and Gordian', *Lat.* 27: 581–97.

—— (1971) *Tertullian: A Historical and Literary Study*, Oxford.

—— (1978) *The Sources of the* Historia Augusta, Collection Latomus 155, Brussels.

—— (1984) 'The Composition of Cassius Dio's *Roman History*', *Phoenix* 38: 240–55.

Barrett, A. A. (1977) 'Sohaemus, King of Emesa', *American Journal of Philology* 98: 153–9.

—— (2002) *Livia, First Lady of Rome*, New Haven, CT.

Benario, H. W. (1958a) ‘Rome of the Severi’, *Lat.* 17: 712–22.

—— (1958b) ‘Julia Domna – mater senatus et patriae’, *Phoenix* 12: 67–70.

—— (1959) ‘The Titulature of Julia Soaemias and Julia Mamaea: Two Notes’, *TAPA* 90: 9–14.

Berchem, D. van (1974) ‘Les Itinéraires de Caracalla et l’itinéraire Antonine’, in D. M. Pippidi, ed., *Actes du IXe Congrès intern. d’Et. sur les frontières rom., Mamaïa, Sept. 1972*, Bucharest, 301–7.

Bersanetti, M. (1946) ‘Il padre, la madre, e la prima moglie di Settimio Severo’, *Ath.* 24: 28–43.

Bird, H. W. (1984) *Sextus Aurelius Victor: A Historiographical Study*, Liverpool.

Birley, A. R. (1969) ‘The Coups d’état of the Year 193’, *Bonner Jahrbücher* 169: 247–80.

—— (1970) ‘Some Notes on HA Severus, 1–4’, *Bonner Historia Augusta Colloquium* 1968/9. Antiquitas 4, Beitr. zur Hist.-Aug. Forsch. 7, Bonn, 59–77.

—— (1971) *Septimius Severus: The African Emperor*, London.

—— (1976) Tr. and introduced, *Lives of the Later Caesars*. The first part of the *Augustan History* with newly compiled *Lives* of Nerva and Trajan, Harmondsworth.

—— (1981) *The* Fasti *of Roman Britain*, Oxford.

—— (1987) *Marcus Aurelius*, ed. 2, London.

—— (1996) ‘Iulia Domna’ in *OCD*^{3}, 777.

—— (1997a) *Hadrian, the Restless Emperor*, London.

—— (1997b) ‘Marius Maximus the Consular Biographer’, *ANRW* 2.34.3: 2678–757.

—— (1999) *The African Emperor: Septimius Severus*, ed. 2, London, 1988, repr. paperback ed., *Septimius Severus*, with additional bibl., London.

—— (2005) *The Roman Government of Britain*, Oxford.

Bleckmann, B. (2002) ‘Die Severische Familie und die Soldatenkaiser’, in Temporini (2002: 265–339).

Bowersock, G. W. (1965) Review of Millar 1964 in *Gnomon* 37: 469–74.

—— (1969) *Greek Sophists in the Roman Empire*, Oxford.

—— (1974) ed., *Approaches to the Second Sophistic*, papers presented at the 105th Meeting of the American Philological Association, University Park, PA.

—— (1975) ‘Herodian and Elagabalus’, *YCS* 24: 229–36.

—— (1990) *Hellenism in Late Antiquity*, Jerome Lectures 18, Ann Arbor, MI.

—— (1993) *Roman Arabia*, Cambridge, MA.

Bowie, E. L. (1970) ‘The Greeks and their Past in the Second Sophistic’, *Past and Present* 46: 3–41 (= M. I. Finley, ed., *Studies in Ancient Society*, London, 166–209).

—— (1978) ‘Apollonius of Tyana: Tradition and Reality’, *ANRW* 2.16.2: 1652–99.

—— (1982) ‘The Importance of Sophists’, *YCS* 27: 29–59.

Braund, D. C. (1984) *Rome and the Friendly King: The Character of the Client Kingship*, London.

Brilliant, R. (1967) *The Arch of Septimius Severus in the Roman Forum, MAAR* 29, Rome.

Broughton, T. R. S. (1929) *The Romanization of Africa Proconsularis*, Baltimore, MD, repr. Westmore, CT, 1968.

Brunt, P. A. (1994) ‘The Bubble of the Second Sophistic’, *BICS* 39: 25–52.

Bruun, C. (1995) '*Pericula Alexandrina*: the Adventures of a Recently Discovered Centurion of the Legio II Parthica', *Arctos* 29: 9–27.
Buraselis, K. (1995) 'Zu Caracallas Strafmassenahmen in Alexandrien (215/16). Die Frage der Leinenweber in P.Giss. 40 II und der *syssitia* in Cass. Dio 77(78). 23.3', *ZPE* 108: 166–88.
Burkert, W. (1972) 'Zur Geistesgeschichtlichen Einordnung einiger Pseudopythagorica', in K. von Fritz, ed., *Pseudepigraphica I*. Entretiens Hardt 18, Geneva, 23–55.
Butcher, K. (2003) *Roman Syria and the Near East*, London.
Cantineau, J. (1931) 'Textes palmyréniens provenant de la fouille du temple de Bêl', *Syria* 12: 116–41.
Càssola, F. (1965) 'Pertinace durante il Principato di Commodo', *PP* 20: 451–77.
Chad, C., SJ (1972) *Les Dynastes d'Emèse*, Beirut.
Champlin, E. (1979) 'Notes on the Heirs of Commodus', *American Journal of Philology* 100: 288–306.
—— (1981) 'Serenus Sammonicus', *HSCP* 85: 189–212.
Charles-Picard, G. (1962) 'Origines e sens des reliefs sacrificiels de l'Arc des Argentiers', in M. Renard, ed., *Hommages à A. Grenier* 3, Brussels, 1254–60.
—— (1966) 'Le Trophée de Varsovie', in *Mélanges offerts à K. Michalowski*, Warsaw, 603–17.
Chastagnol, A. (1994) *Histoire Auguste: Les Empereurs romains des IIe et IIIe siècles*, ed. bilingue latin et française, tr. du Latin par A. Chastagnol, Edition établie par A. Chastagnol, Paris.
Chausson, F. (2000) 'De Didius Julianus aux Nummi Albani', *MEFRA* 112.2: 849–79.
—— (2002) 'Variétés généalogiques. II – *Macer auus maternus* de Septime Sévère', in G. Bonamente and F. Paschoud, eds., *Historiae Augustae Colloquia*, NS 8 (*Colloquium Perusinum, 2000*), Centro interuniversitario per gli Studi sulla '*Historia Augusta*' di Macerata, Munera 18, Bari, 149–70.
Claridge, A. (1998) *Rome: An Oxford Archaeological Guide*, Oxford.
Coarelli, F. (1986) *Roma: Guide archeologiche Laterza*, Rome.
Cooley, A. E. ed. (2000) *The Epigraphic Landscape of Roman Italy*, *BICS* Suppl. 73, London.
Corbier, M. (1974) *L'Aerarium Saturni et l'Aerarium Militare: Administration et prosopographie sénatoriale*, *CEFR* 24, Rome.
Covolo, E. dal and Rinaldi, G. eds. (1999) *Gli imperatori Sever. Storia Archeologia Religione*, Bibl. di Sc. Rel. 138.
Cramer, F. H. (1954) *Astrology in Roman Law and Politics*. Memoirs of the American Philosophical Society 37, Philadelphia, PA.
Crook, J. (1955) *Consilivm Principis: Imperial Councils and Counsellors from Augustus to Diocletian*, Cambridge.
De Lacy, P. (1974) 'Plato and the Intellectual Life of the Second Century A.D.', in Bowersock (1974: 4–10).
De Regibus, L. (1946) 'Contrasti politici alla corte di Lucio Settimio Severo', *Ath*. 24: 130–44.
Dietz, K. (1983) 'Caracalla, Fabius Cilo und die Urbaniciani: Unerkannt gebliebene Suffektkonsuln des Jahres 212 n. Chr.', *Chiron* 13: 381–404.
Dieudonné, H. (1906) 'Numismatique syrienne. Emèse', *RN* Sér. 4, 10: 132–55.

Domaszewski, A. von (1895) 'Die Religion des römischen Heeres', *Westd. Zeitschr. für Gesch. und Kunst* 14, repr. Trier, 1895; in *Aufsätze zur röm. Heeresgeschichte*, Darmstadt, 1975.

—— (1898) 'Der Staatsstreich des Septimius Severus', *Rhein. Mus.* 53: 638f.

—— (1909) 'Virgo Caelestis' (orig. *Orient. Stud. für T. Noldeke* 861–3) and 'Die politische Bedeutung der Religion von Emesa' (orig. *Archiv für Religionswiss.* 12, 223–42) (1908) 223–9), in *Abhandlungen zur römischen Religion*, Leipzig, 148–50 and 197–216.

Downey, G. (1961) *A History of Antioch in Syria from Seleucus to the Arab Conquest*, Princeton, NJ.

Drijvers, H. J. W. (1977) 'Hatra, Palmyra und Edessa. Die Städte der syrisch-mesopotamischen Wüste in politischer, Kulturgeschichtlicher und religionsgesch. Beleuchtung', *ANRW* 2.8: 801–906.

Duncan-Jones, R. P. (1982) *The Economy of the Roman Empire*, ed. 2, Cambridge.

Erdélyi, G. and Fülep, F. (1954) *Katalog der Steindenkmäler*, in *Intercisa* 1 *(Dunapentele-Sztálinváros), Geschichte der Stadt in der Römerzeit*. Arch. Hung. Diss. Arch. Mus. Nat. Hung. NS 33, Budapest, 277–332.

Evans, J. A. (2002) *The Empress Theodora: Partner of Justinian*, Austin, TX.

Fejfer, J. (1992) '*Divus Caracalla* and *Julia Domna*: a Note', *Acta Hyperborea* 4: 207–19.

Fiaccadori, G. (1999) 'Dittico per Settimio Severo e Giulia Domna da Bostra (ILSG XIII 9052 e 9053)', *PP* 54: 152–5.

Fittschen, K. (1978) 'Two Portraits of Septimius Severus and Julia Domna', *Indiana University Art Museum Bulletin* 1.2: 28–43.

Fittschen, K., Zanker, P. and Fittschen-Badura, G. (1983) *Katalog der röm. Porträts in der Capitolinischen Museen u. den anderen kommunalen Sammlungen der Stadt Rom. Beiträge zur Entschliessung hellenistischer u. kaiserzeitlicher Skulptur u. Architektur 3. Kaiserinnen u. Prinzessinnen Bildnisse; Frauenportäts*, Mainz.

Fitz, J. (1967–8) 'When did Caracalla become Imperator Destinatus?', *Alba Regia* 8–9: 285f.

—— (1972) *Les Syriens à Intercisa*, Collection Latomus 122, Brussels.

—— (1977) 'Das Verhalten der Armee in der Kontroverse zwischen Caracalla und Geta', *Stud. zu den Militärgrenzen Roms 2. Vortr. des 10 internat. Limeskongresses in der Germ. Inf. BJ* Beiheft 38, Cologne.

—— ed. (1991) *Die römischen Inschriften Ungarns* 5. Lieferung. Intercisa, ed. J. Fitz, Bonn.

Flinterman, J.-J. (1995) *Politics,* Paedeia *and Pythagoreanism: Greek Identity, Conceptions of the Relationship between Philosophers and Monarchs and Political Ideas in Philostratus'* Life of Apollonius, *Dutch Monographs on Ancient History and Archaeology* 13, Amsterdam.

—— (1997) 'De Sofist, de Keiserin, en de Concubine: Philostratus' Brief aan Julia Domna', *Lampas* 30(2): 74–86.

Frend, W. H. C. (1965) *Martyrdom and Persecution in the Early Church*, Oxford.

Gagé, J. (1934) 'Les jeux séculaires de 204 ap. J.C. et la dynastie des Sévères', *Mél. d'Arch. et d'Hist. de l'École fr. de Rome* 51: 33–78.

Ghedini, F. (1984) *Giulia Domna tra oriente e occidente: le fonti archeologiche*, Rome.

Gilliam, J. F. (1965) 'Dura Rosters and the *Constitutio Antoniniana*', *Hist.* 14: 74–92.

—— (1969) 'On "Divi" under the Severi', in J. Bibauw, ed., *Hommages à M. Renard* 2, Brussels, 284–9.

Gradel, I. (2002) *Emperor Worship and Roman Religion*, Oxford.

Grant, M. (1996) *The Severans: The Changed Roman Empire*, London.

Grosso, F. (1964) *La Lotta politica al tempo di Commodo*, Turin.

——- (1968) 'Ricerche su Plauziano e gli avvenimenti del suo tempo', *Atti dell'Accad. Naz. dei Lincei*, ser. 8, *Rendiconti, Cl. di scienze mor., stor. e fil.* 23: 7–57.

Guey, J. (1953) 'Epigraphica Tripolitana', *REA* 55: 334–58.

—— (1956) 'La date de naissance de l'empereur Septime-Sévère, d'après son horoscope', *Bull. de la Soc. Nat. des Antiquaires de France* 1956: 33–5.

Habicht, C. ed., (1969) *Die Inschriften des Asklepieions. Deutsches Arch. Inst. Die Alterthümer von Pergamon* 8.3, Berlin.

Halfmann, H. (1979) *Die Senatoren aus dem östlichen Teil des Imperium Romanum bis zum Ende des 2. Jh. n. Chr. Hypomnemata* 58, Göttingen.

—— (1982) 'Zwei syrische Verwandte des severischen Kaiserhauses', *Chiron* 12: 217–35.

—— (1986) *Itinera Principum. Geschichte und Typologie der Kaiserreisen im römischen Reich*, Heidelberger althist, Beiträge 2, Stuttgart.

Halsberghe, G. H. (1972) *The Cult of Sol Invictus*, *EPRO* 23, Leiden.

Hammond, M. (1940) 'Septimius Severus, Roman Bureaucrat', *HSCP* 56: 137–73.

—— (1956) 'The Transmission of the Powers of the Roman Emperor from the Death of Nero in A.D. 68 to that of Alexander Severus in A.D. 235', *MAAR* 24: 61–133.

—— (1957) 'Composition of the Senate, A.D. 68–235', *JRS* 47: 74–81.

Hannestad, K. (1944) 'Septimius Severus in Egypt: a Contribution to the Chronology of the Years 198–202', *Classica et Mediaevalia* 6: 194–222.

Hasebroek, J. (1916) *Die Fälschungen der Vitae Nigri und Albini in den S. H. A. Beiträge zur Lösung des Quellenproblems*, Berlin.

—— (1921) *Untersuchungen zur Geschichte des Kaisers Septimius Severus*, Heidelberg.

Haynes, D. E. L. and Hirst, P. E. D. (1939) *Porta Argentariorum. Papers of the British School at Rome* Suppl., London.

Haywood, R. M. (1940) 'The African Policy of Septimius Severus', *TAPA* 71: 175–85.

—— (1962) 'A Further Note on the African Policy of Septimius Severus', in M. Renard, ed., *Hommages A. Grenier*, Collection Latomus 58.2, Brussels, 786–90.

Hekster, O. (2002) *Commodus: An Emperor at the Crossroads, Dutch Monographs on Ancient History and Archaeology* 23, Amsterdam.

Hemelrijk, E. (1999) *Matrona Docta: Educated Women in the Roman Élite from Cornelia to Julia Domna*, London.

Herzog, G. (1918) 'Iulia Avita Mamaea', Iulia Domna', 'Iulia Maesa', 'Iulia Soaemias', *RE* 10.1: 916–23, no. 558; 926–35, no. 566; 940–4, no. 571; 948–51, no. 596.

Hill, P. V. (1964) *The Coinage of Septimius Severus and his Family of the Mint of Rome AD 193–217*, London.

—— (1978) 'The Issues of Severus and his Sons in AD 211', *NC* Ser. 7, 18: 33–7.

—— (1979) 'The Coin-portraiture of Severus and his Family from the Mint of Rome', *NC* Ser. 7, 19: 36–46.

Hitti, P. K. (1951) *History of Syria, Including Lebanon and Palestine*, London.

Hohl, E. (1950) 'Ein politischer Witz auf Caracalla', *Sitzungsb. der deutschen Akad. der Wiss. zu Berlin*, Kl. für Gesellschwiss, Nr. 1.

—— (1956) 'Kaiser Pertinax und die Thronbesteigung seiners Nachfolgers im Lichte der Herodiankritik', nebst einem Anhang 'Herodian und der Sturz Plautians', *Sitzungsb. der deutschen Akad. der Wiss. zu Berlin*. Kl. für Philosophie, etc., Nr. 2.

Horden, P. and Purcell, N. (2000) *The Corrupting Sea: A Study of Mediterranean History*, Oxford.

Instinsky, H. U. (1942) 'Studien zur Geschichte des Septimius Severus', *Klio* 35: 200–19.

Isaac, B. (1990) *The Limits of Empire: The Roman Army in the East*, Oxford.

Jones, A. H. M. (1938) *The Herods of Judaea*, Oxford, repr. 1967.

—— (1971) *Cities of the Eastern Roman Provinces*, ed. 2, Oxford.

Kádár, Z. (1966) 'Julia Domna comme Assyrié Kythereia et Seléné', *Acta Classica Debrecen* 2: 101–8.

Kennedy, D. (1996) 'Syria' in *CAH* 10, d. 2, Cambridge, 703–3.

Kettenhofen, E. (1979) *Die syrischen Augustae in der historischen Überlieferung: ein Beitrag zum Problem der Orientalisierung*, Antiquitas Ser. 3, Vol. 24, Bonn.

Kienast, D. (1996) *Römische Kaisertabelle: Grundzüge einer römischen Kaiserchronologie*, ed. 2, Darmstadt.

King, G. R. D. (2002) 'Archaeological Fieldwork at the Citadel of Homs, Syria, 1995–1999', *Levant* 34: 39–58.

Kuhlmann, P. A. ed. (1994) *Die Giessenen literarischen Papyri und die Caracalla-Erlasse*, Ed., Übersetzung und Kommentar, Berichte und Arbeiten aus der Universitätsbibliothek und dem Universitätsarchiv Giessen 46, Giessen.

Lassère, J.-M. (1975) 'Un Tour d'Elagabale (S.H.A., *Ant. Heliog.* 33.6)', *REA* 77: 131–6.

Leglay, M. (1956) 'Inscriptions de Lambèse sur les deux premiers légats de la province de Numidie', *CRAI* 1956: 294–308.

Lenz, F. W. (1964) 'Die Selbstverteidigung eines politischen Angeklagten. Untersuchungen zu der Rede des Apollonios von Tyana bei Philostratus', *Das Altertum* 10: 95–110.

Leunissen, P. M. M. (1989) *Konsuln und Konsulare in der Zeit von Commodus bis Severus Alexander (180–235 n. Chr.)*, Prosopographische Untersuchungen zur senatorischen Elite im römischen Kaiserreich, *Dutch Monographs on Ancient History and Archaeology* 6, Amsterdam.

Levick, B. (1976) *Tiberius the Politician*, London; ed. 2, London, 2000.

—— (1978) 'Concordia at Rome', in R. A. G. Carson and C. M. Kraay, eds., *Scripta, Nummaria Romana: Essays Presented to Humphrey Sutherland*, London, 217–33.

—— (1982) 'Propaganda and the Imperial coinage', *Antichthon* 16: 104–16.

—— (1990) *Claudius*, London.

—— (1999) *Vespasian*, London.

—— (2002) 'Women and Philosophy at Rome and Beyond', in G. Clark and T. Rajak, eds., *Philosophy and Power in the Graeco-Roman World*, Oxford, 133–55.

Liebeschuetz, J. H. W. G. (2001) *The Decline and Fall of the Roman City*, Oxford.

Lifshitz, B. (1970) 'Notes d'épigraphie grecque, 1 La lettre de Julia Domna aux Ephésiens', *ZPE* 6: 57–60.

Lightfoot, J. L. (2003) *Lucian on the Syrian Goddess*, ed. with introd., transl. and commentary, New York.

Lusnia, S. S. (1995) 'Julia Domna's Coinage and Severan Dynastic Propaganda', *Lat.* 54: 119–40.

McCann, A. M. (1968) *The Portraits of Septimius Severus (AD 193–211)*, *MAAR* 30, Rome.

MacKendrick, P. (1980) *The North African Stones Speak*, London.

Magie, D. (1950) *Roman Rule in Asia Minor to the End of the Third Century after Christ*, 2 vols., Princeton, NJ.

Marasco, G. (1996) 'Giulia Domna, Caracalla e Geta: Frammenti di tragedia alla corte dei Severi', *AC* 65: 119–34.

Mastino, A. (1981) *Le Titulature di Caracalla e Geta attraverso le iscrizioni (indici)*, Bologna.

Mattingly, H. (1951, 1953) 'The Reign of Macrinus', in G. E. Mylonas and D. Raymond, eds., *Studies Presented to D. M. Robinson on his Seventieth Birthday*, 2 vols., St. Louis, MO, 2: 962–9.

Meckler, M. (1999) 'Caracalla the Intellectual', in Covolo and Rinaldi (1999: 39–46).

Meischner, J. (1964) *Das Frauenporträt der Severerzeit*, Inaug. Diss., Berlin.

Merlat, P. (1951) *Répertoire des inscriptions et monuments figurés du culte de Jupiter Dolichenus*, Paris.

Meyer-Zwiffelhoffer, R. (1994) 'Die Münzprägung von Paltos in Syrien', *JNG* 44: 91–111.

Millar, F. G. B. (1962) 'The Date of the *Constitutio Antoniniana*', *Journal of Egyptian Archaeology* 48: 124–31.

—— (1964) *A Study of Cassius Dio*, Oxford.

—— (1968) 'Local Cultures in the Roman Empire: Libyan, Punic and Latin in Roman Africa', *JRS* 58: 126–34.

—— (1977) *The Emperor in the Roman World*, London, repr. with additions 1991.

—— (1983) 'The Phoenician Cities: a Case-study of Hellenisation', *PCPS* 209: 55–71.

—— (1987) 'The Problem of Hellenistic Syria', in A. M. Kuhrt and S. Sherwin-White, eds., *Hellenism in the East: The Interaction of Greek and Non-Greek Civilizations from Syria to Central Asia after Alexander*, London, 110–33.

—— (1993) *The Roman Near East 31 BC–AD 337*, Cambridge, MA.

—— (1998) 'Caravan Cities: the Roman Near East and Roman Long-distance Trade by Land', in M. Austin et al., *Modus Operandi: Essays in Honour of Geoffrey Rickman*, *BICS* Suppl. 71, London, 119–37.

Miller, S. N. (1939) 'The Army and the Imperial House', *CAH* 12: 1–56.

Mitford, T. B. (1950) *New Inscriptions from Roman Cyprus. Skr. Utgivna av Sv. Inst. i Rom. Act. Inst. Rom. Regn. Suec. 15*, Opusc. Arch. 6, Lund, 1–95.

Montalbò, E. (1999) 'I motivi della dinastia e dell' esercito nella monetazione di Giulia Domna', in Covolo and Rinaldi (1999: 343–6).

Moran, J. C. (1999) '193: Severus and Traditional *Auctoritas*', in Covolo and Rinaldi (1999: 31–8).

Moussli, M. (1983) 'Griechische Inschriften aus Emesa und Laodicea ad Libanum', *Philologus* 127: 254–61.

Mundle, I. (1961) 'Dea Caelestis in der Religionspolitik des Septimius Severus und der Julia Domna', *Hist.* 10: 228–37.

Münscher, K. (1907) 'Die Philostrate', *Philologus Suppl.* 10.4: 467–558.

Musurillo, H, (1972) *The Acts of the Christian Martyrs*, Oxford.

Nau, E. (1968) 'Julia Domna als Olympias', *JNG* 18: 49–66.

Naval Intelligence Division Geographical Handbook Series: Syria (1943) [by J. W. Crowfoot, A. N. Sherwin-White, M. D. Emmens], London.

Neugebauer, K. A. (1936) 'Die Familie des Septimius Severus', *Die Antike* 12: 155–72.

Nitta, E. (1989) 'Antroponimi semitici nelle iscrizioni greche e latine della Emesene', Civiltà classica e cristiana 10: 283–302.

Oliver, J. H. (1940) 'Julia Domna as Athena Polias', in *Athenian Studies Presented to W. S. Ferguson*, *HSCP* Suppl. 1: 521–30.

Pallottino, M. (1946) *L'Arco degli Argentari*, I Monumenti Romani, Istituto di Studi Romani 2, Rome.

Palmer, R. E. A. (1978) 'Severan Ruler-Cult and the Moon in the City of Rome', *ANRW* 2.16.2: 1085–120.

Parlasca, K. (1970) 'Eine Iulia Domna-Büste aus der Sammlung Friedrichs des Grossen', *MDAI(R)* 77: 123–31.

Pelletier, A. (1964) 'Les Sénateurs d'Afrique proconsulaire d'Auguste à Gallien', *Lat.* 23: 511–31.

Penella, R. J. (1979) 'Philostratus' Letter to Julia Domna', *Hermes* 107: 161–8.

—— (1980) 'Caracalla and his Mother in the *Historia Augusta*', *Hist.* 29: 382–4.

Pflaum, H.-G. (1960–1) *Les Carrières procuratoriennes équestres sous le Haut-Empire romain*, 4 vols., Paris.

—— (1961) 'Les Gendres de Marc-Aurèle', *JS* 1961: 28–41.

—— (1962) 'Un nouveau gouverneur de la province de Rétie, proche parent de l'impératrice Julia Domna, à propos d'une inscription récemment découverte à Augsbourg', *Bayerische Vorgeschichtsblätter* 27: 82–99.

—— (1979) 'La Carrière de C. Iulius Avitus Alexianus, grand'père de deux empereurs', *Revue des études latines* 57: 298–314.

Pighi, J. B. (1965) *De ludis saecularibus populi Romani Quiritium libri sex*, ed. 2, Amsterdam.

Platnauer, M. (1918) *The Life and Reign of the Emperor Lucius Septimius Severus*, Oxford.

Premerstein, A. von (1913) 'Athenische Kultehren für Kaiserin Julia Domna', *JÖAI* 16: 249–70.

Price, S. R. F. (1980) 'Between Man and God: Sacrifice in the Roman Imperial Cult', *JRS* 70: 28–43.

—— (1984) *Rituals and Power: The Roman Imperial Cult in Asia Minor*, Cambridge.

Purcell, N. (1986) 'Livia and the Womanhood of Rome', *PCPS* 32: 78–105.

Radnóti, A. (1961) 'C. Iulius Avitus Alexianus', *Germania* 39: 383–412.

Raepsaet-Charlier, T. (1987) *Prosopographie des femmes de l'ordre sénatorial (Ier et IIe siècles)*, Acad. roy. de Belg. Cl. des Lettres 4, 2 vols., Brussels.

Rawson, B. (2003) *Children and Childhood in Roman Italy*, Oxford.

Rawson, E. D. (1989) 'Roman Rulers and the Philosophic Adviser', in M. Griffin and J. Barnes, eds., *Philosophia Togata* I, *Essays on Philosophy and Roman Society*, Oxford, corr. repr. 1997, 233–57.

Rey-Coquais, J.-P. (1977) 'Onomastique et histoire de la Syrie gréco-romaine', in

D. M. Pippidi, ed., *Actes du VIIe Congrès intern. d'épigr. Grecque et latine, Constantza*, Bucharest, 171–83.

Robert, J. and Robert, L. (1967) 'Sur des inscriptions d'Ephèse: fêtes, athlètes, empereurs, épigrammes', *Rev. Phil.* 41: 7–84.

Rochette, B. (1997) *Le Latin dans le monde grec. Recherches sur la diffusion de la langue et des lettres latines dans les provinces hellénophones de l'Empire romain*, Collection Latomus 233, Brussels.

Röllig, W. (1973–4) Review of Chad (1972) in *Wiener Zeitschrift für die Kunde des Morgenlandes* 63–4: 283–5.

Ronzevalle, S. SJ (1903) 'Inscription bilingue de Deir el Qala'a', *Revue archéologique* Ser. 4, Vol. 2.2: 28–49.

Roussel, P. and de Visscher, F. (1942–3) 'Les Inscriptions du Temple de Dmeir', *Syria* 23: 173–200.

Rubin, Z. (1975) 'Dio, Herodian, and Septimius Severus' Second Parthian War', *Chiron* 5: 419–41.

—— (1980) *Civil-War Propaganda and Historiography*, Collection Latomus 173, Brussels.

Said, E. (1995 [1978]) *Orientalism: Western Conceptions of the Orient*, with a new Afterword, Harmondsworth.

Salway, B. (1997) 'A Fragment of Severan History: the Unusual Career of . . . atus, Praetorian Prefect of Elagabalus', *Chiron* 27: 127–53.

Scheid, J. (1998a) *Commentarii fratrum arvalium qui supersunt: Les copies épigraphiques des protocols annuels de la confrérie arvale (21 av. – 304 ap. J. C.)*, Rome.

—— (1998b) 'Le Protocole arvale de l'année 213 et l'arrivée de Caracalla à Nicomèdie', in G. Paci, ed., *Epigrafia romana in area adriatica*, Actes de la IXe Rencontre franco-italienne sur l'Epigraphie du Monde rom., 10–11 Nov. 1995, Macerata, 439–51.

Schönert, E. (1965) *Die Münzprägung von Perinthus*, Deutsche Akad. der Wiss. zu Berlin, Schr. der Sekt. für Altertumswiss. 45, Berlin.

Schumacher, L. (2005) 'Die politische Stellung des D. Clodius Albinus (193–197 n Chr.)', *Jahrb. der röm.-germ. Zentralmus. Mainz* 50: 355–69.

Schwertheim, E. (1974) *Die Denkmäler oriental. Gottheiten im röm. Deutschland mit Ausname der ägyptischen Gottheiten*, *EPRO* 40, Leiden.

Seyrig, H. (1932) 'Hiérarchie des divinités de Palmyre', *Syria* 13: 190–5 (= *Ant. syr.* 1 (Paris, 1932) 27–32).

—— (1937) 'Armes et costumes iraniens de Palmyre', *Syria* 18: 4–31 (= *Ant. syr.* 2 (Paris, 1938) 45–73).

—— (1949) 'Sur une idole hiérapolitaine', *Syria* 26: 17–28 (= *Ant. syr.* 4 (1953) 19–31).

—— (1950) 'Palmyra and the East', *JRS* 40: 1–7.

—— (1952, 1953) 'Antiquités de la nécropole d'Emèse', *Syria* 29: 204–50; 30: 12–24 (= *Ant. syr.* 5 (Paris, 1958) 1–60).

—— (1958) 'Uranius Antonin: une question d'authenticité', *RN* Ser. 6, Vol. 1: 51–7.

—— (1959a) 'Caractères de l'histoire d'Émèse', *Syria* 36: 184–92 (= *Ant. syr.* 6 (Paris, 1966) 64–71).

—— (1959b) 'Polémo II et Julia Mamaea', *RN*. Sér. 6, Vol. 11: 45–7.

—— (1963) 'Une idole bétylique', *Syria* 40: 17–19 (= *Ant. syr.* 6 (Paris, 1966) 118–21).

—— (1971) 'Le culte du Soleil en Syrie à l'époque romaine', *Syria* 48: 337–73.

Shahid, I. (1984) *Rome and the Arabs: A Prolegomenon to the Study of Byzantium and the Arabs*, Washington, DC.

Sherwin-White, A. N. (1973) *The Roman Citizenship*, ed. 2, Oxford.

Shotter, D. C. (2003) *Rome and her Empire*, London.

Soproni, S. (1980) 'Die Cäsarwürde Caracallas und die syrische Kohorte von Szentendre', *Alba Regia* 18: 39–51.

Starcky, J. (1975–6) 'Stèle d'Élahagabal', *Mél. Univ. Saint Joseph* 49 *Mélanges offerts à R. P. H. Fleisch, SJ*, 2: 501–20.

Steinby, E. M. ed., (1993–2000) *Lexicon topographicum Urbis Romae*, 6 vols., Rome.

Stoneman, R. (1992) *Palmyra and its Empire: Zenobia's Revolt against Rome*, Ann Arbor, MI.

Sullivan, R. D. (1977a) 'The Dynasty of Emesa', *ANRW* 2.8: 198–219.

—— (1977b) 'Priesthoods of the Eastern Dynastic Aristocracy', in S. Şahin, E. Schwertheim, and J. Wagner, eds., *Studien zur Religion und Kultur Kleinasiens. Festschrift für F. K. Dörner zum 65 Geburtstag, EPRO* 66, Leiden, 2.914–39.

—— (1990) *Near Eastern Royalty and Rome, 100–30 BC*, Phoenix Suppl. 24, Toronto.

Sünskes Thompson, J. (1990) *Aufstände und Protestaktionen im Imperium Romanum. Dies severischen Kaiser im Spannungsfeld innenpolitischer Konflikte*, Bonn.

Swain, S. (1996) *Hellenism and Empire: Language, Classicism, and Power in the Greek World AD 50–250*, Oxford.

—— (1999) 'Defending Hellenism: Philostratus *In Honour of Apollonius*', in M. Edwards et al., eds., *Apologetics in the Roman Empire: Pagans, Jews, and Christians*, Oxford, 157–96.

Swan, P. M. (2004) *The Augustan Succession: An Historical Commentary on Cassius Dio's Roman History, Books 55–6 (9 BC–AD 14)*, American Classical Studies 47, Oxford.

Syme, R. (1968) *Ammianus and the Historia Augusta*, Oxford.

—— (1971) *Emperors and Biography: Studies in the Historia Augusta*, Oxford.

—— (1976) 'Astrology in the Historia Augusta', Bonner Historia-Augusta-Colloquium 1972/4, *Antiquitas* 4.12, Bonn, 291–309.

Temporini, H. ed., (2002) *Die Kaiserinnen Roms von Livia bis Theodora*, Munich.

Teposcu-Marinescu, L. (1994–5) 'A propos du Camée Orghidan', *Dacia* 38–9: 109–19.

Toutain, J. (1943–5 [1951]) 'Communication sur Julia Domna invoquée sous le nom de Dea Caelestis', *Bulletin Archéologique du Comité des Travaux historiques et scientifiques* 44–5: 306–11.

Townsend, P. W. (1938) 'The Significance of the Arch of the Severi at Lepcis', *American Journal of Archaeology* 42: 512–24.

Treggiari, S. (1991) *Roman Marriage: Iusti Coniuges from the Time of Cicero to the Time of Ulpian*, Oxford.

Turcan, R. (1978) 'Le culte impériale au IIIe siècle', *ANRW* 2.16.2: 997–1084.

Van't Dack, E. (1991) 'Commode et ses épithètes *Pius Felix* sous les Sévères', in G. Bonamente and N. Duval, eds., *Hist. Aug. Colloquium Parisinum 1990, Hist. Aug. Coll.* NS 1, Macerata, 311–35.

Wallinger, E. (1990) *Die Frauen in der Historia Augusta*, Öst. Gesellsch. für Arch., Althist.-epigraph. Stud. 2, Vienna.

Walser, G. (1975) 'Die Severer in der Forschung 1960–1972', *ANRW* 2.2: 614–56.

Ward-Perkins, J. B. (1948) 'Severan Art and Architecture in Lepcis Magna', *JRS* 38: 59–80.

—— (1951) 'The Art of the Severan Age in the Light of the Tripolitanian Discoveries', *Proceedings of the British Academy* 37: 268–304.

Whittaker, C. R. (1964) 'The Revolt of Papirius Dionysius, A.D. 190', *Hist.* 13: 348–69.

Williams, M. G. (1902) 'Studies in the Lives of Empresses. I. Julia Domna', *American Journal of Archaeology* NS 6: 259–305.

—— (1904) 'Studies in the Lives of Empresses. II. Julia Mamaea', in H. A. Sanders, ed., *Roman Historical Sources and Institutions*, University of Michigan Studies, Humanistic Series, New York, 67–100.

Winter, B. (2002) *Philo and Paul among the Sophists: Alexandrian and Corinthian Responses to a Julio-Claudian Movement*, ed. 2, Grand Rapids, MI.

Wolff, H. (1976) *Die Constitutio Antoniniana und Papyrus Gissensis 40.1*, Inaug. Diss. Köln, Cologne.

Wuthnow, H. (1930) *Die semitischen Menschennamen in griechischen Inschriften u. Papyri des Vorderen Orients*, Stud. zur Epigr. u. Papyruskunde 1.4, Leipzig.

Young, G. K. (2003) 'Emesa and Baalbek: Where is the Temple of Elahagabal?', *Levant* 35: 159–63.

Ziegler, J. R. (1978) 'Antiochia, Laodicea und Sidon in der Politik der Severer', *Chiron* 8: 493–524.

Zimmermann, M. (1999) *Kaiser und Ereignis. Studien zum Geschichtswerk Herodians*, Vestigia 52, Munich.

Zwalve, W. J. (2001) '*In re* Iulius Agrippa's estate. Q. Cervidius Scaevola, Iulia Domna and the estate of Iulius Agrippa', in L. de Blois, ed., *Administration, Prosopography and Appointment Policies in the Roman Empire*, Proceedings of the first workshop of the international network Impact of Empire (Roman Empire 27 BC – AD 406), Leiden, 28 June–1 July 2000, Amsterdam, 154–66.

Index of places

Index of ancient place names (with provinces, modern names of sites and countries)

Index of persons

Well-known politicians and writers are indexed under the names most familiar to English readers; others by their *nomen* or *cognomen*

General index

Related titles from Routledge

Cornelia
Mother of the Gracchi
Suzanne Dixon

Cornelia - daughter, wife and mother of famous men - won her own enduring place in Roman history. Her sons' political successors, orators, authors and even Roman emperors revered her as 'Mother of the Gracchi'. In a time of moral upheaval and cultural innovation, Cornelia's drive and education equipped her sons for the new age.

Why, asks Dixon, should the mother of revolutionaries continue to be admired - for her prose style, her fertility, her philosophic calm in adversity, her vicarious ambition - by the same arch-conservatives who blamed her sons for the decline of the Republic?

Dixon reminds us that this iconic Roman mother venerated by later ages for igniting her sons' fatal political ambitions and for proclaiming that her children were her 'jewels', was once a woman, not only a myth. She endured the deaths of her own ambitions with the assassinations of her two famous sons ('the Gracchi') in their prime. Her daughter Sempronia, childless widow of a famous general, was the sole survivor of Cornelia's twelve children. Dixon argues that it was Sempronia, dutiful to the end, who kept the family myths alive.

This concise, pocket-sized book plunges the reader into the turbulent Italy of the second century BCE, when Cornelia and her family were at the centre of the culture wars and political upheavals that followed military conquest. Essential reading for anyone interested in women's history, political myth-making or the politics of the Roman Republic.

Hb: 978-0-415-33147-0
Pb: 978-0-415-33148-7
eBook: 978-0-203-39243-0

Related titles from Routledge

Julia Augusti
Elaine Fantham

Julia, the only daughter of Emperor Augustus, became a living example of the Augustan policy. By her marriage and motherhood she encapsulated the Augustan reforms of Rome and helped secure a dynasty.

An unidentified scandal, distorted or concealed in the ancient sources which led to her summary banishment, has discredited Julia, or at least clothed her in mystery. However, studying the abundant historical evidence available, this biography illustrates each stage of Julia's life in remarkable detail:

- her childhood – taken from her divorced mother to become part of a complex and unstable family structure
- her youth – set against the brilliant social and cultural life of the new Augustan Rome
- her marriages – as tools for Augustus' plans for succession
- Julia's defiance or her father's publicized moral regime, and implicit exposure of his hypocrisy by claiming the same sexual liberty he had once enjoyed

Reflecting new attitudes, and casting fresh light on their social reality, this accessible but penetrating portrait from one of the foremost scholars of Augustan literature and history will delight, entertain and inform anyone interested in this engaging Classical figure.

ISBN10: 0-415-33145-5 (hbk)
ISBN10: 0-415-33146-3 (pbk)

ISBN13: 978-0-415-33145-6 (hbk)
ISBN13: 978-0-415-33146-3 (pbk)

Related titles from Routledge

Medea
Emma Griffiths

Medea, the sorceress of Greek myth and Euripides' vengeful heroine, is famed for the murder of her children after she is banished from her own family and displaced by a new wife. Her reputation as a wronged 'everywoman' of Greek tragedy has helped engender her lasting appeal to the modern age. However, this firmly rooted status has also caused many of the intricacies of her timeless tale to be overlooked.

Emma Griffiths brings into focus previously unexplored themes of the Medea myth, along with providing an incisive introduction to the story and its history. Viewed within its context, the tale reveals fascinating insights into ancient Greece and its ideology, the importance of children, the role of women, and the position of the outsider and barbarian.

The critically sophisticated analysis, expressed in clear and accessible terms, proceeds to examine the persistence of the Medea myth through ancient Rome to the modern day. Placing the myth within a modern context and into analytical frameworks such as psychoanalysis, Griffiths highlights Medea's position in current classical study, as well as her lasting appeal. A vivid portrait of a woman empowered by her exclusion from society, alive with passion and the suffering of wounded love, this book is an indispensable guide to a fascinating mythical figure.

ISBN10: 0-415-30069-X (hbk)
ISBN10: 0-415-30070-3 (hbk)

ISBN13: 978-0-415-30069-X (hbk)
ISBN13: 978-0-415-30070-3 (pbk)

Related titles from Routledge

Olympias
Mother of Alexander the Great
Elizabeth Carney

The definitive guide to the life of the first woman to play a major role in Greek political history, this is the first modern biography of Olympias.

Presenting a critical assessment of a fascinating and wholly misunderstood figure, Elizabeth Carney penetrates myth, fiction and sexual politics and conducts a close examination of Olympias through historical and literary sources, and brings her to life as she places the figure in the context of her own ancient, brutal political world.

Individual examinations look at:

- the role of Greek religion in Olympias' life
- literary and artistic traditions about Olympias found throughout the later ancient periods
- varying representations of Olympias found in the major ancient sources.

An absolutely compelling read for students, scholars, and anyone with an interest in Greek, classical, or women's history.

ISBN10: 0-415-33316-4 (hbk)
ISBN10: 0-415-33317-2 (pbk)

ISBN13: 978-0-415-33316-0 (hbk)
ISBN13: 978-0-415-33317-7 (pbk)